Gentlemen and Amazons

Gentlemen and Amazons

The Myth of Matriarchal Prehistory,
1861–1900

———

Cynthia Eller

UNIVERSITY OF CALIFORNIA PRESS
Berkeley   Los Angeles   London

University of California Press, one of the most distinguished university presses in the United States, enriches lives around the world by advancing scholarship in the humanities, social sciences, and natural sciences. Its activities are supported by the UC Press Foundation and by philanthropic contributions from individuals and institutions. For more information, visit www.ucpress.edu.

Epigraphs: Milan Kundera, *The Book of Laughter and Forgetting,* trans. Michael Henry Heim (New York: Viking, 1979), 22. Elizabeth Cady Stanton, "The Matriarchate or Mother-Age," address of Mrs. Stanton before the National Council of Women, February 1891.

University of California Press
Berkeley and Los Angeles, California

University of California Press, Ltd.
London, England

© 2011 by The Regents of the University of California

Library of Congress Cataloging-in-Publication Data

Eller, Cynthia, 1958–
    Gentlemen and Amazons : the myth of matriarchal prehistory, 1861–1900 / Cynthia Eller.
        p.   cm.
    Includes bibliographical references and index.
    ISBN 978-0-520-24859-5 (cloth : alk. paper)—ISBN 978-0-520-26676-6 (pbk. : alk. paper)
    1. Women, Prehistoric.   2. Religion, Prehistoric.   3. Matriarchy.
4. Matrilineal kinship.   5. Patriarchy.   6. Feminist theory
I. Title.
    GN799.W66.E487   2011
    306.85'9—dc22   2010038919

Manufactured in the United States of America

20   19   18   17   16   15   14   13   12   11
10   9   8   7   6   5   4   3   2   1

This book is printed on 50# Enterprise, a 30% post consumer waste, recycled, de-inked fiber and processed chlorine free. It is acid-free and meets all ANSI/NISO (z 39.48) requirements.

For Teresa M. Shaw,
my favorite historian

People are always shouting they want to create a better future. It's not true. The future is an apathetic void of no interest to anyone. The past is full of life, eager to irritate us, provoke and insult us, tempt us to destroy or repaint it. The only reason people want to be masters of the future is to change the past. They are fighting for access to the laboratories where photographs are retouched and biographies and histories rewritten.

—MILAN KUNDERA

The period of woman's supremacy lasted through many centuries— undisputed, accepted as natural and proper wherever it existed, and was called the matriarchate, or mother-age.

—ELIZABETH CADY STANTON

CONTENTS

ILLUSTRATIONS

ACKNOWLEDGMENTS

I like to tell my daughter that I've been working on this book her entire lifetime, and in one sense, that's true. I've paused from this research at numerous points to take on other projects, but the history of matriarchal myth has been the guiding passion of my scholarly work for fourteen years now.

I teach my world religions students that according to the Buddhist worldview, everything is connected: wherever you pick up the fabric of the universe, the threads eventually lead everywhere else. For me, matriarchal myth is where I pick up the fabric of the universe. It looks like a narrow interest, but the threads lead everywhere, and I continue to enjoy following them outward and back again.

A number of people and institutions have been kind enough to support my love affair with ideas of prehistoric matriarchy and goddess worship. Most notably, the Center for the Study of Religion at Princeton University has given me an institutional home—twice as a Visiting Fellow and for many years as an Affiliate Fellow—that has proven invaluable. Generations of graduate students and visiting scholars have endured my rough drafts and provided helpful feedback. I am particularly grateful to Robert Wuthnow and Anita Kline, who have always made me feel at home at Princeton.

Support from the National Endowment for the Humanities allowed me to work intensively on this and related projects during the 2004–05 academic year. Montclair State University offered a sabbatical leave in 2007–08, during which I was able to complete the manuscript.

Numerous friends and colleagues read through earlier versions of the manuscript, or just as usefully, listened to my woes and helped me rethink the organization of the project. In this regard, I would like to especially thank David

Benfield, Mary Bly, Lauren Bryant, Deborah Campbell, Robert Fraser, Ronald Hutton, Elizabeth Leake, Lizzie Reis, Rosemary Radford Ruether, Teresa Shaw, Arlene Stein, Lise Vail, and Sylvia and Robert Wolfe. Uwe Bergermann and the members of his Reading German class at NYU's Deutsches Haus guided me patiently through the mysteries of the German language. In the world of translation, Uwe taught me to fish, which was impressive indeed; but I am also everlastingly grateful to those who just caught the fish and handed them to me. For assistance with French translations, I thank Heidi Katz and Pamela Klassen; for German, Marion Grau, Tamara Schoenbaum, Vondah Sheldon, and the truly amazing Anne Phillips-Krug; for Italian, the brilliant Rosa Zagari-Molinari.

Reed Malcolm of the University of California Press has been patient with me past all reasonable expectations, as have Kalicia Pivirotto, Jacqueline Volin, and Susan Carter, a superb copy editor.

For keeping the home front running smoothly, I thank Jon Greene, Coline Chaumont, Janne Andresen, and Gülşah Kuzakçı. All my love to Jon Greene, Sophie Eller, and Lucy Eller for giving my heart its true home.

The Travels and Travails of Matriarchal Myth

In 2003, Dan Brown became an overnight success and a media sensation with the publication of *The Da Vinci Code*. The novel is formulaic: a thriller. Before the reader can adjust her chaise longue and slather on her sunscreen, our hero, Dr. Robert Langdon, is falsely accused of a heinous crime at the world-famous Louvre Museum in Paris. A beautiful, intelligent Frenchwoman—Sophie Neveu—appears and helps Langdon escape. At first, he does not even realize that he is the intended prey of the authorities. Chases ensue, on foot, by automobile, and by airplane. The mystery begins with strange signs accompanying the murder of Jacques Saunière, a curator at the Louvre, and spirals out from there. Our hero, a Harvard "symbologist," does not have the leisure to sit and cogitate, as he is undoubtedly accustomed to doing back home in the Widener Library stacks. No, he has to run fast and think faster. Not only must he be clever and quick, he must also be physically agile—even forceful—and attuned to the twisted channels of the minds of criminals, religious fanatics, eccentric historians, cunning priests, and corrupt officials . . . all of whom turn out to have a lot in common, since they are on the side of evil. Whom can he trust?

As Western Christian history unravels before him, the apparently good turn out to be evil, and vice versa. Jesus, Christian readers may be relieved to learn, is good, very good. So is his mother, the Virgin Mary. So far so . . . Catholic. But wait: don't start to genuflect yet! Yes, Jesus is good, and his mother is good, but so is his wife! That's right, Jesus's wife, Mary Magdalene. And his great-great-great-etc. granddaughter, our hero's beautiful sidekick and skilled code cracker, Sophie Neveu. If you've never heard of Jesus's wife—or you had, but thought she was a reformed prostitute and devoted disciple, but not a "special friend" of our

Lord—don't feel bad. It's a news flash for most of us, because the world's most powerful and secretive institution (the Catholic Church, naturally) has conspired to keep this information from Jesus's flock for nearly two thousand years. Only a few, the elect, the Leonardo da Vincis of the world, have kept the flame of truth alive for future generations, hoping that one day all Christians will be able to accept the full humanity of the Christ.

After *The Da Vinci Code* raced to the top of the best-seller list, it prompted a culture-wide discussion, from Internet opinion-fests to sermons and Sunday school lessons. It was a boom time for New Testament scholars, who were abruptly handed an audience clamoring to know if any of the novel's revelations could possibly be true. Had Jesus been married? Did he have children? Was Mary Magdalene actually sitting at the table with Jesus and his disciples in Leonardo da Vinci's painting of the Last Supper? Had the Knights Templar carefully preserved secrets too combustible to be acknowledged by the Catholic Church for thousands of years of Christian history? Was there a secret society called the Priory of Sion dedicated to protecting the truth about Jesus and his bloodline? Could the Catholic Church—which everyone seemed ready enough to believe was sufficiently conniving to hide inconvenient truths from its lay members—successfully keep something like that secret? And if it were true that Jesus had been married and had children, what would it change? Everything? Or only a few details, none of them faith shattering? Indeed, was it possible that the new Jesus, the post–*Da Vinci Code* Jesus, could be even better suited to modern sensibilities than the old one?

The Da Vinci Code broke upon the consciousness of most readers not only with the predictable force of a fast-paced thriller, but with the bracing air of unanticipated iconoclasm. And yet part of the appeal of *The Da Vinci Code*'s plot is that it is not really new at all: it is simply the elephant of six-blind-men fame suddenly seen from a different angle. The main fixtures of *The Da Vinci* Code are familiar. With the exception of the alluringly subterranean elements of Opus Dei and the Priory of Sion, they are drawn from Christian high culture: Jesus, Mary Magdalene, the Emperor Constantine, the Catholic Church, the Holy Grail, Leonardo da Vinci, the Louvre, Westminster Abbey. All these people, places, symbols, and organizations are ones we feel proud to be aware of, to embrace as our cultural heritage. Dan Brown tosses them into the air for the action of his novel. But when they come down, they do not form the old familiar picture. Nor do they end up as a heap of unrelated scraps. The puzzle pieces that seemed to admit of only one possible configuration emerge, after a twist of the kaleidoscope, in another light, forming a new, equally symmetrical, and appealingly fresh pattern.

It is the Christian story retold, but with a few key changes. First, the Catholic Church is not the body of Christ on earth. It is wealthy, powerful, sneaky, and bent on retaining its paternalistic authority over its flock by doling out Christian truth in the bite-size servings it believes its children are capable of swallowing (a very Protestant view of Catholicism!). Second, on the fully human, fully divine spectrum debated by the early church councils, Jesus swings dramatically toward the fully human. And he does so in a very significant way: by loving a woman and having a child with her. From this one deft fictional device (toyed with earlier in the rock opera *Jesus Christ Superstar* and Nikos Kazantzakis's novel *The Last Temptation of Christ*) comes a river of theological innovation, all apparently quite intriguing to the modern mind. Christianity is redeemed from its ascetic moralism. We get to keep Jesus, but throw out everything we as a culture have come to find distasteful about Christianity: dogma, institutional authority, the secondary status of women, and a moral preference for chastity over sex. The Holy Grail, sought after by zealous Christians for centuries, turns out to be the sexual, reproductive body of a woman. Sex is good; women are, at the very least, equal to men; and Christianity has its Goddess again.

Wait . . . a Christian Goddess? Now that's not something I learned about in Sunday School. Even if Jesus was married, as the novel contends, where does "the Goddess" come in? Jesus's mother, the Virgin Mary, has been knocking pretty hard on the door of deification for the past thousand-plus years of grassroots Christian culture, but she is still not regarded as a goddess by people who want to keep their Christian noses clean. To complicate matters, the popularity of the Virgin Mary was waxing strong in Western history at the same time that, according to Dan Brown's novel, "the sacred feminine" was being ground under the boot heels of the cassocked gentlemen of Rome. It doesn't seem likely that they would have extended so much ecclesiastical and theological support to the Virgin Mary if she were the secret Christian Goddess. And if the Virgin Mary does not qualify as the "lost Goddess" of Christianity, it is not immediately clear how Mary Magdalene could so qualify in her stead.

The Da Vinci Code is never very precise on this point. Its theological vision is somewhat muddy (perhaps forgivable, given the genre). Throughout, *The Da Vinci Code* stresses the presence of pagan symbols and elements in Christianity, which are gleefully discovered in famous cathedrals all over Europe by the novel's hero.[1] It describes a pre-Christian, "ancient" religion of nature worship and gender balance, "yin and yang," that assures "harmony in the world." Da Vinci himself, according to Langdon, was "in tune with the *balance* between male and female," believing that "a human soul could not be enlightened unless it had both male and female elements."[2]

This gender balance is the official line, but from the outset, the novel emphasizes the "feminine" at the expense of the "masculine." The good Dr. Langdon is writing a book titled *Symbols of the Lost Sacred Feminine*. Saunière, the curator at the Louvre whose murder drives the book's plot, is described as "the premiere goddess iconographer on earth," with "a personal passion for relics relating to fertility, goddess cults, Wicca, and the sacred feminine." Indeed, Saunière "dedicated his life to studying the history of the goddess."[3] The Priory of Sion, the secret society said to have preserved the truth about Jesus's marriage to Mary Magdalene, is not described as a Christian group upholding the ancient notion of divine gender balance in the face of a male-dominated Church. It is a—even *the*— "pagan goddess worship cult."[4] Meanwhile, the Emperor Constantine is said to have been responsible for "waging a campaign of propaganda that demonized the sacred feminine, obliterating the goddess from modern religion forever."[5] It is the "feminine-worshipping religions" that are the target of persecution, not some ideally balanced male-and-female religion. And the central tragedy of Western history is the church-driven conversion of the world, in Dan Brown's phrase, "from matriarchal paganism to patriarchal Christianity."[6]

Jesus's humanity and Mary Magdalene's central role in early Christianity is positioned as a rediscovery of true Christian history, a redressing of the Christian church's gender imbalance and a long overdue correction to its anti-sex morality.[7] But *The Da Vinci Code* actually goes further than this: it reclaims paganism at the expense of Christianity. Once "bad" Christianity—essentially, the Catholic Church—is separated from "true" Christianity, all that's really left is the person of Jesus.[8] This Jesus does not emerge as the Christ, the Messiah, or even as a particularly astute rabbi. Rather, he is the sacrificed pagan hero-king, the consort of the Goddess, who appears in the person of his wife, Mary Magdalene. The Judaism of Jesus and his bride never appears in any guise other than as a variant of paganism, yet another of the many ancient religions devoted to fertility and goddess worship, the mating of male and female in sacred sexual union. Indeed, the Star of David, which we are told is ignorantly read as the central symbol of a monotheistic Judaism, turns out to represent two deities. It is a superimposition of male and female signs "marking the Holy of Holies, where the male and female deities—Yahweh and Shekhinah—were thought to dwell."[9]

To me, this is what makes *The Da Vinci Code* so fascinating as a cultural phenomenon: it is a novel that imagines a sex-positive, harmonious ancient world, purportedly balanced between the genders but focused on "the sacred feminine"; and it blames religion—specifically Christianity—for the invention of male dominance. Even more striking to me is that this novel was received with incredible enthusiasm by a twenty-first-century, nominally Christian audience. People *loved* this book, as gushing commentary all over the Internet attests.[10] In what did its appeal lie?

Whatever the appeal of *The Da Vinci Code* was to its readers, it is something that has been appealing for quite some time now. For *The Da Vinci Code* is yet another variant of a story I call the myth of matriarchal prehistory: the belief that women held greater power and place in times past than they do today; that male dominance, at least in the form we've known it in the past couple of millennia, is a comparatively new invention; that the gender of the deities a culture worships is indicative of which human sex it values more; and that we now stand at an important world historical turning point where gender relations are concerned. As Sophie Neveu's grandmother tells Harvard symbology professor Robert Langdon at the close of *The Da Vinci Code:* "The pendulum is swinging. We are starting to sense the dangers of our history . . . and of our destructive paths. We are beginning to sense the need to restore the sacred feminine. . . . You mentioned you are writing a manuscript about the symbols of the sacred feminine, are you not? . . . Finish it, Mr. Langdon. Sing her song. The world needs modern troubadours."[11]

And the world has them aplenty, most of them not making any pretense of hiding behind a fictional narrative, as Dan Brown does.[12] For the past forty years, matriarchal myth has had quite a hearing, especially among feminists and neopagans. Feminists have found in matriarchal myth license to hope that just as male dominance had a beginning in ancient times, it can have an end too: that the oppression of women is not our only cultural heritage, but merely our most recent.[13] Neopagans have relished telling a countercultural myth that reverses many of the value signs of Western culture, counting polytheism, magic, nature, sex, the body, and women among its greatest goods.

Others have also found succor in matriarchal myth. Afrocentrists such as Chiekh Anta Diop and Ifi Amadiume have assigned Mother Africa the role of the Goddess. In Africa, they say, benevolent matriarchs presided over the birth and long, peaceful history of humanity. It was in the north, in Asia and Europe, where warlike, patriarchal cultures emerged, viewing woman as "only a burden that the man dragged behind him."[14] Another version of matriarchal myth, narrated in Jim Mason's *An Unnatural Order,* asserts that the fall of humanity came with the development of agriculture, which "broke the primal bonds with the living world and put human beings above all other life."[15] Especially damaging, says Mason, was the domestication of large animals to provide work, milk, and meat. Mason's central concern is animal rights, but significantly, his story is also gendered: it is men who absorbed the lesson taught by animal domestication most readily and who applied it to the females of their own species, reducing them to economic and sexual slavery.

A few even quirkier takes on matriarchal myth emerged in the last decade of the twentieth century, each with its own peculiar focus. In *Food of the Gods,* Terence McKenna reminisces about the good old days, with their good old drugs (primarily marijuana and psilocybin), which made woman-centered prehistory a blissful place to hang out and get high. He laments the rise of patriarchy and its use of bad drugs (alcohol, cocaine, and sugar) that make everyone fretful and men nasty and domineering. William Bramley, author of *The Gods of Eden,* takes matriarchal myth to its logical extreme. He argues that all was bliss on earth until we were colonized by extraterrestrials (the "Custodians") who brought war, disease, hierarchy, and, of course, male dominance. Other proponents of matriarchal myth have even suggested that earth was populated solely by females until male extraterrestrials landed with their alien Y chromosomes and irretrievably polluted the human gene pool with the virus of maleness.

In spite of its countercultural flavor, the myth of matriarchal prehistory has also been mainstreamed, appearing in world history textbooks, news magazines, and other popular media. Some, such as author Jacqueline Shannon, stick with the feminist message. Her reason no. 8 for "why it's great to be a girl" is that "anthropologists and archaeologists credit females with the 'civilization' of humankind" because they "dragged men, kicking and screaming, out of savagery into the New Stone Age."[16] Former U.S. vice president Al Gore, arguing for sane environmental policies in *Earth in the Balance,* notes that a prehistoric "reverence for the sacredness of the earth" may have been tied to "the worship of a single earth goddess, who was assumed to be the fount of all life and who radiated harmony among all living things."[17] Even the glossy magazine *Healing Retreats and Spas* got in on the action in 2000 with "The Goddess Issue," offering healthy eating with Demeter; aromatherapy "to nurture the goddess in everyone"; prenatal yoga ("Embodying the Goddess"); and an article titled "Season of the Goddess: Rediscovering the Divine Feminine," proclaiming that "the goddess was once a universal icon with countless names, faces, and attributes."[18]

Anyone who lived through the women's liberation movement of the 1960s and 1970s knows that during those decades gender came, for a time, to be of overwhelming cultural and political interest. We were collectively absorbed in rethinking the rightful roles of women and men, from the kitchen to the boardroom to the sanctuary. That imagined alternative histories of sex relations flowered as the women's movement explored its contours in the 1970s and 1980s is to be expected. What is perhaps more surprising is that our love affair with matriarchal myth in its variant forms still continues today (as witness *The Da Vinci Code* phenomenon). And though it has been easy—and sometimes politically expedient—to forget this, matriarchal myth did not erupt onto the scene as a made-to-order feminist myth at the first conference of the National Organization for Women in 1966, or in the heady years immediately after. Matriarchal myth—the belief that women's status has declined dramatically, has changed completely, since a male takeover some three thousand years ago—has been a staple theme in Western thought for nearly a century and a half and has carried a variety of meanings and messages. The genesis of the myth as we know it today is easy to locate. In 1861, a Swiss lawyer and scholar of the classics, Johann Jakob Bachofen, published a book titled *Das Mutterrecht: Eine Untersuchung über die Gynaikokratie der alten Welt nach Ihrer Religiösen und Rechtlichen Natur* (Mother Right: A Study of the Religious and Juridical Nature of Gynecocracy in the Ancient World).[19]

Bachofen's interest in woman-rule grew out of a tradition existing from classical times up through the mid-nineteenth century. Throughout this period, people were fond of telling stories of female-dominant societies, usually drawing explicitly on Amazon myths from antiquity. But Bachofen's *Mutterrecht* did something new. It claimed that Amazons were not oddities, prisoners either of the overheated human imagination or of a few isolated spots on the globe where women had set up their own societies without men. Instead Bachofen claimed that myths of Amazons, along with a lot of other mythical and archaeological evidence, added up to clear proof that in its infancy, humankind was actually gynecocratic: ruled by women. Only later did men seize the power that characterized most of recorded history and the western European society in which Bachofen and his contemporaries lived.

Bachofen was only the beginning. In his own lifetime Bachofen was quickly shunted aside to make room for other proponents of matriarchal myth, some of whom invented the idea independently of him. Leading the charge in Great Britain was the Scottish lawyer John Ferguson McLennan. Just four years after *Das Mutterrecht* was published, McLennan released *Primitive Marriage,* a very different sort of study from Bachofen's, but one that also "discovered" women's central role in prehistory. Enthusiasm for the matriarchal theory spread quickly and was essentially adopted as historical truth by the emerging discipline of anthropology, not only in Great Britain, but to a lesser extent, in the United States and continental Europe as well. From the mid-1860s through to the 1890s, the question was not so much *whether* "primitive" and prehistoric societies were matriarchal, but in what way. Then, beginning in 1884 with the publication of *Origin of the Family, Private Property, and the State,* by Friedrich Engels (communist organizer and longtime collaborator with Karl Marx), the myth of matriarchal prehistory was taken up as effective political ammunition by both communists and first-wave feminists, and later by fascists as well.[20]

The myth of matriarchal prehistory was largely set aside by anthropologists in the early years of the twentieth century. Matriarchal myth lost the center stage it had enjoyed in the last decades of the late nineteenth century and would not regain it until the late twentieth century, under feminist auspices. However, these two efflorescences of matriarchal myth are intimately, even lineally, related. For when the discipline of anthropology disavowed matriarchal myth, others picked it up: some in the academy and many outside, bringing with them wildly diverse political, psychological, and scholarly interests. In the first half of the twentieth century, matriarchal myth traveled across continents, between academic disciplines, from the political right to the political left and back again. The myth did not attain the common cultural currency it held in the late nineteenth century, which it would find again in the late twentieth. But it was still on the move. It made itself at home among sexologists, psychoanalysts, poets, mythographers, and archaeologists, to name a few, and served as a foundational myth for the emerging religion of Wicca beginning in Britain in the 1950s. Meanwhile, in nations striving to remain true to Marxist principles—Soviet Russia and Maoist China—matriarchy was what archaeologists and anthropologists were supposed to find when they entered the field (because Engels said they would), and find it they did.

When second-wave feminists "discovered" matriarchal myth in the late twentieth century, they did so primarily by reading the work of their forebears, from nineteenth-century anthropologists up through the scattered variants of matriarchal myth that had sprung up in multiple pockets of the social fabric in the intervening decades. The reconstructions of prehistory that feminists found most convincing were archaeological, and they made ample use of both old and new archaeological findings to support their argument that patriarchal society and patriarchal gods were a recent development. But pretty much every available approach to matriarchal myth was interleaved into the emerging feminist myth. The existence of goddess-worshipping, nonpatriarchal societies was confirmed for its proponents through myth, folklore, psychology, poetry, even dreams and past-life recollections. Given the many proponents of matriarchal myth who came before them, only rarely did they have to create their material *ex nihilo*. What we are looking at, then, is a modern conversation spanning many decades, many generations, and many political orientations. *The Da Vinci Code* is just another link in the chain.

When seen in historical perspective, what is most intriguing about the myth of matriarchal prehistory is not so much its recent feminist message, but rather the robustness and flexibility of the myth itself. Matriarchal myth is a thread that runs brightly through the intellectual life of the West, testifying to the confusion, conflict, and political interest surrounding the topic of gender. "What if?" the myth asks, over and over again across the decades. What if women rather than men ran the world? What if the very things that have been seen as women's social disabilities—pregnancy, childbirth, lactation—were once regarded as the chief characteristics of the divine? What if the battle of the sexes were laid to rest and women and men cooperated to create a benevolent, harmonious social world? What if God were Goddess? The myth of matriarchal history is, at heart, an enormous thought experiment, a play with reversals, an endeavor to visualize a past radically different from the present. And though its fulcrum is gender, the pivot around which history turns, matriarchal myth takes up all manner of human concerns in its reach: sex, religion, economy, politics; art, food, language, child rearing, science . . . all have been tagged with the labels "feminine," "matriarchal," or "goddess" at some point in the last century and a half. As an orientation—or reorientation—toward human history, matriarchal myth has been made to speak to nearly every aspect of human existence.

Today it is difficult to see the myth of matriarchal prehistory as anything other than feminist. What possible motive, if not a feminist one, could inspire such zeal to find a woman-centered utopia in the past? What possible take-home message could matriarchal myth have, other than its obvious one, that male dominance is a major historical mistake that must be corrected immediately, if not sooner? But matriarchal myth has not always carried a feminist message, nor have its narrators primarily been women.

This book examines the first era of matriarchal imagining in the modern West, one that permeated late nineteenth-century culture as thoroughly and effectively as contemporary matriarchal myth did in the late twentieth century. Late nineteenth-century narrators of matriarchal myth were almost all men. Indeed, when late nineteenth-century women took up matriarchal myth, they borrowed it from the men who came before them, changing relatively little in the process (the opposite of today's situation, in which men like Dan Brown follow in the footsteps of late twentieth-century women such as Marija Gimbutas and Riane Eisler, who have anchored the current era in the history of matriarchal myth).[21] Among late nineteenth-century narrators of matriarchal myth, the rise of male dominance was more often viewed as an improvement in human social relations than as a catastrophe. Patriarchy was typically seen as another rung up the ladder of human progress from its beginnings in "savagery." But even in these earliest manifestations, matriarchal myth draws our attention to emerging fault lines in Western culture's understanding of gender and sex inequality. The very fact that patriarchy was not regarded as universal and inevitable by the late nineteenth-century men who pioneered matriarchal myth indicates that a more nuanced and ambivalent attitude toward gender was emerging.

For all their bravado—and it was sometimes extreme—the matriarchal myth of late nineteenth-century men did not outlast them. As George Stocking points out, none of the evolutionary anthropologists who dominated matriarchal discourse during the Victorian era has today "the obvious world historical significance of a Marx, or the general intellectual historical significance of a Freud. . . . Nor have they the discipline-forming historical significance of a Weber or a Durkheim; none of them offers a general theoretical standpoint. . . . Nor would they be regarded today . . . as major investors in the general intellectual capital of the modern human sciences."[22] Ironically, the matriarchal myth of Bachofen's *Mutterrecht*, little celebrated when it was published, had a slightly longer shelf life than that of British anthropologists, as it gradually won fans on both the political left and right in continental Europe in the early years of the twentieth century. But neither Bachofen nor the British anthropologists, neither Friedrich Engels nor first-wave feminists, successfully pushed their matriarchal narrative forward to those they considered their proper intellectual heirs. Those that followed them in their chosen fields either disowned matriarchal myth entirely—sometimes with real vitriol—or else, like the Soviets, who preserved the matriarchal myth of Engels, half-heartedly kicked it along while turning their real intellectual passions in other directions.

The dramatic decline of matriarchal myth among anthropologists at the end of the nineteenth century is generally attributed to intellectual advances resulting from more and better ethnographic work and changing methodologies for addressing questions of human social relations, whether prehistoric, historic, or contemporary. But I believe that the heyday of matriarchal myth in the nineteenth century passed largely because the questions it addressed—having to do with marriage, women's rights, and Victorian sexual attitudes—fell out of vogue, and the whole theoretical apparatus of an evolutionary shift from matriarchy to patriarchy went with it, like the baby with the bathwater. Theories of matriarchal prehistory did not attain the same sort of prominence again until a similar set of questions—about women's rights and sexual attitudes, among other things—again engaged the public, this time in the United States in the 1970s.

Indeed, one of the most interesting aspects of the nineteenth-century debate about matriarchy among Victorian men is the way that it prefigures twentieth-century feminist debate. Both return relentlessly to the same story of evolving human social life; both have a small set of confirming cases to which they appeal again and again (though in the nineteenth century, these were mainly ethnographic, and in the twentieth century, they were mainly archaeological); both are diligent about refining the particulars of their story and will debate relatively minor points without ever calling into question the larger enterprise; and both are populated by a handful of truly brilliant, synthetic minds, along with a veritable army of lesser devotees, pedantic detail-mongers, and other camp followers. Lastly, both have presented a story compelling enough that others with divergent political interests have found ways to bend it to their own use. In the late twentieth century, women owned matriarchal myth, though they shared it with others who did not always have the same political agenda. But in the late nineteenth century, men owned the myth: they defined it and refined it, most of them pretending to scholarly disinterestedness as they nevertheless vigorously interrogated the origins, legitimacy, and future of sex inequality.

THE "MYTH" IN MATRIARCHAL MYTH

By now, it must be apparent that I regard this narrative of matriarchal human origins as a myth, but what does that mean? The term *myth* has a tortured history. For several centuries now, scholars from a variety of disciplines have devoted years of their professional lives to coming up with adequate definitions of myth.[23] With the right definition, it has been hoped, myths could be made to yield up their true meanings, what has animated them and made them objects of respect, and sometimes reverence, by those who tell them. As with the term *religion*, the meaning of *myth* is both obvious and obscure. We feel we know a myth when we hear one, just as we usually feel comfortable identifying the presence of religion in cultures vastly different from our own. If we can keep our gaze in soft focus, it really isn't very difficult to know when we have encountered a myth or a religion. But scholars are notoriously dissatisfied with the soft-focus lens. And as soon as one attempts to define terms like *myth* or *religion* with any precision, they squirm away with impressive agility. It's like trying to catch fish with your bare hands. You might get lucky, but more likely, you'll just get wet.

This is when one is after a value-neutral, phenomenological definition of myth. Most people do not experience myths as value-neutral. Either they love myths, or they hate them . . . or they love-them-and-hate-them, depending on which stories are being called myths. In any given cultural milieu, one can find people who yearn for myth with a lover-like desperation, who want to imbue every aspect of life, from the individual to the communal, with the "mythic" view, which seems to them the only one capable of capturing the essence of being and experience (a view especially associated with romanticism). On the other hand, it is just as easy to find those who think that myth is, in a word, ridiculous, and can't imagine what redeeming value could exist in such absurdly fanciful stories.

Imagine being herded into a concert hall to hear a performance of avant-garde classical music. Some members of the audience will be swooning with aesthetic ecstasy while others will want to cover their ears and run away. This may have something to do with individuals' musical education or lack thereof, or the fine-tunedness of their ear. Certainly those who love the music will claim that. But maybe it as simple as saying that there is no accounting for taste. Like avant-garde classical music, "myth"—that is, the big broad category of myth (myths, "mythic awareness," "mythic consciousness," etc.)—tends to be polarizing. It has been so since ancient times, when some Athenians lovingly recited and acted out their culture's myths, while others, such as Xenophanes, Herodotus, and even Socrates, dismissed the same myths as dangerous foolishness.

In the West, attempts to define *myth* have occurred within and alongside internal Christian controversies regarding the authority of scripture. Once having been exposed to other cultures' myths, Christians could not miss the similarities of foreign myths to biblical stories: similarities in style, cultural use, and sometimes even in content. But Bible stories were "true": they had been revealed by God. The myths of other cultures were just stories believed in by credulous "primitives."[24] Since then, however neutrally scholars have sought to define *myth,* the term has never successfully been pried loose from its shadowy antipodes: "history," "science," and "truth." Nor has *myth* escaped its longstanding connotations of "fiction," "story," and "legend." In our commonsense use of the word "myth" there lingers the assessment of Sir James George Frazer that myths are "mistaken explanations of phenomena, whether of human life or of external nature."[25]

Certainly it is possible to regard a myth as simultaneously untrue and enormously significant, as conveying important truths in the type of vehicle best suited for this purpose.[26] Many Jews and Christians, for example, are now routinely taught that the first chapter of the book of Genesis is not a historical account of exactly how God created the universe and human beings in six days; rather, it is a metaphorical, symbolically rich story that we tell in order to illuminate the nature of God and God's intentions for humanity. Some proponents of matriarchal myth have taken exactly this step with the myth of matriarchal prehistory, claiming to speak of matriarchal origins in order to spark thought, inspire, or clarify and question what we ordinarily think of as "reality." Like the Romantic philosophers Schelling and Schlegel, these matriarchalists regard myth as "sublimely transrational," as "a vehicle of deeper truths than those conveyed by scientific, denotative discourse."[27] But for most people, it remains difficult to completely disassociate the label "myth" from determinations of truth or falsity.

For the sake of the present discussion of matriarchal myth, the question of its accuracy as a factual account of human prehistory (and history) could simply be bracketed and set aside for the duration. Whether matriarchal myth is true or false, or true in parts and false in others, is, to one way of thinking, irrelevant to engaging with the story's history, its changing contours, and its enduring appeal. While one *could* do this, I choose not to. To me, it matters whether the account of matriarchal origins is factual or not. It tells us what the myth's narrators have been up to for all these years. Have they been scientifically reconstructing the history of human society on earth? Or have they been making up stories that fill their cultural and psychological needs?

At a deep epistemological level, depending on how nihilistic you are or how much you distrust "science," these two options may be the same: we may think we are engaging in rigorous intellectual, scientific thought when we are simply making up stories we find pleasing. Our intellectual abilities and our capacity for disinterestedness are limited. We cannot know exactly what happened in prehistoric times. Beyond a few particulars, we cannot really know what happened in historic times either, nor can we precisely identify the extent to which our wish to believe certain things about ourselves has prejudiced our reconstruction of the "facts" of history. History is an imperfect science, if it is a science at all.

But this sort of nihilism, I would argue, applies only at the extreme limits of human thought. Short of that, there are better and worse histories, ones that conform more closely or not to the evidence we have at hand. And as histories go, the matriarchal theory is very weak. There is little evidence to support it, and it is generally unconvincing to anyone not already wanting very much to believe it. The proffered evidence is said to prove a lot when it proves little or nothing; even when it sometimes better supports other interpretations of history. I have treated this issue at length in a previous book *(The Myth of Matriarchal Prehistory: Why an Invented Past Won't Give Women a Future)*, and so I will not reiterate it here.[28] Matriarchal myth is a fascinating cultural phenomenon, and I want the freedom to treat it as one without having to shout down those who would balk at the notion that it is anything other than a true account of human social life on earth. We have little reason to believe that the story of our matriarchal, goddess-worshipping past (or a gender-egalitarian past, for that matter) is true. Therefore, we have good reason to believe that the matriarchal story first and foremost reflects our cultural needs and desires, and those of its earlier narrators.

So when I call the matriarchal theory "myth," I do indeed mean that it is not true, that it is fictional, that as an account of human social history, it fails elementary evidentiary tests. I will not be attempting to hide this "bias," this evaluation of the historical likelihood of society having once been universally matriarchal or gender-egalitarian up until patriarchy burst onto the stage of human history, unbidden, unwelcome, and utterly unprecedented. But in the present context I am far more interested in how the story is used, how it has been passed from one narrator to another, and what it says about Western culture's recent wrestlings with gender.

Fortunately, scholarly, value-neutral approaches to myth, slippery though they can sometimes be, take exactly this approach: they observe the existence of a story people hold to be important and then look to see how the story is deployed, what interests (or whose) it supports, and how it functions in society. In a pithy phrase, Bruce Lincoln sums up this view: "Myth is ideology in narrative form."[29] The matriarchal theory of human origins and history fits scholarly definitions of myth beautifully. It is a story told repeatedly, in different versions and by different narrators, and it is granted a high degree of moral authority by its narrators.

Let us begin with the issue of repetition. Myths are told again and again, in different contexts, and across generations. Unlike one of Faulkner's short stories, for example, a myth "is not identical with any given text." It is, as French structuralist Lévi-Strauss has it, the sum of all its different versions, long and short, told in many contexts, with varying details and interpretations.[30] Myths have "strong contrasts" (as, for example, matriarchy and patriarchy, goddess and god) that help to make them easy to memorize and retell. Their principal narrative elements stand out clearly against one another.[31]

Myths are also characterized by the importance granted to them. They are considered more credible and influential than other sorts of stories; they are believed to speak about what matters most. As Bruce Lincoln puts it, myths convey not just truth, but *"paradigmatic* truth"; they evoke "the sentiments out of which society is actively constructed."[32] Myths seek to order the world, to give it meaning. As such, myths tend to take, for their subject matter, things that are painful, inexplicable, or both.[33] Sex inequality, I would argue, is painful, for both women and men, which is why it crops up in myths over and over again.[34] Honestly, it does not take a moral genius to see that women are treated unfairly in patriarchal societies. Even people highly socialized to believe that sex inequality is natural, unavoidable, and morally right can find it troubling. An explanation for this inequality is required.[35] Matriarchal myth, I suggest, is an effort to provide this explanation, to make sense out of the painful ambiguities of sex inequality. It does this, intriguingly, whether the narrator is in favor of sex inequality or against it, whether sex inequality is seen as a reality to be accepted in good grace or as a hideous abomination of the natural order.

As it has been told and retold by successive generations, matriarchal myth itself has been altered and adapted to suit the interests of its varied narrators.[36] But this is only half the story. Matriarchal myth has shifted about in all sorts of ways over the course of the past 150 years. Yet it has also remained quite hauntingly the same story throughout its circuitous travels in Western thought and politics. Its grammar, its plot elements, its structuring devices are all very, very similar in its different tellings. The fact that such contradictory agendas have all found safe harbor in the confines of matriarchal myth is itself remarkable. It is testimony, I believe, to the shared bank of assumptions about gender made by most thinkers in the West, no matter what their political perspective. As such, the myth of matriarchal prehistory provides a superb case study for probing Western assumptions and ambitions regarding gender: both what is (largely) shared and what is contested. The core tropes of the myth show us the former; the morphing details show us the latter.

2

Amazons Everywhere

Matriarchal Myth before Bachofen

The gynococracy or government of women was quite universally spread for it existed not only among the Scythians, Sarmatians and Amazons in particular but it occurred in both Asias where the warlike women who had been their mistresses had set the style for all the women living under their empire of making themselves rulers over their husbands although they were not all so warlike or so far separated from men as those who gloried in living far from them and seeing them only at set times.

—JOSEPH LAFITAU

Prior to the publication of Bachofen's *Das Mutterrecht,* most of the Western world was convinced that the patriarchal family was the original human society, since it was laid out as such in the book of Genesis.[1] Bachofen was the first to offer something very different, a coherent narrative that gave women and goddesses primacy in an early phase of human history only to stipulate their complete overthrow by a later social system that favored men and male gods. However, Bachofen did not create this version of prehistory *ex nihilo.* He had a lot of preexisting matriarchal material to work with. Amazon stories had been very popular from ancient times forward, indicating a continuous interest in exploring gender reversals. And especially in the eighteenth century, philosophers were beginning to experiment with time lines of human social development that they believed had universal applicability. All that remained was for someone to alchemize gender reversals into an evolutionary historical account. By 1861, the stage was beautifully set: all that was left was to bring up the lights and let the show begin.

THE ENDURING APPEAL OF THE AMAZON

Variants of matriarchal myth have been found all around the world. For example, a Kikuyu myth from Africa traces the origin of the people to a family of nine sisters whose husbands all agreed to live under a matriarchal system. This system continued for generations. The men's lot was a harsh one. They had to tolerate humiliation and injustice at the hands of the ruling women and were expected to remain sexually faithful to their spouses, although their wives were at liberty to take multiple husbands. The men wished to rebel but were not as physically strong as their wives. Finally, the men plotted to impregnate all their wives simultaneously. While the women were indisposed, the men took over. They have been in power ever since.[2] Similar myths have been identified in South America, Africa, Oceania, and Australia. One type of such myths associates social power with the possession of sacred flutes, trumpets, or other ritual paraphernalia. These objects are held exclusively by men, but legends say they were originally the possession or even the creation of women, who held the social power associated with them until the ritual objects were stolen by the men.[3]

Several ancient Greek myths also tell of women's loss of power in what amounts to a patriarchal revolution. The most famous of these is a rather late and fragmentary account of the naming of the city of Athens. It is attributed to Varro in Augustine's *City of God*. According to this narrative, an olive tree and a spring of water issued forth in the city that became known as Athens. The residents were told by Apollo that the olive tree was from Athena and the spring from Poseidon, and that the citizens should name their city after one of these deities. All the women voted for Athena and all the men for Poseidon, and because the women of Athens outnumbered the men (by one), Athena won the vote. This enraged Poseidon, who flooded the land. Apollo recommended that in order to assuage Poseidon's anger, the Athenian men should take away women's right to vote, refuse to call them Athenians, and stop the practice of naming their children after their mothers.[4]

The nineteenth-century men who invented modern matriarchal myth did not have access to many non-Western myths of the loss of women's power, most of which came to the attention of outsiders only after the turn of the twentieth century. But they were exceedingly well versed in classical texts and so were familiar with stories like that of the naming of Athens. Interestingly, however, the classical resources most favored for Western experiments with gender reversals prior to Bachofen's work were not matriarchal myths, but stories of the Amazons. The Amazons did not represent a female-dominant past that occurred prior to the takeover of men, and thus cannot truly be counted as matriarchal myths. Amazons were geographically, not chronologically, separate from normative society. Just where they lived was never settled in the classical era. When ancient explorers did not find Amazons in the lands where legend said they lived, they did not sacrifice their belief in Amazons; they merely said the Amazons lived a bit farther off.[5]

Classical scholarship has long been dogged by the question of whether or not the Amazons actually existed. Quite often, it was simply assumed that they did, because they were treated so familiarly and their stories told so frequently in classical Greek culture. Amazons are common in ancient Greek art, drama, and mythology, appearing in everything from plays to histories to medical treatises, as well as innumerable vase paintings. Stories of Amazons date back to Homer and were referenced repeatedly through the time of Alexander the Great and even beyond. In Asia Minor, where the Greeks believed that most Amazon societies were situated, Greek cities were often named after Amazons who were said to have been entombed there.[6] Amazons were thought to hunt on horseback, fight wars, and wear clothing usually reserved for men. More colorfully, it was said that Amazons could not marry until they had killed a man (or sometimes, three men) in battle.[7] Amazons raised their daughters but killed, enslaved, or abandoned their sons. Most often, their societies were said to be made up exclusively of women and their children, but occasionally they were depicted as including adult men, who were carefully kept in submission to their wives.[8] The common notion that Amazons cut off their right breast, the better to draw their bowstrings, seems to stem from an etymological error: the ancient Greeks interpreted the word *amazon*—which doesn't seem to have been a Greek word at all—as deriving from the Greek roots *a-mazon*, meaning "without a breast." In actuality, Amazons are never depicted in ancient Greek art with fewer breasts than the standard two.[9]

Among classicists today there is a virtual consensus that the Amazons did not exist, at least not in anything like the form attributed to them in Greek myth. They are, like centaurs and giants, regarded as fictional antagonists in the battles of the ancient world. Their special role, say classicists, was to teach Athenians and other "civilized" peoples that the rule of women was freakish, dangerous, and certainly not to be risked in any form. Stories of the Amazons did not, as one might imagine, cause the peoples of antiquity to conclude that female dominance or equality might be acceptable, given that it was already being successfully practiced by the Amazons. Instead, the Amazons were set up as the archetypal reversal of all that was good and right in patriarchal society. In fact, the Amazons were always eventually routed by the Greek heroes, no matter how bravely they fought. As the orator Lysias concludes in a speech delivered in 389 B.C.E. in honor of those killed in battle, "When matched with our Athenian ancestors they [the Amazons] appeared in all the natural timidity of their sex, and showed themselves less women in their external appearance than in their weakness and cowardice."[10]

Although the Amazons were in all likelihood fictional, they continued to exercise a powerful fascination long after the demise of classical Greek civilization. For many generations, from the fall of the Roman Empire up to Bachofen's

FIGURE 1. A fifteenth-century depiction of Amazons from *The Nuremberg Chronicle,*
by Hartmann Schedel

invention of modern matriarchal myth, Amazon tales continued to be widely
told. Classic Amazon myths were embroidered upon with relish, and new Amazon myths were created, again with the usual moral lesson of masculine triumph.[11] The first author to truly celebrate the Amazons and mourn their passing was the Venetian writer Christine de Pizan, often lauded as the first Western
feminist writer. In her 1405 book *Le Livre de la Cité des Dames* (The Book of the
City of Ladies), Pizan depicted the Amazons as autonomous women whose existence proved that all women are in fact capable of wielding social and military
power. She claimed that the reign of the Amazons was "extremely long-lived,"
lasting for over eight hundred years. Turning to the Amazon stories of her medieval peers, Pizan asserted that the male authors were blind to the clear implication of their own stories, arguing that it was not men who emerged triumphant in these tales, but rather women.[12] As early as the fifteenth century, then,
the possibility of a feminist interpretation of Amazon stories had emerged.

Pizan's positive valuation of Amazons was unusual, however, both in her own time and for the following five centuries. Amazons typically evoked far more ambivalent emotions, which at least partially accounts for their continued appeal. The best-known postclassical Amazon stories were those found in the Amadís cycle, a series of chivalric romances recounting the adventures of the knight Amadís and his son Esplandián. The first four books in the Amadís cycle were published in 1508 in Spain through the efforts of Garcia Rodríguez de Montalvo, who claimed—probably accurately—to be producing editions of tales that dated in their oral forms to the thirteenth and fourteenth centuries. Montalvo also claimed—probably inaccurately—to be discovering additional tales about Amadís in buried chests brought from Constantinople. The origin of the stories was disputed at the time and is still questioned today, with the Portuguese, Spanish, and French all embracing the original romances as their own. Throughout the sixteenth century, new volumes were added to the series by Spaniards Feliciano de Silva and Pedro de Luján, and then by Italian and German authors, who produced several more sequels, adding up to a total of twenty-four volumes. The Amadís stories were enormously popular. By 1650 the initial four-volume *Amadís de Gaula* had been reprinted 267 times in Spain alone and, according to one German publisher, sold more briskly in German than did the writings of Martin Luther.[13]

Amazons are not the principal characters in the Amadís cycle. The heroic knights are the protagonists in these stories, and like the ancient Greeks, they battle all sorts of enemies, including fantastical creatures such as giants and headless men. Amazons make significant appearances, though. They are not true heroines: they ultimately lose in battle. One commentator describes Montalvo's Amazons as "silly, vain, over-dressed, erotic, helpless, cruel, and inept," among other adjectives.[14] These Amazons are, significantly, not Christians, as are all the knights of the Amadís cycle (who regularly thank God for their victories and attend church for sermons and confession).[15] As Alison Taufer argues in her essay "The Only Good Amazon Is a Converted Amazon," the paganism of the Amazons is an important aspect of their characterization in the Amadís cycle. The Amazons, the stories suggest, can become proper civilized women if only they will convert to Christianity. Montalvo, Silva, and Luján all work with variations of a narrative motif in which an Amazon queen, at war with the Christian knights, is eventually persuaded that the Christian God is the true God.[16] For example, Calafia, the Amazon queen who features in Montalvo's *Sergas de Esplandián* (the fourth book in the Amadís cycle), is won over to Christianity through the chivalry of Amadís, who refuses to attack her, but simply "fights defensively until he can capture her weapons without wounding her." Calafia is treated with great honor after she is taken prisoner, and she falls in love with the handsome Esplandián, the son of Amadís. Esplandián marries another, but Calafia converts to Christianity anyway, explaining, "As I have just seen the order of your law, and the great disorder of others, it is very clear that you follow the truth, and we, lies and falsehood." Upon her conversion, Calafia announces that her people will no longer live without men and engage in promiscuous sex with strangers, but will follow the "normal habits of procreation between men and women." Presumably they also give up the habit of feeding their male infants to their pet griffins.[17]

The popularity of the Amadís tales was intimately entwined with the conquest of the Americas. The Indians that the conquistadores encountered in the New World—like the fictional Amazons—were always described as polytheistic pagans who needed to be offered the chance to accept Christianity (unlike Jews and Muslims, who were intractable enemies of the faith, having rejected Christianity).[18] But for medieval Europeans the Amazons were not only *like* Indians, a fictional substitute for them . . . they *were* Indians, living in the Americas among other native tribes. European conquistadores frequently claimed that they encountered Amazons in the lands they explored. Some even specifically set out in search of the legendary Amazons, spurred on by sponsorship from monarchs such as Queen Isabella of Spain. Columbus, Cortés, Orellana, Guzmán . . . all returned from their voyages to the New World with stories of islands populated solely by women who kill or give away their infant sons and who are possessed of incredible wealth.[19] In the late sixteenth century, the English explorer Sir Walter Raleigh returned from a voyage to South America to report on the existence of Amazon tribes that were very like their ancient Greek counterparts:

> But they which are not far from Guiana do acompanie with men but once in a yeare, and for the time of one moneth, which I gather by their relation to be in Aprill. And that time all Kings of the borders assemble, and Queenes of the Amazones, and after the Queenes have chosen, the rest cast lots for their Valentines. This one moneth, they feast, dance, & drinke of their wines in abundance, and the Moone being done, they all depart to their owne Provinces. If they conceive, and be delievered of a sonne, they returne him to the father, if of a daughter they nourish it, and retaine it, and as many as have daughters send unto the begetters a Present, all being desirous to increase their owne sex and kind, but that they cut off the right dug of the brest I do not finde to be true. It was farther told me, that if in these wars they tooke any prisoners that they used to accompany with those also at what time soever, but in the end for certaine they put them to death: for they are said to be very cruell and bloodthirsty, especially to such as offer to invade their territories.[20]

Some medieval scholars and explorers believed that the Amazons of Greek antiquity actually migrated to South America after the death of their queen Penthesilea, so that the Amazon tribes described by the conquistadores were in fact the descendants of the ancient Amazons of Greek mythology.[21] Taking the existence of these female-dominant tribes for granted, the conquistadores gave the name "Amazon" to the longest river in South America, and they named California after the fictional Amazon queen Calafia from Montalvo's *Sergas de Esplandián.*[22]

Greek and New World Amazons served essentially the same purpose for those who told tales of them: to imagine an inversion of the narrator's culture and provide a means of approaching "savage" cultures.[23] Although the Amazon was a popular figure in medieval and Renaissance times, and sometimes treated generously within a text, her independence of men was not to be tolerated. By the end of the narrative, she had to be safely restored to her place in a male-dominant world. This can be seen in Edmund Spenser's famous sixteenth-century novel, *The Faerie Queene,* which wrestles with the question of the proper place of women by pitting two fighting women—Britomart and Radigund—against each other. Radigund is an Amazon queen, ruling a city of women. She holds men prisoner and dresses them in women's clothes in order to demean them. One of the men she has imprisoned is Artegall, Britomart's lover. Britomart comes to the Amazon city to rescue Artegall. When she finds him dressed in women's clothing, she is terribly embarrassed. If he is to be her husband, his masculinity must be restored.[24] So Britomart triumphs over Radigund in battle, releases Artegall, and then changes the laws of Radigund's city,

> changing all that forme of common weale,
> The liberty of women did repeale,
> Which they had long usurpt; and them restoring
> to mens subiection, did true Iustice deale[25]

End of story . . . almost. For Britomart does not actually put *herself* in subjection to her man, Artegall. She appoints magistrates for Radigund's city and makes them swear their fealty to Artegall, but she herself remains in charge. As Spenser explains:

> Vertuous women wisely understand,
> That they were borne to base humilitie,
> Unlesse the heavens them lift to lawful sovereaintie.[26]

Though women's rule is consistently portrayed as dangerous and lawless, the Amazon figure nevertheless allowed medieval and Renaissance-era men to create space for the concept of female social and military authority. This was necessitated by the actual rule of women like Queen Elizabeth. Patriarchal rule was rationalized as necessary by portraying the female-only military societies of the Amazons as dangerous and unnatural, a threat to male power. Yet the power, even the rule of a woman, could be accepted if it were regarded as the exception to an otherwise firm principle of women's subordination to men. The Amazon was an ambivalent figure: dangerous and horrible, certainly; but also brave, powerful, magisterial. Elizabethan compilations detailing the lives of "worthy women" always culminated in Elizabeth I; but they began with Penthesilea, Hippolyta, Artemisia, and other Amazon queens from classical Greek legends.[27]

The early Renaissance was a high watermark in Amazon storytelling, but fascination with legends of woman-rule continued into the modern period in Europe. In 1730, the Abbé Desfontaines, a French scholar, published a novel relating the adventures of Gulliver's son, who lands on the imaginary island of Babilary, where women hold social power and use it to oppress men.[28] In *Candide,* first published in 1759, Voltaire parodies the usual Amazonian formula by sending his fictional hero to South America to learn about civilization from the Amazons.[29] In the eighteenth and nineteenth centuries, the Amazon figure underwent a minor rebirth in the hands of German writers, some of whom exerted a direct influence on Bachofen.[30] Goethe, for example, read the Amadís cycle (which was reissued in Leipzig in 1782 in an abridged form). He even wrote a poem titled "Der Neue Amadis," writing to Schiller in 1805 to share his enthusiasm for the Amadís stories.[31] Other German writers aspired to writing or rewriting Amazon legends and exploring the "Männin" (masculine woman) theme, which was common in German literature during this period.[32]

The culmination of the continuing interest in Amazons in German literature came in 1808 with the publication of the play *Penthesilea,* by Heinrich von Kleist. Penthesilea, an Amazon queen killed and loved by Achilles (yes, in that order) is a heroine of classical Greek mythology. In his play, Kleist changes the story. He has the two protagonists falling in love before the death scene, and he adds a much more detailed account of the history of the peculiar matriarchal community headed up by Penthesilea. According to Kleist's drama, the Amazons were once ordinary married women. They became a *Frauenstaat,* a nation of women, only after their menfolk were killed in battle. Kleist continually emphasizes this accidental quality of Penthesilea's Amazon state. Throughout the play he portrays Amazonism as confounding and perverting women's true nature, a state of affairs that becomes abundantly clear as the drama unfolds between Penthesilea and Achilles.[33]

In Kleist's telling, Penthesilea falls in love with Achilles from the moment she sees him. This instantly creates a conflict within her between the warlike Amazon nature she has been forced by circumstance to cultivate, and her true nature, the one that Kleist views as inescapable: her feminine desire to be subservient to a man. Immediately upon seeing Achilles, Penthesilea starts to plead with the gods to "throw that youth, so hotly coveted, / Tumbling into the dust before my feet." But in the next breath she warns, "A shaft of death / Is sharpened for the one who dares lay hand / Upon his head . . . / I'd sooner lose my own heart's blood than his."[34] Achilles is similarly attracted to Penthesilea, and he simultaneously wants to hurt and humiliate her, specifically to

FIGURE 2. A classical representation of Achilles and Penthesilea, from the late fifth century B.C.E.; the original bell krater on which these figures are painted is kept at the National Archaeological Museum of Spain in Madrid

"set a crown of gashes on her forehead / And drag her through the streets by her sleek hair."[35]

As Penthesilea contemplates the beautiful and heroic Achilles, she begins to reflect that her martial talents might not be so important after all . . . at least not so important as her womanly charm:

> And let this body, full of warmth and life,
> Be thrown upon the open field in shame.
> Let me be served as breakfast for his dogs,
> As offal for the hideous birds. Let me be
> Dust instead of woman without charm.[36]

Still, she is not reconciled to giving up her weaponry:

> Accursed if I should live to see the shame!
> Accursed if ever I receive a man
> Not honorably conquered with a sword![37]

Achilles finds this attitude puzzling and asks Penthesilea this:

> What is it that incites you, dressed in bronze
> From head to foot, and like a Fury filled
> With blinding rage, against the tribes of Greece;
> You who need but serenely show yourself
> In all your loveliness to see the race
> Of men kneel down before you in the dust?[38]

Once Penthesilea and Achilles have the leisure to sit and talk and declare their undying love—after Achilles defeats Penthesilea in battle—they begin to bicker over where they should ultimately live, her place or his. Unfortunately they are interrupted by the Amazon army, which arrives to free Penthesilea, who does not actually want to be rescued. There follows a tragic miscommunication: Achilles calls Penthesilea out in single combat, planning to throw the battle so that she can have the satisfaction of a faux victory before she follows him home to bear his children. Penthesilea misunderstands and believes Achilles has betrayed her. So Penthesilea goes into battle consumed with bloodlust. She tears Achilles to pieces, sets her dogs on him, and then sinks her teeth into his chest.[39] When she recovers herself, she is bewildered:

> What! I? You mean I—him?—Beneath my dogs—?
> You mean that, with these hands, these little hands—?
> And with this mouth, these lips that swell with love—?[40]

Upon realizing what she has done, Penthesilea kills herself with a handful of arrows.

This, as we will see shortly, is just the sort of ending that Bachofen imagined for the Amazons of antiquity, though he preferred to stop short of the murder-suicide. Instead, he sees the Amazons gratefully surrendering their armament and embracing their true feminine nature, in subordination to men.

EARLY ETHNOGRAPHY

Another step toward matriarchal myth came with the beginnings of ethnography in the eighteenth century. As Europeans colonized other continents, some took the time to report on local customs before (or in some cases, instead of) destroying them. Europeans were thus fed a steadily increasing diet of information about other cultures, a diet that simultaneously expanded and threatened their sense of what human society was and could be. Some of this information pertained to relations between the sexes. The Spanish conquistadores reported that they found Amazons everywhere, but none of their claims were sustained. Later explorers, colonizers, traders, and missionaries, however, provided more credible reports to those "back home." These reports included such exotica as free sexual relations among women and men, people going about half-clothed, and, perhaps most surprisingly, women possessing freedoms and responsibilities never granted them in European culture. These reports fired the European imagination.

Where the status of women was concerned, the most striking testimony came from Father Joseph François Lafitau, a Jesuit missionary working with the Mohawks of Sault St. Louis, outside of Montreal, in the early eighteenth century. His *Les Moeurs des Sauvages Amériquains* (Customs of the American Indians) describes Iroquois society as a gynecocracy, or "government of women" (a departure, he admits, from the opinions of other European observers of the Iroquois, who believed "that only the men among the Indians are really free and that the women are only their slaves"):

> It is they [the women] who really maintain the tribe, the nobility of blood, the genealogical tree, the order of generations and conservation of the families. In them resides all the real authority: the lands, fields and all their harvest belong to them; they are the soul of the councils, the arbiters of peace and war; they hold the taxes and the public treasure; it is to them that the slaves are entrusted; they arrange the marriages; the children are under their authority; and the order of succession is founded on their blood. The men, on the contrary, are entirely isolated and limited to themselves. Their children are strangers to them. Everything perishes with them.[41]

Lafitau did not stop with this observation; he had a much larger theory to prove, one that included chronological and geographical components. Lafitau had an extensive classical education as part of his preparation for the priesthood. He was familiar with Herodotus, Strabo, and Pausanias, among others, and with what they had to say about the cultures of the ancient Mediterranean.[42] In particular, Lafitau was drawn to what Heraclides of Pontus had said about Lycian women: that they exercised authority over their husbands, just as Lafitau believed the Iroquois women did.[43] Lafitau could not conceive of such an odd custom being independently invented on two sides of the world, so he posited a huge migratory scheme according to which the Iroquois were the direct descendants of the ancient Lycians, who were before that the descendants of Japhet, expelled from the Promised Land by the Hebrews. These descendants of Japhet were gradually driven into Greece in one direction and across Asia in the other, from whence they came to the New World and then eventually across the continent to eastern North America, where Lafitau met them as the Iroquois nation.[44]

In early efforts to systematize material acquired through ethnographic observation, assumptions similar to Lafitau's were made: that the human race was once one (created in the Garden of Eden), only to be dispersed—relatively recently—after the great flood. Interestingly, some of these efforts to collect the then available data on human difference gave prominent place to the status of women. A case in point is the encyclopedic tome *An Investigation of the Theories of the Natural History of Man,* written by William Frederick van Amringe, a New York lawyer, in 1848. Van Amringe set out to understand everything about the human race via the methods current at the time: craniology, anatomy, anthropology, analogies with other animal species, and so on. Throughout, van Amringe pressed home the point that there was not a single human species, but several, different in nature and not to be mixed. He summarizes the respective natures of these human species as follows: "The Shemite [European] is constitutionally calm, cheerful, dignified, benevolent, sentimental, and thoughtful. The Ishmaelite [Arab] is reserved, austere, gloomy, cruel, vindictive, and voluptuous. The Japhethite [East Asian] is quiet, orderly, industrious, courteous, indifferent, and insincere. And the Canaanite [African] is indolent, careless, sensual, tyrannical, predatory, sullen, boisterous, and jovial."[45]

These species were created by God for who knows what providential purposes. (Van Amringe seems to be at a complete loss to explain God's motives.) That they are separate species is a fact sealed for van Amringe in the different standards of beauty upheld by each. For example, van Amringe claims that Ishmaelite men desire women who are obese, have oily skin, and have "teeth projecting beyond the lips"; the Shemite, by contrast, likes his women to have small hands with tapering fingers, "slightly dimpled over the joints, and rosy at the tips," and "a slight tendency to increase of flesh." Such differences in standards of beauty among humans "were designed by the Creator for the double purpose of giving specific character to each species, and to keep each species distinct from every other."[46]

One of the most striking differences between these distinct species of humans is, for van Amringe, their varying attitudes toward women. It is here that we get some hint of the matriarchal ideas that would soon blossom forth in the theories of Bachofen. Van Amringe begins his chapter on the history of women by highlighting the female contribution to the development of the race: "If man, by reason of his masculine, physical, and spiritual powers, occupies the foreground in the transactions of the world, woman by reason of her spirituality, is the secret cause to produce those transactions. If female influence is passive rather than active, it is not the less powerful." This sounds like a traditional "power behind the throne" notion, but van Amringe quickly goes on to say that women's influence is active as well as passive and that "no doubt can be entertained . . . that the influence of woman must have been anterior to any improvements of the original condition of man." In fact, he says, social development tracks absolutely parallel to improvements in the status of women: "From the New Hollander who secures his wife by knocking her down with a club and dragging the prize to his cave, to the polished European who fearfully, but respectfully and assiduously, spends a probation of months or years, for his better half, the ascent may be traced with unfailing accuracy and precision."[47]

Van Amringe hopes that all human species might rise to civilization by improving their treatment of women, reflecting that "whatever may be the rudeness or savageism of a people; however low they may be sunk in morals and intellect; if they have only permitted their women to stand upon the same level with themselves, the hope may be reasonably entertained of elevating him." And yet van Amringe's hopes are continually dashed by history, as lower human species seem surprisingly resistant to the European example. Van Amringe's particular target is the Ishmaelites, or Mohammedans. Their sexual relations, he claims, are characterized by "tyranny, cruelty, and absolute inequality"; and though "the Turks" have had six hundred years to benefit from the shining example of the Europeans, they have not "undergone the slightest change" in this respect.[48] For van Amringe, as for Lafitau, an enhanced social status for women is a geographically circumscribed phenomenon.

DEVELOPING AN EVOLUTIONARY TIME LINE

Lafitau's theory was steeped in the classics, informed by ethnography, and tinged with curiosity about the possibility (or actual existence) of female dominance. Van Amringe, writing over a century later, privileged women's contribution to civilization, declaring that the status of women was the marker by which we could judge social progress. Both these men anticipated Bachofen, but they lacked two characteristic features of the modern articulation of matriarchal myth: they did not place anything on a historical time line, and their theories were not universalizing (that is, they applied only to certain human groups). For Lafitau, matriarchy traveled around the globe but never altered significantly with the passage of time, nor would it give way to patriarchy at some specific point. Gynecocracy was not "our" ancient heritage, but only the peculiar custom of ancients and savages whose practices had degenerated from the perfection of Eden. For van Amringe, the only human species able to make use of feminine wisdom and its elevating effects were the Shemites, the Europeans, while all other species remained resistant to this resource (for mysterious reasons known only to God).

In contrast, the Scottish moral philosophers of the late eighteenth century, especially Adam Ferguson and John Millar, began to develop the sort of evolutionary time line of gender relations that would become essential to matriarchal myth for both Bachofen and the British evolutionary anthropologists of the late nineteenth century. Even Ferguson and Millar can be said to have been anticipated by the English political philosopher Thomas Hobbes, writing in the seventeenth century. Hobbes diverged from many of his philosophical contemporaries by denying that male supremacy was the natural or original order of things: "Whereas some have attributed the Dominion to the Man only, as being of the more excellent Sex; they misreckon it. For there is not always that difference of strength or prudence between the man and the woman, as that the right can be determined without War." It could be inferred that Hobbes believed that women fought and lost a battle for sex dominance in a time before the creation of the state, much as they do in most versions of the myth of matriarchal prehistory. But within the confines of Hobbes's theory, this could not have been a very organized battle. Women could not have joined together to assert social dominance any more than men could, since everyone operated as individuals in the "war of all against all" that constituted the "state of nature."[49]

Hobbes raised a related point that would later become a key feature of the myth of matriarchal prehistory: the power that uncertainty of paternity bestows on women. As Hobbes explains: "In this condition of meer Nature . . . the Dominion is in the Mother. For in the condition of meer Nature, where there are no matrimoniall lawes, it cannot be known who is the Father, unless it be declared by the Mother; and therefore the right of Dominion over the Child dependeth on her will and is consequently hers."[50] For Hobbes, these observations had little import for his overarching thesis on the development of human society, but the Scottish philosophers who followed him found such notions far more significant.

Adam Ferguson, in his *Essay on the History of Civil Society,* written a century after Hobbes's treatise, focused on Lafitau's observations of the Iroquois "gynecocracy." However, he completely reversed Lafitau's scheme of global migrations. As Ferguson stated, "If nations actually borrow from their neighbours, they probably borrow only what they are nearly in a condition to have invented themselves."[51] Gynecocracy, which Ferguson considered a cultural invention, belonged to a particular stage of cultural evolution: the lowest. In the earliest era Ferguson could imagine, when property consisted of "the food of to-morrow" and the tools for obtaining it, everything was vested in women, who also had sole custody of the children, "with little regard to descent on the father's side."[52] Ferguson was at pains to distinguish gynecocracy—which he understood as inheritance through women—from female dominance. Women held property in the lowest cultural stages, he said, because property was not valued. It signified labor and was "a subject with which the warrior does not choose to be embarrassed."[53]

In *The Origin of the Distinction of Ranks,* John Millar of Glasgow offered a similar, though more fully elaborated, time line of gender relations. He made a brief bow toward degenerationism in a footnote, saying that the "original institutions" of human beings, revealed by God, had been subsequently lost by some peoples.[54] But Millar's overriding theme involved evolution of a sort that would come to dominate intellectual thought a century later:

> When we survey the present state of the globe, we find that, in many parts of it, the inhabitants are so destitute of culture, as to appear little above the condition of

brute animals; and even when we peruse the remote history of polished nations, we have seldom any difficulty in tracing them to a state of the same rudeness and barbarism. There is, however, in man a disposition and capacity for improving his condition, by the exertion of which, he is carried on from one degree of advancement to another; and the similarity of his wants, as well as of the faculties by which those wants are supplied, has every where produced a remarkable uniformity in the several steps of his progression.[55]

Millar assumes then that his people, the Scots, were once like "brute animals" (though they had advanced a good deal farther than some of the other peoples of the world).

Millar is ambivalent—and self-contradictory—on the question of "the rank and status of women" (a topic that occupies an entire chapter of his work). At the beginning of Millar's story, "in the ages most remote from improvement," women "are degraded below the other sex, and reduced under that authority which the strong acquire over the weak." The customs and economy of the time work against women: lack of clothing is "extremely unfavourable to the rank and dignity of the women"; and men's desire for sexual intercourse—through which women derive "consideration and respect . . . in a polished nation"—is all but absent. Indeed, sexual desire is "barely sufficient for the continuation of the species," since "it cannot be supposed . . . that the passions of sex will rise to any considerable height in the breast of a savage . . . [who] must have little regard for pleasures which he can purchase at so easy a rate."[56] Yet like Ferguson and Hobbes before him, Millar suggests that motherhood provided women with a status and authority that was inaccessible to their male counterparts: "If a woman has no notion of attachment or fidelity to any particular person . . . the child which she has borne, and which she maintains under her own inspection, must be regarded as a member of her own family." Under these circumstances, children "can hardly fail, during a considerable part of their life, to regard their mother as the principal person in the family. This is in all probability the source of that influence which appears to have been possessed by women in several rude and barbarous parts of the world."[57]

Citing women's influence over children is not tantamount to claiming that ancient societies were matriarchal, but for Millar it leans strongly in that direction and bears little relation to his earlier statements about women's "degradation." Noting that "among the ancient Britons . . . the women were accustomed to vote in the public assemblies," Millar speculates that this situation came about because "the rude and imperfect institution of marriage, and the community of wives . . . must have prevented the children from acquiring any considerable connexion with their father, and have disposed them to follow the condition of their mother, as well as to support her interest and dignity. When a woman, by being the head of a large family, is thus advanced to influence and authority, and becomes a sort of female chief, she naturally maintains a number of servants, and endeavours to live with suitable splendour and magnificence."[58]

Women's lot in "rude societies"—which doesn't sound all that bad, if women do indeed get to vote and have servants—improves, at least as far as Millar is concerned, as society evolves: "When men begin to disuse their ancient barbarous practices, when their attention is not wholly engrossed by the pursuit of military reputation, when they have made some progress in arts, and have attained to a proportional degree of refinement, they are necessarily led to set a value upon those female accomplishments and virtues which have so many different ways to multiply the comforts of life. In this situation, the women become, neither the slaves, nor the idols of the other sex, but the friends and companions."[59] Millar praises the practice of social intercourse between the sexes, suggesting that without the "polish" that women give to conversation and the expression of thoughts and sentiments, men's culture deteriorates proportionately: "Hence it is, that the Greeks, notwithstanding their learning and good sense, were remarkably deficient in delicacy and politeness, and were so little judges of propriety in wit and humor, as to relish the low ribaldry of an Aristophanes."[60]

Unfortunately, including women in public life can go too far, Millar notes, and he warns that such a turning point may have arrived. "In a simple age," says Millar, "the free intercourse of the sexes is attended with no bad consequences; but in opulent and luxurious nations, it gives rise to licentious and dissolute manners, inconsistent with good order, and with the general interest of society."[61] Here Millar presages the circularity of the myth of matriarchal prehistory as it develops under Bachofen: women are said to have possessed a freedom and authority in prehistoric times that they have had no opportunity to regain until the present moment . . . but that would only be regained now at society's peril.

The neat, staged, grand narratives of human history that would later come to dominate matriarchal myth had even clearer predecessors in thinkers who chose not to spend significant time speculating on gender relations in earlier ages of the human race. Giambattista Vico's *New Science,* published in 1725, ordered human history as a progression from "habitat" to "settlement" to "society."[62] Charles de Secondat, the baron of Montesquieu, developed a similar three-stage evolutionary sequence in his 1748 *Spirit of the Laws.* This sequence consisted of savagery, barbarism, and civilization—a typology we will meet again, when it comes laden with matriarchal freight—with savages described as "generally hunters" who were organized into "dispersed clans," while barbarians were "herdsmen and shepherds" coming together in "small nations."[63] Closer to Ferguson and Millar's Scottish home was Adam Smith, who established a history of economic development that numerous later thinkers would use as a template for articulating a history of gender relations.[64] Smith demarcated "four distinct states which mankind pass through":

"1st, the age of hunters, 2dly, the age of shepherds, 3dly, the age of agriculture, and 4thly, the age of commerce."[65]

MATRIARCHY AND THE SOCIALIST IMAGINATION

If anyone can be said to have directly anticipated Bachofen, that person would be François Marie Charles Fourier.[66] In Fourier, many of the building blocks of matriarchal myth are firmly in place: a staged, evolutionary progression, with surviving remnants of earlier stages found in "savage" cultures; a devolution of women's status with some degree of reclamation anticipated in the future; and a frank advocacy of a particular political position based on the lessons of prehistory. Indeed, Fourier might be remembered as the founder of matriarchal myth, if he hadn't been so terribly odd.

Fourier (1772–1837) lived in France, doing most of his writing after 1803. The son of a cloth merchant, Fourier attempted a career in business, at which he failed miserably. Thereafter he supported himself at odd jobs while devoting his time to writing scathing critiques of "civilization" and in particular, marriage and the family. Described as a "utopian socialist," Fourier is believed by many to have been clinically insane. Indeed, his writings suggest at the least a vivid imagination, if not actual psychosis.[67] Fourier had a grandiose sense of himself, claiming that "before me, mankind lost several thousand years by fighting madly against Nature. . . . I am the first who has bowed before her . . . she has deigned to smile upon the only mortal who has offered incense at her shrine; she has delivered up all her treasures to me."[68]

According to historian Priscilla Robertson, Fourier named the fundamental law of nature to be "attraction," and he advocated the founding of ideal communities called "phalansteries," in which individuals could "obey their healthy passions" without being bound to families, "which held people in such a grip that they were mostly miserable."[69] These phalansteries would reinstate the freedom— both sexual and economic—that marked Fourier's first, "Edenic" stage of human history. Modifying scripture, Fourier suggested that human beings were created as young adults and placed in a number of locations on earth rather than in the single garden described in Genesis. Due to increasing population pressures, Edenism gave way to Savagery (which saw the birth of marriage and private property), then to the Patriarchate, Barbarism, and finally Civilization (the stage during which Fourier considered himself unfortunate to live). Most of the evolutionists who followed Fourier, including matriarchalists, were content with three to five stages in their evolutionary sequences,[70] but Fourier followed the fifth stage, Civilization, with no fewer than twenty-seven more. Two stages worked as intermediaries leading to the eighth stage, the "dawn of happiness," which would in turn

FIGURE 3. François Marie Charles Fourier (1772–1837), French utopian socialist

inaugurate seventeen stages of "blessed Harmony." The final seven stages in Fourier's scheme would recapitulate the first seven, in reverse order, until, after a brief return to Edenism, the planet would die.[71] Like Bachofen after him, Fourier attributed both inevitability and progress to his evolutionary scheme, arguing that it is "our destiny . . . to advance; every social period must progress towards the one above it."[72]

Most notably for our purposes is that Fourier stated repeatedly that the degree to which a society was progressive or regressive could be most easily and surely determined by the freedom and status of women, and further, that a society could morph itself into the next stage by changing its treatment of women. *"The extension of privileges to women,"* Fourier stated categorically and emphatically, *"is the general principle of all social progress."* He attributed this mechanism to God: "Now God recognises as freedom only that which is extended to both sexes and not to one alone; he desired, likewise, that all the seeds of social abominations such as savagery, barbarism, civilisation, should have as their sole pivot the subjection of women, and that all the seeds of social well-being such as the sixth, seventh, eighth periods should have no pivot but the progressive enfranchisement of the weak sex."[73]

According to Fourier, women in the Edenic stage are completely free and equal. What marks the end of this stage and the beginning of Savagery is the institution of marriage, in which men are given control over women, while women are left to do the majority of the labor. From here the status of women declines, as does the status of most men; the Patriarchate (Fourier's third stage) is characterized by small-scale slavery, and Barbarism (Fourier's fourth stage) is characterized by large-scale slavery. Civilization brings an incremental improvement for women, as marriage becomes monogamous, and wives—particularly those of ruling men—gain status as the mistresses of large households. This did not do much to redeem Civilization in Fourier's eyes, however. Any improvement in women's status was tiny compared to the plunge women endured in the fall from Edenism. But the phalansteries Fourier hoped to see created *would* make a real difference for women. In them, Fourier recommended that boys and girls be dressed alike from infancy to encourage equal opportunities for both. Women's domestic servitude would be ended through the provision of central kitchens and nurseries where people of either sex could do the work that pleased them. And to guard against a de facto reinstitution of "women's work," Fourier determined that no more than seven eighths of all workers in any profession should be of the same sex. Fourier anticipated only great things for the women of the future, who he insisted would, "in a state of liberty," "excel man in all functions of the mind or the body which are not the attributes of physical force."[74]

A key influence on Fourier's thought was ethnographic reportage. There is no evidence that Fourier read Lafitau's work on the Iroquois, though of course it is possible. However, he was certainly familiar with reports about life on Tahiti, probably in the form of letters from Philibert Commerçon, a French naturalist who traveled there in the 1760s. In fact, learning of the sexual customs of Tahiti might have been what sent Fourier down the singular intellectual path he was to travel. Fourier dates his initial epiphany regarding the curses of civilization to 1799. It was then that he began to speak of the Edenic stage, which he believed survived in Tahiti in the practice of *"phanérogamie simple,"* or "free love."[75]

Émile de Girardin, a French thinker writing fifty years after Fourier, likewise sought to initiate substantial changes in relations between the sexes. In *La Politique Universelle: Décrets de l'Avenir,* published in 1852,[76] de Girardin addressed what he perceived to be a problem of monumental proportions in European society: the high proportion of illegitimate births and the underprivileged status of illegitimate children. De Girardin proposed to redress this problem through legislation demanding that all children be given their mother's name and property. Women were to be declared "equal"—though de Girardin assumed that women granted equality would choose to raise children without direct recompense in the home of a working husband.[77]

INFLUENCES ON BACHOFEN

Bachofen was aware of de Girardin's book and hoped that his own work on mother right would shed further light on the institution of matriliny.[78] He was probably not influenced by Fourier or by Commerçon's reports on Tahiti, but he was at least aware of the work of Lafitau and the Scottish philosopher Adam Ferguson.[79] Undoubtedly, however, Bachofen was most deeply moved toward his matriarchal scholarship by his predecessors, teachers, and peers within the German academic world, especially the two streams represented by Hegel and the early German Romantics. Bachofen's intellectual antecedents will be discussed further in the next chapter, but it should be mentioned here that some of his predecessors in philology, jurisprudence, and the classics were also exploring topics related to gender though without reaching the same conclusions as Bachofen.

Particularly important in this regard was the work of Friedrich Gottlieb Welcker, who held a chair in *Altertumswissenschaft* (the study of antiquity), first at the University of Göttingen and later at the University of Bonn. Bachofen met Welcker in Rome in 1842 or 1843, when both were engaged in research there.[80] Welcker's *Die Aeschylische Trilogie,* published in 1824 in Darmstadt, foreshadowed Bachofen's intense interest in Aeschylus's *Oresteia,* which Bachofen repeatedly cites in *Das Mutterrecht* as his single most important proof-text for the existence of ancient matriarchy. Welcker also discusses other classical sources, including "the murder of the men by the women on the island of Lemnos,[81] matriliny among the Lycians, the customs of Epizephyrian Locri, the Amazons, the legend of the daughters of Minyas at Orchomemus, [and] the Danaids," all of which made it into *Das Mutterrecht.*[82]

Another direct predecessor of Bachofen was Eduard Gerhard, an archaeologist who founded the Institute for Archaeological Correspondence in Rome and who was curator of the Altes Museum in Berlin. In 1855, Gerhard published a two-volume work, *Griechische Mythologie,* which analyzed classical symbols and raised the possibility that the various goddesses of the ancient Greek pantheon might have been manifestations of a single primordial Goddess who had been worshipped in preclassical times.[83] Though obviously focused on Greece, Gerhard freely drew parallels between Greek mythology and the myths of Egypt, India, Persia, Assyria, Babylon, Phoenicia, Germany, and Scandinavia in order to make his case regarding the meaning and purpose of Greek myths.[84] Welcker, Gerhard, and others brought the intense interest in Amazons and gender reversals that had flourished since medieval times into an academic context. They returned to the actual classical sources and asked what these stories might have meant in their own time—unlike the authors of the *Amadís cycle* and writers such as Kleist, who continued to take literary license with Amazon myth. Previous speculation about Amazons by Europeans had conceptualized Amazons as the Greeks saw them: they were aberrations, exceptional cases. The Amazons were to women what centaurs were to horses. In the early nineteenth century, this view began to change, and at least some scholars came to understand the Amazons—or at least the symbolism of Amazons—as an integral part of the normative culture of ancient Greece.[85]

Whether Amazons were portrayed as vengeful and misandrous, as they often were, or as free and capable, as writers like Hobbes, Lafitau, and Fourier presented them, strong women were a recurring theme in Europe from ancient through late modern times. The fascination these women held for European men, complemented by emerging theories of human social evolution and religious and historicizing interpretations of myth (with which Bachofen was directly familiar), provided a rich stew from which Bachofen was able to extract the complex and ultimately intoxicating broth of the myth of matriarchal prehistory. Unlike classical Greek images of woman-rule, the matriarchal societies Bachofen postulated for prehistoric times were not unnatural, frightening, or tragic—in fact, they were often quite appealing. Still, according to Bachofen, matriarchy was strictly a thing of the past. It would seem that matriarchal myth contained the ambivalence and anxiety that men experienced at the prospect of gender reversals—previously evident in the popular Amazon myths—by banishing them to a former era. But in the process, the myth of matriarchal prehistory created an era of woman-rule far more substantial, universal, and long-lived than anything Amazon myth had ever been able to conjure, and this provided a new forum for thinking through more complex visions of sexual difference and social power.

3

On the Launching Pad

J. J. Bachofen and 'Das Mutterrecht'

*I propose to investigate all aspects of matriarchal culture, to disclose its
diverse traits and the fundamental idea which unites them. In this way I
hope to restore the picture of a cultural stage which was overlaid or totally
destroyed by the later development of the ancient world.*

—JOHANN JAKOB BACHOFEN

JOHANN JAKOB BACHOFEN, 1815–1878

Bachofen has been described by one of his twentieth-century disciples, Berta
Eckstein-Diener, as a "soft, corpulent Basler patrician with a wonderful, half-
open child's mouth [and] over a million Swiss francs, a professor of Roman law
with many honorable titles and an almost inconceivable knowledge . . . about the
feminine age under the hem of history."[1] This sketch captures the essentials: Bachofen's birth into wealth and status, his extensive education, and the work for
which he is most remembered—his investigation into "the feminine age under
the hem of history": matriarchal prehistory.

Bachofen was born into a conservative, wealthy, patrician Basel intent on retaining its self-determination as a canton within the Swiss confederation. The
Bachofens were a prominent family, related by marriage to most of the other important families of Basel. According to biographer Andreas Cesana, Bachofen in
mid-life was quite possibly the single richest man in Basel.[2] The Bachofens' wealth
came from their silk ribbon manufacturing firm, long an institution in the city. In
the years just before Bachofen's birth, the family lived above the firm's shops and
offices in the *Weisses Haus,* along with the firm's unmarried employees.

The Basel into which Bachofen was born was steeped in medieval tradition,
but the city was undergoing dramatic change. Between 1779 and 1880, the population of Basel leapt from fifteen thousand to sixty-one thousand, and by the latter half of the nineteenth century, workers were denouncing old relationships of

FIGURE 4. Johann Jakob Bachofen (1815–78) as a young man

patronage and joining together to strike for better conditions and higher wages. These were tumultuous times, but if they touched Bachofen himself, they must have done so mostly subconsciously, for his letters describe Basel as provincial and boring: "An enormous centrifugal force dissipates everything and nothing significant happens." And: "One day here is very much like another. We get up in the morning, consume four meals, then go to bed again."[3]

Bachofen enjoyed a cosmopolitan education that took him to Germany, France, and England; he also traveled to Italy and Greece. Yet throughout his life, Bachofen remained wedded to his native city. Bred to take his place in Basel's public life,[4] Bachofen demonstrated his willingness to adhere to this plan, writing one of his earliest compositions, in 1831, on the subject of patriotism.[5] He began his studies at the University of Basel in 1834, studying history and classical philology (historical linguistics), but moving shortly thereafter to Berlin, where he pursued philology and *Altertumswissenschaft* (the study of antiquity) under Leopold Ranke, August Böckh, and Friedrich Karl von Savigny. These areas of scholarly inquiry were his first and last love, but family plans for his future career as a Basel jurist spurred Bachofen to focus on the law. He transferred to Göttingen, where a tutor drilled him so that he could pass his examinations and thereby complete his legal education. Still, he continued with his scholarly work on Roman law, inspired by his work with Savigny. After taking his degree in law, Bachofen spent a year in Paris, apprenticed to a French lawyer, and another year in England studying English law in London and Cambridge. Bachofen returned to Basel in 1841 and was immediately appointed to a chair of Roman law at the University of Basel.[6]

From the start, Bachofen's appointment was controversial. As a member of the wealthy conservative elite, Bachofen clearly did not need the salary the position provided, and the opposition press did not hesitate to publish this fact. The press further criticized the university for continuing to appoint faculty in traditional fields like philology and law (which often had "more professors than students"), while "modern subjects" such as the natural sciences, economics, political science, and foreign languages were severely underfunded. Bachofen quickly caved in to the pressure and stopped drawing a salary for his teaching. In 1844, he resigned his position completely.[7] He nevertheless remained devoted to Basel. As he notes in his autobiography, "No one here who has studied can avoid participation in public affairs . . . much less one who has succeeded in acquiring a doctorate in law . . . and who, as the tradesman likes to put it, doesn't have anything to do."[8] Bachofen accepted a part-time appointment as an appeals judge in Basel's criminal court and briefly served on the university's governing board before a falling out with a colleague prompted his resignation from that post.[9] Afterward, as before, he spent the bulk of his time studying classical literature, history, and archaeology.

Bachofen was a dedicated and indomitable researcher. After his resignation from the University of Basel, he became increasingly isolated from academic life, rarely attending scholarly meetings, publishing his own work in extremely limited editions, and regarding himself as without predecessors.[10] The legacy of Bachofen's independent work was an impressive record of publication (including his most renowned work, *Das Mutterrecht)* and ten thousand pages of unpublished papers that were donated to the library at the University of Basel.[11]

In Bachofen's early years, ancient Rome stood as his ideal republic, as it did for many others of his generation of intellectuals. This was certainly true of Bachofen during his legal studies (he wrote his doctoral dissertation—in Latin—on Roman law), but when he embarked on his first trip to Italy, in 1842, Bachofen found himself most attracted to mortuary art and cemeteries, whose "profound emotion" and "warm humanism" contrasted sharply with what Bachofen called "the poverty and aridity of our world today." By focusing on mortuary art, Bachofen felt drawn beyond the patrician Rome he had idealized to some deeper, "Eastern" heritage: "Italy descended from its remote pedestal where it had been held captive by scholars for so long. . . . While Rome's founder had been introduced to me as a true Italian Adam, I now saw in him a very modern figure, in Rome the capstone and the downfall of a cultural period of one thousand years."[12] The study of Roman law now seemed trivial and vain to Bachofen.[13] So he set off once more in search of "the immortal footprints" *(den unsterblichen Fußstapfen)* in all things, but increasingly, in the earliest things, for it was his opinion that "just as one might expect from those who are so close to their eternal origin, the earliest people thought soundly and appropriately."[14]

This interest in the earliest and the oldest led Bachofen to travel to Greece in 1851, where he focused his attention not on classic monuments such as the Athenian Acropolis, but on the most archaic sites. He was "positively enamored" of anything that appeared to indicate "oriental influence." By 1853, back in Basel, Bachofen was working out an idea of a "primordial feminine goddess," clearly inspired by archaeologist Eduard Gerhard, whom he had met in Rome. Bachofen relied heavily on Gerhard's work as he began his research for *Das Mutterrecht,* exchanging letters with him about possible matriarchal elements in Greek myth.[15] Bachofen developed his views throughout the mid-1850s as he sought to find the deepest layer of human religion, resting in "the creative potency of the earth," which he deemed to be "nearly everywhere conceived as something female."[16]

By the end of 1855, Bachofen had assembled the last pieces of the narrative he would articulate in *Das Mutterrecht:* placing the key stages of prehistoric and classical religion on a historic, evolutionary trajectory and explaining the mechanisms of change between these stages. Bachofen went public with his new theory in 1856 at a meeting of the German Philological Association in Stuttgart, where he gave a lecture titled "Über das Weiberrecht" (On the Law of Women).[17] The initial reception at this lecture was apparently positive. As historian Jonathan Fishbane reports, "The mood was one of fascination and the excitement of an archaeological-like find beneath the layers of ancient culture."[18] Bachofen then began work on a manuscript he first called *Gynaikokratie* (The Rule of Women). In trying to sell it to a German publisher, Bachofen stated—echoing Fourier— that "the position of women in human society is of paramount significance for the insight into the cultural condition of every age."[19] The book was finally published in 1861 by Stuttgart's Krais and Hoffman under the title *Das Mutterrecht: Eine Untersuchung über die Gynaikokratie der Alten Welt nach Ihrer Religiösen und Rechtlichen Natur* (Mother Right: A Study of the Religious and Juridical Aspects of Gynecocracy in the Ancient World).[20]

Many have speculated on the source of Bachofen's interest in matriarchy. Reviewers are fond of pointing out that Bachofen lived at home with his mother

FIGURE 5. Johann Jakob
Bachofen, author of
Das Mutterrecht
(published in 1861)

and did not marry until after her death, when he was fifty years old.[21] Bachofen's
mother, Valeria Merian, is typically portrayed as a strong, beautiful woman, so
attractive and so devoted to her sons that they were loathe to leave her embrace,
and so capable that they developed an unusual—for the time—respect for wom-
en's abilities. But Lionel Gossman has suggested another possible explanation for
Bachofen's attachment to his mother: Bachofen had a younger sister who died in
childhood as the result of an accident that may have been her mother's fault.
Gossman suspects that Bachofen's mother, far from being extremely attentive,
may have been distant with her sons because of her lifelong grief and guilt over her
daughter's death. It may have been this that kept Bachofen living in her shadow,
awaiting her recognition.[22]

These are intriguing speculations, but ultimately unnecessary ones. As we have
seen, Bachofen was not the first to become interested in the possibility of powerful

women and matriarchal societies, nor was he by any means the last. We shall have to look more deeply to find the motivations that led Bachofen and so many other men to labor in the fields of matriarchal myth. But first, some groundwork is in order: Bachofen's vision was a unique one, and one that has had a lasting influence on matriarchal thought, so it is important to become acquainted with some of its details.

THE CHRONOLOGY OF HUMAN HISTORY IN BACHOFEN'S *DAS MUTTERRECHT*

Das Mutterrecht is not an easy work to summarize, especially not briefly. It is a sprawling, poorly organized work, difficult to follow in German and certainly no easier in translation.[23] This is perhaps best demonstrated by the fact that Bachofen's commentators summarize *Das Mutterrecht* in contradictory ways: not only do they draw different conclusions from Bachofen's work, but they cannot even agree on the most fundamental facts of what Bachofen is saying. It is almost as though they have not been reading the same book, except for the continual evocation of terms like "Demetrian matriarchy" and "hetaeric tellurism," which are peculiar— and peculiar to Bachofen. Clearly, something is amiss, and it begins in *Das Mutterrecht* itself. Thus it is impossible to render a precise overview of Bachofen's chronology or of the evidence and sentiments that underlie it. But Bachofen is nothing if not repetitive, and some themes come through loud and clear. It is on these that I will concentrate.

Bachofen's basic scheme consists of five stages of human evolution: hetaerism, Demetrian matriarchy, Dionysian matriarchy, Amazonism, and the Apollonian age. Though Bachofen is clear that this *is* an evolution—beginning "at the lowest, darkest stages of human existence" and ending at "the luminous heights of immortality and immateriality"[24]—it is not the clean, gradual, developmental process one later encounters among the evolutionary anthropologists. Every shift from one stage to the next is accompanied by violence and resistance, for, as Bachofen explains, "In all things it is abuse and perversion that provide the greatest stimulus to development."[25] Evolution crashes against stasis over and over again throughout Bachofen's chronology, and every victory is contested, incomplete, and continually threatened by the forces of regress. At least in theory the outcome is certain, since these evolutionary stages are universal; mother right, Bachofen says, "does not belong to a specific people but to a specific cultural period."[26] The outcome doesn't *feel* certain, though: opposing forces are forever arrayed on opposite extremes, each demanding full allegiance to their own program, with no possibility of compromise.

This chronology and the manner of its progression is classically Hegelian. Bachofen's history proceeds dialectically, as two opposing principles battle for a new synthesis, which can only give rise to another set of opposing principles that must again do battle. Furthermore, the contest, for Bachofen as for Hegel, is one between Matter and Mind, with all of human history grappling mightily and painfully away from the former and toward the latter. It is, in the words of Stanley Edgar Hyman, "Bachofen's greatest vision: humanity ceaselessly struggling, and in the struggle rising from the muck to the heavens."[27] Bachofen gave Hegel's abstract and intangible theory a body, an actual human history drawn from documentary sources.[28] But even more significantly for our purposes, Bachofen extrapolated from Hegel's matter/mind distinction a great proliferation of dualisms: earth and sun, darkness and light, vengeance and law, left and right, passive and active, east and west, and—can you guess?—female and male.[29]

It is this last dualism that provides the fuel on which the myth of matriarchal prehistory runs. The principal content Bachofen gives to this distinction is that of materiality, which is "feminine," and spirituality, which is "masculine."[30] As these two principles duke it out on the field of human history, they are conveniently embodied in women and men, and thus each new era, each stage in Bachofen's scheme, can be understood in terms of the prevailing relations between the sexes. And because history is moving out of matter and toward spirit, it also moves inexorably—if fitfully—from the rule of women to the rule of men, and from Mother Goddess to Father God.

Disrupting this neat schema at the very beginning (and Bachofen is masterful at disrupting his own theories), the first stage in Bachofen's chronology is hetaerism,[31] which, in spite of its female connotations (from the Greek *hetaera*, or courtesan), is characterized by the rule of men. This is the era of complete materialism, with no glimmer of "Spirit" or "Mind," when "pure natural law" (*ius naturale*)—a sort of "might makes right" philosophy—is at its height. Lacking the institution of marriage, children are "sowed at random," after the manner of "uncultivated swamp vegetation, reeds and rushes." (The swamp is Bachofen's favorite recurrent metaphor for the hetaeric stage.)[32] This primeval tribe is characterized by "communal ownership of women," and it is the strongest man who dominates. As Bachofen explains:

> Every clan has its tyrant. This authority is based on the law of fecundation. Since there is no selection within sexual relations, individual paternity does not exist. Everybody has only one father, the tyrant. All are his sons and daughters and he owns all property. . . . There is no deviation from *ius naturale* in this stage in which a single man is dominant. The tyrant obtains all of his rights from the woman; he inherits only from his mother's womb. . . . This mother right does not imply gynecocracy. In the lowest stage, the male is dominant.[33]

In other words, the hetaeric stage is matrilineal, but not matriarchal.[34]

Bachofen typically regards hetaerism as a miserable, brutal time. Yet in this darkness is one "bright spot in life," one "light in the moral darkness," and it is motherhood. In one of what historian Lionel Gossman calls his "sudden irruptions of highly imaginative and poetic prose,"[35] Bachofen writes:

> The relationship through which humanity first attains to civilization, that which serves as the starting point for the development of every virtue, the formation of each nobler aspect of existence is the model of motherhood which comes into being as the divine principle of love and unity, of peace amidst a life full of violence. By nurturing the fruit of her womb, woman learns earlier than man how to extend her loving care beyond the limits of her own self and to protect and support another creature's existence. All social progress, all devotion, all ministration to the living and respect for the dead emanates from her.[36]

It is this mother love that forms the heart of the second stage of Bachofen's chronology: Demetrian matriarchy. This is the true matriarchy, characterized not only by matrilineal transmission of status and property, but also by the rule of women *(Gynaikokratie).*[37] It came into being when women rebelled against the excessive sexuality of men and demanded the right to be monogamous. As Bachofen states: "It cannot be doubted that gynecocracy has developed out of—and been consolidated and preserved through—the conscious and continuous resistance of woman against the hetaerism that demeans her. [She is] the defenseless object of men's abuse. . . . exhausted by men's lusts, women are the first to feel the need for regulation and a purer ethic."[38] By force of arms, in what Bachofen calls the first period of Amazonism, women instituted marriage and took control of society, asserting the "higher rights of motherhood" and opposing the "sensual demands of physical strength" possessed by men. Each woman claimed the right to court and choose her own husband, after which she "rules over him."[39] The "wild swamp vegetation" of hetaerism gave way to "ordered agriculture . . . a regulated cultivation of the soil."[40]

Agriculture is Bachofen's dominant metaphor for the Demetrian matriarchy, though there is no clear sense—as there will be in later versions of the myth of matriarchal prehistory—that matriarchy emerges as a result of the development of agriculture. Instead, agriculture stands for the type of procreation that matriarchy initiates: no longer randomly sowing his seed in the swamp of communally owned women, man now "opens the woman's womb, lays his seed for the purpose of generation . . . [and harvests] the child from the maternal garden," just as "the tiller . . . plows the earth, lays the seed, and finally harvests the fruit."[41] This equation—woman as earth, man as seed—is the root of matriarchal religion for Bachofen. The earth gives birth, and women give birth; in an era when human beings most value the material, it is only natural, so the argument goes, that they would worship the earth and reverence women.[42] In spite of men's careful culti-vation of women's wombs, according to Bachofen, fathers remain relatively un-important during the Demetrian age, providing only an instrumental function. As Bachofen says in a phrase that echoes down through the history of matriar-chal myth, "The father is always a legal fiction; the mother, in contrast, is a physi-cal fact."[43]

Bachofen reads Demetrian matriarchy as a great cultural advance. Women could not lead humanity out of the realm of the material, as women "only know of the physical life," and even at the highest levels of development, "woman is not capable of ridding herself of material nature."[44] But women did bring materialism to its highest, most civilized peak, its logical conclusion. The "maternal womb" teaches woman to "stretch beyond the limits of her own personality and subordi-nate the feeling of satisfied sensual desire in the sexual union," while men cling to "purely physical pleasures" as they are dragged kicking and screaming into mother right and marriage.[45]

Within the embrace of the Demetrian matriarchy, the tyrannical strong man of the hetaeric stage melts into a little boy who requires the "firm guiding hand" of the mother.[46] Eliding the stage of hetaerism as though it never existed or was of no account, Bachofen issues this formulaic statement: "In a word, the woman is first a mother, the man a son."[47] As Bachofen explains at greater length: "Matri-archy is necessary to the education of mankind and particularly of men. Just as the child is first disciplined by his mother, so the races of men are first disci-plined by woman. The male must serve before he can govern. It is the woman's vocation to tame man's primordial strength, to guide it into benign channels."[48] And in this vocation, the women of the Demetrian matriarchy excelled. Again, Bachofen waxes eloquent: "The gynecocratic world period is indeed the poetry of history, by virtue of its sublimity, through its heroic grandeur, even through the beauty to which it is elevated by woman; because it encourages bravery and a knightly ethos among men, gives significance to feminine love, and demands discipline and chastity of young men."[49]

But just as boys grow up, so the Demetrian matriarchy gives way to the Diony-sian age, in which men take on the role of women's lovers. Bachofen describes Dionysus as the "radiant son," the first of the solar gods who will lift humanity out of the night of matriarchy.[50] It is worth pausing to take closer note of how Bachofen perceives sonship. In terms that we, under the influence of Freud, would deem Oedipal,[51] Bachofen marvels at the "awesome metamorphosis of Nature" that is repeated "in the birth of every infant boy," when "the man emerges from the woman." According to Bachofen, this transmogrification inspires particular awe in the mother, who is "astonished by the new phenomenon": "She recognizes in the creation of the son the impregnating force to which she owes her mother-hood. With delight her gaze lingers on the form. The man becomes her darling, the he-goat her bearer, the phallus her constant companion." Bachofen describes the mother's eroticized worship of her son as "the highest expression of matriarchy." From here Bachofen fantasizes an incestuous role for the mother's son, one which he ascribes to Dionysus in *Das Mutterrecht*. Dionysus is the "fructifier of the mother": "Having been the begotten, he himself becomes the begetter. And always in relation to the same woman—sometimes as mother, sometimes as wife. The son becomes his own father."[52]

Bachofen characterizes the Dionysian age as emerging in pointed opposition to mother right, with its assertion of the primacy of "male-phallic nature" *(männlich-phallischen Natur)* and the domination of women by men within monogamous marriages. Dionysus is aware of and enamored with his ability to kindle life, and "searches relentlessly for a woman whom he may impregnate." But this does not last: "The same god that brought down the woman from her Amazonian heights and broke her ancient power, the same god once again places authority in her hands, first through the religious consecration with which he imbues her, then through the erotic-sensual life associated with his service."[53] Whatever his relationship to paternity, Dionysus remains within the web of the material; that is, the feminine. He is "forever moving between rising and setting, growth and decay . . . yearning to merge with feminine matter."[54] For Bachofen, this cannot be a positive development. In fact, Bachofen frequently compares the Dionysian age unfavorably to Demetrian matriarchy, which "was the source of high virtues and of a stable and well-ordered, if narrow-minded, existence," whereas the Dionysian age concealed "the decay of social life and of morality that furthered the demise of the old world more than any other cause." As Dionysian men returned in some measure to the hetaeric age, Bachofen suggests that they ultimately lost the respect of their women, who "came to despise them."[55]

This growing disrespect for their dissolute menfolk, combined with the fact that not all women successfully accommodated themselves to the Dionysian age, precipitates a second stage of Amazonism in Bachofen's time line. Unlike the first, which Bachofen interprets as "a step forward toward a purer form of life," this Amazonian rebellion against paternity is "a regression and perversion."[56] It is basically matriarchy out of hand, women gone wild. In a last-ditch effort to wrest power back from men, Amazonian women go to war, constructing the female-only societies familiar from Greek legend and medieval European tales.

Bachofen narrates the Amazons' eventual defeat as a result of superior male military prowess, but more importantly, as women's weakness in the face of the seductive powers of Dionysian men. Bachofen is dismissive of this female turnaround, noting "the difficulty that female nature has in behaving with moderation and measure." He celebrates the defeat of Amazonism as a restoration of right relations between the sexes, decrying the Amazons as "man-hating, man-killing, war-like virgins" *(männerfeindlichen, männertötenden, kriegerischen*

Jungfrauen).[57] Though they "towered over men," says Bachofen, they essentially ended by prostituting themselves. In thrall to Dionysian phallicism, they became obsessed with stimulating lust in men at the expense of all culture and morality.[58] Bachofen's Amazons swing wildly between a desire to kill men and a desire to submit to their manly charms.

The Amazons' loss proves in the end to be their gain. In Bachofen's descriptions of the final downfall of Amazonism, one can hear the echoes of Kleist's *Penthesilea:* "The woman recognizes the man's higher strength and beauty to which she gladly bends. Tired of her Amazonian grandeur, which she was able to sustain only for a short while, she willingly renders homage to the man who gives her back her natural purpose. She understands that it is love and fertility and not manhating belligerence that constitute her destiny. Now she willingly follows the one who, through his victory, has brought her salvation."[59] The defeat of Amazonism establishes, for the first time, what Bachofen deems "the true equality of the sexes." His idea of equality is a curious one, since it is premised on the superiority of men and their domination over women. To explain this relationship, Bachofen likens women to the moon, and men to the sun: "The moon has no light of its own, it borrows all its light from a greater heavenly body. Woman is like the moon, material. However, man is like the sun, spiritual. . . . The man's spiritual principle dominates. The woman realizes that she must borrow her loveliest luster from him."[60]

The final triumph over mother right is secured by the Apollonian age, which brings with it a new notion of paternity. Ironically, this paternity has little to do with the male role in conception. Far from it. Unlike Dionysian paternity, which is sexual and material, Apollonian paternity is spiritual, of the mind alone. Apollonian paternity is most powerfully demonstrated for Bachofen in the practice of testamentary adoption in ancient Rome. Apollo "liberates himself entirely from any connection with woman" and forges paternal relationships with others independent of any blood relation.[61] By virtue of its "immateriality," Bachofen declares this "the triumph of paternity," which "allows the intellect to rid itself of material phenomena . . . and rise above the laws of material life. . . . Maternity is related to the physical side of man, the only thing he shares with animals: the paternal-spiritual principle relates to man alone."[62] With the "Apollonian-metaphysical principle," says Bachofen, humanity reaches "the permanent and complete defeat of the maternal principle" and "the decisive conquest of woman."[63]

Bachofen becomes quite expansive on this point: when "mother right remains with the animals and the human family moves on to father right," the spirit is "purified of the slag of matter by fire."[64] Since women are slag, inextricably wedded to matter, they have reached the end of their evolutionary usefulness with the victory of Apollonian paternity. Henceforward, women, and the goddesses that embody feminine nature, can only serve as a drag against the evolutionary tide. This they do: Bachofen regards the growth of goddess cults in ancient Rome (especially those of Isis and Cybele) as an illustration of "how difficult it is for people at all times and under the authority of various religions to overcome the weight of material nature and to reach their highest destiny, the elevation of worldly existence to the divine paternal principle."[65]

Freed from matter and the overwhelming power of the blood tie of maternity, the Apollonian age is set to develop a new, superior form of justice—no small matter for Bachofen, who, it must be remembered, came to his work on matriarchy as a legal scholar. According to Bachofen, law under Demetrian matriarchy protects the sanctity of blood relation, which is the bedrock of mother right. When considering this aspect of matriarchy, Bachofen leaves behind the hymns he sings to the Demetrian age elsewhere in *Das Mutterrecht* and lets go with a vituperative denunciation of matriarchy's "sinister, abominable, and hopeless cult of unforgiving chthonic power." Maternal law is "gory," "gruesome," and "merciless."[66] The era of mother right is a "bleak, somber, barbarous time . . . where every murder triggered another, where spilled blood was washed away with the blood of another."[67] As Bachofen concludes, "Mother right is the bloodiest of all laws," as it must be, since only the naive fail to recognize that the "insatiable thirst for blood" is an essential part of women's nature.[68] No wonder, then, that Bachofen welcomes the turn to the sun of Apollonian paternity, under which law becomes a civilized process of adjudicating competing claims.[69]

The example par excellence of this shift is, for Bachofen, the trial of Orestes, as narrated in Aeschylus's *Oresteia*.[70] Aeschylus's tragedy was based on a legend told by Homer in the *Odyssey*, later retold in different versions by the Greek poets Stesichorus and Pindar.[71] The basic plot of the *Oresteia* revolves around a series of murders within the house of Agamemnon, the king of Mycenae. Agamemnon sacrifices his daughter Iphigenia to the gods to calm the winds so that his ships may safely sail off to war. Upon his return, Clytemnestra, Iphigenia's mother, kills Agamemnon in revenge for his having killed their daughter.[72] Finally Orestes, their son, avenges Agamemnon's death by killing his mother, Clytemnestra. This is where early versions of the story end, but in Aeschylus's version, the drama is just beginning. Orestes finds himself pursued by his mother's avenging furies *(erinyes),* who wish to punish him for his act of matricide. His case comes before a tribunal in Athens, over which Athena presides. Orestes's defense is offered by Apollo, who claims: "The mother is not the true parent of the child / Which is called hers. She is a nurse who tends the growth / Of young seed planted by its true parent, the male." To underscore his argument, Apollo points to Athena: "Present, as proof, the daughter of Olympian Zeus: / One never nursed in the dark cradle of the womb." (According to Greek mythology, the goddess Athena was born from Zeus's head.) The tribunal—composed of Athenian citizens—votes on whether to convict or acquit Orestes in the murder of his mother, and the vote is tied. Athena breaks the tie by voting to acquit, stating, "No mother gave me birth. Therefore the father's claim / And male supremacy in all things . . . wins my whole heart's loyalty."[73]

The *Oresteia,* as Bachofen interprets it, is the purest distillation of the shift from mother right to father right: the blood vengeance demanded by Clytemnestra's *erinyes,* representatives of mother right, is denied in a court of law that upholds the principle of paternity as the energizing seed against that of maternity as the passive, gestating earth. One could hardly hope for a clearer literary narration of the themes that Bachofen addresses.

Of course, there is a circularity here: Bachofen did not conceive of the theory of mother right, only to stumble across this particularly acute example of matriarchal themes in, of all places, classical Greek myth. The *Oresteia*—among many other texts—*instructed* Bachofen in the myth of matriarchal prehistory; it was taken as evidence for prehistoric matriarchy.[74] How could this be, when Aeschylus's work was a play, and not a historical text? For Bachofen this posed no difficulty. The myths Aeschylus relied on in composing the *Oresteia* were, for Bachofen, clues—read properly—to even more ancient times. Indeed, the majority of Bachofen's evidence for prehistoric matriarchy comes from classical myth.[75] This presents a puzzle: in 1855, when Bachofen began work on *Das Mutterrecht,* classical myths were hardly new texts, nor were they newly rediscovered. They had been around for many centuries and had been read over and over with diligence and scholarly acumen. If they in fact encoded a historical phenomenon of mother right, previous scholars had failed to notice this. But then, they were not working with Bachofen's personal agenda or, usually, his theory of myth.

BACHOFEN AND THE INTERPRETATION OF MYTH

Bachofen was through and through a classicist: he read classical texts, admired classical times, and sought to understand classical precedents. In this he was a man, not quite of his own times, but of a generation or two prior.

The culture of classical Greece was of such great importance in the German-speaking world in the middle of the eighteenth century that a well-known book on this period of German history is titled simply *The Tyranny of Greece over Germany.*[76] Johann Joachim Winckelmann, a German scholar of Roman antiquities, set the tone in the 1760s with his works on ancient art and literature from around the Mediterranean. He regarded ancient Greece as a *sui generis* wonder and helped to kick off the *Hellenomanie* that captivated late eighteenth-century German intellectuals.[77] This was the environment in which Bachofen's intellectual life took root. Others of his generation moved away from the classicist obsessions of their academic mentors, but Bachofen stayed the course, at least until after the publication of *Mutterrecht*.[78] Though he made occasional ethnographic references, these were merely footnotes to his greatest interest: classical myth; and through myth, religion; and through both, the truth about human prehistory.[79]

Classical myths, for Bachofen, were reliable tools for the recovery of prehistory. These myths were of course written texts, and thus not prehistoric at all. But working on the assumptions that myths preserved earlier oral traditions and that the realm of religion is inherently more conservative than family life or government, Bachofen believed he could use these myths as tools to uncover the deep past.[80] As he asserted, "They say that myth is like quicksand, making it impossible to gain a foothold. However, this complaint does not apply to myth itself, but to the approach taken to it. Variform and changing in its outward appearance, myth does follow certain laws and is as rich and reliable in concrete results as any other source of historical knowledge."[81] Bachofen considered myths to have distinct advantages over other texts as a means of reconstructing history because they were not the work of a single author, but rather the distillation of "a collective experience in the light of religious faith."[82]

In Bachofen's estimation, then, myth was a sober, accurate historical document. According to Lionel Gossman, Bachofen likened himself to a "cautious sailor hugging the shoreline," engaged in a method of "empirical observation."[83] If one accepts Bachofen's definition of myth, his actually *is* a prudent approach to exploring prehistory. Of course, how Bachofen gets from the actual text of the myth to the historical reality it represents is a somewhat mysterious process, for if myth is history, it is a history that must be decoded out of its fantastic narrative presentation.[84] Bachofen is never precise about how he gets from one place to the other, though get there he does, with assurance and alacrity. Intuition and imagination play a role, as Bachofen readily admitted: "There are two paths to every realization: the longer, slower, more arduous one of rational combination and the shorter one that is traveled with the force and velocity of electricity, the path of fantasy which, inspired by the sight and the immediate touch of ancient remains, instantly grasps the truth without any mediating links. In terms of life and color, that which is acquired on the second path is mightily superior to the products of the intellect."[85] This intuitive method played out in Bachofen's reconstruction of ancient matriarchy. For example, the insight that "our origin is from clay and marsh" (the primeval swamp of the hetaeric stage) is a "memory" that, according to historian Philippe Borgeaud, came to Bachofen "as a personal experience in the course of his meditation on funerary symbolism."[86] Another method of interpretation Bachofen relied on was attending to the emotional tone of myths. For example, Bachofen could be certain that mother right preceded father right because "the very vigor of Roman patriarchy implies an inimical principle that had to be combated and ousted."[87]

Some commentators view Bachofen's understanding and interpretation of myth as his most important scholarly contribution, vastly more significant than his "highly speculative, generally discredited work on mother right."[88] In ways—and certainly by his own estimation—Bachofen *was* pioneering a new method of myth interpretation.[89] But he was also drawing on a school of mythography that had developed in the late eighteenth and early nineteenth centuries, just before and during his formal education. This solidly German tradition bequeathed to Bachofen "a predisposition to an intuitive global understanding of the wisdom of classical and preclassical societies" and inculcated in him the basic principle of euhemerism:[90] "that myth always centres round a kernel or core of historical truth, misrepresented by false symbolism and literary embellishments."[91]

The first herald of this new Germanic approach to myth came in the late eighteenth century with the work of Christian Gottlob Heyne, a professor of *Altertumswissenschaft* who had an unusually long career at the University of Göttingen (from 1763 to 1812).[92] Heyne discarded the then mainstream notion that myths were simply fantasy, impossible stories bearing no relationship to reality. Instead, he believed he could tap myths for their deeper meanings, and sometimes for the history they encoded.[93] Heyne did not naively equate myth with history, but he believed that the latter could be detected in the former at least part of the time. Myths were of two types: they either elaborated versions of historic events or they were *philosophemes,* stories that offered explanations for natural phenomena or taught moral lessons.[94] Their distinctive narrative form, filled with divine and supernatural characters, Heyne attributed to the fact that their authors were "primitives," utilizing a "natural and necessary mode of expression during the 'childhood of the human race.'"[95] To understand myths properly, Heyne concluded, one had to understand the people and cultures that gave birth to them. Only then could they be translated for modernity.[96]

In Heyne there was already a touch of a looming Romanticism, a yearning for the deep soul of classical Greece, which could be seen only imperfectly behind the screen of its myths. This yearning, alongside a true historicist agenda, was even more pronounced in the work of Heyne's contemporary, Johann Gottfried Herder (1744–1803).[97] Herder was a localist and a relativist; he dismissed claims of human universalism and was even disinterested in the nation-state, then a topic of great interest among European intellectuals. Instead he sought after the *Volksgeist,* each people's unique way of thinking and expressing itself, which could be detected in its customs, language, laws, and, of course, in its mythology.[98] Anticipating the Romantic movement he helped to create, Herder emphasized emotion at the expense of rationality, arguing that it was the "vital forces" of a people, its poetry and its religion, that determined its national character. Unlike Heyne, Herder did not think of one culture as superior to another on an evolutionary scale. Each culture had its own genius, its own flavor, and each should be appreciated in its own context and by its own standards.[99] If anything, a younger culture was superior to an older one, since it had not "slipped into the evils of luxury and civilization," but instead was caught in its moment of greatest creative and poetic growth.[100]

Romanticism caught fire in Germany as the eighteenth gave way to the nineteenth century, bringing with it a new zeal for exploring myth, which was thought to encapsulate truth and reveal it to those who listened properly.[101] The Romantic movement was initially dominated by a handful of thinkers in two cities, Jena and Berlin, who were inspired by Herder, Goethe, and the *Sturm und Drang* school of literature, and who were further spurred on in their aspirations by the dramatic events of the French Revolution.[102] The German Romantic movement did not retain any real coherence after its founders moved on to other places and pursuits, so historians sometimes limit its life span quite severely, applying it to only a few individuals and a few texts between 1795 and 1810, or even more narrowly, between 1796 and 1800.[103] These dates are misleading, however. Romanticism was very influential throughout the first half of the nineteenth century. Even after it died down, it continued to be revived by people like Bachofen (who is regarded by some as "a belated representative" of Romanticism and by others as "the Romantic par excellence" in which "the entirety of the German Romantic movement found its highest expression").[104] The Romantic movement pervaded all manner of literary genres and academic disciplines in Germany: it was a mood as much as a methodology, an orientation to the world as much as a hermeneutic tool. Certainly it was a key element in how German scholars approached the study of mythology and the classics in the time leading up to Bachofen.

Romanticism came to Bachofen secondhand, principally through professors of the *Historische Schule* with whom he studied at the University of Berlin. The *Historische Schule,* whose chief representatives were Friedrich Karl von Savigny, August Böckh, and Leopold Ranke, opposed themselves to the *Philosophische Schule,* whose principal spokesperson was G. W. F. Hegel. Hegel and the professors of the *Historische Schule* had more in common than it might at first seem,[105] but in the early decades of the nineteenth century, they saw themselves as opposites. It was the *Historische Schule* that took on the ideals of the Romantic movement.[106] When they approached historical material, they sought to experience it empathically, conjuring up its long-deceased original authors, rather than simply recording it or analyzing it linguistically. In this, the esteemed philologist August Böckh led the way. Böckh repeated a series of lectures on philology at the University of Berlin for nearly fifty years, from 1818 to 1865, lectures that Bachofen attended in the 1830s. Böckh consistently expressed his frustration with fellow philologists and critics who questioned the immediacy with which he encountered past languages, myths, and peoples.[107] "Complete understanding," Böckh insisted, "is reached in response to a feeling," which "can cut the Gordian knot of uncertainty."[108] Böckh was not deterred by materials like myths, which seemed to disguise their meanings behind fabulous or unbelievable story lines. As he explained, "the farther the representation of character departs from history, the more does it require historical interpretation."[109] The interpreter needed to be willing to give him- or herself up to the author of a text and wait for illumination to spring forth.[110]

Certainly Bachofen came to work in just this mode, letting intuition guide his interpretation of antiquity and reacting with annoyance, even outrage, when other philologists reached different conclusions or questioned his methods.[111] Bachofen was clearly influenced by Böckh, but he made the more lasting connection with his famous mentor in the field of jurisprudence, Friedrich Karl von Savigny.[112] Savigny, like Böckh, took a characteristically Romantic attitude toward his subject matter; in this case, jurisprudence. Like philology, jurisprudence sounds like a rather stale, narrow field of study, but in the early nineteenth century, it was anything but that. Roman law was not only ancient law, but also contemporary law. Germany was then in the process of codifying its legal system, and one of the main sources upon which it drew was Roman law, which Savigny and many others claimed had been continuously practiced in Europe up through the Middle Ages.[113] Furthermore, Savigny took an expansive view of law, seeing it as a key to culture, government, national identity, and even philosophy.[114] It was a living thing, a distillation of the life of a people, not a matter of philosophy and abstract reasoning; it was "organically connected with the nature and character of a people."[115] Bachofen did not follow Savigny in every particular; in an 1854 autobiographical essay that he addressed to Savigny, Bachofen noted several areas in which he differed from his mentor (one of which was politics, Bachofen having taken on a conservative stance upon his return to Basel after his studies).[116] Nevertheless, it is clear that Bachofen absorbed Savigny's Romantic sense that both myth and law could be read as expressions of a people's core nature and fundamental values.

If there is one scholar who can be said to have directly anticipated Bachofen's approach to myth, it would be Georg Friedrich Creuzer, professor of philology and ancient history at the University of Heidelberg, a friend of Savigny and Böckh, and author of an extremely controversial text first published between 1810 and 1812 titled *Symbolik und Mythologie der Alten Völker* (Symbolism and Mythology of Ancient Peoples).[117] *Symbolik* made an enormous impression on the principal Romantic thinkers of the day. Friedrich Schlegel claimed that Creuzer had "newly founded" the science of myth.[118] Creuzer, in turn, was an enthusiastic reader of everything produced by the Romantic movement, inspired in part by his scandalous love affair with the poet Karoline von Günderode, who was obsessed "with the infinite, with the orient, and with self-destruction"—all Romantic preoccupations—and ultimately with her own self-destruction, since she stabbed herself to death at age twenty-six after Creuzer ended their affair and returned to his wife.[119] Some commentators have been so impressed with the Romanticism of Creuzer's work that they have designated Heidelberg as the center of "religious romanticism," as opposed to the "literary romanticism" that sprang up in Jena.[120]

The principal theme of Creuzer's *Symbolik* was ancient Greek religion, which he cast in a more sinister and mysterious light than had earlier scholars. Creuzer inflamed the field of philology by claiming that the true essence of Greek religion was not Greek at all, but Indian. Creuzer argued that the Brahmins of India, having devised an esoteric set of symbols to encapsulate their profound religious insights, traveled as missionaries to Asia Minor, Egypt, and eventually to Greece and Italy. To teach the Greeks, who lacked some of the wisdom and subtlety of the East, the priests were forced to articulate their religious truths in a narrative rather than symbolic mode. Once the symbols of the wise men from the East were corrupted by their translation into myth, they came to lose their deeper religious meaning. A religion that in India was monotheistic devolved into the Greek pantheon, with its wide variety of heroes and heroines, gods and goddesses.[121] In spite of myth's degenerative influence on religion, Creuzer continued to believe that myth was instrumental in transferring beliefs, teachings, and history to new generations, and also that myths could be mined for archaic information many centuries after they ceased to be living stories.[122]

Bachofen was industriously reading and taking notes on Creuzer's *Symbolik und Mythologie der Alten Völker* while traveling in Greece in 1851, and numerous extracts from *Symbolik* are found in the Bachofen archives in Basel. Bachofen's sequence of Dionysian and Apollonian prehistoric stages was prefigured in Creuzer's division of ancient Greek religion into the Dionysian, representing multiplicity and matter, and the Apollonian, representing unity presiding over the material forms of nature.[123] Bachofen followed Creuzer in stressing "the dark underside of ancient civilization" and exploring Oriental influences in ancient Greek culture rather than celebrating Hellenism as an indigenous European marvel, as scholars like Winckelmann had done a century before. And again like Creuzer, Bachofen paid little attention to the chronological sequence of ancient texts, preferring to impose his own chronology on them.

Bachofen did not adopt Creuzer's vision wholesale. For example, he rejected the theory that traveling priests from India were the origin of classical Greek religion.[124] Here Bachofen followed Creuzer's colleague, Karl Otfried Müller, also a former student of Böckh, and the inheritor of Heyne's chair in philology at Göttingen. Bachofen attended Müller's lectures at Göttingen after he left his studies at the University of Berlin, so he was directly familiar with Müller's work. Unlike Creuzer, Müller believed that Greek myth was native to the Greeks and that, as Herder had argued earlier, it encapsulated the essence of a people, the Greek

Volksgeist.[125] Müller had a lot of support in this. Creuzer had alienated many of his peers by reducing the Greeks to barbarians while elevating ancient India and Persia as the true sources of religious genius. Müller reversed Creuzer's course, claiming that "the Greek mind, even in . . . the earliest of its productions, appears richer and more various in its forms" and takes "a loftier and a wider range than is the case in the religion of the oriental neighbours of the Greeks," whose cyclic traits "must in the end have wearied and stupefied the mind."[126]

Müller also differed from Creuzer in regarding myth not as a deliberate creation of elites, but as "the fruit of an unconscious collective process." Myth was not a degeneration from a prior, more immediate symbolic connection with religious truth, but rather was a part of the same cultural universe, invented and understood via a "mythopoetic faculty" alive in all human cultures and at all levels of society. If anything, myth sometimes clarified what was too vague, too easy to misread, in symbolic communication.[127] However, Müller regarded myth as having to do with "inner life" and was less inclined to find in it an encoded history, as Creuzer, and later Bachofen, did. In reading myth as history, then, Bachofen was clearly more in league with Creuzer than with Müller, though he clung to Müller's undiluted form of *Hellenomanie.*[128]

It needs to be stressed here that Bachofen wrote *Das Mutterrecht* more than forty years after Creuzer and Müller published their major works. The insistence, in Müller's words, that "a certain rapture is necessary for the student of mythology,"[129] was well out of vogue by the 1840s, when Bachofen first set pen to paper, and certainly by the 1860s, when he was publishing *Das Mutterrecht.*[130] A revolution in thought had passed Bachofen by, partly because he was located in Basel rather than in Germany; partly because he was a lone wolf researcher who lacked a scholarly community; and mostly because he was Bachofen, looking backward rather than forward, believing that modernity was losing sight of all that mattered most, and that the smartest thing to do culturally, politically, and academically was to put on the brakes. Bachofen was—or as an adult, became—a conservative in the classical sense, wishing to retain traditional institutions and forestall rapid change.

Bachofen was also behind the times in his belief that universal histories could be unearthed and formulated. "After 1850," notes George Williamson in *The Longing for Myth in Germany,* "the Romantic paradigm continued to justify the collection of anecdotes and fragments, but hopes for final synthesis were quietly abandoned."[131] Perhaps this was true for most scholars, but certainly not for Bachofen, who was just warming up to the challenge of presenting a stirring new synthesis whose contours could be discovered in classical myth. In an era when the study of myth and history had become highly rationalist and specialized and earlier approaches were denounced as mysticism, Bachofen forged ahead with the academic agenda of an earlier generation. In his study of antiquity, Bachofen was after something—many things, actually—that he felt was lacking in his own age. Somehow, for him, all these became tied up in the figure of Woman. The ambivalence Bachofen felt toward Woman (or maybe just women, though I have no intention of attempting to sort out the idiosyncratic wrinkles in Bachofen's psyche) managed to gather up in its wake Bachofen's profound ambivalence toward Christianity, democracy, and the modern era, and set an odd, variegated cornerstone for the contemporary Western myth of matriarchal prehistory.

PROGRESS AND NOSTALGIA: BACHOFEN ON WOMEN, RELIGION, HISTORY, AND GOVERNMENT

Who are women, for Bachofen? As we have seen, they are first and foremost mothers. And motherhood, in Bachofen's scheme, gives women a striking bivalence: they are forever enmeshed in the material, being born only to bear again in turn, tied as strongly to death as to life. ("Only woman mourns the demise of the material," says Bachofen, since it is "she who through conception and birthing fulfills the destiny of the material.")[132] Yet, it must be recalled, it is women—as mothers—who first lift man out of the material, out of the primeval swamp in which he has been rutting and wallowing without a thought for the morrow. In one of the great transformation mysteries that Bachofen assigns to women, mothers enter the material, live it fully, and through it give rise to the spiritual.

The tension between these two depictions of femininity is plain: first, woman is a fool for mourning the death of matter; next she is a spiritual genius, precisely through her attention to matter and mourning.[133] These two views of women compete with each other throughout the pages of Das Mutterrecht: woman is both "femme fatale" and "harbinger of culture"; she is the "clue to the fallen and to the elevated in human nature." As Bachofen himself put it, "Each innovation towards the worse in human conditions proceeds from woman. . . . also the initiative for the elevation from sunken conditions lies in the hands of women."[134]

At the time Bachofen wrote Das Mutterrecht, he was heir to a long European and biblical tradition of viewing women as magnetically suspended between virginity and whoredom, always ready to swing one way or the other depending on their choices—or, more accurately, men's interpretations of their choices. The ambivalence Bachofen exhibits toward women may be lamentable, but it cannot be very surprising. Still, Bachofen is notable for the way in which he simultaneously maintains both views, sometimes at their extremes.[135] If Das Mutterrecht is "a paean to the marvel of women," as one of Bachofen's later reviewers claims, it is also a slap in the face.[136]

In reading Bachofen's oeuvre, however, the insult takes a backseat to the compliment, the gutter to the pedestal. In spite of his evolutionary time line leading inexorably to father right, Bachofen's dominant mood toward women is adulatory:

women have achieved great things, excelling where men could not. Again—and ironically—this is part and parcel of women's virtuosity in the material realm. As Bachofen explains: "Mystery is the true essence of any religion, and wherever woman spearheads the realms of cult and life, she will take delight in nurturing the mysterious. Her natural disposition connects the sensual and the transcendental; her close kinship is with natural life and the material, whose perpetual death evokes in her the need for consolation and spiritual hope." Religion is where woman shines, exerting "the greatest influence on men and on the education and morality of civilization through her natural inclination toward the supernatural, the divine, that which defies any law, and the miraculous."[137]

Women's connection to religion is extremely important in Bachofen's scheme because religion itself is crucial. In the *Origin of the Family, Private Property, and the State*, Friedrich Engels complained that "Bachofen believes at least as much as Aeschylus did in the Erinyes, Apollo and Athena; for, at bottom he believes that the overthrow of mother right by father right was a miracle wrought during the Greek heroic age by these divinities."[138] This is overstating the case: I think it is clear that Bachofen did not believe in the actual existence of Apollo and Athena, but it is extremely easy to lose sight of this while reading his work, so removed is it from anything lower than Mount Olympus. One could easily gain the impression that Demeter herself presided over the age of the mother and that Apollo bestowed father right upon Rome.

Since his primary texts are classical myths, it might be thought that Bachofen merely lifted a concern with religion from these texts, but it appears that cause and effect move in the opposite direction. Bachofen was already committed to religion as the locus and instrument of important social change and so he sought out texts to support his views. Bachofen is completely open about his position, declaring that "there is only one mighty lever of all civilization, and it is religion." "Every great step in the evolution of humankind takes place within the realm of religion," he says, "which is always the most powerful, and in primordial times the only, bearer of civilization."[139]

Bachofen was himself, by all accounts, a good, god-fearing Calvinist Protestant,[140] an identity that sat uncomfortably beside his obvious admiration for paganism. "Uncomfortable" possibly describes Bachofen better than any other word could. One of his favorite phrases, popping up again and again throughout his writings, is "neither this nor that." One minute engaged in a rhapsodic hymn to Demetrian matriarchy and in the next decrying its regressive materiality, one minute triumphantly proclaiming the victory of father right and in the next bemoaning the loss of mother right, Bachofen could never find the chair in which he really wanted to sit.

Amidst all this nay-saying, however, there were certain claims Bachofen made consistently, ones which he either believed in fully, unquestioningly, or which he could not bring himself to explicitly question. Foremost among these was Bachofen's conservatism. Bachofen mourned "the old relationships of love and trust, hierarchy and respect" that in his eyes characterized traditional European society, and feared the "material demands of the undifferentiated mass of the equally entitled." Bachofen's early attraction to ancient Rome was based on what he regarded as the perfection of a patrician order that nineteenth-century Europe, with its spiraling demands for democracy and equality, was inexorably dissolving.[141] As Lionel Gossman explains, "Democracy, nationalism and socialism . . . seemed to Bachofen three evils that were about to plunge the world back into a new age of barbarism. . . . Democracy, to him, meant—sooner or later—demagogy and despotism."[142] Bachofen put it this way: "Democracy always paves the way for tyranny; my ideal is a republic ruled, not by the many, but by the best citizens."[143]

Bachofen took a very dim view of the world in which he was forced, by dint of his birth in nineteenth-century Basel, to live. While Bachofen reserves a burst of enthusiasm for the triumph of Apollonian paternity in ancient Rome, he never summons up anything more than stoic acceptance for his own era, in which he lives, by his own account, as *der Einsiedler,* a recluse, an anchorite.[144] Bachofen was "a stranger in modernity" in part because he did not accept the modern world's belief in progress, in a history that reached ever upward toward some glorious endpoint.[145] At face value, this seems completely contrary to his project in *Das Mutterrecht,* which follows a "victorious path from bottom to top, from the material night to the light of a heavenly spiritual principle."[146] But this evolutionary strain in Bachofen, in which history can be seen as "a process of redemption," is overwhelmed by his Hegelian preference for ongoing struggle, for dualisms never resolved once for all time, for "timeless human values" that can only flourish under conditions that constantly "ebb and flow."[147] *Das Mutterrecht,* for all its promulgation of a five-stage, upward-traveling dialectic, reads not so much as a tale of victory, but as one of transition and crisis, repeatedly reaching forward and sliding back.[148]

In the midst of this relentless struggle, which in Bachofen's own time and by his own reckoning was sliding back rather than reaching forward, where could one go for succor? For Bachofen, the answer was clear: one went backwards. Bachofen first went back to ancient Rome, a time, he felt, of cultivated elites. When this proved inadequate, he simply went back further, to the reign of the benevolent matriarchs, until he found himself, as Lionel Gossman puts it, "irrevocably in the past, indeed on the other side of historical time, in prehistory."[149]

It is too simple, and quite inaccurate, to say that what Bachofen found in the past was a model for the present. Though he thrilled to the discovery of Demetrian matriarchy and longed to immerse himself in it, he never failed to return to his own "well-educated but enfeebled times," which in the final analysis he could only reckon as an improvement over the ancient age of mother right. It was with father right that human history, properly speaking, began: through the elevation from material to spiritual, humanity first attained the ability to create on an intellectual level. Bachofen counted it as "foolish" to "look back nostalgically from the end of evolution towards its beginnings" and believed that a return to the age of the mothers would result in the bestialization of man. No matter how good Bachofen sometimes made barbarism look, he still called it barbarism, and he steadfastly refused to critique civilization per se. "We must not condemn civilization," he stated, "or give it over to pre-cultural conditions"; to attempt this would be "the most disastrous of all stupidities."[150]

In this Bachofen revealed yet again an affinity with Hegel over his opponents in the *Historische Schule* at the University of Berlin. Everything in Bachofen seems to ally him with the Romantics: his passion for the ancient, for myth, for woman as mother, for what Ludmilla Jordanova in *Sexual Visions* calls "the fascination with the erotic, the funereal, and the demonic."[151] But for all that they were singing the same song, Bachofen and the Romantics parted company in two highly significant ways. First, the Romantics were antifoundationalist. Coming in the wake of the Enlightenment, they cast off the notion of a first principle and rejected universal or metaphysical accounts of human life. Instead, they staked their claim with national and cultural specificity.[152] Bachofen, in contrast, told a universalizing story. Human history proceeded in stages. These stages were not the property of any specific culture, but belonged to human infancy and childhood as such. The process had its own internal logic, moving in an evolutionary, progressive, and ultimately irreversible direction. This is the spirit of Hegel. It is not the spirit of Herder, Savigny, or Creuzer.

Second, the Romantics, in their evocation of what Gossman calls "the hidden object of curiosity and desire" ("the excluded, the alienated, the repressed, the feminine . . . nature, the Orient, woman, the people, and the hidden past") were actively seeking a way out of the constraints of rational thought and patriarchal, bourgeois culture.[153] Bachofen, as we have seen, refused the seductive call for escape. Patriarchy, father law, was a positive development, he insisted. Again like Hegel, and unlike the Romantics, the Orient is for Bachofen merely the Occident's "own petrified past," not a beacon drawing it toward the wisdom of the East.[154] For both men history is a struggle between opposing dualisms—matter and spirit, female and male, Dionysus and Apollo, Orient and Occident—with the former inevitably yielding to the latter. Bachofen's sober attitude, his conviction that whatever its attractions, the present was superior to the past, was Hegelian, not Romantic. Indeed, Bachofen sounded very much like Freud would a generation later, profoundly sympathizing with the id and the child, but never wavering in his conviction that adulthood required the sublimation of infantile impulses.

Still, the past was more alive, more tempting, for Bachofen than it was for Hegel. His brave words notwithstanding, Bachofen's yearning to escape his own age and return to the land of the mothers is palpable. In an 1864 letter to philologist Heinrich Meyer-Ochsner in Zurich, Bachofen wrote, "The French say openly that the present situation is a golden age compared to the previous one. May God preserve us, they say, from a return to freedom. . . . Such people need despotism and are happy in it." By 1870 he was remarking to Joseph Marc Hornung, a professor friend in Lausanne: "I have never felt more vitally than I do today the price of a work which pulls our thought out of the events of the day and imposes silence to sad reflections on the lugubrious spectacle which the history of civilized Europe presently offers. The epoch of Mother-right seems now to me less barbarous, an age of gold compared to the century of the chassepots."[155]

Though Bachofen deemed nostalgia for the matriarchal era a disastrous stupidity, *Das Mutterrecht* is simply awash in it. His is the posture of the good and loyal son: he gives "his pious, filial attention" to "the Mothers, the dead," and like his sometime counterpart, Jules Michelet, he ensures that "honored, consoled . . . and blessed, they [the Mothers] might return in peace to their tombs."[156] Bachofen takes on this task not dutifully, but with passion: "In the light of the current state of things, [the matriarchal era] looks like fiction. But the most superior poetry, more vibrant and touching than any fantasy, is the reality of history. Humankind has experienced fates that we are not able to imagine." Bachofen's epiphanies in ancient Italian cemeteries leave him pining for "abandonment without reserve to the most luxuriant life of the senses . . . [in which] no idea of struggle, of self-discipline, of sin and repentance disturbs the harmony of a life at once sensual and transcending sensuality."[157]

However, Bachofen's nostalgia for the rule of women and a life of materiality in no way rewrites him as a feminist before his time.[158] Instead, it returns him to the orbit of Romanticism. As George S. Williamson explains: "The persistent gap between mythical hope and prosaic reality . . . [leads] to that most Romantic of emotions: longing *[Sehnsucht]*. . . . Sentiments of nostalgia, longing, or exile were indeed a common feature of European culture in the decades following the French Revolution, as writers sensed the profound distance that divided them from the world of their childhood and, by extension, from the seemingly unified and tradition-bound societies of the distant past."[159]

The Romantic movement, and Bachofen along with it, held an admiring but ultimately trivializing view of women. For one thing, women were celebrated almost entirely within their traditional spheres of childbearing and domesticity. As Rita Felski explains: "In the texts of early Romanticism one finds some of the most explicitly nostalgic representations of femininity as a redemptive refuge from the constraints of civilization. Seen to be less specialized and differentiated than man, located within the household and an intimate web of familial relations, more closely linked to nature through her reproductive capacity, woman embodied a sphere of atemporal authenticity seemingly untouched by the alienation and fragmentation of modern life."[160] For the Romantics, "the feminine" sat out-side history, outside the life of the public. It lived, changeless and uniform, where it could serve as a resource for the present and future. But it could never—must never—act on its own account.[161]

Nostalgia, whatever personal enjoyments it offers, is hardly an emotion that disrupts the status quo. Anthropologist Renato Rosaldo describes nostalgia as "a particularly appropriate emotion to invoke in attempting to establish one's inno-cence and at the same time talk about what one has destroyed."[162] Nostalgia is the balm of tempestuous times, a remedy for the feeling that we have moved too quickly to overwrite our past and have inadvertently left something behind. In Bachofen's desire to go back—back to the mother and to prehistory—and in his condemna-tion of the present, there is no *imperative* to go back, as Bachofen's commitment to a conservative, patrician, patriarchal Europe clearly shows. Rosaldo describes this as "imperialist nostalgia" in which " 'we' (who believe in progress) valorize inno-vation, and then yearn for more stable worlds, whether these reside in our own past, in other cultures, or in the conflation of the two. . . . when the so-called civi-lizing process destabilizes forms of life, the agents of change experience transfor-mations of other cultures as if they were personal losses."[163] Bachofen spent the better part of his lifetime and his scholarly work mourning this loss, turning to the women of the matriarchal age as to a loving mother in whom resides, as he repeatedly said, "all concern for the living and grief for the dead."[164]

BACHOFEN'S LEGACY

Bachofen did not enjoy much fame in his lifetime. He "was either ignored com-pletely or disregarded as a misguided eccentric," writes Gossman, "one of hun-dreds of obscure classical philologists in the provincial cities of German-speaking Europe."[165] Though his early presentations of the thesis of *Das Mutterrecht* were received with enthusiasm, the book itself caused little stir. It was only lightly reviewed, and it was entirely ignored by the more respected journals.[166] Then hot on its heels in 1865—and without any direct contact with Bachofen or his work—came John F. McLennan's *Primitive Marriage:* a very different sort of study, but one that also "discovered" women's central role in prehistory. It was McLennan's version of prehistoric gender relations and the many permutations developed by his colleagues that dominated scholarly and even popular discussion in the last third of the nineteenth century. In fact, versions of McLennan's matriarchal myth achieved a status of near-dogma in the emerging discipline of anthropology, while Bachofen's *Mutterrecht* descended to the status of footnote.[167]

The only evolutionary anthropologist who took an interest in Bachofen—establishing a correspondence with him and soliciting his opinions on matters of mutual interest—was Lewis Henry Morgan, an American. Though Morgan was undoubtedly influenced by Bachofen, it could not have been by much, for Morgan did not read German (a fact he admitted apologetically to Bachofen), and *Das Mutterrecht* was not available in English.[168] Indeed, the influence seems to have mainly gone the other way. By 1870, Bachofen was aware of anthropological interest in theories of mother right. He consumed the growing literature by evolutionary anthropologists, reading more than six hundred different authors. He contemplated a revised edition of *Das Mutterrecht* that describe "the remains of the maternal system surviving in all the peoples of the world." Failing that, in 1878, he set himself a much more modest task: a study of "the role of the maternal uncle in the development of the human family"—the sort of preoccupation far more characteristic of the evolutionary anthropologists than of Bachofen's earlier work. Bachofen ceased to be a trailblazer and instead became a camp follower. In 1880 he dedicated his *Antiquarische Briefe* to "Herr Lewis H. Morgan in Rochester (New York) . . . out of gratitude for the manifold instructions which I received."[169]

Bachofen continued to receive token acknowledgment from other proponents of matriarchal prehistory, but as likely as not, they were quickly followed by critical rants about Bachofen's scholarship (or lack thereof), his leaps to unwarranted conclusions, and—always—his turgid prose.[170] Bachofen was called an ideologue, a novice, a romantic, a fool . . . while the stars of McLennan and his ilk continued to rise. Some, more sympathetic, undertook to include Bachofen in "the neopositivistic fold" of British evolutionary anthropology, but this was a place where Bachofen—with his interest in religion, his endless metaphors and correspondences, his dialectic of constant struggle, his nostalgia for the rule of women, and above all his pervasive Romanticism—could never belong.[171]

On the continent, the reception of *Das Mutterrecht* was little better. Élisée Reclus, a French anarchist often considered to be a follower of Bachofen, praised Bachofen's "deep erudition" and "subtle interpretations of an obscure symbolism" that demanded "much learning and patient inquiry, and even a special cast of mind." But he also suggested that readers might be "frightened away by Mr. Bachofen's ponderous science."[172] Alexis Giraud-Teulon, a professor of history and jurisprudence at the University of Geneva, was more enthusiastic about Bachofen's work, accepting it more or less at face value and promoting it through his own writings (such as his 1868 work, "La Mère chez Certaines Peuples de l'Antiquité").[173] However, even Giraud-Teulon hesitated to accept Bachofen's findings as having universal applicability to human prehistory, and he eventually equivocated on the extent of women's supremacy within matriarchal societies, sometimes claiming that matriliny was mainly a technicality of family organization, while at other times claiming that "uterine blood lines" resulted in the subordination of fathers and husbands within the family.[174] Likewise, though Émile Durkheim accepted Bachofen's basic premise of a period of matrilineal kinship, he was unwilling to draw any great significance from it, and his explicit criticism of Bachofen's work dampened its influence in the French-speaking world.[175] For himself, Bachofen seemed to accept these criticisms in stride, grateful for any attention that might be interpreted as "rescuing his work from obscurity."[176]

Even the German-speaking world discounted Bachofen's work. Apart from a brief correspondence with the German anthropologist and matriarchalist Josef Kohler in the mid-1880s, Bachofen was ignored for more than a quarter century, until a new edition of *Das Mutterrecht* was reprinted in 1897.[177] Upon Bachofen's death in 1887, the local press in Basel published only the briefest of obituaries. One newspaper contained an announcement placed by the family, while another ran a short notice saying that Bachofen was hardly known in the city of his birth and residence, and that he had "for years lived in seclusion, devoting himself entirely to his studies and to the fine arts."[178]

This is not to say that Bachofen's work dropped into the sea of European intellectual debate without leaving a ripple. A number of thinkers were influenced by Bachofen; some of them even admitted it. Cosima Wagner's diary notes how much her husband Richard (the famed operatic composer) was impressed by Bachofen's 1870 work, *Die Sage von Tanaquil.* Cosima recalls Richard exclaiming "What a world that was! What does ours look like beside it?"[179] As would be true all the way through the twentieth century, however, Bachofen's work was rarely put to the uses that Bachofen himself intended. Bachofen's discussion of Dionysian and Apollonian civilizations inspired Friedrich Nietzsche, who lived in Basel when he wrote *The Birth of Tragedy,* and who was a regular guest at Bachofen's home.[180] But Nietzsche embraced the Dionysian age, in direct contradiction to Bachofen's sober respect for the more civilized Apollonian age. And Nietzsche did not hesitate to abandon both Basel and the pursuit of philology, while Bachofen remained wedded to both up to his death.[181] Prior to the turn of the twentieth century, Bachofen's *Mutterrecht* was most often summed up in words like these: "the rhapsody of a well-informed poet [rather] than the work of a calm and clear-sighted man of science."[182]

Yet Bachofen's significance to matriarchal myth is greater than it first appears. As one peruses the many versions of matriarchal myth that have circulated since Bachofen published *Das Mutterrecht,* if there is a single most striking feature, it is their abundant variety across all measures: methodology, definition of matriarchy, lessons drawn for contemporary society, and so forth. Given this variety, Bachofen serves as the perfect synecdoche, for Bachofen himself was such a mass of contradictory theories and passions that depending on what page you turn to in his oeuvre, you can find an idealist or a materialist; a feminist or a patriarchalist; a reactionary or a revolutionary. Radicals of the right and left both eventually turned to Bachofen because their respective social agendas *were in there*. Feminists and their enemies could both champion Bachofen because their varying visions of appropriate gender relations *were in there*. No one took on Bachofen's entire program because, it seems, only Bachofen himself could hold such a morass of sentiments and ideas in productive tension with one another. But anyone could reach into that same morass and come up with something they found useful, and this is precisely what later matriarchalists did. Even when they had no perceived or real connection to Bachofen's work, partisans of the myth of matriarchal prehistory have continued to echo Bachofenian ideas down through the decades to the present.[183] In Bachofen can be found most of the seeds of thought that eventually colonized the entire territory of matriarchal myth.

Bachofen retains another important significance to matriarchal myth: his broad influence on feminist matriarchal thought of the late twentieth century. This is perhaps the last place one would expect to find Bachofen's influence. Bachofen is barely cited by feminists, virtually never read, and on those rare occasions when he is invoked, it is mostly to note that he was not himself a feminist, but a male supremacist, one whose work can be dispensed with in its entirety. In a move similar to that made by most nineteenth-century evolutionary anthropologists, feminist matriarchalists continue to name Bachofen as the originator of matriarchal theory, but only on a technicality: he got there first.

Unlike nineteenth-century anthropologists, however, feminist matriarchalists *are* influenced by Bachofen, having adopted many of his assumptions into their own reasoning. How was such a miracle accomplished, if they are loathe to read his work and condemn him as a misogynist? The feminist partnership with Bachofen is thanks primarily to the offices of Carl Jung, whose work *is* read—and much admired—in the most powerful branch of contemporary matriarchal theory: feminist spirituality. If there is anyone who has come close to taking on Bachofen's entire program, complete with its tensions, contradictions, philosophical orientation, and political agenda, it is Jung and his followers.[184]

There is an irony here, for Jung can hardly be counted a matriarchalist, any more than Bachofen can; and in ways, even less so. Given Jung's decided preference for ahistorical interpretation and his general disinterest in things female (save as representations of the anima, and that typically in the male psyche), his influence on feminist matriarchal myth should be attenuated, to say the least.[185] But through the clever patchwork that is the hallmark of matriarchal myth (one could argue that it is the hallmark of most thought), contemporary feminist matriarchalists draw on Jung's worldview, and through him to Bachofen's, while lifting their historical trajectory of gender relations from other sources. Bachofen's ideas reverberate—even when unattributed and greatly transformed—throughout the history of matriarchal myth.[186] In 1861, Bachofen stepped onto the stage of a messy, chaotic play of intellectual forces, and delivered the first—and one of the most impassioned—arias to the matriarchal age. He was quickly swept back into the chorus, where he lived out the rest of his life, never to know how many would pick up the themes of that aria, or in what strange ways they would employ it.

4

The Matriarchal Explosion

Anthropology Finds Mother Right (and Itself)

All the evidence we have goes to show that men were from the beginning gregarious. The geological record distinctly exhibits them in groups— naked hunters or feeders upon shell fish leading a precarious life of squalid misery. . . . As among other gregarious animals, the unions of the sexes were probably in the earliest times, loose, transitory, and in some degree promiscuous.

—JOHN FERGUSON McLENNAN

While Bachofen labored away in relative isolation in Basel, a thriving fraternity of matriarchalists—including some of the most respected scholars of the day— was gathering in England and Scotland. As George Peter Murdock reflected in 1931, "The authorities for many years were all but unanimous in accepting the priority of mother right."[1] This great interest in matriarchy coincided with the development of the discipline of anthropology in Britain. It could even be argued that it *formed* the discipline of anthropology. The matriarchal thesis and the debates it provoked were a key foundation upon which anthropology established itself.[2] The matriarchal thesis emerged with pronounced vigor in the final third of the nineteenth century, becoming the au courant version of human social history within a decade after it was first proposed.

As George Stocking comments in *Victorian Anthropology,* a survey of the works of British anthropologists "suggests that not all things human were of equal interest to them."[3] What *was* of interest were two cultural institutions: marriage and religion.[4] Of course, these were Bachofen's main interests, too. Bachofen and the British anthropologists further shared a vision of human history as a staged evolutionary process from an unsavory, irreligious promiscuity toward the twin beacons of monogamy and monotheism that Christian European culture was taken to represent. But the flavor of their theories was distinctly different. Bachofen's matriarchal prehistory was a bacchanalia sponsored by Greek gods and goddesses, serving up wildly oscillating versions of humankind's enduring struggle between Matter and Mind, whereas the matriarchal prehistory of the British anthropologists was a sensible walk through a natural history museum, with stops at various exhibits for a docent lecture. British matriarchalists imparted their share of drama to prehistory, to be sure: fantasies of group marriage and totem sacrifice were standard fare. But the transitions that were in Bachofen's narrative marked by armed conflicts and unexpected reversals of fortune were in British anthropological narratives the gradual accomplishments of the child who, having mastered crawling, pulls herself up and begins to walk.

The writings of Bachofen and the British anthropologists emerged from very different cultural and intellectual traditions. Their matriarchal theories differed substantively, and more importantly, were built on different bodies of evidence. British anthropologists noted examples from the classics, as Bachofen had before them (especially the ever-favorite *Oresteia*),[5] but these were more literary allusions than proof-texts. Instead, the early anthropologists rested their case almost entirely on ethnographic material and associated speculations, something Bachofen barely took note of until after the publication of *Das Mutterrecht*.[6]

It is likely that in the late 1850s and early 1860s, Bachofen was working on some variant of the biblical timescale, believing that all human history—from the hetaeric swamp to Demetrian matriarchy to modern Basel—had to be shoehorned into a span of roughly six thousand years.[7] On such a timescale, classical sources reached very far back into human history. "Primitive" tribes were mainly irrelevant to Bachofen's enterprise anyway, since it was not *their* prehistory that Bachofen sought, but rather his own: the prehistory of the "cultural mainstream" that yielded up the Roman Empire and nineteenth-century European culture.

The anthropological matriarchalists, in contrast, were united in their conviction that human prehistory reached back hundreds of thousands of years, forming a span vastly larger than the relatively brief period of human literacy beginning with biblical scripture and the classics. This revolution in thinking had multiple and far-reaching effects, but certainly one of these was the new significance it gave to the "odd" customs of "savage" peoples. In the era of empire, some subject peoples ranked higher than others. There were "civilizations"—albeit not as advanced as the European—such as those in the Middle East, South Asia, and the Far East. But then there were "savages," most notably the indigenous populations of Africa, Australia, and the Americas, but also including tribal groups from northern Europe to the southern tip of Asia and everywhere in between. It was with the "savages" (or "primitives") that the British anthropologists were principally concerned. With the discovery of human antiquity, these peoples, formerly deemed to be at best the very distant and very backward cousins of Europeans (wayward descendants of Noah who had fallen off the map of human progress), quite suddenly sprung to life as reincarnations of Europeans' very own great-

great-great- (etc.) grandparents. They became proportionately more fascinating as a result.

Also, once "they" ("savages") were recognized as "our" (Europeans') ancestors, interest in their idiosyncrasies gave way to a quest to identify their similarities, via what came to be called "the comparative method."[8] Prior to this, anthropology tended to focus on curiosities and to ascribe such similarities as they found among the various peoples of the world to prehistoric migrations—what became known as the "diffusionist" model.[9] But as anthropologists began to examine "primitives" for evidence of their own prehistoric cultural development, cross-cultural similarities became important proofs of the basic correctness of the doctrine of evolutionism—which was appealing in its own right, since it suggested that all human (pre)history led up to Victorian England, the cutting edge, if not the absolute summit, of sociocultural evolution. The belief that similar ideas—Adolf Bastian's *Elementargedanken*—could be found all over the world lent credence to the belief that "our" ancestors (or a reasonable approximation of them) were alive and well in such places as aboriginal America and Australia. They could even be found, anthropologists discovered, among the peasants and the urban lower classes of Europe, whose folklore quickly became an object of anthropological study. Thus differences among peoples were no longer placed on a geographic map of cultural diffusion, but on a chronological time line of human cultural development much more universal and precise than anything Bachofen had imagined.[10] This shift had an enormously salutary effect on the discipline, which began to receive "that liberal share of public interest which was withheld from it as long as it was believed that it could do no more than record the curious customs and beliefs of strange peoples."[11] Anthropology was now "the science of history," and it tried with all its might to live up to that moniker, establishing itself on a par with the other natural sciences.[12]

For the British anthropologists, taking the opportunity to explore their own ancestry in the cultures of living "savages" produced the rather startling finding that their ancestors had given women a place in society that was quite different from the place they occupied in Victorian England. In general, the British anthropologists were not nearly so enthusiastic as Bachofen in imputing powers and liberties to women under mother right.[13] McLennan, author of the seminal *Primitive Marriage,* made this explicit: "Admitting him [Bachofen] to be correct in thinking that women, revolting from hetairism, introduced monogamous marriage, surely it is a pure dream of the imagination that they effected this by force of arms."[14] The anthropological matriarchalists differed internally on the question of women's status, but none came out so strongly as Bachofen had in claiming prehistoric ascendancy for women, and very few pressed past some form of sexual equality under which women and men had complementary, equally valued roles. Some even asserted—at least at times—that the woman in "the so-called matriarchate" had "no power," but only "gave her name to her child."[15] If a consensus developed among anthropologists, it was late in coming, after most of the fire of the matriarchal explosion had died down.[16] The status of women, it turned out, was a relatively fine point over which matriarchalists could differ without endangering their fundamental agreement about the characteristics of prehistory and the transformations that led to "civilization."

This is not to say that the status of women was an altogether unimportant question for the anthropological matriarchalists. But they were cushioned from overt conflict first because they all agreed that things were *different* for prehistoric women (and their living counterparts in "savage" society), and second because things were definitely and dramatically different for prehistoric *men*. And it was men, after all, who were the primary creators and consumers of matriarchal myth in the late nineteenth century. Not surprisingly, they tended to see themselves in their ancient forefathers more readily than in their ancient foremothers. Whatever life may have been like for their ancient foremothers, their ancient forefathers' experience—living in the house and the lineage of their mother— could never have been what the evolutionary anthropologists themselves experienced as Victorian men.

Another reason for the anthropologists' comfort with a fluid and imprecise definition of "matriarchy" was that much of their attention was directed not toward changing forms of government or social power, but toward shifts in sexual mores. Sex, in the imagination of the Victorian anthropologists, always involved women. But the actual conditions and experiences of these women's lives could be more or less glossed over in favor of the anthropologists' greater interest in women as they appeared to and interacted with men. For British anthropologists, prehistoric women existed almost wholly within the confines of sex, marriage, and family: the same places that Victorian men encountered the only women they recognized as truly women (as opposed to servants and working-class women, who were—literally and figuratively—placed in a different class).

Indeed, the most striking feature of the late nineteenth-century anthropological debate is its obsession with a short list of relatively exotic cultural features, all centered around sex, reproduction, and marriage (with marriage understood mainly as a site for sex and reproduction).[17] (No wonder, then, that the matriarchal thesis gained such currency. It was, as Robert Fraser notes, "connected with that . . . Victorian wet dream—the 'looser sexual relations' that supposedly went along with it [matriarchy].")[18] Again and again, the British anthropologists came back to the purported sexual promiscuity or group marriage of "the primitive horde"; polyandry and "visit marriage" (in which husbands lived with their mothers rather than their wives); "marriage by capture" (in which men either pretended to or actually carried off their brides); incest; the couvade (in which men took to their beds when their wives gave birth); indeterminate paternity (either as a result of ignorance of the mechanics of sex and reproduction or, more commonly, as a result of the aforementioned rampant sexual promiscuity); and the assumed peculiarities of maternal kinship (matriliny, matrilocality, and the avunculate, in which a woman's children were cared for by her brother rather than her husband). Like medieval scholars arguing over how many angels could find purchase on the head of a pin, Victorian anthropologists wrestled endlessly over how many mothers and fathers a single child could claim as a result of group marriage.

Reading through this debate over matriarchy—which Marvin Harris calls "one of the most heated and useless discussions in the history of the social sciences"—is both amusing and touching.[19] Although many of their questions continue to be debated in the field of anthropology (mostly under the rubric of "kinship"), the atmosphere is much altered from the era of the discipline's emergence. Social anthropology was in love with itself in the late nineteenth century, and it shows. The writings of these matriarchalists are filled with a sense of discovery, of thrilling adventure in lands undreamed of by their fathers and mothers, and with the imperialist confidence that the world was theirs to improve. What is amusing from an early twenty-first-century perspective is how seriously they took themselves, how certain they were that they were uncovering scientific truths about human culture and society. Evolutionary anthropology and its pet theory of matriarchal prehistory, once it had its day, tended to go the way of poodle skirts rather than the way of fine wine.[20] As the field of cultural anthropology shifted in the early twentieth century, differences between cultures, rather than their similarities, came to be highlighted; theorizing gave way to fieldwork; disconfirming data became more interesting than confirming data. Iconoclasm became the order of the day. Cultural anthropology as we know it today is a fairly timid discipline, offering much data, some suggestive hypotheses, and a lot of caution when drawing even narrow conclusions. But in the late nineteenth century, anthropology was bold: it made sweeping conclusions with fearless zest, certain that it was not merely speculating, but lifting timeless laws of human evolution out of the living ground of "rude" societies.[21] To be thought of as doing anything less was an insult.

HENRY SUMNER MAINE'S PATRIARCHAL THEORY

It may appear curious to begin this review of late nineteenth-century anthropological theories of matriarchy with a scholar who saw nothing but patriarchy as far back as he looked. But it was in reaction to Maine's 1861 text, *Ancient Law*, that the first generation of British anthropologists wrote.[22] Maine was a promising young scholar of the classics at Cambridge University before he turned to the law. A series of lectures he delivered to law students in the 1850s formed the basis of *Ancient Law,* which was received with much admiration and led to positions at the University of Calcutta, Oxford University, and in the end, his alma mater, Cambridge. Throughout his career as a historian, jurist, and colonial officer, Maine continued to articulate his vision of a progressive development in law from the virtual ownership of most people by the patriarch of a large family unit to increasing legal autonomy for individuals. Maine's *Ancient Law* marks the end of one era—perhaps even its pinnacle—and the beginning of another.[23] In Maine can be found an intriguing juxtaposition of the old thesis that human society was "originally" patriarchal along with hints of things to come:[24] a growing openness toward evolutionary argumentation, the use of ethnography as evidence, and a focus on the institution of marriage (and through it, on the prehistoric status of women). Maine further anticipated the British anthropologists in his perception that the key unit of ancient societies was not the individual—as it had been for many previous European thinkers, such as Hobbes, Rousseau, and Mill—but the extended family (or, in matriarchalist terms, the clan).[25] Though Maine gave his unstinting support to the patriarchal theory, he nevertheless created a significant portion of the space in which British matriarchal myth would later grow.[26]

Maine began with the assumption that human society was from the beginning patriarchal and that its most basic unit was heterosexual monogamous marriage.[27] His mode of reasoning was that of comparative jurisprudence. Using the oldest known codes of law, including the Hebrew Bible, the Hindu Laws of Manu, and the Twelve Tables of Rome, Maine projected back from them toward a more ancient, not-yet-literate past. According to historian Robert Fraser, Maine held that "Roman jurists had simply enshrined existing social rights," and thus Roman law reflected "the historical realities of early Italian life."[28] A man of his times, Maine regarded his method as parallel to that of the geological sciences (then enjoying a heyday), opening *Ancient Law* with the statement that "the early forms of jural conceptions . . . are to the jurist what the primary crusts of the earth are to the geologist. They contain, potentially, all the forms in which law has subsequently exhibited itself."[29] What lay in the crust of ancient law was the doctrine of *patria potestas,* in which, as Maine explains, "the eldest male parent—the male ascendant—is absolutely supreme in his household. His dominion extends to life and death, and is as unqualified over his children and their houses as over his slaves." In fact, it is only this eldest male parent, he who exercises *patria potestas,* who is recognized by the law, along with those few sons and grandsons who one day might inherit the patriarch's power. Law in ancient Rome is "scanty," Maine argues, because "it is supplemented by the despotic commands of the heads of households." Women are therefore treated by ancient law only as the wards or possessions of men, for they can never aspire to *patria potestas.* Critically, for

FIGURE 6. Henry Sumner Maine (1822–88), English jurist and author of *Ancient Law,* a work that supported the priority of patriarchal social structures

those anthropologists who were to follow, Maine asserted that descent never occurred through the mother.[30]

Although at the time Maine was widely read as an apologist for patriarchy, he was anything but that. He was at pains to show in *Ancient Law* how the patriarchal family was a unit manufactured first by society and later by law, but not by nature. In recounting clever end runs around patriarchal law that were invented by underclasses in the Roman Empire, Maine obviously roots for women's liberation. Moreover, a central "law of development" that Maine claimed for the evolution of jurisprudence was one of increasing freedom and privilege for women. The endpoint of these increasing freedoms—soon to arrive in England, by Maine's reckoning—was the final and complete assimilation of the legal position of women to the legal position of men. Maine supported this process directly through his writings, some of which were circulated in the early 1870s by feminists campaigning for legal reform in women's property rights.[31]

What is perhaps most notable about *Ancient Law,* given how quickly it would be all but supplanted by the matriarchal notions of early anthropologists, is how completely Maine neglects the ethnographic record. In this, *Ancient Law* is more similar to *Das Mutterrecht* than its anthropological heirs.[32] Like Bachofen, Maine wrote without any explicit acknowledgment of the intellectual revolution that was fast bringing a tremendously extended time-depth to human prehistory. *Ancient Law* appears to work on the assumption that human history begins in the Garden of Eden and extends only a few millennia to the present. Maine neither mentions Darwin nor seems to have been influenced by him.[33] The same could not be said of those who overturned his work.

JOHN FERGUSON McLENNAN: THEORIST OF MARRIAGE AND CONNOISSEUR OF THE BIZARRE

John Ferguson McLennan, "an Edinburgh attorney with a keen amateur interest in ethnology,"[34] set British anthropology along the road it was to tread for the next thirty-five years with his 1865 *Primitive Marriage,* written in direct refutation of Maine. McLennan was never a very successful lawyer, and though he studied at Cambridge, he never received a degree there. Though his scholarship was widely admired—or at least cited—he was never given an academic position. Nevertheless, his *Primitive Marriage* made waves, and set many people thinking in new ways.[35] If all the evolutionary anthropologists were fascinated with peculiar (in British eyes) forms of marriage, McLennan still stood out from the crowd with his disquisitions on endogamy, promiscuity, exogamy, marriage by capture, fraternal polyandry, and the like. McLennan fed the Victorian appetite for sexual oddities while seizing up and running with the banner of cultural evolutionism, then still in its infancy. McLennan's story of the long, strange trip of human cultural evolution was original in a way that even Bachofen's—which was certainly novel—was not. Without significant exposure to the Amadís cycle of Amazon legends, the emerging mother goddess theories of German Romanticism, or even the quasi-matriarchal theories of his own Scottish forebears,[36] and with no knowledge of Bachofen's *Mutterrecht,*[37] McLennan created such a singular narrative that it is difficult not to stand in awe of him, even when laughing out loud at the absurdity of many of his claims.

McLennan very much believed in his own theories—there was nothing tentative about him—and he was purportedly very nasty when crossed. Robert Lowie characterizes him as having "a pugnacity that barred fairness to opponents";

FIGURE 7. John Ferguson
McLennan (1827–81),
Scottish attorney and
author of *Primitive
Marriage,* which kicked
off the mania for
matriarchal theory in
Great Britain

Peter Rivière describes him as "a man with an original idea, . . . a willingness to propound it tenaciously, an immediate and violent reaction to the slightest criticism, and a crusading intent to destroy all opposition."[38] Indeed, McLennan took on Herbert Spencer in an 1877 *Fortnightly Review* article, and after a brief response, Spencer withdrew from the debate, complaining that McLennan had "introduced into his rejoinder a tone which renders it undesirable to continue this discussion."[39] At the end of his life, McLennan was busy at work writing *The Patriarchal Theory,* in which he aimed to finally obliterate Sir Henry Maine's argument that patriarchy was original to human society.[40]

McLennan and Maine are frequently compared to each other, since they wrote at the same time and in such dramatic counterpoint, but they could not have been more different. In *The History of Ethnological Theory,* Lowie describes Maine as "the embodiment of serene wisdom coupled with unusual subtlety" while noting that McLennan "impresses us by the bumptious vigor of his intel-lect."[41] Lowie is hardly an unbiased observer (he was rather single-mindedly de-voted to wiping the stain of universalism and evolutionism from anthropology's face), but the contrasts between Maine and McLennan are nevertheless sharp. Maine was a successful attorney, a professor at both Cambridge and Oxford Uni-versities, a legal member of the Viceroy's Council in India, and the recipient of a knighthood; McLennan tried (with the help of individuals like Morgan, Maine, and Lubbock) to get an academic post, but one never came his way. He was de-scribed as "a poor speaker" and an inadequate lawyer. He was no doubt also crippled by his undisguised contempt for the legal system. Coming from a "hum-bler background" than Maine, McLennan was what might be called a "scrapper." Meanwhile, Maine glided through life, cushioned by his considerable status and wealth.[42]

Before 1865, McLennan had written the article on law for the eighth edition of the *Encyclopedia Britannica,* along with an article or two discussing ethnographic interests. These earliest efforts betrayed no sign of the elaborate theory that was to spring forth full-blown in *Primitive Marriage* and continue virtually unchanged until McLennan's death in 1881. It is not clear just what flipped the switches in McLennan's mind, but according to George Stocking, it is likely that McLennan's sudden interest in the evolution of human marriage was precipitated by the dis-covery of "the extreme antiquity of man," and in particular by Charles Lyell's *The Geological Evidences of the Antiquity of Man,* published in 1863. Lyell, a geologist—and a Scotsman and attorney, like McLennan—had long resisted any interpreta-tion of archaeological findings that lent credence to the existence of the human race prior to its scriptural creation by God in roughly 4000 B.C.E. But in 1859, Lyell finally "yielded to the pressure of it," taking the vast majority of scholars with him into this new, vastly expanded territory of human prehistory.[43]

It is difficult to overestimate the enormity of the impact caused by the discov-ery of human antiquity (or more properly, the abrupt general assent given to the theory of human antiquity, since the idea had been in the air for at least a century before).[44] The discovery of human antiquity was even more revolutionary in that it occurred virtually simultaneously with the Darwinian revolution.[45] Prior to 1859, there was general agreement that the human race was "extremely modern" (as Lyell claimed as late as 1855), and most reckoned human history on the biblical time line. Furthermore, the biblical creation date of 4000 B.C.E. actually re-stricted human history to the years after the flood, when all peoples of the earth were wiped out save Noah and his family, an event typically dated to 2350 B.C.E.[46] Of course, as with any intellectual revolution, there were those who recognized the significance of human antiquity immediately, and those who tarried behind. McLennan was emphatically in the first camp. In his 1869 article "The Early His-tory of Man," four years after the publication of *Primitive Marriage,* McLennan describes the biblical timescale as "pernicious" and sets out to dismantle it with all the evidence at his fingertips.[47]

That McLennan saw fit to devote so much time and effort to defending the proposition of human antiquity indicates not only that it was still controversial in the 1860s, but also that human antiquity was crucial to McLennan's intellectual framework. The superstructure of *Primitive Marriage* could not have stood upon the foundation of the biblical timescale. Even as the antiquity of humankind came to be accepted as fact, McLennan could not rest, for he had another biblically based fire to put out: the doctrine of degenerationism. According to degenerationist theory—and to the Bible, as degenerationists interpreted it— "men had originally one religion and one set of God-given values, but as they migrated to the margins of the earth, coped with new environments, and time passed, they tended to forget, their stock of cultural ideas degenerated, and they lost touch with the one true religion and culture."[48] The British anthropologists, beginning with McLennan, were unanimous in rejecting degenerationism outright, arguing that while there were abundant examples of "savage" peoples rising to barbarism and even to civilization, examples of "civilized" people becoming savage were exceedingly scarce.[49]

These were fighting words in the 1860s. As Marvin Harris explains, "In the context of the times, to assert that there had been a general movement from savagery to civilization was to avow that the Biblical account of the origin of institutions was wrong and that history could be understood without calling upon God as an active historical agent."[50] McLennan himself was eager to avoid this implication, or at least the appearance of it: "The progress we contend for is wholly divine as much as it is wholly human. What is at issue is the mode of the divine operation."[51] But everything in British evolutionary theory drove toward a disruption of biblical authority and a plainly reduced role for God. This was threatening to Christian leaders; it did not appeal to the British populace, either. As Julia Wedgwood, Darwin's niece, wrote in 1863, "There is something dreary in the indefinite lengthening of a savage and blood-stained past."[52] But for the evolutionary anthropologists, the idea of human antiquity flung open a new door on the past—and by extension, on the present—and they were more than eager to rush through.

With what would they fill up all that newly discovered time, the time before "civilization," when humans apparently hunted woolly mammoths with crude stone tools? With what else than evolutionary stages, custom made to lead humankind from its now surprising origins: no longer God's pièce de résistance, but a humanoid creature barely different from the apes (from which Darwin was now saying humans evolved)? McLennan's evolutionism was premised—as was all evolutionary anthropology—on a type of human universalism in which people would everywhere traverse the same stages, whether slowly or quickly.[53] This development was, importantly, a moral one: later stages were not superior simply in technological terms, but in value-laden ones. Though never very specific about what constitutes moral superiority, McLennan exhibits no doubt that the British have it and "primitives" do not. He claims that "it matters not what moral standard we take, when we study the history of the rules now constituting it we shall have a similar account to give of them. They are the lower the farther back we go."[54]

Discovering the evolutionary stages of human social life was of necessity an armchair enterprise. McLennan might have traveled to visit "primitives" in situ, had he wished. But he could never have made sufficient observations to support his theories. All the evolutionary anthropologists, including McLennan, were disparaged by later anthropologists for their lack of field research,[55] but this truly was outside their project. A year in Tahiti might have helped McLennan to be more sensitive to the complexities of other cultures, but it could not have given him the data to speculate on universal evolutionary stages. Lowie chastises McLennan for practicing "dialectics *in vacuo*," for speculating "about conditions not only unknown but unknowable," but this critique comes from a later era. When McLennan erupted on the scene with *Primitive Marriage*, speculation was the name of the game, and McLennan, with his "fragmentary, chaotic brilliance" and "audacious conceptual originality" played it very well.[56] Still, it cannot be denied that much of the ethnographic evidence McLennan relied upon was faulty. Rivière notes that most of the ethnographies McLennan cited were "the writings of classical or medieval authors and the rest the accounts and tales of travelers, soldiers, and sailors; today not one of them would be regarded as an adequate source of ethnographic evidence."[57]

Promiscuity, the lowest of human customs, according to McLennan, stands at the beginning of his evolutionary time line. It was this image of the "Primitive Horde,"[58] more than McLennan's succeeding stages, that made the strongest impact on nineteenth-century anthropology. McLennan was not able to find any existing "savages" who even approached the group grope he fantasized for human prehistory (nor were those matriarchalists who followed him), so he was required to step outside his announced method of lining up existing peoples on a chronological time line.[59] Instead, McLennan sought to establish the promiscuity of early humans by looking back farther, into the animal kingdom, where sexual relations were, by Victorian standards anyway, promiscuous.[60]

What followed from these promiscuous sexual relations was, in McLennan's thinking, "kinship through females only," because "blood-ties through fathers could not find a place in a system of kinship, unless circumstances usually allowed of some degree of certainty as to who the father of a child was."[61] This was, in fact, the only way in which McLennan could imagine maternal kinship arising, because "that . . . the children of a man and woman living together as husband and wife should be subject to the mother's authority and not the father's, be named after her and not after the father, be her heirs and not the father's, is simply incredible."[62] Uncertain paternity, for McLennan, was due primarily to promiscuity, not to any ignorance of the connection between sexual intercourse and conception (as it was for many later narrators of matriarchal myth). Describing paternity as "an undoubted blood-tie," McLennan claims that it "must have been thought of soon after that [blood-tie] through mothers." But paternity still went unrecognized, McLennan claimed, because "when the idea of it [paternity] was formed it could only receive development into a system of kinship on certain conditions which were not easily satisfied"—namely sexual monogamy for women.[63]

McLennan gives only sketchy details on the nature of life in the primitive horde, but it was no golden age, especially for women. Like other anthropological matriarchalists, McLennan imagined that in a state of promiscuity, males would be "the primary benefactors in the exchange" while females would be "the unwilling objects."[64] This male supremacy is quite clear in McLennan's statement that promiscuous groups "would hold their women, like their other goods, in common." Even the presence of children, attached strictly to their mothers and not their fathers, did not dilute this supremacy, for the children as well "would belong to the horde." Yet elsewhere McLennan gave women a higher status, noting that there is "no case . . . producible of a woman being ill-treated under a form of marriage which assigns to her the headship of the family."[65]

Either the promiscuous horde did not thrive for long, or McLennan found it relatively uninteresting, because his theory quickly skips along to later stages that developed out of two fundamental difficulties besetting the horde: first, the men of each group argued over their women, splitting into feuding groups; and second, there weren't enough women to go around, which further increased intertribal hostilities.[66]

But why should there be any scarcity of women in primitive society? McLennan's answer was female infanticide.[67] In "this early struggle for food and security," with its attendant need for "braves and hunters," it would be "in the interest of every horde to rear, when possible, its healthy male children." Females, "less capable of self-support, and of contributing, by their exertions, to the common good," would be a burden on the group and would thus be killed in infancy during times of scarcity. Primitive men realized that this may not have been a particularly clever thing for them to do when it dawned on them that they had no one to marry (though this was, to McLennan, only one of "the multitude of facts which testify to the thoughtlessness and improvidence of men during the childish stage of the human mind"). But instead of desisting from the practice of female infanticide, primitive men resolved their problem by either agreeing to share one woman amongst themselves (polyandry) or by "prey[ing] upon one another for wives" (what McLennan termed "marriage by capture").[68] McLennan marshaled numerous examples to support his claim that early men stole their wives from other groups, including mock battles in marriage ceremonies in which the bridegroom steals the bride from her family, the payment of dowries, prohibitions against marrying close relations, and even the common European custom of the father "giving away" the bride in marriage ceremonies.

Marriage by capture gave way, more generally, to exogamy (a term coined by McLennan): the custom of marrying outside one's own group. For "usage, induced by necessity"—that is, the practice of stealing women from other groups— "would in time establish a prejudice among the tribes observing it . . . against marrying women of their own stock."[69] McLennan read this as a positive development, not only for society as a whole, but also for women. As Elizabeth Fee explains McLennan's reasoning, "The sheer physical effort involved in wife-capture must have made the men proud of their new possessions. This pride and consequent possessiveness led to the strengthening of the bond between man and wife and to the beginning of marital 'love.' . . . Marriage was born in 'brutal violence and unwilling submission,' yet the very control of man over woman opened the possibility of love between the sexes."[70]

The other option—and a competing story line in McLennan's narrative—was polyandry. It, like marriage by capture, led to paternal kinship over the long run. McLennan distinguished between two types of polyandry: "archaic" and "fraternal" (although he most often referred to them by the names of the living groups who were supposed to have practiced them: "Nair" and "Tibetan"). In the first, many unrelated men married a single woman, who either maintained her own household or resided with her parents. Under this system, kinship continued to be exclusively maternal. But the other type of polyandry consisted of several brothers marrying one woman. This was the "germ of father right." Fraternal polyandry prepared the way, said McLennan, "for a species of marriage still less rude, in which the woman passed from her family, not into a house of her own, but into the family of her husbands, in which her children would be born, and to which they would belong."[71]

The last step to father right in McLennan's schema was certainty of individual paternity. McLennan connected this to a number of developments, including property, sedentism, and a restoration of the numerical balance between the sexes (once primitive men figured out that killing female babies was not in their best long-term interests). He speculates that "the earliest examples of such married life as would give certainty of male parentage would probably be furnished by the chiefs of tribes, who might have the power to secure to themselves one, or perhaps several wives." These chiefs would in time "find more imitators, and their cases would furnish a model for an improved system of succession." But foremost among the causal factors for father right was property: "a practice of sons succeeding, as heirs direct, to the estates of fathers," which effectively ended maternal kinship.[72] At this point, McLennan was able to tack on Maine's chronology of marriage and family law to the end of his own time line. He deemed

Maine's analyses accurate for patriarchal society (if neglectful of all that came before).[73]

For McLennan, unlike Bachofen, the trajectory of evolution is quite unambiguously progressive. McLennan never exhibits nostalgia for maternal kinship (or even primitive promiscuity, though it made for spicy parlor conversation), and counts each stage as another step upward: "Any regulated relation of the sexes is an advance on promiscuity; the Tibetan polyandry, in which the co-husbands are brothers, is an advance on the Nair," and so on. The fact that maternal kinship yielded to paternal kinship is no historical accident. It is a moral imperative resulting from "the superiority of the male sex," which "everywhere tended to establish" father right.[74] Father right was an advance for women as well, according to McLennan. They lost sexual freedom and some of the power that they had in polyandrous households, but in return they, like Bachofen's primeval women, were increasingly freed from excessive sexual advances. Interestingly, though, McLennan does not see the evolution of marriage culminating in Victorian monogamy, the status quo with which he was familiar and which Bachofen regarded as the apogee of the evolutionary trajectory. Rather, he imagines continued evolution, through which marriage laws gradually concede equality of rights to women, thereby "improving a system which still preserves too many features of the husband's absolute supremacy as head of the agnatic family."[75]

Thus began a new chapter in the myth of matriarchal prehistory, one with only the slimmest of connections to its Bachofenian genesis. McLennan stated categorically that Bachofen "saw the fact that kinship was anciently traced through women only, but not why it was the fact." Bachofen, for his part, complained in a letter to Morgan that McLennan's work was "very insufficient" and suggested that "historical inquiries do not admit of being treated as cases in a court of strict justice, by reasoning of a barrister."[76] Whatever the principals had to say about it, it was McLennan's theory that became the flavor of the century.

MOVING BEYOND McLENNAN: SIR JOHN LUBBOCK'S MATRIARCHAL MYTH

The first real departure from McLennan's theory—and not an enormous one—came with the work of Sir John Lubbock. Like McLennan, Lubbock did not have a university post—he was a banker—but unlike McLennan, Lubbock had a lot of political clout and social prestige. Like his father before him, Lubbock combined the practical pursuits of banking with amateur scientific work. His father made contributions to astronomy and mathematics, while Lubbock himself worked in entomology and archaeology in addition to his anthropological work advancing the matriarchal theory. At the age of thirty-six, Lubbock was elected as a member

FIGURE 8. John Lubbock (Lord Avebury, 1834–1913), British
banker and amateur archaeologist and anthropologist

of Parliament. Eventually he was elevated to the peerage, and he selected the name
"Lord Avebury" after the Neolithic monuments he had worked to preserve.[77]

Lubbock's anthropological work was clearly indebted to McLennan. In his
1870 book *The Origin of Civilisation,* Lubbock focused on marriage, beginning
with promiscuity and evolving to monogamy. He found room for several of
McLennan's key ideas within his theory (exogamy, marriage by capture, and female infanticide) and argued strongly in favor of evolutionism and against degenerationism. He took exception to Bachofen, as McLennan did, for his "absurd"
notion that women instituted matriarchy through force of arms.[78] But Lubbock
was still his own man. He appealed more frequently to ethnographic evidence
than did McLennan (though the evidence Lubbock used was no more reliable),
tweaked McLennan's time lines for the development of various forms of marriage, discounted polyandry altogether, regarded female infanticide as irrelevant

to marriage customs, and was an even more zealous advocate of the doctrine of evolutionism than McLennan had been.[79]

Lubbock's basic schema is the familiar one: "The natural progress of ideas is, first, that a child is related to his tribe generally; secondly, to his mother, and not to his father; thirdly, to his father, and not to his mother; lastly, and lastly only, that he is related to both." Marriage begins in "the lowest races" as "Communal Marriage," or promiscuity; it then becomes a temporary alliance that "exists only till the birth of the child, when both man and woman are free to mate themselves afresh"; it then progresses to a state where "the man buys the woman, who becomes as much his property as his horse or his dog." Under these conditions, says Lubbock, mother right prevails for quite some time, simply because there is a closer "natural" tie between mothers and their children than that between fathers and their children.[80]

But as one might suspect, when women are being bought like horses and dogs, their status is not stellar.[81] However, Lubbock does not valorize male domination as McLennan and Bachofen do: men take power because they can, not because they must or should. As Lubbock explains: "It seems to me perfectly clear that the idea of marriage is founded on the rights, not of the woman, but of the man, being an illustration of 'the good old plan,/ That he should take who has the power, / And he should keep who can'."[82]

It is an extension of this power that begins the transition to father right. Patriarchy develops in a two-step process: first, marriage becomes either polygynous or monogamous, and second, fathers claim the right to pass property on to their own children (rather than their sister's children, as Lubbock suggests they would have under a system of mother right). What Lubbock terms "individual marriage" (as opposed to group marriage) evolves because of its several advantages: "the impulse which it would give to, and receive back from, the development of the affections; the convenience with reference to domestic arrangements; the natural wishes of the wife herself; and, last not least, the inferior energy of the children sprung from 'in and in' marriages."[83]

If, as Lubbock claims, marriage is a male invention, in men's best interests, why does it accord with "the natural wishes of the wife herself"? To answer this question, Lubbock appeals to an imagined transitional time when a tribe included both native-born women and women captured from other groups. He imagines native and captured women observing each other and assessing the relative merits of their respective positions. Native women are "nominally no doubt free," but they are nevertheless "subject to the attentions of all their tribesmen—attentions no doubt often very unwelcome, but yet which could not be rejected without giving bitter offence." They also lack the advantage of having a single man devoted to procuring "food, shelter, and protection" for them. Captive women, in contrast, are "so to say slaves," but they enjoy "the protection, and in many cases . . . the secured affection, of one man." In Lubbock's eyes, captive women have it better. Native women perceive this too, and they "exchange their nominal freedom, and hazardous privileges, for the comparative peace and security" enjoyed by captive women. In truth, though, the decision is not theirs: it is men who, according to Lubbock, "extend the right of capture" and "apply it to all those [women] belonging to their own [tribe]."[84] This "individual marriage" opens the door for patriliny, which also turns out to conform with "natural wishes": in this case, those of the man, who wishes to see his property passed on to his biological children.[85]

Lubbock consistently portrays evolution as the outcome of good common sense. When he observes that not all groups have evolved to the degree that the British have, he implies that not all peoples are endowed with abilities sufficient to line up their "natural wishes" with social progress. This was, as stated earlier, a significant departure from the degenerationist theory of human development, one with important implications. As long as "savages" had degenerated from a former shared elevated condition, the imperative—at least biblically speaking—was to lift them up, to give them the advantages that "civilized" peoples had either retained or won back since the fall of the Tower of Babel. Once "savages" were understood to be ancestors who because of their inherent limitations had never tasted civilized pleasures, it became more reasonable to rule over them without worrying about improving their condition. Especially as Darwinist thought began to enter into anthropology—largely through Lubbock's efforts[86]—it was possible to believe that "savages" were not merely accidentally excluded from civilization, but racially unfit for it. In this manner, evolutionary anthropology provided an excellent resource and rationalization for administration of the British colonies, one that McLennan had been less eager to point out.[87]

Lubbock is perhaps most noteworthy among the evolutionary anthropologists for his undisguised, undiluted horror for "savage nations."[88] A charter member in the "'too offensive for description' school of ethnography," Lubbock continually apologized to readers for describing savage customs, which must be "very repugnant to our feelings."[89] Lubbock equates savages with children: savages "do not act without reason . . . though their reasons may often be bad ones," but "like children, [savages] have no steadiness of purpose." This presents an unfortunate obstacle for ethnographers, who must observe and record the activities of these childlike people who can neither act wisely nor explain their actions. As Lubbock complains, "The mind of the savage, like that of the child, is easily fatigued, and he will . . . give random answers, to spare himself the trouble of thought."[90]

One gets the impression that Lubbock would have preferred to have nothing to do with "savages," that even reading others' accounts of their lives pained him. But the study of savage society was a necessary means to a glorious end: obtaining proof positive of the doctrine of evolution, entailing the firm knowledge that though "we" began as savages, we moved on, and we can continue to climb ever upward on the ladder of progress.[91] Lubbock detailed the benefits of rejecting the degenerationist theory:

> If the past history of man has been one of deterioration, we have but a groundless expectation of future improvement: on the other hand, if the past has been one of progress, we may fairly hope that the future will be so too; that the blessings of civilisation will not only be extended to other countries and to other nations, but that even in our own land they will be rendered more general and more equable; so that we shall not see before us always, as now, countrymen of our own living, in our very midst, a life worse than that of a savage; neither enjoying the rough advantages and real, though rude, pleasures of savage life, nor yet availing themselves of the far higher and more noble opportunities which lie within the reach of civilised man.[92]

Lubbock's vision of global noblesse oblige had its underbelly, though: if on the one hand it sought to lift "rude" races up, on the other hand it was quite capable of looking upon their destruction with equanimity. If "savages" were unable to "evolve" (or, failing that, to permit themselves to be raised up), then it was no loss if they were crushed under the wheels of progress. No one was at fault; it was just the way—the evolutionary way—the world worked. And, although the general trajectory of history is progress, there are exceptions. As Lubbock explains: "I do not of course mean to say that every race is necessarily advancing: on the contrary, most of the lower ones are almost stationary. . . . but it seems an almost invariable rule that such races are dying out. . . . on the other hand, improving nations increase in numbers, so that they always encroach on less progressive races."[93] So saying, Lubbock rescues British colonialism from any moral obligation to preserve the lives or lifestyles of "savage" peoples. Once their customs have been adequately cataloged to provide insight into "our" prehistoric ancestry, these peoples are no longer needed.

SURVIVAL OF THE FITTEST: HERBERT SPENCER CHAMPIONS PATRIARCHY

This very savage (pun intended) usage of the emerging consensus on human antiquity and evolution became known as "social Darwinism," though in reality it had little connection to Darwin or his theories.[94] Its greatest advocate was sociologist Herbert Spencer, a self-made philosopher who won his way into the finest intellectual salons of England of that era. He was raised as a Quaker, and his dissenting religious roots left him free to question authority and advocate political liberality, though ironically he ended by becoming quite conservative, especially where the rights of women were concerned. By the mid-1870s, twenty-five years into his career, Spencer adhered to the increasingly orthodox view that prehistoric human society was promiscuous, characterized by maternal kinship, and populated by women utterly unlike those who lived in Victorian England. Spencer was tremendously popular during his lifetime. At the height of his career, more than a million volumes of his writings were in print in numerous languages, and he was eventually nominated for the Nobel Prize in Literature. Elizabeth Fee describes him as "England's most revered nineteenth-century philosopher, polymath, and staunch supporter of the harsher bourgeois values." His fame did not long outlive him. Spencer was "a dilettante in social anthropology," but then most anthropologists of the era were dilettantes in the sense that they were all working with second- and third-hand ethnographic reports and forming grandly speculative theories in the time they had left over from their legal or business careers. Spencer's task was particularly ambitious, though: he sought to blend the lessons of anthropology and biology (and philosophy and geology) into "his own system of systemic philosophy." In the process of working on this task, Spencer did much to popularize evolutionary anthropology as developed by McLennan and Lubbock, including its conception of prehistoric gender relations.[95]

What Spencer contributed to the growing anthropological discussion was a free use of the language of biology to undergird concepts of social evolution. In the hands of McLennan and Lubbock, the myth of matriarchal prehistory involved an evolutionary process that was largely triggered by social causes and social development. Humans learned, over the course of millennia, how best to order their society, gradually discovering that marriage had advantages over promiscuity, that patriliny was superior to matriliny, and that private property was better than communal ownership. With Spencer, changes in human society carried a more profound sort of inevitability than they had with other narrators of matriarchal myth, for progress was based not on humankind's evolving sagacity, but on the mechanisms of natural selection. Cream—white and male—would rise to the top, with no special effort made to insure that result.

One of the things Spencer naturalized—that is, attributed to biological causes—was male domination, which he regarded as the evolutionary product of a series of adaptations that gradually freed the human race from the hoary strictures of mother right.[96] Spencer managed this through his theories of sex difference. Sex difference was of course not new to matriarchal myth; it is at the core of every version of the myth of matriarchal prehistory and was well established in England in the 1870s, when Spencer was writing on the topic. But where Bachofen, McLennan, and Lubbock discussed sex differences primarily in terms of received opinion (e.g., women hate sex) and of women's and men's different reproductive roles, Spencer found sex differences in every cell of each human being, and in every facet of social life. The biological spin Spencer put on matriarchal myth was not very influential for the evolutionary anthropologists who came immedi-

FIGURE 9. Herbert
Spencer (1820–1903),
British polymath and
popularizer of social
Darwinism

ately after him—they mostly stayed within an earlier framework that stressed the
tangible impact of reproductive differences on social relations—but Spencer certainly presaged a boldly biologistic type of matriarchal myth that was to become
dominant in the twentieth century.

Spencer begins his history of the human race with the now customary promiscuous horde, where children are attached only to their mothers: a place unfit
for woman or man, in Spencer's judgment. This matriarchal time is characterized, he says, by "the abject condition of women," though it turns out that this
abjection is due solely to the fact that women were engaging in sex regularly with
more than one man—which, for Spencer, meant that women were oppressed and
miserable. "The system of kinship through females arises where unions of the
sexes are temporary or unsettled," Spencer explains. He never satisfactorily explains why, but he asserts that matriliny makes government impossible—which
may be why the promiscuous horde is also unfit for men. Government becomes

possible, Spencer believes, in "the patriarchal group." Patrilineal descent provides "a union of efficiency with supremacy" that bodes well for the further evolution of the human race.[97] The next evolutionary step is taken as monogamy comes to replace polygyny. Spencer hypothesizes that this occurs when men begin to choose a favorite from among their wives and demote the others "to the status of slaves or concubines."[98] With the development of monogamy, Spencer perceives "the zenith of evolutionary development," where men desire only one woman and gradually give up "the desire to command"—which, he asserts, was "essentially a barbarous desire."[99]

This entire development can be successfully argued without any real resort to biologistic thinking, beyond noting, as McLennan had before him, that under circumstances of sexual promiscuity, paternity cannot be determined. Spencer went further, however. His prehistoric matriarchy represents a time in which women's and men's tasks were considerably less distinct than in Victorian England. Women and men, Spencer asserted, were even less different biologically in times past, approximating one another in brain size and physical strength.[100] But as the human race evolved, women encountered "a somewhat earlier arrest" of evolution, "necessitated by the reservation of vital power to meet the cost of reproduction." Evolution sees to it that women become smaller and weaker . . . and also stupider. As Spencer explains, "Man has advanced somewhat alone in the intellectual evolution of the race." This is a trend that Spencer wishes to see continue (of course—it is an evolutionary trend and therefore both inevitable and beneficial). "If perfection is to be the aim of our efforts," Spencer claims, "it will be best advanced by further divergence of male and female characteristics."[101]

Interestingly, Spencer's version of sex differences includes a rather large environmental component. Biology makes women smaller and weaker, but culture also has an effect on sex inequality, sometimes through the very simple mechanism of oppression. According to Spencer, the sexed division of labor, for example, is in part determined "by the ability of the males to force on the females the least desirable occupations," since "the stronger will ill-treat the weaker . . . imposing on them all the disagreeable tasks they are able to perform." This gives rise to a culturally constructed discrepancy in status between women and men. Living in this environment causes women to develop certain characteristics, among them "the desire for approval and the capacity to deceive." Spencer's attention to culturally constructed forms of domination is assimilated to biological sex difference through Spencer's belief in the inheritance of acquired characteristics (a theory developed by botanist Jean-Baptiste Lamarck and widely accepted at the time Spencer was writing). When women are forced through male domination to become subservient, the argument goes, subservience becomes "adaptive." It is then passed on to succeeding generations of women, not only as a convenient quality to learn for survival in a patriarchal society, but also as a biological trait. After enough generations of male domination, women become biologically programmed for subservience.[102]

This was the mature Spencer; in his earlier works, Spencer had been quite vocal in support of women's equality, declaring that "if he were to marry he would forget, if he could not destroy, the legal bond." In *Social Statics,* published in the early 1850s, Spencer advocated full political rights for women and asked, with a healthy skepticism, "Who can tell us where the sphere of the woman actually lies? Considering that the customs of people differ from each other so widely, I would like to know how it can be proved that the sphere we assign to her really is here, that the limits we set on her activity are exactly the proper bounds?" But by the time Spencer adopted anthropological notions about matriarchy and turned them to his own use, he was quite beyond any lingering feminist notions.[103] Like Lubbock—and unlike McLennan—Spencer thought it pointless to bemoan the inevitable disparities between different races, classes, and genders. He was all for men behaving like gentlemen and treating the ladies well, but he expressed neither hope nor desire for reversing women's evolutionary trend toward increased inferiority to men.

REPORTING FROM THE FIELD: LEWIS HENRY MORGAN

At the other end of the spectrum from Spencer was Lewis Henry Morgan, an American anthropologist from Rochester, New York, who mostly ignored arguments from biology or natural selection, relying instead on ethnographic material and hoping for improvements in women's condition. Like McLennan and Maine, as well as Bachofen, Morgan was first a lawyer, pursuing his ethnographic research as an independent scholar.[104] The point of distinction most frequently made between Morgan and his British colleagues is that Morgan engaged in his own field research.[105] This point is overdrawn. Morgan was indeed determined to gain firsthand exposure to other "primitive" cultures, but he still did his most important work from the armchair. Nothing he claimed for the history of the human race was reliant on his own observations in the field. Furthermore, Morgan's field research was comparatively limited. In the post–Margaret Mead age, the general public tends to visualize anthropological fieldwork as an intensive interaction with another culture, involving acquisition of language skills and residence with these other peoples for long periods of time. This is in fact what anthropological fieldwork became in the early twentieth century, but this is not what Morgan did. His fieldwork was much more limited in duration, sometimes consisting of no more than a day or two's visit to a Native American tribe (though his exposure to the Iroquois near his native Rochester, New York, was of longer duration).[106] Besides, for his project, Morgan needed much more information than he could acquire firsthand. He set out to get this larger pool of information

FIGURE 10. Lewis Henry Morgan (1818–81), American anthropologist and author of *Ancient Society*, an account of human prehistory that was especially influential for communist and socialist versions of matriarchal myth

by directly soliciting the observations of others. It was this, more than his own fieldwork, that distinguished Morgan from his British peers.

Morgan began his work entirely independently of the British matriarchalists. Early investments in the mining industry in Michigan gave Morgan sufficient wealth to pursue his ethnographic pastime. By 1846, Morgan had become particularly intrigued with the kinship terminology of the Iroquois, which was quite unlike that of Anglo-American culture. He was curious to know what other types of kinship terminology existed and how they were distributed on a global scale. Morgan's enthusiasm was sparked by his belief that kinship terminology was extremely slow to change and could thus serve as a fossilized relic of prehistoric forms of family relations.

Initially Morgan was an ardent diffusionist. Like Lafitau before him, he thought the customs of the Iroquois so peculiar that they could only be accounted for by discovering from whence the Iroquois originally migrated. Morgan suggested that since a kinship system similar to that of the Iroquois was found among the Tamils of India, they "must spring from the same stock": "When the discoverers of the New World bestowed upon its inhabitants the name of *Indians,* under the impression that they had reached the Indies, they little suspected that children of the same original family, although upon a different continent, stood before them. By a singular coincidence error was truth."[107] Morgan sought support for his diffusionist theory by developing a questionnaire designed to map out the kinship terminologies of a variety of ethnic groups. With the help of the Smithsonian Institution, the U.S. State Department, and several missionary boards, Morgan managed to distribute this questionnaire widely in the late 1850s and early 1860s to diplomats and missionaries all over the world. Eventually, Morgan received 139 responses that he was able to use to compile his *Systems of Consanguinity and Affinity of the Human Family,* published in 1871.[108]

By the time Morgan was completing this book, he was reaching out in a new theoretical direction that was to culminate with the publication of his magnum opus, *Ancient Society,* in 1878. In this book, Morgan's early loyalty to diffusionism as an explanatory device for kinship systems gave way to a thoroughgoing evolutionism. Where he previously believed kinship systems to be static, carried like so much baggage from one continent to another, he now saw them as dynamic, changing as cultures moved through several predictable evolutionary stages. Some have suggested that Morgan's turnaround was based on the data pouring in from his worldwide survey of kinship terminology,[109] but it seems more likely that Morgan was motivated by the discovery of human antiquity. Indeed, Morgan begins *Ancient Society* with this sentence: "The great antiquity of mankind upon the earth has been conclusively established." From this Morgan draws the familiar conclusions:

> It can now be asserted upon convincing evidence that savagery preceded barbarism in all the tribes of mankind, as barbarism is known to have preceded civilization. The history of the human race is one in source, one in experience, and one in progress. . . . Since mankind were one in origin, their career has been essentially one, running in different but uniform channels upon all continents, and very similarly in all the tribes and nations of mankind down to the same status of advancement. It follows that the history and experience of the American Indian tribes represent, more or less nearly, the history and experience of our own remote ancestors when in corresponding conditions.[110]

In *Ancient Society* Morgan argued that several social variables ran parallel to development in kinship systems. Of these, three were key: government, property, and technology. Morgan conceptualized these parallel developments in a tripartite scheme of savagery, barbarism, and civilization (borrowed from

Montesquieu), which he further broke down into lower, middle, and upper stages (except for "civilization," which was singular). Each stage is demarcated first by modes of technology. For example, the middle stage of savagery begins with the advent of fishing and the use of fire; the upper stage of barbarism begins with the smelting of iron ore; civilization begins with the invention of alphabets and writing.[111] This materialist thread runs throughout Morgan's work. Though government and family have their own internal developments that are not dependent on changes in the "arts of subsistence," they are nevertheless always coordinated with technological changes, a fact that made his work especially attractive to communist thinkers.[112]

In spite of this nascent materialism, Morgan spends the bulk of *Ancient Society* tracing evolutionary progressions for forms of marriage and government. And since Morgan's notion of government is full of gentes, phratries, and other forms of kinship, it is fair to say that family organization is Morgan's central interest. After a brief section entitled "Growth of Intelligence through Inventions and Discoveries," Morgan turns to "Growth of the Idea of Government," beginning with a chapter titled "Organization of Society upon the Basis of Sex," and including a penultimate chapter titled "Change of Descent from the Female to the Male Line." Like his British predecessors, Morgan begins with "indiscriminant [sic] mating characterized by the absence of sexual possessiveness and jealousies." This is the lower stage of savagery. In the middle stage of savagery, the "consanguine" family is introduced, in which parent/child incest is prohibited. The "punaluan" family of the upper stage of savagery extends this prohibition to brother/sister incest (between siblings who are related through their mother). A non-exclusive pairing marriage follows ("syndyasmian") in the lower stage of barbarism, in which marriage lasted only as long as "the pleasure of the parties" endured. The middle stage of barbarism brings the patriarchal, polygynous family. In concert with McLennan, Morgan sees patriarchal marriage and male dominance arising with the first opportunity to ascertain paternity with certainty: that is, when women became monogamous. For Morgan (though not for McLennan), women's chastity was largely the result of the increasing scope of the incest taboo, which was heretofore responsible for all the earlier shifts in marriage customs as well. When more and more partners are ruled off-limits, "the ever-increasing difficulty of obtaining wives . . . [leads] to the acquisition of women by violence or by purchase." It is at this juncture that the ancient "gyneocracy" is defeated and patriliny is instituted. It is followed by the upper stage of barbarism, which introduces monogamous, exclusive marriage.[113]

Although Morgan is no fan of the promiscuous horde, he does not suggest—as his British colleagues do—that women are victimized by men's voracious sexual appetites. Instead, Morgan argues that "women in the promiscuous and matrilineal stages were either equal to, or dominant over, men, and were in control of sexual relations, descent, and property." Women were "status superiors in their own households," and "the work of women and men was accorded equal value." Up through the syndyasmian family in the lower stage of barbarism, women retained headship of the gens, which Morgan deemed the most important social organization and the basis of government.[114] But subsequent developments were detrimental to the status of women. In contradiction to his general scheme of evolution as progress, Morgan makes it quite clear that the move from matriliny to patriliny is not unambiguously positive. He believes that the patriarchal family offers growing room for individuality, but he is clearly distressed at the way in which women and children are subordinated to the male head of the family. Not only are women and children unable to reap the benefits of a growing individualism, they are stripped of their former status and autonomy and reduced to the status of slaves. In particular, Morgan is appalled by the treatment of women in classical Greece, remarking that it "remains an enigma that a race with endowments great enough to impress their mental life upon the world, should have remained essentially barbarian in their treatment of the female sex at the height of their civilization." Morgan attributes the downfall of Greece and Rome in part to their failure to "develop their womanhood" and reflects approvingly on gains women subsequently made within monogamous marriage.[115] This is a development that Morgan wishes to see continue. Indeed, he regards it as "destined to progress still further, until the equality of the sexes is acknowledged, and the equities of the marriage relation are completely recognized." In the future, Morgan thought, the rising status of women would be an index of how far the institution of the family had progressed.

Morgan's evolutionism had a touch of advance and retreat, a hint of the *Sturm und Drang* more characteristic of Bachofen than the other evolutionary anthropologists. And like Bachofen, Morgan expressed a degree of nostalgia for matriarchal times. However, Morgan was far more sanguine about the future than Bachofen. Morgan hoped for "a recurrence, but on a higher level, of the freedom, equality and brotherhood characteristic of the ancient *gens*."[116] Coming from outside the British epicenter of evolutionary anthropology, Morgan bridged the worlds of England and continental Europe. He was able to forge an intellectual link with Bachofen, as none of the British anthropologists were able to do, probably because he was more comfortable with the notion of women's former social power than were his British counterparts.[117] And initially, anyway, Morgan was in easy conversation with McLennan, who shared his vision of increasing freedom and rights for women in the future.

Eventually, however, a heated war of words developed between McLennan and Morgan. Morgan left McLennan's pet theory, marriage by capture, out of his account of the evolution of the family in *Ancient Society* and, in his appendix, offered some rather cutting remarks about McLennan's theory of exogamy.

McLennan countered Morgan in a new edition of *Primitive Marriage,* to which he appended a nasty retort claiming that Morgan had been anticipated by Lafitau, that he misunderstood the nature of kinship terminology (it was a "mere mode of addressing persons that had no bearing on family or descent"), and that he was ignorant of important sources on the Iroquois.[118] In spite of McLennan's attacks, Morgan's reputation grew, in England and elsewhere.

Morgan also had the unique honor of being the first proponent of matriarchal myth to inspire other anthropologists to go into the field and find evidence to support his theories. Foremost among these were Alfred L. Howitt and Lorimer Fison. Both were Englishmen who had traveled to Australia to prospect for gold. When gold mining turned out to be unprofitable, Howitt turned first to droving cattle and later became "a seasoned explorer," while Fison became a Wesleyan missionary to Fiji. Fison learned of Morgan's work when one of Morgan's questionnaires reached him in 1869. Fison supplied details of Fijian and Tongan kinship systems, and began a "long and warm correspondence" with Morgan, defending his theory of the evolution of kinship systems and developing a passionate hatred of McLennan and Lubbock on Morgan's behalf. Howitt joined in, corresponding with Lubbock, McLennan, Morgan, and others, and coauthoring (with Fison) the 1883 article "From Mother-Right to Father-Right," which appeared in the *Journal of the Royal Anthropological Institute.* The special task Howitt and Fison set for themselves was to explain the mechanisms through which "uterine succession" was superseded by "descent through males." They claimed to find evidence of group marriage, possibly of the "punaluan" type, among Australian tribes that had totemic clans which restricted marriage between certain persons. Though they regarded this as "ancient rule" rather than "present usage," Howitt and Fison believed they had proven Morgan's theory. More particularly, Howitt and Fison did their best to rule out cultural diffusion as the impetus for the adoption of father right. They argued for a natural, evolutionary "disinclination on the part of the heirs of a man's body to surrender the inheritance to his sister's children" and the husband's eventual insistence "on the strict fidelity of his wife to himself under severe penalties." When paternity was secured, they said, father right emerged victorious.[119]

WILLIAM ROBERTSON SMITH AND THE ARABIAN CASE

Meanwhile, McLennan's influence lived on in the form of an almost slavishly devoted disciple: William Robertson Smith, a professor at Cambridge University. Smith was instrumental in extending the reach of McLennan's theories, both by championing them within an academic environment and by applying them to his own area of research, the Hebrew Bible.

FIGURE 11. William
Robertson Smith
(1846–94), Scottish
philologist who
delineated survival of a
matrilineal family system
among the Arabs

Like Spencer, Smith's influence in his own time vastly outstrips the degree to which he is remembered today. Smith was "an intellectual prodigy," rising to become a professor of Hebrew at the seminary of the Free Church of Scotland in Aberdeen by the age of twenty-three. He studied with the famous biblical critics Paul Lagarde and Julius Welhausen in Germany, and attracted large crowds back home in Scotland for his lectures on the Old Testament, his audiences delighted by his command of the nuances of ancient languages. In 1875, Smith wrote the "Bible" entry in the *Encyclopedia Britannica,* which questioned whether Moses was in fact the author of the first five books of the Hebrew Bible. For this, Smith was put on trial for heresy in one of the last such trials conducted in Great Britain. Though he was not convicted and maintained throughout the trial that he believed in the divine inspiration of scripture—Smith was removed from his post at the seminary. In the aftermath of the heresy trial in the early 1880s, Smith relocated to Cambridge University, where he assumed a post as professor of Arabic.[120]

Smith had met McLennan at the Edinburgh Evening Club in the early 1870s and was instantly enthralled with his theories, which, as Robert Fraser notes, Smith took up "with almost indecent alacrity." Smith was particularly keen on following up on McLennan's hunch that there were remnants of a matriarchal kinship system among the Arabs. Setting out "to vindicate theories he was already inclined to believe," Smith found precisely what he was looking for: that "kinship through the mother alone was originally the universal rule of Arabia, and that kinship through males sprang up in polyandrous groups of kinsmen which brought in wives from outside but desired to keep the children of these alien women to themselves."[121] Smith published the results of his research in 1885 in a book titled *Kinship and Marriage in Early Arabia*.[122]

The hallmark of Smith's work was his reliance on "reasonable inferences" to prove that the chain of events postulated by McLennan occurred in ancient Arabia. For example, after presenting ethnographic evidence that early Arab men were inclined to "share" their wives sexually with visiting friends and kinsmen while still counting all their wives' children as their own, Smith concludes that nothing else can account for this curious practice but the prior existence of fraternal polyandry. This is, he says, a reasonable inference that "meets all the conditions of a legitimate hypothesis." When problems crop up with the evidence, Smith retreats to the theory, which he regards as already having been adequately established by McLennan. For example, after a diligent search, Smith finds only a few examples of Arab tribes with feminine names. But far from allowing this to deter him from claiming universal prehistoric mother right, Smith explains, "Everywhere as society advances a stage is reached when the child ceases to belong to the mother's kin and follows the father. Accordingly we may be tolerably sure that the law of female kinship was once much more widely spread than appears from the recorded instances of tribes with female eponyms." The fact that there are any feminine names at all, he later suggests, "goes to shew that at some time or other there was either a different law of kinship, or a possibility of forming a tribe on another principle than that of unity of blood."[123]

Paternity—or its absence—is key to Smith's time line for the development of the institution of marriage, as it was for McLennan. Smith notes, "That a child is of his mother's blood is a fact that at once forces itself on the observer when he begins to think at all," and any notion of fatherhood must come far later. As supportive evidence, Smith offers the fact that designating the father in Arabic would require "a participial form of the root *w-l-d*," but the "most general Arabic word for kinship" is *rahim*, or womb. Smith takes this to prove "beyond all question" that the Arabic language "developed in a condition of life in which physical fatherhood was not the basis of any important social relation."[124]

Though Smith adopts the stages of McLennan's theory with precision, his interpretations are somewhat different. For example, Smith's vision of prehistoric times is one of great freedom for women. In the earliest forms of marriage that Smith postulates for Arabia, "the woman remained with her kin and dismissed her partner at will, the children belonging to the mother's kin and growing up under their protection." Unlike McLennan, Smith never gives any hint that women are unhappy with this arrangement or that they are required to have more sex with more men than they would like. He describes the "origin of polyandry" as "a state of morality in which no weight is laid even on temporary fidelity to one man, where there is no form of marriage with one husband at all, but every woman freely receives any suitor she pleases." Neither does Smith ever suggest that women are better off with the arrival of patriarchy, when they are confined to marriage with a single male partner. Women in patriarchal Arabia become, Smith says, no more than property. In fact, Smith deems the "subjection of women to their husbands" in Arabia "as a virtual captivity," begun when they actually were captives, stolen from competing tribes, just as McLennan postulated. Smith is far from suggesting that patriarchy was a total disaster for women; it was merely a temporary step backward. Men, apparently motivated by benevolence, eventually give women a more comfortable status in society and in marriage. Patriarchy evolves, and women's lot improves. Smith emphasizes "the alleviations which the prophet [Mohammed] introduced in the hard condition of married women" and credits "the influence of higher civilizations" (among which he names Palestine, Persia, and Mohammed's "own city of Mecca").[125]

For Smith, then, the evolution of marriage was not unambiguously good, as it was for McLennan, with each stage making an advance upon the "rudeness" of the stage that came before. Otherwise, Smith's work is almost wholly derivative of McLennan's. Still, these few key differences between the two men demonstrate that even early on, there was room for a variety of political positions under the umbrella of the myth of matriarchal prehistory. Evolution meant progress, but for some, such as Smith, the path upward sometimes included a smidgen of Bachofenian retreat.

Smith's most important contribution to matriarchal myth was the simple fact that he was a well-known public figure whose first area of expertise was philology (historical linguistics) rather than anthropology. With the exception of the idiosyncratic Bachofen, philologists in both England and Germany took comparatively little interest in matriarchal theory. From the vantage point of the twenty-first century, Victorian philologists are nearly forgotten, while Victorian anthropologists are admired—with qualifications—as pioneers. At the time, though, the status equation was reversed, and Smith's attention, as a philologist, to matriarchal myth did much to enhance it in his contemporaries' eyes.[126] Along with his interest in matriarchal myth, Smith developed ways of thinking about myth and ritual, and more to the point, the relationship between the two, that would be profoundly influential for later advocates of the matriarchal theory.

Most significantly, Smith conveyed matriarchal myth to his intellectual protégé, Sir James George Frazer. Frazer, like Smith, had a wide and deep education
in the classics and the ancient languages associated with them, having trained at
Trinity College, Cambridge, in the classics before embracing anthropology.[127] It
was E. B. Tylor's *Primitive Culture* that persuaded Frazer to change directions in
1883, shifting from a dissertation on Plato and a translation of Pausanias's *Descriptions of Greece* to the work on totemism, magic, and religion that would dominate his professional life.[128] Later that same year Frazer met Smith, newly arrived
at Cambridge University. The two men struck up an immediate friendship, no
doubt strengthened by their shared ties to Scotland and the Free Church.[129] In
1890, Frazer published the first version of the book that was to define his professional life and captivate a generation: *The Golden Bough*. The initial work was
composed of two volumes and was dedicated to Smith "in gratitude and admiration."[130] A third volume was added in a 1900 edition, and then, between 1906 and
1915, an edition containing twelve volumes was released, to which was added a
supplement in 1936, near the end of Frazer's life.[131]

In 1912 Salomon Reinach commented that a "sufficient epitaph" for Smith
would be "*genuit Frazerum*."[132] Indeed Frazer's fame soon eclipsed that of Smith,
and in his later publications, Smith was thanking Frazer effusively for acquainting
him with "primitive habits of thought."[133] However, the first edition of *The Golden
Bough* does not even mention the then hot topic of matriliny,[134] so Frazer's story
belongs more to the twentieth than to the nineteenth century. In later editions of
The Golden Bough, where Frazer did address "kinship through females" as an
important aspect of human prehistory, he explicitly denied that there had ever
been a time of women's power or exclusive goddess worship. Though this should
disqualify him from being a player in the history of matriarchal myth, Frazer
(like Jung after him) is actually key in the transmission of matriarchal myth from
the nineteenth to the twentieth centuries. Frazer inspired a love of ritual and folklore among his readers, many of whom found the potentially matriarchal elements
of his story far more enticing than Frazer himself did. For example, in the early
twentieth century, Jane Ellen Harrison lifted matriarchal myth from anthropology
and gave it new life within the classics, largely as a result of her reading of Frazer.
Later, in the mid-twentieth century, the Wiccan movement, infatuated with Frazer's notions of the goddess and the dying king, the fertile field and the cycle of the
seasons, created a new religion that successfully transmitted matriarchal myth to
the feminist movement of the late twentieth century. It became as popular there as
it had been in the late nineteenth century among anthropologists. Thus, although
Smith added comparatively little to matriarchal myth, his acquaintance with
Frazer provided the vehicle by which Smith's matriarchal ideas would travel down
the decades.

E. B. TYLOR AND THE ANTHROPOLOGICAL
SEAL OF APPROVAL

Edward Burnett Tylor, widely viewed as the founder of modern anthropology, is a highly instructive figure in the story of British matriarchal mythology. Tylor's earliest work, in the 1860s and 1870s, made little or no note of the matriarchal thesis. But in 1889, in what has been described (somewhat anachronistically) as "the very first cross-cultural study," Tylor supported the priority of mother right.[135] Toward the end of the nineteenth century, Tylor began to suspect that claims about matriarchal prehistory were overly ambitious and perhaps misplaced. When anthropology as a whole disavowed the myth of matriarchal prehistory, Tylor did too.[136] This would be fairly unremarkable if Tylor were just another third-rate amateur ethnologist, but Tylor was *Tylor,* and his (albeit temporary) acceptance of the matriarchal thesis left an indelible mark on the discipline of anthropology that could never truly be washed away, no matter how much later anthropologists may have desired to do so.

Born into a "prosperous middle-class London Quaker merchant family," Tylor came to anthropology from a non-academic background. He did not attend university, but was instead an apprentice in a brass foundry. It was only as a result of "delicate health" that Tylor left the foundry to travel. He visited the United States and Cuba, where he met his fellow countryman, Henry Christy, a banker who had been engaged in amateur archaeology in the "bone caves" of central France. Christy invited Tylor to go to Mexico with him, and the two set off together. Tylor never did any formal fieldwork in Mexico, but he developed a sensitivity to cultural detail that made him less willing than his fellow anthropologists to skim over messy or contradictory data in his zeal to establish an intriguing theory.[137]

Tylor was an unapologetic evolutionist, arguing along with his peers that there was no evidence for the theory of degenerationism. Humans, Tylor said, no matter how far separated, evolved through similar—and in theory, predictable—stages of development. Before coming to the defense of the myth of matriarchal prehistory in 1889, Tylor had already given it a wonderful gift in his theory of "survivals," presented at length in his 1871 book, *Primitive Culture*. The theory of survivals held that human cultures exhibit "processes, custom, opinions, and so forth [including "games, popular sayings . . . superstitions, and the like"], which have been carried on by force of habit into a new state of society different from that in which they had their original home, and . . . thus remain as proofs and examples of an older condition of culture out of which a newer has been evolved."[138] Scholars had certainly made use of the theory of survivals before Tylor came upon the scene, but Tylor coined the term and did the most to popularize the theory, uniting the data of folklore and ethnography and offering a tie-in to the then prestigious discipline of geology. Cultural "survivals," said Tylor, compared favorably

FIGURE 12. Edward Burnett Tylor (1832–1917), prominent British anthropologist who favored, and later discarded, the matriarchal theory

to geological fossils, and like fossils, Robert Fraser explains, "it mattered not if . . . [they] came from Ceylon or from Tibet," since "at some time or another that particular historical stratum must have bent round and joined on to the land mass of Roman [Western] history."[139]

Tylor's matriarchal theory was never strongly developed and was derived from McLennan and Bachofen.[140] In "On a Method of Investigating the Development of Institutions" in 1889, and later in "The Matriarchal Family System" in 1896, Tylor spoke freely of exogamy and marriage by capture, and searched for the evolutionary moment in which mother right gave way to paternal kinship. With multiple charts and graphs, Tylor tried to demonstrate correspondences between types of residence (matrilocal, patrilocal, or "removal," in which a new couple sets up their own home); avoidance customs (according to which certain individuals may not be allowed to look at, speak to, or otherwise recognize specific relatives-in-law); marriage by capture; exogamy; and the practice of couvade.[141] Tylor began a new trend by counting instances of these customs; he could state, for example, that 65 tribes practice matrilocality, 76 practice "removal," and 141 practice patrilocality. His compilation of data led him to believe—or, more accurately, confirmed what he was already inclined to believe—that paternal kinship was an evolutionary development out of maternal kinship. Societies practicing paternal kinship, he said, exhibit "trifling" and apparently "motiveless" customs that are intelligible only when seen as survivals from an era of mother right. Contrariwise, societies practicing maternal kinship do not have any such survivals from a time of father right. Therefore, Tylor concluded, it is obvious that maternal kinship came first, and was followed, after a time of transition and upheaval, by paternal kinship.[142] In concert with most of his British peers, Tylor did not imagine that women "govern the family" in matriarchal society (this honor going to her brothers and uncles), but he did concede that "in these communities women enjoy greater consideration than in barbaric patriarchal life."[143] Still, true moral progress lay along the path of evolution. For Tylor, better things lay ahead, in spite of any setbacks suffered along the way (such as, presumably, the oppression of women).[144]

In an odd way, Tylor marked both the pinnacle and the end of the reign of mother right in Anglo-American anthropology, much as Maine had done for the earlier patriarchal theory. Like Maine, Tylor summed up the position of his day, and, again like Maine, he subtly (if unintentionally) subverted it by exhibiting new ways of thinking about and investigating human history that would soon serve opposing theories. Indeed, when the time came, Tylor was willing to discard the more audacious claims of the theory he had formerly championed.

But in the 1880s, that time had not yet arrived. Matriarchal myth reigned as dogma within British anthropology. From there it spread out to the cultural mainstream and made itself useful to people with a variety of philosophical and political perspectives on gender. Where it caught on most tenaciously was with communists and feminists, both of whom championed matriarchal myth and, with various twists and turns, passed it along to subsequent generations of the faithful throughout the twentieth century.

5

Making Matriarchal Myth Work

Communists and Feminists Discover
the Mother Age

This rediscovery of the primitive matriarchal gens as the earlier stage of the patriarchal gens of civilized peoples has the same importance for anthropology as Darwin's theory of evolution has for biology and Marx's theory of surplus value has for political economy. . . . The matriarchal gens has become the pivot on which the whole science turns; since its discovery we know where to look and what to look for in our research, and how to arrange the results.

—FRIEDRICH ENGELS

The political use of matriarchal myth was a natural fit in the wider social context of the late nineteenth century. "The woman question" (*die Frauenfrage,* in German), as it was typically known in that era, was the focus of intense debate,[1] especially as it swept up with it concerns about sexuality that were ultimately to mark the end of the Victorian era. Preoccupations with sex and gender (encoded by the Victorian anthropologists in the terms *kinship, marriage,* and *family*) combined from the beginning with questions about greater social structures (the anthropologists' "totemic clans" and "phraetries"). As political unrest in Europe peaked, opposing factions used matriarchal myth to reach diametrically opposed conclusions about the future of society. The conservatism of Bachofen and the generally liberal attitudes of the Victorian anthropologists diverged ever farther across the political spectrum in both directions as matriarchal myth became the treasured property of communists, feminists, and eventually—in the twentieth century—fascists.

Of course, no one prior to this came at matriarchal myth innocent of a political agenda. One need not dig very deep to see how the various versions of the myth of matriarchal prehistory were colored by their narrators' assessment of the society in which they lived, and the forms of government they deemed best suited to human progress. But they did not lift up the evolutionary history they traced as providing reason in itself to adopt any particular position on "the woman question," the proper future of sexual relations between men and women, or the most fruitful form of government. While Bachofen and the many evolutionary anthropologists had their own divergent political perspectives, they accepted that the story—which was after all conceived of as an accurate history of the human race—left room for competing public policies. Just as Darwinian theories of human evolution are today accepted by both Democrats and (some) Republicans, anarchists and communists, so too did the earliest theorists of matriarchal myth leave room for the possibility that different individuals could draw different moral lessons from the scientifically proven existence of a matriarchal past. This changed rather dramatically as non-academics took up matriarchal myth for the first time in the 1880s. They were much more inclined to see history moving with a purpose and rhythm that could yield only one reasonable normative conclusion: their own.

These political uses of matriarchal myth are also notable for the magnetic pole shift they brought to the narrative. Though both Bachofen and the anthropologists demonstrated varying amounts of respect, appreciation, and nostalgia for earlier, more matricentric forms of society, they were unanimous in their belief that the principal thrust of human history was forward and upward from a "savage" past to a "civilized" future.[2] When matriarchal myth was taken up by socialists and first-wave feminists, it quickly became a myth of regress rather than a myth of progress, a clarion call for revolution and revival of an ancient past rather than a stoic hand at the helm of the Western capitalist empire. Political activists saw in matriarchal myth the blessed creation, devastating fall, and eventual restitution of human society, and it aroused a quasi-religious fervor in them that evolutionary, progressive forms of matriarchal myth had not been able to muster. Prehistory was no longer the primordial muck out of which humanity had painfully and nobly extracted itself, but an alternative vision of what human society could be. Political activists took the historicizing element inherent in matriarchal myth and used it not only to account for present society but also to make its constructed—and therefore changeable—nature clear. This is the valence that proved to be much more salient in matriarchal myth in the late twentieth century, as matriarchalists went to the past to seek not only genealogy, but also precedent.

FRIEDRICH ENGELS AND *THE ORIGIN OF THE FAMILY, PRIVATE PROPERTY, AND THE STATE*

The entrée proper of matriarchal myth into communist and socialist circles came with the publication of Friedrich Engels's *Origin of the Family, Private*

FIGURE 13. Karl Kautsky (1854–1938), Czech socialist journalist, popularizer of Marxist theory, and author of "The Origin of Marriage and the Family," published in 1882

Property, and the State in 1884. Technically, Engels didn't get there first. He was preceded by Karl Kautsky, a young socialist journalist who published an article titled "Die Entstehung der Ehe und Familie" (The Origin of Marriage and the Family) in 1882. However, Kautsky wrote at the behest of Engels, and when Engels didn't agree with Kautsky, Engels essentially took over and wrote the communist manifesto on marriage and the family himself.

Kautsky came to his socialism as a student at the University of Vienna in the late 1870s. Prior to this, his only political commitment had been the intense Czech nationalism of his family, who had lived in Prague before moving to Vienna when Karl was seven years old. Kautsky's socialism quickly disqualified him for the career toward which he was aiming—that of a teacher—for "being both a servant of the state as a teacher and an opponent of the state as a socialist" was somewhere between impractical and completely impossible. Searching for an alternative, Kautsky was offered a subsidy by the wealthy German socialist Karl Höchberg to settle in Zurich and write for the newspaper *Der Sozialdemokrat*.[3]

In this early period, Kautsky wrote on a variety of topics reflecting both his own interests and those of his mentors, first Höchberg and later Engels. Before Kautsky became acquainted with the works of Marx—which he would spend his professional life interpreting for a popular audience[4]—he read Darwin and Spencer.[5] Indeed, some have suggested that Kautsky's entire body of work could be best described as "Darwino-Marxism." Bringing Darwin and Marx together was no easy task. Social Darwinists, from Spencer onward, generally assumed that the principles of Darwinism supported a capitalist economy. "Survival of the fittest" seemed a maxim of endless competition, far from socialist ideals of mutual support and community.[6] Kautsky argued otherwise as he worked to lay the foundations and then build the edifice of a truly "scientific socialism."[7]

One of Kautsky's earliest articles was on population increase, food supply, and the work of Thomas Malthus. Kautsky sent this article to Engels—it served as his introduction to him—in late 1880. Engels's reply to Kautsky's work was lukewarm, but he encouraged Kautsky to come and visit him in London, saying, "You are quite right to come here. . . . it has become very necessary to you to come away from the uncritical atmosphere in which the entire current German-produced historical and economic literature decays." Kautsky spent the late spring of 1881 in London, currying favor with Marx and Engels. With Engels, this approach appeared to work. Engels did not have a terribly high opinion of Kautsky's work, calling him "a born pedant and hair-splitter," but he found him to be "an extremely good fellow" and seemed to enjoy his company. Marx was less impressed, saying that Kautsky "is a mediocrity with a small-minded outlook . . . very conceited . . . belongs by nature to the tribe of the philistines but is otherwise a decent fellow in his own way." Marx suggested that Engels took "a much milder view of this Kauz since he proved himself a very talented drinker."[8]

In the spring of 1881, Kautsky was at work on a study of protective tariffs, a topic given him by Höchberg. Kautsky shared the results of this research with Engels, but by the fall of 1881, he abruptly dropped the topic when Engels suggested that he investigate the origins of the family and marriage, a move that Höchberg was also encouraging by directing Kautsky to the works of McLennan and Bachofen. Kautsky saw his investigations into the evolution of marriage as well within the orbit of socialism, though as he later remembered of this time, "I was the only one in the party doing research on marriage and the family."[9] Kautsky completed his study of the origin of marriage and the family in the spring of 1882. He took his manuscript to the University of Jena in the hopes of convincing

Ernst Haeckel, a well-known social Darwinist whose writings had inspired Kautsky, to award him a doctoral degree on the basis of this work. Haeckel seemed impressed with Kautsky's study, but was told by the university authorities that he could not award a degree for work that was so far afield from his own specialization in zoology.[10] Instead the manuscript was slated for publication in three parts in the journal *Kosmos*.[11]

There is little in Kautsky's "Die Entstehung der Ehe und Familie" that would identify it as socialist. It reads very much like other treatments of the topic penned by German intellectuals in the last decades of the nineteenth century. Kautsky was responding in part to Bachofen, and like others, he both praised and damned him. Specifically, he described Bachofen as "sophisticated," but quibbled with him over the status of prehistoric women. Kautsky—like the British anthropologists before him and upon whom his work was also dependent— found it difficult to believe that women actually ruled society, as Bachofen had claimed. The notion of Demetrian matriarchy was thus closed off to him.[12] Kautsky also took exception to Bachofen's first stage, that of hetaerism. Though he consistently refers to the "hetaeristic Mutterrecht" as the first stage of human social life, Kautsky was clearly not envisioning the sexually perfervid swamp of Bachofen's imagination nor the sexual free-for-all the British anthropologists described as "primitive promiscuity." Kautsky began instead with the assumption of sex equality: "Within the tribe," he declared, "complete sexual freedom obtained," and "the woman, being free and equal, stood under the protection of the community just as much as the man." However, owing to feelings of jealousy, as well as women's desire to choose individual men for themselves, this sexual freedom "did not lead to communal marriage where every man had marital rights with regard to all women of the tribe, but rather to . . . monogamous, easily dissoluble, more or less loose alliances."[13]

Kautsky hesitated to regard this early stage as matriarchal, though he made the usual allowances for a closer connection between mother and child, which would naturally result in a matrilineal kinship system. True mother right was, for Kautsky, only possible with the development of private property. It was this same condition that allowed for the development of father right. Kautsky was quick to discount any clear evolutionary sequence from one to the other. Both, he said, sprang from the original condition of hetaerism, but from there, some cultures went through a stage of marriage by capture while others did not; some developed polyandry while others moved straight to monogamy; some, indeed, passed over a matriarchal phase altogether, adopting patriarchal customs as soon as they developed private property.[14]

Engels read Kautsky's article on marriage and the family in 1883, and responded to it in a series of letters. Never did Engels accept anything Kautsky said that he was not already prepared to accept. Throughout his letters to Kautsky,

Engels takes the tone of the older and wiser mentor correcting the errors of his overly enthusiastic and perhaps overconfident pupil. Engels complained in particular of Kautsky's rejection of *die Gemeinschaft der Weiber* (the sharing of women among the men of the tribe) in favor of his vision of serial monogamy. Engels was quite insistent on the existence of a period of indiscriminate sexual relations, and he was particularly annoyed with Kautsky's assertion that sexual jealousy would have played any role at all in early human social relations. Engels assumed, probably rightly, that Kautsky adopted this view from Darwin. Engels had no interest in giving Darwin credit for knowing anything about the topic of prehistoric marriage ("Darwin is as little an authority in this field as with regard to economics"), though Engels himself borrowed from Darwin when it suited him.[15]

In his response to the second installment of Kautsky's article, Engels became even more didactic. He claimed that Kautsky contradicted himself, that he went over the sources far too quickly, that he indulged in unfounded speculation and generalization, and that he "paid too much attention to the opinions of the so-called anthropologists." Engels suggested that Kautsky would come to "very different conclusions" if he were to continue in his study of the origins of marriage and the family, and specifically that he would eventually come to see that Bachofen was right about the original "sex collective" (even though he was right for all the wrong reasons).[16] By September of 1883, Engels was declaring that his time was too valuable to be spent reading Kautsky's ruminations on the family. He told Kautsky that to treat the subject properly, he would have to do a great deal more research, to go back and revisit "the whole evolution of the topic." He didn't seem to believe Kautsky capable of this and instead congratulated him on moving on to other subjects, such as biblical times and colonization, that he might be able to handle more adequately.[17]

When Engels came to write about marriage and the family in 1884, he clearly felt he owed no intellectual debt to Kautsky. And Kautsky, it would seem, felt the same, though perhaps his reflections on Engels's *Origin* were colored by a combination of an authentic hero worship and a more prosaic need to honor one of the principals of the first generation of materialist philosophy. In a tribute to Engels published after his death in 1895, Kautsky heralded *The Origin of the Family, Private Property, and the State* as nothing less than a marvel; Engels had saved Morgan's work from oblivion, filled in its historical gaps, put it "into the frame of the Marx-Engels materialistic conception of history," and blended it into "one uniformly developed series, the pre-historic and historic," all "in the little book of 146 pages."[18]

In fact, Engels developed few original thoughts in *The Origin*; fewer than Kautsky had in "Die Entstehung der Ehe und Familie," to tell the truth. Engels's account of human prehistory was almost wholly dependent on the work of Morgan,[19] with a little help from Bachofen.[20] The lessons he drew from this prehistory

FIGURE 14. Friedrich
Engels (1820–95),
longtime collaborator
with Karl Marx and
author of *Origin of the
Family, Private Property,
and the State*

(and history too, for that matter) were in near complete harmony with the principles of dialectical materialism already worked out in collaboration with Karl
Marx.[21] All Engels did was to place the Marxist theory of economic development—
previously limited to a rather short span of human history—on a longer, highly
gendered timetable.

As it turned out, this was a lot. Marxism—particularly where it concerned
women—would never be the same. Economic developments, with which Marxism
had long concerned itself, were forever after (if fitfully) interlocked with issues of
gender and women's emancipation.[22] Matriarchal myth would never be the same
either, as with a few deft touches, Engels remade the narrative as a fully fledged
golden age myth, with the painful period of human history cushioned comfortably
on either end with times of peace, plenty, and freedom for all. Prehistoric matriarchy was rendered as an ideal, its disruption as a tragedy, and its return—although
of course in a greatly refashioned form—a passionately longed-for utopia.

Engels's watershed book, with its long-lasting impact, very nearly went unwritten. As we have seen, through the end of 1883 Engels showed no inclination to tackle these topics, contenting himself with criticizing the work of Kautsky. It was the death of Marx that spurred Engels to undertake his own study of the origins of marriage and the family. Marx had been reading the works of the most prominent Victorian anthropologists in the years before his death in March of 1883, continuing his long-standing interest in ethnography. He did not write anything on the topic during the last ten years of his life,[23] but he left behind notes on his readings,[24] and was especially drawn to the work of Morgan.[25] Later commentators have argued that Marx was himself contemplating a book on the topic. After his death, Marx's daughter Eleanor began organizing her father's notes and papers with the help of Friedrich Engels. In February of 1884, Engels wrote to Kautsky, bemoaning the fact that he could not "work up the material" from Marx's notes on ethnography; given his busy schedule, he could not "even think of it." But by late March, Engels had set to work on *The Origin* and by May it was finished.[26] He sent the manuscript to Kautsky for possible publication in *Die Neue Zeit,* a journal Kautsky founded with several other notable socialists in 1883 with the goal of providing historical and philosophical perspectives on Marxism ("scientific socialism").[27] It was ultimately decided that the work would not get past the Prussian censors and should therefore be published through other channels. Kautsky gleefully imagined the reaction of "our bourgeoisie" upon reading about the sexual license of the first stage of human social life described by Engels in *The Origin.*[28] Clearly, he was not one to hold a grudge over their disagreement on this important point in their respective versions of the matriarchal theory.

There is no question that Engels saw himself as Marx's posthumous ghostwriter, describing his own work as "a meagre substitute for what my departed friend no longer had time to do."[29] But the historical record suggests that Engels's role in the authorship of *The Origin* was rather more substantial than this. As accustomed as we are today to speak of "Marx-and-Engels" in a single breath, *The Origin* had only one author, and it was not Karl Marx. Indeed, nothing in Marx's writings, published or otherwise, suggests that he accepted the idea of a prehistoric matriarchy.

As early as "The German Ideology" (written, but not published, in the mid-1840s; that is, well before Bachofen's *Das Mutterrecht*), Marx and Engels had sketched out a history beginning with a primitive communist society that came to an end as a result of its internal contradictions, as other social forms were to do in subsequent stages of human social life (e.g., feudalism, and in the future, capitalism).[30] This primitive society was not matriarchal. Nor did Marx and Engels evince any interest in anything more ancient. In fact, they taunted German historians for paying any attention at all to preliterate eras, claiming that

FIGURE 15. Karl Marx (1818–83), German philosopher and economist

when they run out of positive material and when they can serve up neither theological nor political nor literary rubbish, [they] do not write history at all, but invent the "prehistoric era." They do not, however, enlighten us as to how we proceed from this nonsensical "prehistory" to history proper; although, on the other hand, in their historical speculation they seize upon this "prehistory" with especial eagerness because they imagine themselves safe there from interference on the part of "crude facts," and, at the same time, because there they can give full rein to their speculative impulse and set up and knock down hypotheses by the thousand.[31]

In "The German Ideology," Marx and Engels reckoned on the basis of the six-thousand-year biblical timescale. Later, after the discovery of human antiquity, Marx softened his judgments on the utility of reconstructing human prehistory. But Marx read the evolutionary anthropologists critically, scribbling marginalia indicating that he was unprepared to adopt their vision of prehistory wholesale.

Even after reading Morgan, McLennan, Lubbock, and Bachofen, Marx demurred on several basic theses of the story, including the existence of "primitive promiscuity" (which he deemed "nonsense") as well as the conclusion that irregular sexual relations would of necessity have resulted in matrilineal kinship systems (which he suspected were a local and not a universal phenomenon).[32]

Once Marx was gone, Engels did not feel compelled to share Marx's caution. Engels was fascinated—like his anthropological brethren—with the prospect of filling up the newfound era of prehistory with evolutionary stages proceeding ever closer to the nineteenth-century present, creating a "scientific" time line for the development of human civilization. Engels still gave the credit to Marx, though. In a speech at Marx's graveside, Engels compared Marx to Darwin: "Just as Darwin discovered the law of development of organic nature, so Marx discovered the law of development of human history." Engels put the same level of confidence behind the "scientific" results of evolutionary anthropology: "Just as Cuvier could deduce from the marsupial bone of an animal skeleton found near Paris that it belonged to a marsupial animal and that extinct marsupial animals once lived there, so with the same certainty we can deduce from the historical survival of a system of consanguinity that an extinct form of family once existed which corresponded to it."[33]

For the purposes of writing the scientific economic history of humanity on this new timescale, there was one figure who stood out from the others for Engels: the American anthropologist Lewis Henry Morgan. As noted, Marx was well disposed toward Morgan,[34] certainly as compared with Bachofen and the other Victorian anthropologists. But Engels was positively worshipful, describing Morgan's work as "epoch-making."[35] The reason why is clear: Morgan's schema, unlike those of McLennan or Lubbock, was explicitly laid out in reference to changes in material technology. Morgan proposed connections between kinship, technology, government, and class division, and suggested reasons why each stage was bound to evolve into the next, hinting at the process of dialectical change so central in Marx's thought.[36] Engels overestimated the extent to which Morgan was a materialist, seeing all social change as ultimately propelled by economic change.[37] Still, there was an obvious overlap that Engels sought to exploit. Also, as an American, Morgan appealed to Engels in a way that the other evolutionary anthropologists could not, for Engels saw in Morgan a fellow outsider in the British intellectual marketplace. Engels consistently exaggerated Morgan's outsider status, complaining in the preface to the 1891 edition of *The Origin* that "the chauvinistically inclined English anthropologists are still striving their utmost to kill by silence the revolution which Morgan's discoveries have effected in our conception of primitive society, while they appropriate his results without the slightest compunction."[38]

The other chief influence on Engels as he wrote *The Origin* was Bachofen. The simple fact that Marx and Engels actually *read* Bachofen is significant, since the most influential British anthropologists did not, at least not in any depth.[39] Marx especially must have felt a sense of recognition reading Bachofen. Though the two men came from different classes, religions, and nations, and had arrived at radically opposed political positions, they had come up through the same German university system around the same time. They were both well schooled in the classics and steeped in Hegelianism, Enlightenment philosophy, and German Romanticism. Both spoke of "mastering nature" as a noble and quintessentially human goal.[40]

But poor Bachofen never really stood a chance with Marx or Engels. If Morgan could generously, if somewhat unreflectively, be regarded as a materialist, Bachofen was plainly an idealist. As Engels sneeringly complained at the very outset of *The Origin,* Bachofen made "religion the lever of world history," a sentiment that would read as pure folly to anyone taking a socialist position in the late nineteenth century.[41] In spite of his pointed criticisms, Engels referred to Bachofen as a "mystic of genius" who started "a real revolution." Engels credited Bachofen with being "the first to replace the vague phrases about some unknown primitive state of sexual promiscuity by proofs . . . that the original position of the mothers, as the only certain parents of their children, secured for them, and thus for their whole sex, a higher social status than women have ever enjoyed since."[42]

Given that *The Origin* relies so heavily on Morgan's *Ancient Society* and credits Bachofen's innovations only to dismiss him as a purveyor of "fancies,"[43] it may seem an overstatement to say that Engels's *Origin* melded the two principal forms of matriarchal myth that had emerged by the time he sat down to write. But Bachofen's influence on *The Origin* is pervasive even where it is uncredited. This is especially the case with Engels's descriptions of primitive matriarchal communism, which are far more exalted and vivid than anything Morgan ever wrote. For Engels, the "lower" stages of society give women a position that is "not only free, but honorable," where mothers "are held in high respect." Later Engels speaks in the same uncompromising—and un-British—tone as Bachofen when he declares that early societies were characterized by "the supremacy of the women."[44] Bachofen's nostalgic romance with a matriarchy that could never be recreated became Engels's dream of an idyllic past destined to be revived in the future.

Even before engaging with Bachofen's and Morgan's works, Marx and Engels had envisioned the earliest communal societies as differentiated by gender. In "The German Ideology" they referred to a sexed division of labor, confined, at this point "to a further extension of the natural division of labour imposed by the family."[45] In *The Origin,* Engels elaborates: "The division of labor is purely primitive, between the sexes only. The man fights in the wars, goes hunting and fishing, procures the raw materials of food and the tools necessary for doing so. The woman looks after the house and the preparation of food and clothing, cooks, weaves, sews. They are each master in their own sphere: the man in the forest, the woman in the house."[46] Interestingly, in describing this earliest stage of human life, Engels relied more on Darwin than Morgan,[47] and couched his analysis in the language of biology rather than that of history.[48] At the most basic level, then, Engels held that the relationship between men and women is fixed by biological laws and cannot be expected to change. But at another level, Engels argued that gender relations are conditioned by history. If all prehistoric women are imaginatively left shuttling between the kitchen and nursery, there is nevertheless significant change over the course of history, and thus room for transformations in gender relations, particularly in the realm of marriage. What was "a sacred, eternal, and unchallengeable institution" to most Victorians became, in Engels's *Origin,* a shifting, unstable institution subject to the exigencies of differing modes of production.[49]

"The German Ideology" distinguished between two basic modes of production: production and reproduction, "of one's own in labour and of fresh life in procreation."[50] Once the family exists as a social relationship, however, reproduction becomes simply another nexus of production, not qualitatively different from any other. It is certainly not a second institution running parallel to economic development, as it becomes for Engels in *The Origin,* written thirty-eight years later.[51] As Engels explains:

> According to the materialistic conception, the determining factor in history is, in the final instance, the production and reproduction of immediate life. This, again, is of a twofold character: on the one side, the production of the means of existence, of food, clothing and shelter and the tools necessary for that production; on the other side, the production of human beings themselves, the propagation of the species. The social organization under which the people of a particular historical epoch and a particular country live is determined by both kinds of production: by the stage of development of labor on the one hand and of the family on the other.[52]

By making this move, Engels is able to interpolate various forms of the family as part and parcel of a materialist history of humanity. He can take on the entire apparatus of the consanguine family, the punaluan family, and so on, as developed by Morgan, and impose this directly onto a Marxist time line of economic development.[53] Group marriage (a concept that, as we have seen, was ridiculous to Marx) becomes a cornerstone in Engels's theory,[54] and as a result, an integral part of Marxist anthropology for many decades to follow. And gender—a concept that was to Marx self-evident and not particularly interesting—is freed up to become a topic for political debate and the grounds for the communist adaptation of matriarchal myth.

Engels's views on prehistoric gender relations were not particularly revolutionary.[55] According to Engels, women's roles in primitive communal society were limited to caretaker and domestic goddess. At least these roles were respected. As Engels explains, "In the old economic household, which comprised many couples and their children, the task entrusted to the women of managing the household was as much a public, a socially necessary industry as the procuring of food by the men."[56] The transformation in Engels's schema occurs with the institution of the patriarchal family. As he explains, "Household management lost its public character. It no longer concerned society. It became a private service; the wife became the head servant, excluded from all participation in social production." This was, in Engels's famous phrase, *"the world historical defeat of the female sex."*[57]

Engels has difficulty theorizing the transition to patriarchy. As Maurice Bloch explains in *Marxism and Anthropology,* "When Engels postulated a pre-class stage when there were no conflicting principles and everything was sweetness and light, he had no Marxist way by which to explain historical change." The essential element of internal contradiction was missing, so there was nothing to trigger a new synthesis. In *The Origin,* Bloch argues, Engels imagines a prehistoric matriarchy operating on biological, Darwinian principles of natural selection, which can evolve only as nature would have it unfold. It is only with the advent of "the family, private property, and the state" that history per se begins and then develops through predictable stages of material production. Being forced to theorize a shift from natural/biological to social/constructed is a trap that Marx recognized and into which he assiduously endeavored not to step.[58] For Marx, history was always social history, made by humans interacting with one another, and it was so from the beginning. But for Engels, as for most champions of matriarchal myth, it was important to maintain a stable ideal seated in prehistory as a referent through which to understand the present—this time of history and change—and upon which to model the future: a second period of comparative timelessness, of utopia realized, in which change would be unnecessary. This matriarchal myth clearly mimics the Judeo-Christian account: an original society, completely "natural," is launched upon a tempestuous period of dynamic change owing to human choice to seek knowledge or wealth. In such stories, from there, only one very good choice—whether for Jesus or communism or matriarchy—is needed to restore humans to the perfection of the original utopia.

Like all matriarchalists, though, Engels needs to find a path from prehistory into history; he does so through two mechanisms, one associated with production and the other with reproduction. On the side of production, Engels traces the advent of father right to the practice of pastoralism. The herding of animals, says Engels, produced surplus wealth, and as "the taming of the animals in the first instance and their later tending were the man's work," it was men who accumulated this wealth.[59] This gave men the economic leverage they needed to create the patriarchal family, from which all the misery of history followed in a chain reaction. However, Engels ultimately credits women—in the realm of reproduction—with creating the conditions of their own oppression through "pairing marriage," which set the stage for monogamy and the privatization of reproduction and the family. Like Bachofen, whom he cites, Engels attributes the innovation of monogamy to women's "longing for the right of chastity, of temporary or permanent marriage with one man only, as a way of release" from what Engels regarded as the "oppressive and humiliating" nature of group marriage for women.[60] At first, says Engels, pairing marriage is a private, noninstitutionalized arrangement that doesn't affect property or labor relations within the matriarchal clan. But once the basic form of nuclear family units was in place, men could claim the growing surplus wealth produced by pastoralism for themselves and their children—who were for the first time assuredly theirs, now that sexual relations were monogamous (for women, if not for men, who, as Engels notes, never agreed that fidelity would be their lot in life).[61] Women lost the primary sphere of control that had been theirs under tribal conditions, and their formerly public labor in the household became private servitude under their husband. Eventually women's status was so degraded that the wife was merely "the slave of his [her husband's] lust and a mere instrument for the production of children."[62] Engels declares this to be the first instance of economic class, when a benign, "natural" division of labor between the sexes develops into an "antagonism between man and woman in monogamous marriage." Along with economic class comes class oppression.[63]

This first class oppression was hardly the last in the history Engels traced in *The Origin*. The early practice of linking production directly with consumption yielded to the possibility of production for exchange: rearing extra animals not for their meat or milk, but for the prospect of trading them for other items of value. New types of production—especially handicrafts—heightened the practice of exchange to the point where a new class emerged, a mercantile class that was not productive at all, but merely facilitated exchange among the various productive sectors of society.[64] Need for more labor, more production, gave rise to the practice of war, through which slaves were procured.[65]

What Engels did *not* say about matriarchal civilizations is that they involved goddess worship or women serving as the religious functionaries (priestesses) of their societies. This would have been contrary to Marxist theory regarding religion. If women were in fact powerful in prehistory, they would have had no need for religion to compensate them for lacks in their earthly lives. In general, Marx and Engels refrained from commenting on religion in prehistoric societies, the sole exception being Marx's statement in his notebooks to the effect that the presence of powerful goddesses in the ancient Greek and Roman pantheons was in part motivated by the memory of the women of earlier primitive societies. But Marx then says that "the other half" of the explanation for the appearance of these powerful goddesses is an "inversion of their actual position in Greek society; it is also the justification in the mythology of their constraint in that low position, and the expression of the hopeful fantasy of its betterment in another world."[66] We will have to look beyond Marx and Engels to see the reappearance of a strong theory of prehistoric goddess worship in matriarchal myth.

In spite of the disaster effected by the patriarchal family, Engels was on board for a happy ending, like all his matriarchalist peers. He did not align himself with Bachofen, who anticipated further refinement of a system of male domination, or with those liberal Victorian anthropologists who envisioned an orderly progression toward enfranchisement within the existing socioeconomic structure. Instead, Engels predicted a new era of women's equality that would be realized only after the toppling of capitalism. Divested of its economic underpinning, male dominance would utterly collapse.[67] Engels refrained from giving a precise account of what post-capitalist gender relations would look like, but that didn't stop him from offering tantalizing speculations:

> With the transfer of the means of production into common ownership, the single family ceases to be the economic unit of society. Private housekeeping is transformed into a social industry. The care and education of the children becomes a public affair; society looks after all children alike, whether they are legitimate or not. This removes all the anxiety about the "consequences," which today is the most social—moral as well as economic—factor that prevents a girl from giving herself completely to the man she loves. Will not that suffice to bring about the gradual growth of unconstrained sexual intercourse and with it a more tolerating public opinion in regard to a maiden's honor and a woman's shame?[68]

Indeed, sexual freedom seems to be one of Engels's favorite themes regarding a coming age of gender equality, as seen in this excerpt from *The Origin:*

> What we can now conjecture about the way in which such relations will be ordered after the impending overthrow of capitalist production is mainly of a negative character, limited for the most part to what will disappear. But what will there be new? That will be answered when a new generation has grown up: a generation of men who never in their lives have known what it is to buy a woman's surrender with money or any other social instrument of power, a generation of women who have never known what it is to give themselves to a man from any other considerations than real love, or to refuse to give themselves to their lover from fear of the economic consequences.[69]

Prior to *The Origin,* the attitudes of Marx and Engels toward women were fairly conventional for their time. Certainly neither man was a feminist. Marx, for example, is known to have proclaimed his preference for male over female children on more than one occasion. Upon the birth of his daughter Franziska in 1851, he wrote to Engels, "My wife was delivered of a girl, unfortunately, and not a *garçon.*"[70] Then when his daughter Jenny bore a son in 1881, he wrote her a letter of congratulation, adding, "I prefer for myself the 'male' sex for the new generation that is born at this turning point of history,"[71] indicating that even late in his life Marx did not expect women to play as dramatic a role as men in the downfall of capitalism. When asked in an 1865 parlor game with his wife and daughter to name the virtues he prized most in men and in women, he answered "strength" and "weakness," respectively.[72]

What was true in Marx's personal life carried over to his political life. In 1866, both Marx and Engels approved a statement by the German section of the International Workers Association that read, in part, "The rightful work of women and mothers is in the home and family caring for, supervising, and providing the first education for the children, which it is true presupposes that the women and children themselves receive an adequate training. Alongside the solemn duties of the man and father in public life and the family the woman and mother should stand for the cosiness and poetry of domestic life, bring grace and beauty to social relations and be an ennobling influence on the increase of humanity's enjoyment of life."[73] This doesn't sound feminist to most twenty-first century ears, but in the late nineteenth century it was one feminist viewpoint. The "special" gifts of women (usually as mothers) were portrayed in glowing terms, and the sanctity of the domestic sphere was supposed to be protected so that its purportedly beneficial effects could ripple out from home to public life. So the fact that Marx and Engels were committed to protectionist laws that would prevent women from working need not disqualify them as feminist-friendly. But even protectionist laws were of less concern to Marx and Engels than the engaging prospect of refining a theory and history of economic determinism. Gender was never high on their agenda.[74]

One has to wonder, then, why gender equality became so surpassingly important in Engels's *Origin* in 1884. As we have seen, Marx's views did not change prior to his death. Engels was clearly striking out on his own. Charles Fourier could not have been the inspiration. In *The Communist Manifesto* of 1848, Marx and Engels were rather dismissive of the "Fourierists" and their phalansteries. While describing Fourier and his supporters as revolutionaries, they accused Fourier's followers of being reactionary, trying "to deaden the class struggle and to reconcile the class antagonisms" while separating themselves off into "pocket editions of the New Jerusalem."[75] Bachofen and the Victorian anthropologists are the obvious place to look for the roots of Engels's incipient feminism, but Engels's interest in their work is most likely effect rather than cause.

The direct instigation for Engels's sudden interest in women's rights—and for the writing of *The Origin*—was almost certainly the enormously popular *Woman and Socialism,* written by German labor leader August Bebel. *Woman and Socialism,* in its first edition, had not even a glimmer of hope for women's future in a purported matriarchal past.[76] But it did talk of women: how capitalism failed them while communism could free them. In one of the odd twists characteristic of the history of matriarchal myth, Bebel, having inspired Engels's interest in women's status, later adopted Engels's matriarchal speculations from *The Origin* and took them to a vastly wider audience than they otherwise would have known.

THE FIRST CHAPTER OF AUGUST BEBEL'S
WOMAN AND SOCIALISM

Woman and Socialism, a wildly popular book, appeared in different editions both before and after Engels's *Origin,* and it is easy to see the influence each had upon the other. It seems probable that Engels took the title of *The Origin* from a statement Bebel made at the outset of the second edition of *Woman and Socialism* (then titled *Woman in the Past, Present and Future*), published in 1883: "Thus marriage arose [and] the foundations of private property, of the family, tribe and state, were laid."[77]

August Bebel was a German labor leader who by the late 1870s was already highly regarded throughout the socialist movement. Bebel was born in 1840 to a Prussian officer and his wife, who quickly added two younger sons to their family. Bebel's early life was marked by poverty and loss. His father died of consumption when he was four years old; his mother married her husband's brother, who beat the children until he too succumbed to consumption a mere two years later, just after the death of Bebel's youngest brother. Bebel's mother was forced to move in with her mother, where she supported the family by sewing military gloves. After her own long bout with consumption, Bebel's mother died when he was thirteen years old. Bebel was forced to withdraw from school. He and his brother Carl were each taken in by one of their maternal aunts and began apprenticeships. Bebel trained as a turner, working fourteen hours a day on a lathe to produce building materials. In his late teens, Bebel began traveling from town to town throughout German-speaking Europe (Austria, Switzerland, and Germany), meeting other journeymen and finding employment with local turners. When he was eighteen, Bebel's brother Carl died, leaving him the sole survivor of his immediate family. At the age of twenty, Bebel took the last of his long journeys when he walked by foot from Salzburg to Leipzig, where he was to live and work for most of his adult life.[78]

Bebel began his political life after he settled in Leipzig, when he convinced his five fellow turners to strike, demanding better lunches, shorter hours, and improved sleeping accommodations. He was still in his early twenties when he helped to found the League of German Workers' Associations in 1863. This was the same year he married Julie Otto, who was to keep his turner's shop, his home, and his political work going during his many stints in jail for treason against the German Empire and violations of the Anti-Socialist Laws. Bebel became a leader of heroic proportions, heading up the German Social Democratic Party and being elected to the Reichstag again and again throughout his adult life. His picture hung on many a living room wall in Germany, and his books—especially *Woman and Socialism*—were devoured by people from all walks of life.[79]

FIGURE 16. August Bebel (1840–1913), German labor leader and author of *Woman and Socialism*

Bebel's interest in women's issues began early in his political life. He was an invited guest at the first German Women's Congress in 1865,[80] and for some years in the mid-1860s was a close associate of Moritz Müller, a businessman and factory owner who was at the time a leading figure in the feminist movement.[81] It was not until the 1870s, though, that Bebel began to develop the feminist convictions that would characterize his politics for the remainder of his life. Just prior to this, in 1869, Bebel had written a draft program for the Social Democratic Party that called for universal suffrage for men, but not for women. His view was the conventional protectionist one. He envisioned a future in which women need not "compete with men economically" but would instead "assume the position where they belong by nature and right, in the family, in order to raise children and manage the household."[82] By the mid-1870s, Bebel was self-consciously including women in his audience ("Whenever I say readers I mean as a matter of course the reader of both sexes") and giving voice to what today would be called a social constructionist view of gender ("One still hears everyday the nonsense about women's natural callings, which are defined exclusively in terms of domesticity and the family").[83] Abandoning his earlier protectionist views, Bebel advocated the development of traditionally "masculine" virtues in women and vice versa.[84] In 1876, Bebel began lecturing on the topic of "the position of women in the present State and with regard to Socialism." By his own report, these lectures were standing room only and were received with great enthusiasm by both women—who were exhorted to influence their husbands' votes—and men.[85] In 1879, the first edition of Bebel's *Die Frau und der Sozialismus* (Woman and Socialism) was published, a declaration of women's equality to men and an unapologetic call for full political and economic rights for women.[86]

Having left school at fourteen, Bebel was self-taught. The first socialist writings that inspired Bebel were those of the German socialist Ferdinand Lassalle, and it was not until the late 1860s and early 1870s that he read anything at all by Marx or Engels.[87] Bebel's feminist writing began in the mid-1870s when he was in prison for conspiracy to commit treason and insulting the emperor. He authored a fourteen-page essay, *Über die Gegenwärtige und Künftige Stellung der Frau* (On the Present and Future Position of Woman).[88] Bebel himself notes that he "was induced to write it" by his "study of the French socialistic and communistic Utopias," principally those of Fourier.[89] *Woman and Socialism* was written during another term in prison, from 1877 to 1878, "for insulting the chancellor and denouncing militarism."[90] Significantly, his other literary production during this prison term was a biography of Fourier.[91]

Virtually from the moment it came out, *Woman and Socialism* was a classic. The praise heaped upon it by Bebel's contemporaries included remarks like these:

> "For us young socialists Bebel's book was not just a programme, it was a gospel."
> "It was from this book that the proletarian masses derived their socialism."
> "[It was] the veritable bible for young Socialists."
> "[It] undoubtedly created a greater belief in socialism in the popular mind than Karl Marx's biting criticism of bourgeois economics was ever able to."[92]

Alexandra Kollontai, a communist leader during the Russian Revolution, called *Woman and Socialism* "the woman's Bible," while Clara Zetkin, who was to succeed August Bebel as the leading socialist authority on women, rhapsodized that *Woman and Socialism* was "more than a book, it was an event, a deed."[93]

It is remarkable that in the late nineteenth century, a book with the term *woman* prominently featured in both text and title should be "a major socialist primer"[94] for budding socialists, male and female alike. No doubt part of the book's appeal was that it was almost immediately banned under Germany's 1878 Anti-Socialist Laws, and therefore had the thrill of the forbidden. As Marx's daughter, Eleanor Marx-Aveling, wryly remarked about the prohibition on *Woman and Socialism,* "This has increased at once the difficulty of obtaining the book, and the number of those that obtain it."[95] The first edition was 180 pages long and was written as one long essay, with little structure or organization. An additional imprisonment from 1882 to 1883 (for distributing prohibited leaflets) allowed Bebel to produce a significantly revised and expanded edition of 220 pages that was released under the title *Women in the Past, Present and Future.* The revised title was aimed— unsuccessfully—at avoiding the ban on socialist literature. In spite of the ban, the book attained a wide release; it was printed in Leipzig, smuggled into Zurich, and from there distributed throughout central Europe.[96] Translations into virtually all European languages appeared very quickly.[97] Over its fifty-three editions, eight of which involved substantial revisions, the book grew to 472 pages in length and represented four decades of Bebel's thinking and research on the topic.[98]

What is significant for our purposes is the shift that occurred between the second edition, published in 1883, and the third edition, published in 1884. In the first two editions, Bebel claimed that women had always and everywhere been oppressed by men; in the third and all subsequent editions, he offered the account of matriarchal prehistory given by Engels in *The Origin.* The second edition of *Woman and Socialism* begins with this sentence: "From the beginning of time oppression has been the common lot of woman and the labouring man."[99] The edition published after Engels's *Origin* revises this first sentence to read: "Woman and the workingman have, since old, had this in common—*oppression.*"[100] But then Bebel the orator comes to the fore, proclaiming, "The favorite phrase—a phrase that the ignorant or impostors daily smite our ears with on the subject of the relations between man and woman, and between the poor and the rich—'it always has been so,' and the conclusion drawn therefrom—'it will always be so,' *is in every sense of the word, false, superficial and trumped-up.*"[101] From there, Bebel sallies forth to tell a happier story, the tale of a matriarchal past. This is little more than a summary of Engels's *Origin,* with prominent attention given to Morgan and Bachofen, and it is a story with which Bebel is soon done. For fewer than forty pages Bebel skips back and forth repeatedly between matriarchy and the mechanisms that brought it to an end before moving decisively to the study of patriarchal societies for the remainder of his book.[102]

In summary, the sequence in the communist adaptation of matriarchal myth is this: Engels—who was generally little interested in matters of gender prior to his entrée into the field in 1884—was given the necessary incentive to write *The Origin* because of the enormous popularity of Bebel's *Woman and Socialism.* Bebel, in turn, took Engels's account of prehistory to be the accurate one and substituted it for his own in later editions of the book.

Orthodox Marxists have suggested that Engels wrote *The Origin* not because he wanted to cash in on Bebel's literary gold mine, but because he noticed that Bebel was expounding falsehoods about prehistory and wanted to see these corrected.[103] There is little evidence of this. The relationship between Bebel and Engels was friendly and collegial, extending to personal letters and family visits, and during the time Engels was writing *The Origin,* he and Bebel corresponded about other matters without ever mentioning their varying accounts of human prehistory.[104] It seems likely that the two men saw their works as complementary rather than competing. Bebel's book, for all that it begins with "women's past," with prehistory and ancient history, is mainly a straightforward socialist analysis of capitalist society and a call for its demise, with gender frequently demoted to subtext (which helps to explain why the book could function as a socialist primer).[105] Engels's *Origin,* in contrast, did not delve into an analysis of present capitalist society—this having been covered at great length in other works by him and Marx—but offered a detailed treatment of prehistory.[106]

There would have been no reason for Bebel to question Engels's account of humanity's matriarchal past. Engels had read the ethnographies; Bebel had not. Engels was working from Marx's notes; Bebel was not. Engels was a scholar, a "university man"; Bebel had no formal education beyond grammar school. Engels was self-consciously a philosopher of socialism; Bebel was a proletarian and an activist. Engels saw himself (and Marx too, of course) as an original thinker, a theoretician; Bebel saw himself as a popularizer of socialist theory for the working masses, to whom he could speak in their own language. Naturally Bebel would have accepted Engels's authority on the matter of the prehistoric status of women.[107]

In spite of his near total dependence on Engels's *Origin,* Bebel does introduce a few small innovations into his tale of matriarchal origins. The first is his treatment of Christianity. In his discussion of women's status in earlier societies, Bebel is eager to save early Christianity from the general opprobrium meted out to patriarchal society. In later editions of *Woman and Socialism,* Bebel writes that Christianity "personified opposition against the beastly materialism that prevailed among the rich and mighty ones in the Roman empire; it represented rebellion against the oppression and disdain of the masses." With an anti-Semitic twist, Bebel lays Christianity's attitude toward women at the doorstep of Judaism: "Since it [Christianity] sprang from Judaism that knew woman only as an oppressed being, and since it was biased by the biblical conception that she is the source of all evil, it preached the disdain of woman; it preached abstinence and destruction of the flesh."[108]

Another innovation in Bebel's matriarchal myth is his accepting attitude toward prehistoric sexuality. As we have seen, sex is a constant referent in matriarchal myth. In the eyes of Bachofen and the Victorian anthropologists, chastity is a great advance over the steamy scenes of total licentiousness they imagine for prehistory (though one has to suspect that the mere fact that they *talk* about promiscuous sex, even as they conspicuously shudder at the prospect, was enticing). A few of the Victorian anthropologists made primitive promiscuity—or at least some happy medium between that and sexual repressiveness—sound slightly appealing. And Engels of course opened the door to a frank appreciation of the prospect of sexual freedom in the future. But Engels stopped well short of endorsing free sex as the natural conclusion of matriarchal myth, if only by crediting women, as Bachofen had done, with inventing the pairing marriage as a restriction upon the too complete abandon of group sex.

Bebel, in contrast, took on the role of apologist for primitive promiscuity. Freely acknowledging that by late-nineteenth century standards, primitive sexuality appears as "a monstrosity, a mire of immorality," Bebel asks his readers to step back and adopt an attitude of cultural relativism: "As each stage in social development has its own methods of production, thus each stage also has its own code of morals, which is only a reflection of its social conditions. Morals are determined by custom, and customs correspond to the innermost nature, that is, to the social necessities of any given period." Bebel derides the opponents of matriarchal myth for failing to take this relativistic attitude toward sexuality, accusing them of an inability to see beyond "their bourgeois prejudices."[109] Bebel says quite pointedly that his contemporaries have it wrong when it comes to their attitudes toward sexuality: "Of all the natural desires that are a part of human life, beside the desire for food in order to live, the sexual desire is strongest. The impulse of race preservation is the most powerful expression of the 'will to live.' This impulse is deeply implanted in every normally developed human being, and upon attaining maturity its satisfaction is essential to physical and mental welfare."[110] Elsewhere, Bebel suggests that sexual abstinence is the cause of numerous physical and mental illnesses, including suicide. He does not end as a proponent of unrestrained sexuality; in fact, he argues that too much sex is even more detrimental than not enough.[111] But Bebel was the first to temper his horror at primitive promiscuity with a strong dose of criticism of present attitudes toward sexuality, a theme that became central in twentieth-century versions of matriarchal myth.

The practical upshot of Bebel's inclusion of Engels's version of matriarchal myth in the later editions of his *Woman and Socialism* is that these theories found their way to a large and varied group of socialists and feminists over the next thirty-plus years, during which time *Woman and Socialism* continued to enjoy great popularity.[112] Though Engels's *Origin* is more widely read today, it was positively lost in the shadow of Bebel's *Woman and Socialism* during the late nineteenth century.[113] Bebel offered all the matriarchal theory that the average socialist reader either wanted or needed. Knowledge that there were previous matriarchal societies was encouraging. Beyond that, the interest was in women's present op-pression and hope for future equality.

The theory of matriarchal origins bore the imprimatur of both the premier surviving socialist theorist (Engels) and one of the most prominent socialist ac-tivists (Bebel); it was also taken up by others in the movement. In France, Paul Lafargue, the head of the French Communist Party and husband to Marx's daugh-ter Laura, did what Bebel had done in Germany. Lafargue's *La Propriété, Origines et Evolution,* much indebted to Engels's *Origin,* was published in 1895. If any-thing, it was more stridently confident about women's supremacy in prehistoric societies than Engels's book had been.[114] Lafargue also reintroduced Bachofenian ideas about prehistoric women serving as religious functionaries. He writes of the "awesome role of priestess and guardian of the mysteries that woman had in the primitive community," a role he expected women to assume again in a com-ing communist utopia.[115] Another prominent socialist, Heinrich Cunow, offered a mild critique of *The Origin,* arguing that Engels was mistaken when he put women's child-bearing capacities into a separate category as a qualitatively dif-ferent form of productivity (a criticism with which Marx would likely have agreed).[116] But neither of these men displaced or even added much to the work of Engels and Bebel. Later, socialist and communist women entered the discussion of matriarchal myth as well, though oddly, they tended to be less enthusiastic than their male counterparts and even began a series of compromises that helped to end the first reign of matriarchal myth within communist circles. In this they were clearly different from their liberal sisters, who did not hesitate to make use of matriarchal myth in their quest to gain equality for women.

FEMINISTS ON THE FIRST WAVE

Socialist and communist leaders were the first narrators of matriarchal myth to draw unambiguously feminist lessons from the story, to regard patriarchy as downfall rather than progress. In spite of Bebel's earnest efforts, however, femi-nism did not truly take hold in the growing workers' movement of the late nine-teenth century. Ironically, as we will see in a later chapter, female socialist lead-ers, as well as male ones, put the feminist agenda on the back burner. Liberal and radical feminists in England, and especially in the United States, took a firmer hold on matriarchal myth, but it was never more than a small minority of first-wave feminists who promoted the myth. Some who did were prominent activ-ists; others were more off-beat, more esoteric in their interests, experimenting with theosophy and Goddess worship. Thus there was variety in first-wave femi-nist adaptations of matriarchal myth in spite of the fact that most first-wave feminists—both leadership and rank and file—never took an interest in the sta-tus of women in prehistoric times. This is ironic, since ideas of matriarchy and ancient goddess worship were more mainstream in the late nineteenth century than they would be in the late twentieth century, when feminists became more intent on bending matriarchal myth to their own purposes. Yet the stories told by these earliest feminist proponents of matriarchal myth are surprisingly similar in content to those told by second-wave feminists beginning in the 1970s. This is not the result of direct transmission. Second-wave feminists relied on some of the same sources as first-wave feminists (though they had access to many new ones as well), but they did not rely on first-wave feminists themselves.[117] Nevertheless, almost to the letter, these two generations of feminists, separated by nearly a century, told the same basic narrative of matriarchal utopia and its overthrow. Many things changed over those hundred years: notions of gender roles, feminist theory, and of course the breadth of our knowledge of prehistory. But the themes of feminist matriarchal myth remained intact.

Those liberal and radical feminists who adopted matriarchal myth in the last years of the nineteenth century did not borrow it from Engels or Bebel, as their socialist sisters did, but rather from Morgan and the British anthropologists. Some feminists in continental Europe read and embraced Bachofen,[118] while others criticized him,[119] but Anglo-American feminists merely referred to Bachofen's work without demonstrating any real knowledge of it.[120] When feminist narrators of matriarchal myth enunciated a materialist account of history, they mainly repeated arguments originally made by Lewis Henry Morgan.[121] More often, they drew on the work of the British anthropologists, repeating soon-to-be arcane notions about "marriage by capture" and "fraternal polyandry" as described by John Ferguson McLennan in *Primitive Marriage*.[122] Even Elizabeth Cady Stanton, who spent comparatively little time defending the matriarchal thesis—though she clearly accepted it—dwelled on the sort of ethnographic examples of which the Victorian anthropologists were so fond.[123] Like their predecessors, first-wave feminists also made use of classical sources. Stanton, in a late echo of Lafitau, even deemed the Touaregs of northern Africa to be descendants of the supposedly matriarchal Lycians of the classical era.[124] First-wave feminists seemed most enamored of Vesta and Cybele, the great mother goddesses of the Roman Empire, but were also eager to include feminine deities from throughout the ancient world, and Hindu goddesses, with whom British women were just then becoming acquainted.[125]

The most obvious change first-wave feminists made to the myth of matriarchal prehistory was the same one that socialist narrators made: they turned a myth of progress into a myth of regress. Human civilization starts well and then deteriorates, instead of starting badly and improving over time. But socialist concerns with technology, property, and government were left aside as first-wave feminists zeroed in on gender and sex as the most salient—or sometimes the only—driving force in the grand tides of human history. Once one

FIGURE 17. Elizabeth Cady Stanton (1815–1902), American feminist activist
and sometime partisan of the matriarchal theory

sets economic and other considerations on the back burner, matriarchal myth
becomes an even more intensely bipolar story than it was in the hands of its first
narrators. Gender, in the minds of virtually all proponents of the myth of matriarchal prehistory, is a dualistic proposition: people are either female or male,
and that is believed to make all the difference. Once society is characterized
foremost by its choices regarding the relationship between females and males,
there are really only three options available: male dominance, female dominance, and sexual egalitarianism (with, perhaps, some gradations in between).
The addition of other considerations, such as the role of private property, can
complicate things. For example, in *The Origin,* Engels walks the reader through
at least four different economic stages in human history and suggests that there
could have been many others as well.[126] Morgan, describing a sequence of kinship and productive technologies, quickly came up with seven stages. Liberal
feminists, in contrast, stuck single-mindedly to the struggle for social equality

between the sexes, making it difficult for stages to proliferate as they had for other matriarchalists.

Most changes first-wave feminists made to the matriarchal myth they inherited were matters of emphasis. But four modifications stand out as more extensive than this. Oddly enough, given later history, the principal innovation first-wave feminists brought to matriarchal myth was the further integration of Darwinian evolutionary theory into the narrative.[127] First-wave feminist narrators of matriarchal myth were evolutionists, along with the rest of the liberal intelligentsia in Victorian culture. For them, much more so than for socialist matriarchalists, the historical decline in women's status had to be reconciled with their evolutionist assumptions. First-wave feminists managed this dilemma by trading cultural evolution for biological evolution and specifying that females, rather than males, led the way. The sociobiology that the Victorian anthropologists only touched on before abandoning matriarchal myth altogether was seized upon by first-wave feminists as confirmation of their theories about the development and ultimate fate of gender relations.

To this feminists made a second modification, creating a stronger role for motherhood than any before them, save Bachofen perhaps, had attempted. Cultural as well as biological, motherhood as understood by these first-wave feminists could explain virtually everything about the paradise that was lost and might again be reclaimed.

The third modification first-wave feminists made to matriarchal myth was the inclusion of a prominent role for religion as both evidence for and a major catalyst for the shift from matriarchy to patriarchy. Except in rare cases, this was not a straightforward adaptation of Bachofen, but a new version of how goddess-centered, priestess-maintained religions prevailed in prehistoric times, and how their replacement by god-centered, priest-maintained religions spelled an end to the matriarchal era. Dionysus and Apollo had no role to play in this story; it was the reign of Yahweh that was problematic.

The fourth shift had to do with the purported promiscuity of "primitive" societies. Flatly rejecting the Victorian anthropologists—and siding with Bachofen's notion of Demetrian matriarchy, whether they knew it or not—first-wave feminists insisted that the women of the matriarchal era restrained the expression of human sexuality to monogamous marriage.

Charles Darwin, with his clear statements about male superiority and the evolutionary fitness of male dominance,[128] doesn't seem the likeliest character to inspire dreams of prehistoric matriarchy among first-wave feminists. And yet in the preface to *The Evolution of Woman*, published in 1894, Eliza Burt Gamble, a schoolteacher and suffragist from Michigan, claims that it was not until 1886, when she first read Darwin's *The Descent of Man*, that she "became impressed with the belief that the theory of evolution, as enunciated by scientists, furnishes

FIGURE 18. Eliza Burt Gamble (1841–1920), American suffragist and author of *The Evolution of Woman* and several books on ancient and contemporary religion

much evidence going to show that the female among all the orders of life, man included, represents a higher stage of development than the male."[129] This was *after* she read the works of the British anthropologists, which, for whatever reason, failed to light her feminist imagination.

First-wave feminists construed Darwin as providing evidence for prehistoric matriarchy primarily through his theory of sexual selection. Unlike natural selection, which works on both sexes simultaneously, sexual selection is said to be responsible for sex-specific adaptive traits. As Darwin explains: "Sexual selection depends on the success of certain individuals over others of the same sex, in relation to the propagation of the species. . . . It is a struggle between individuals of one sex, generally the males, for the possession of the other sex. The result is not death to the unsuccessful competitor, but few or no offspring."[130] Darwin's classic example of sexual selection is the brilliant plumage of the peacock, used to attract—for mating purposes—the comparatively drab peahen. When it came to human beings, though, Darwin placed the emphasis not on female choice and male displays of attractiveness (as with the peacock and peahen), but on male-male competition for mating rights with women, who are given little or no choice but to submit to the winning male. First-wave feminist matriarchalists rejected this emphasis and focused instead on the element of female choice in sexual selection, asserting that this was obvious scientific proof that the evolutionary destiny of the human race lay in women's hands. Eliza Burt Gamble made this connection, asserting that "sexual selection . . . resembles artificial selection, save that the female takes the place of the human breeder."[131] In the early twentieth century, for some feminists, this quickly became a full-out eugenics program. For example, Frances Swiney, president of a local branch of the National Union of Women's Suffrage Societies in England and one of the most prolific supporters of the matriarchal thesis, spoke of eugenics in frankly racist terms, enjoining her peers to inculcate in their sons' minds "that racial pride which would scorn union, however transitory, with a woman of a lower race," so that "the great Anglo-Saxon nation" could "keep its blood-royal pure and undefiled."[132]

However, Swiney belongs to a later chapter of the history of matriarchal myth, after the turn of the twentieth century. She was among the few British women championing the feminist potential of matriarchal myth during the first wave of the feminist movement. For the most part, those feminists who became excited about the story of matriarchal prehistory were Americans. Elizabeth Cady Stanton and especially Matilda Joslyn Gage, both leaders in the women's suffrage movement, used matriarchal myth rhetorically to argue for women's rights. Women could be trusted to manage social power, they said, because they had done so for many millennia during the infancy and childhood of the human race.

Like most nineteenth-century narrators of matriarchal myth, first-wave feminists believed that women's character inhered first and foremost in motherhood, certainly in prehistoric times, and usually thereafter as well. This was no mere fact of parturition and lactation, as many of the British anthropologists had construed it. Motherhood was a morally superior form of human interchange. It was the guiding light of humanity as it made its struggling way upwards out of savagery—if savagery it was, and how could it be, if there were mothers, then as now? This idealization of motherhood was of course much the same as Bachofen's: a romantic, Victorian vision of Mother as the sweet, suffering, all-giving source of human love. As mothers, women were believed to be, in a timeless way, a superior type of being. As Eliza Burt Gamble put it, "Maternal love . . . is divine, uncreated, eternal."[133]

But this immutability rubbed uncomfortably up against the historicizing element in evolutionism, which, as we have seen, was as popular with first-wave feminists as it was with their male peers. If evolutionary rhetoric was to prove successful for feminist ends, motherhood had to be historically created via developmental processes inhering in biological givens, and this "progress" had to take place against a backdrop of (albeit temporary) decline: the triumph of patriarchy.

FIGURE 19. Matilda
Joslyn Gage (1826–98),
American suffragist and
early champion of the
prehistoric religion of
the Goddess

The most urgent matter of business in reconstructing prehistory along feminist lines was to displace the theory that "man the hunter" was responsible for the evolution of humanity to its present height, and instead give that honor to mothers. Elizabeth Cady Stanton rose to this challenge. In a speech to the National Council of Women in February 1891, she offered the opinion that "the wily hunter, who lived on uncooked food and slept on the ground, wherever night found him," was involved in "rude activities" that "developed but few of his faculties." Meanwhile, Stanton said, women of the same era were "learning the great lessons of life" through care for their newborn children: "What love and tenderness helpless infancy calls out; what intelligence and activity its necessities compel; what forethought and responsibility in providing for herself and children it involves."[134]

Motherhood didn't just initiate the first steps toward human community; feminist matriarchalists saw it as the ultimate ground of virtually all technologies and institutions that Victorian-era society held valuable. Prehistoric women had discovered fire, invented pottery, and domesticated plants and animals, not to mention developing medicine, language, theology, and philosophy. And they did all this while cultivating "the arts of peace, and the sentiments of kinship, and all there was of human love and home life."[135] In general, the ideal of motherhood for these early feminist matriarchalists had to do with the actual practices of mothering: feeding, tending, rearing . . . as one might expect from a matriarchal myth striving to lodge some of its truisms in anthropological evolutionism, in which behavior plays such a strong role.[136]

This glorification of mother love was so rhapsodic that it gave way rather easily to the divinization of motherhood in the form of the Great Mother Goddess. Most first-wave feminists spoke of the worship of a mother goddess in prehistoric times, or at least claimed that the pantheons of prehistoric cultures were dominated by goddesses in preference to gods.[137] Often the anthropological doctrine of "survivals" was invoked to suggest that women's role in ancient Greek, Roman, and Teutonic religions was the remnant of their far greater power during the time of the matriarchy.[138] Of the first-wave feminist advocates of matriarchal myth, it was Matilda Joslyn Gage who treated the purported goddess religions of matriarchal prehistory at greatest length. Gage was, among American feminists, one of the most radical, especially as she grew older and came to identify the church as a cornerstone of patriarchy, one with which feminists could brook no compromise. Most significant for the later history of feminist matriarchal myth, Gage claimed that according to matriarchal religion, nature is permeated with the sacred. She began to assemble a set of what she took to be symbolic referents to the goddess: the circle, the sphere, the egg, a ship or ark, and so forth.[139]

The most pronounced change first-wave feminists made to the picture of matriarchal society they had inherited from their male predecessors was to claim unequivocally that the earliest societies were not hotbeds of sexual promiscuity, but islands of calm, measured monogamy overseen by naturally chaste women. Aside from a comment made in passing by Elizabeth Cady Stanton to the effect that fatherhood was unknown prehistorically because sexual relations were "transitory and promiscuous," first-wave feminists were united in their conviction that the widely held notion of primitive promiscuity was a fantasy in the minds of male anthropologists. Drawing on no evidence whatsoever (or at least none that they cited), they asserted that monogamy was the creation of the matriarchate.[140] Men did not create monogamy to ensure that any progeny were their own biological offspring, or because they began to favor one concubine over another. Rather, it was women who created monogamy, and they did so as a result of their natural impulses as women. Eliza Burt Gamble, for example, universalizes monogamy not only as a female human trait but as one characteristic of "the orders of life below mankind" in which female sexual selection predominates. She explains that whereas "the male is ready to pair with any female, she, on the other hand, when free to choose, can be induced to accept the attentions only of the one which by his courage, bravery, or personal beauty has won her favors."[141]

First-wave feminists did not imagine a prehistoric monogamy exactly like the one they knew in the Victorian era. Carefully avoiding the impression that they were advocating sexual freedom, they constructed a matriarchal era that made room for serial monogamy and divorce, and that attached no particular value to virginity.[142] Promiscuity, the hallmark of the earliest human societies for earlier theorists, was instead applied by first-wave feminists to the patriarchy: "The sacrifice of woman to man's baser passions has ever been the distinguishing characteristic of the Patriarchate," wrote Matilda Joslyn Gage.[143]

Like later feminist narrators of matriarchal myth, first-wave feminists had trouble explaining why a patriarchal revolution would have occurred, given that the matriarchal era was so peaceful and prosperous. Eliza Burt Gamble wrestles with this mystery, wondering that "as a stream may not rise higher than its source, or as the creature may not surpass its creator in excellence, it is difficult to understand the process by which man . . . has become superior to woman." Most first-wave feminists did not follow the evolutionary anthropologists' lead in blaming the patriarchal revolution on men's discovery of biological paternity. As we have seen, prehistoric ignorance of paternity is generally attributed to two possible causes: either people didn't understand the mechanism of conception, or they were so sexually promiscuous that they could never know who an individual child's father was. First-wave feminists appear to have credited prehistoric humans with understanding that conception required sexual intercourse. And having stipulated that matriarchal peoples were monogamous, first-wave feminists implied that the paternity of individual children was easily identified. So instead these feminists looked to social factors to explain the transition to patriarchy, settling most often on slavery, war, or both. Elizabeth Cady Stanton found the headwaters of patriarchy in wars of conquest and wars for territory, from which women withdrew, since these violated "the tenderest sentiments of their nature." Willing only to be "angels of mercy to minister to the wounded and the dying," women stood aside while man took over as "ruler, tribal organizer, tribal father."[144] Ultimately Gamble followed McLennan in postulating a growing practice of "marriage by capture," in which women reigned supreme within their own tribes, but men, who wandered farther from home, made use of the opportunity to take captive women from other tribes and to treat them as slaves rather than as mothers of the tribe. Soon all women had to fear being taken captive and had to rely on the protection of their menfolk, thus instituting patriarchy.[145]

It is no wonder that first-wave feminists found matriarchal myth attractive. In a few bold narrative strokes, it seemed to set the feminist movement free from the charge of their critics that male dominance was biological and eternal, and therefore inevitable and unchangeable. But at the same time that matriarchal myth introduced a strong note of historicism to gender relations, it incorporated cutting-edge biological theories that would make their political arguments potentially more convincing to an educated audience of the late nineteenth century. Matriarchal myth neatly undid the patriarchal knot held in place by centuries of philosophy and natural science regarding sex and gender, and it did so with the sort of good story that could easily function as a rhetorical device to arouse commitment to the feminist cause.

All this was done self-consciously. First-wave feminists were well aware of what they were trying to accomplish in their adoption of matriarchal myth, and seemed to find it genuinely puzzling that others did not draw from it what they believed were the obvious conclusions. If female dominance, or even sexual egalitarianism, had at one time been the rule, then male dominance could not, by definition, be the only possibility for the human race. Matriarchy in the past provided precedent for matriarchy—or at least something different from patriarchy—in the future.

Furthermore, first-wave feminists claimed that women had held a position at the forefront of human society for a very long time. For optimal use-value as a feminist myth, it was necessary that the matriarchy dwarf the patriarchy in duration. And by common feminist consensus, it did. Late nineteenth- and early twentieth-century feminists rarely dealt in dates, which at any rate were under significant dispute as scientists debated the antiquity of humankind. Elizabeth Cady Stanton did take a stab at estimating the actual spans of matriarchal and patriarchal time: "Without going into any of the fine calculations of historians, as to the centuries of human growth, I would simply state that some agree on about 85,000 years. They assign 60,000 to savagery, 20,000 to barbarism, and 5,000 to civilization." However, Stanton made it clear that the numbers didn't matter much in the face of a larger truth: "These facts are only interesting to show for how long a period, in proportion, women reigned supreme."[146]

First-wave feminist proponents of matriarchal myth regarded their conclusions about prehistory as scientific. If proof was not yet available on all points of the narrative, it soon would be. Matilda Joslyn Gage, in keeping with the spirit of the times, was enthusiastic on this point:

The last half century has shown great advance in historical knowledge; libraries and manuscripts long inaccessible have been opened to scholars, and the spirit of investigation has made known many secrets of the past, brought many hidden things to light. Buried cities have been explored and forced to reveal their secrets; lost modes of writing have been deciphered, and olden myths placed upon historic foundations. India is opening her stores of ancient literature; Egypt, so wise and so famous . . . has revealed her secrets; hieroglyphs, inscribed temples, obelisks and tombs have been interpreted; papyri buried 4,000 and more years in the folds of bandage-enveloped mummies have given their secrets to the world. The brick libraries of Assyria have been unearthed, and the lost civilization of Babylonia and

Chaldea imparted to mankind. The strange Zunis have found an interpreter; the ancient Aztec language its Champollion, and the mysteries of even our western continent are becoming unveiled. Darkest Africa has opened to the light; the colossal images of Easter Island hint at their origin; while the new science of philology unfolds to us the history of peoples so completely lost that no other monument of their past remains. We are now informed as to the condition of early peoples, their laws, customs, habits, religion, comprising order and rank in the state, the rules of descent, name, property, the circumstances of family life, the position of mother, father, children, their temples and priestly orders; all these have been investigated and a new historic basis has been discovered. Never has research been so thorough or long-lost knowledge so fully given to the world.[147]

Simultaneously heralding human history as a story of evolution and regarding the patriarchy as a tremendous devolution was a bit tricky. Perhaps this is why, at the height of enthusiasm for evolutionary thought in the late nineteenth century, so many first-wave feminists were not inspired by matriarchal myth in spite of the stirring speeches of Stanton and Gage.

One way of managing the competing types of evolution and devolution is visible in what I have come to think of as the Goldilocks version of matriarchal myth: Mama's matriarchy was "too female," Papa's patriarchy was "too male," but the future, belonging to Baby, was going to be "just right." This view was implicit in the work of several of the Victorian anthropologists (notably John Ferguson McLennan and Lewis Henry Morgan). These men deemed patriarchy to be an advance, but they were nostalgic—as Bachofen had been—for mother right, and argued, sometimes forcefully, that the future must and should lead to greater rights and an improved status for women. In her commentary on Genesis 3 in *The Woman's Bible,* Elizabeth Cady Stanton states the Goldilocks version of matriarchal myth most succinctly: "Recent historians tell us that for centuries woman reigned supreme. That period was called the Matriarchate. Then man seized the reins of government, and we are now under the Patriarchate. But we see on all sides new forces gathering, and woman is already abreast with man in art, science, literature, and government. The next dynasty, in which both will reign as equals, will be the Amphiarchate, which is close at hand."[148]

Matriarchal myth never caught on as the *mythe du jour* in the women's movement of the late nineteenth century, notwithstanding the presence of articulate and highly placed spokeswomen. A number of feminists continued to enthuse about prehistoric matriarchy during the first fifteen years of the twentieth century, including prominent figures like Charlotte Perkins Gilman. But in the late 1800s, the myth stayed largely in male hands. It would continue to do so—with a few important exceptions—up until the arrival of the second wave of feminism in the late 1960s and early 1970s.

6

Mother Right on the Continent

We are on very good ground to argue that the Germanic tribes had the mother right, no matter what the other arguments are. . . . Either the Germans themselves or their ancestors at one point did not acknowledge any other relation than that through mothers alone.

—LOTHAR DARGUN

At the same time that socialists and first-wave feminists were experimenting with the political uses of matriarchal myth, its popularity within anthropology spread from England to the continent. Anthropologists in continental Europe came to matriarchal myth a bit later and less enthusiastically than the British anthropologists had, mostly owing to differences in the development of the discipline in their respective countries. Though they brought matriarchal myth to new, mostly German-speaking audiences, they added comparatively little to the matriarchal discussion, and did not create much excitement for matriarchal myth in the general public. In Great Britain, the matriarchal debate was consuming: no British anthropologist felt free to ignore it, and the majority embraced it, at least for a time. On the continent, matriarchal myth sprang up mostly in isolated pockets, in the work of individual scholars, rather than dominating the anthropological discipline as a whole. This more lackluster approach to matriarchal myth on the continent meant not only a slower beginning, but a later end. While British anthropologists barred the door on matriarchal myth around the turn of the twentieth century, continental anthropologists continued to produce a trickle of matriarchal writings that no one took the trouble to critique. And ironically, although British anthropologists were more fervid in their disavowal of matriarchal myth, thinkers in other fields picked up their work and continued to spin out fresh versions of matriarchal myth based on it throughout the twentieth century.

In contrast, when the dribble of matriarchal myth on the continent finally gave out in the early twentieth century, virtually no one looked back on this earlier work. To be sure, new versions of matriarchal myth thrived on the continent beginning with a Bachofen revival in the 1910s and 1920s, through fascist and völkisch versions in the 1930s and 1940s, and feminist versions in the 1980s. But twentieth-century matriarchalists on the continent did not look back to the work of the central European anthropologists who preceded them. They went straight to Bachofen, to German poets and musicians, and, when in a more theoretical mood, to Morgan and the British anthropologists. In short, the anthropologists discussed in this chapter left no lasting mark on the history of matriarchal myth.

Early matriarchal myth on the continent carried stronger echoes of Bachofen than did matriarchal myth in England and America. This was only partly because Bachofen was still read by German and French scholars. It had more to do with the fact that continental scholars were heir to the same intellectual traditions in historiography and the interpretation of myth that Bachofen had been. Nevertheless, since it was British anthropology that had staked the greatest intellectual claim to matriarchal myth in the late nineteenth century, most continental matriarchalists were more in the debt of McLennan, Lubbock, and Morgan than Bachofen. They concentrated on the development of marriage and forms of kinship, and for the most part exhibited little interest in Bachofen's prime mover, religion. Unlike the British, matriarchalists on the European continent engaged in a fiercer debate over women's status in prehistoric society. This never caused them to divide their ranks, but there was a greater range of opinion than that found among the British anthropologists, who were hesitant to claim any profound power or privilege for women in matriarchal society.

The most exciting and significant development in matriarchal myth on the continent was the publication of *Woman and Socialism* in 1879, Friedrich Engels's *Origin of the Family, Private Property, and the State* in 1884, and the editions of Bebel's *Woman and Socialism* that followed upon it. However, Engels was little regarded among anthropologists, and Bebel even less so. Engels's self-consciously political use of matriarchal myth alienated most anthropologists, who wore the disinterested robes of "science" like a suit of armor as they labored to reconstruct human prehistory. Engels did not find a home among anthropologists until the communist revolutions in Russia and China made his *Origin* required reading for anthropologists in those countries.

For the most part, anthropologists on the continent followed the themes that Bachofen and the British anthropologists had set in motion, weaving together the threads of ethnographic accounts of kinship terminology and myth to reconstruct a prehistoric world with mothers at the center.

ETHNOLOGY IN GERMANY

Most matriarchalists on the continent were from Germany or neighboring countries, and they took their principal worldview from the German version of anthropology rather than its British cousin—even as they lifted much of the actual

FIGURE 20. Adolf Bastian (1826–1905), German ethnologist
and world traveler

content of matriarchal myth from the British anthropologists. British and German anthropologists were in conversation with one another in the late nineteenth century, but their foundational assumptions were not the same.[1] For one thing, the term *anthropology* was usually reserved in Germany for physical anthropologists: the sort of researchers who were measuring skulls rather than recording myths and kinship terms. *Ethnology* was the preferred term for cultural anthropologists in Germany, and no one epitomized the discipline more than the prolific and much-admired Adolf Bastian.[2]

Bastian was born in 1826 into a well-to-do family in Bremen. He experimented intellectually during his youth, attending five universities and studying both jurisprudence and the natural sciences. He eventually trained as a doctor at Würzburg, where he studied under Rudolf Virchow, a famous physical anthropologist and soon-to-be friend and colleague. But upon graduation, Bastian did not set up a traditional medical practice. He was keen to see the world, and so he signed on for a stint as a ship's doctor and was on the move for the next eight years. An abbreviated list of his destinations includes Australia, New Zealand, the west coast of South America, Mexico, the United States, China, southeast Asia, India, Syria, Egypt, South Africa, Portugal, Spain, Turkey, Russia, Sweden, and Norway.[3] This was only the beginning of Bastian's travels; in total, he traveled for a full twenty-five years of his life. Bastian was a man of independent means, and though he regularly returned to Germany and worked there, he never stayed for long. He planned his voyages with specific goals in mind, usually to collect materials for the Museum für Völkerkunde in Berlin, of which he was the director.[4] But he still traveled with open eyes and an open mind, spending more time absorbing and reflecting than collecting. His wayfaring never ended. In his late seventies, he traveled to India and then the West Indies, still acquiring materials for the museum in Berlin. He died far from home, in Trinidad, in 1905.[5]

In his intervals back home, Bastian published at length, though not always comprehensibly (his biographer, Klaus-Peter Koepping, refers to Bastian's "turgid prose" and the "conceptual muddle" of his work). In addition to reports on his travels, Bastian engaged in the comparative anthropology popular at the time and was diligent in reviewing and reporting on British ethnographic work—and a great deal else besides—for a German audience. Bastian was at his most influential in the 1860s and 1870s, when the discipline of ethnology was just emerging in Germany and matriarchal myth was coming to life in Britain.[6] Most German anthropologists practiced other professions, pursuing their cultural studies as self-described amateurs (as was the case in England). Bastian long thought of himself as a geographer rather than an ethnologist (though he later helped to delineate the field of ethnology in its relationship to the humanities and natural sciences).[7] Twenty-five percent of the members of the prominent Berliner Gesellschaft für Anthropologie, Ethnologie und Urgeschichte, which Bastian founded with Virchow, were medical doctors, and most of the other members were military officers, government officials, and businessmen rather than professional academics.[8] As in England, German ethnologists aspired to construct a "scientific" study of human culture bound to strict standards of neutral observation and analysis.[9] Because of their positivist views, ethnologists like Bastian set themselves at odds with the philological disciplines that had supported matriarchal speculation in the German-speaking world up through and including Bachofen. Bastian and his peers were not the products of the intensive classical education that typified German secondary and university education in the early half of the nineteenth century. They were immersed in the natural sciences, even as they sought to speak on the historical questions formerly dominated by philologists.[10]

German ethnologists under the influence of Bastian began their study of human culture with quite different assumptions from those of the cultural anthropologists in England. Most were anti-evolutionist. They simply did not set out, as the British scholars did, with the assumption that humanity emerged in a low animalistic condition and gradually made its arduous way to civilization in incremental steps (with many human groups, of course, never arriving there at all, or only with the help of European missionaries and colonial officers). The significance of this cannot be overestimated. Evolutionism was a foundational assumption in the work of British anthropologists from the time that the matriarchal theory was first brought forward by McLennan in 1865. With its time lines, its staged development, and its ascent to civilization and patriarchy, matriarchal myth fit perfectly with the mind-set of the British Empire. This was not the case in Germany, which prior to the mid-1880s was not an imperial power and held no colonies abroad. To be sure, Germans benefited from the imperialism of others. They could claim European status and a quasi-colonialist identity wherever they went in the world. But they were not themselves involved in, as Matti Bunzl and H. Glenn Penny put it, "acquiring lands and peoples for the purpose of political and economic domination,"[11] and that made a difference in how they initially approached the study of "primitive" societies.

Indeed, *primitive* was not the term of choice in German ethnology for describing the peoples who were the object of their study. Instead the term was *Naturvölker*: natural peoples (as opposed to their term for themselves, *Kulturvölker*: cultural peoples).[12] The term *Naturvölker* called up many connotations in the late nineteenth century, and different shades of meaning applied depending on who was using the word. On the face of it, it sounds as though *Naturvölker* are people without culture, people surviving on mere animal instinct, while in contrast, *Kulturvölker* have taken a hand in controlling their own destiny. The value implications are obvious. In an article titled "Adventures in the Skin Trade," historian Andrew Zimmerman argues that while British anthropologists could easily feel superior to "primitives," they nevertheless saw them as human beings at "a very early stage of a universal process of human development." According to Zimmerman, Germans placed the *Naturvölker* entirely outside of history, excluding from the outset any possibility that they might develop or change over time to become more "civilized."[13] Other historians have disagreed with Zimmerman, understanding the term quite differently. Klaus-Peter Koepping notes that by etymology and usage, *Naturvölker* was tinged with a Romantic view; *Naturvölker* were closer to "a virtuous state of nature," uncontaminated by the depredations of so-called civilization. Such people were not without culture in a bad sense, but in a very positive one.[14]

Bastian and his contemporaries' usage of *Naturvölker* seems to have been more nuanced than either of these scholars would have it, and is very revealing of the basic assumptions of the German ethnological enterprise. *Naturvölker,* for Bastian, did not lack culture or history; their cultures had all the same elements as those of "civilized" peoples *(Kulturvölker),* with the single exception of written language. And all that the absence of written language meant was that the *Naturvölker* had to be studied with the special methods developed by ethnologists rather than the more traditional tools of history and philology.[15] Bastian saw the study of *Naturvölker* as a crucial scientific enterprise (and not just because they were there to study, although this was clearly a motivation for Bastian, an inveterate collector of artifacts and cataloger of cultures).[16] Bastian was after a broader scientific finding when he sought out comparative information on human cultures. The story for which he wanted data was not an evolutionary one. Rather, Bastian wanted to know what all human beings shared in common. The *Naturvölker* promised to shed light on this question, not only because they were human, but because, according to Bastian, they were simpler than the *Kulturvölker*.

Here Bastian believed himself to be following good scientific protocol. He argued that studying the *Naturvölker* was the anthropological equivalent of biologists learning about cell behavior by examining the simplest plants. Just as lessons learned from algae could be applied to the study of complex plants like trees, so the *Naturvölker* would reveal truths of human nature and society that would apply equally to the *Kulturvölker*. The *Naturvölker,* said Bastian, provided "a limited field of observation which could be compared to an experiment in a laboratory."[17] Because the *Kulturvölker* exhibited far greater complexity, it was more difficult to isolate fundamental elements of human culture in their societies. Bastian believed that focusing on *Naturvölker* would allow ethnologists to clearly see the building blocks of human culture rather than being distracted by the enormous structures the *Kulturvölker* had constructed with those same blocks. The *Naturvölker* were not evolutionarily earlier, nor were they without their own history. They were just simpler, smaller than the *Kulturvölker*.[18]

Bastian sought to identify what he called the *Elementargedanken:* the elementary ideas of humanity. Beginning with the assumption that all peoples everywhere share the same basic human nature, Bastian hoped to define just what that nature entailed in terms of human cognition and human culture. What he expected to find was the "monotonous sub-stratum of identical elementary ideas" that underlay "the psychic unity of social thought" expressed in "the basic elements of the body social."[19] Bastian knew from firsthand experience that human cultures are not identical. But this, he believed, was owing to the fact that culture was variously mediating the basic forms of human thought, which "lay hidden behind consciousness."[20] In their role as mediators for the *Elementargedanken,* Bastian regarded human cultures as different but equal.[21] His views were shared by the majority of prominent German ethnologists working in the last forty years of the nineteenth century.[22] They believed, for example, that race was "a category of physical, rather than cultural or mental, variation" and that "regardless of somatic and cultural differences, all peoples showed approximately the same basic mental capacities." Differences between them were not due to the level of their evolutionary advance, but rather could be put down to "diverse environmental factors and historical accidents."[23]

Not incidentally, Bastian and his colleague Virchow also rejected Darwinian evolutionism, saying it was speculative, and in Bastian's words, the results of "fantasies" from the "dreams of mid-day naps."[24] Of course many in the Victorian era took exception to Darwinism, but where British anthropologists typically found its theories intellectually exciting, many German ethnologists did not, referring to it pejoratively as the *Affenlehre*—the "monkey doctrine."[25] A number of reasons have been proposed for this, including the desire to avoid any appearance of sympathy toward the socialist and communist movements, which were partial to evolutionary theory; suspicion of any theory coming out of Britain; and the usual religious scruples.[26] But intellectual traditions in Germany also played a role. Historiography in Germany since the time of Herder was characterized by its attention to specific histories, to the *Volksgeist* of individual peoples.[27] From this perspective, knowing what "stage" a society was in couldn't tell you that much about its people. Human cultures were too rich and various for that. Further dampening enthusiasm for matriarchal myth on the continent was the fact that Bastian himself seemed to have wholly conventional views about women's status cross-culturally, regarding it as everywhere subordinate.[28] Evolutionism did have a toehold in Bastian's thought, though. He occasionally speculated on the rise of institutions like the family and the state, and more routinely claimed that human cognition evolved from a "sensual and emotive stage"—characterized by animism—to a more metaphysical approach to understanding the world.[29] But Bastian's evolutionism, such as it was, was nothing in comparison to that of his fellow anthropologists in England.

In short, German ethnology did not really provide the best soil for matriarchal myth to take root and thrive. However, it was not wholly closed off to the basic tenet of matriarchal myth: that gender relations could have been different in prehistoric times. And though Bastian rejected Darwin, many writers and thinkers on the continent did not. A handful of ethnologists struggled to map out histories of human sexuality and marriage that began with chimpanzees and marched forward all the way up to nineteenth-century Europe. The matriarchal myth these ethnologists promoted was less unilinear, less deterministic, and more open to cultural variation than that popular in England. It also remained in more comfortable conversation with non-matriarchal theories about human origins.[30]

THE GERMAN SYNTHESIS: JULIUS LIPPERT'S
VERSION OF MATRIARCHAL MYTH

One of the most comprehensive treatments of matriarchal myth on the continent came in the mid-1880s with the work of Julius Lippert. A prolific independent scholar of working-class origins who supported himself as a schoolteacher, Lippert

FIGURE 21. Julius Lippert (1839–1909), Czech historian and
author of *The History of the Family* and *The Evolution of Culture*

published two books on matriarchal myth: *Die Geschichte der Familie* (The History
of the Family) in 1884 and *Kulturgeschichte der Menschheit in Ihrem Organischen
Aufbau* (translated into English under the title *The Evolution of Culture*) in 1886.
Lippert's treatment was essentially a materialist one. The second of his two books
on prehistoric matriarchy may have been written in response to the work of Engels and Bebel, although it is just as likely that Lippert was inspired directly by
Morgan, as Engels himself had been.

   Lippert tied religious change to social developments and gendered power, re-
introducing an aspect of matriarchal myth that had largely fallen out of vogue
after Bachofen.[31] He recovered Bachofen's references to classical sources, which
amounted to no more than a footnote in the matriarchal myth of other German
ethnologists. Lippert's theory is also notable for its relative—though not complete—
lack of interest in sex differences. At the opposite end of the spectrum from
Darwinian British intellectuals like Spencer, Lippert attributes matriarchy to the
basic exigencies of reproduction rather than to any more elaborate vision of

inherently masculine and feminine traits. Patriarchy develops because men see an opportunity to grab social power—produced by changes in the means of subsistence—and they take it.

The earliest stage in Lippert's matriarchal myth is communistic. What bonds people together is their "common mother or maternal ancestress," who eventually becomes spiritualized as a goddess.[32] Like Bachofen before him, Lippert sings hymns of praise to the mother and her child, and even more importantly, to their shared blood, a *Blutsverwandtschaft* (blood kinship) from which the father is excluded.[33] During the earliest stage of human society, all activity is devoted to "the food-quest." Initially, the sexes do not play different roles in procuring food. As "chance collection" of foodstuffs gives way to knowledge and forethought, adults begin to tutor the young, but again, according to Lippert, there is no sexed division of labor. Sexuality, he claims, was wholly promiscuous: "With the primary instinct dominant, the women of a primitive family must have been regarded as a gift of fortune in which each member had an equal share as in other goods provided by nature." As long as promiscuity is the rule, Lippert says, a child is attached to its mother alone.

Lippert is quick to add that "the men of the tribe by no means possessed a right of property or dominion over the person of the woman," but it is hard to credit this. First, all members of the tribe are male in Lippert's construction, since it seems doubtful that each woman in the tribe "had an equal share" in every other woman, who was "regarded as a gift of fortune" to her. Second, the men have "a common and equal legal title to the enjoyment of her sexual favors." This is irrespective of the woman's wishes; elsewhere Lippert notes that "the suit of no guest" may be refused by the young girl, since "as the tribal member of olden times he had a right to her favors." Obviously they are not "favors" if she does not have the right to refuse to give them.[34]

Promiscuity is first modified, in Lippert's evolutionary schema, when mother/child incest is forbidden because of "the authority naturally associated with the position of mother." As limits are placed on promiscuity, men have to produce something better than their tribal membership card to have sexual relations with women. Women, says Lippert, begin to barter sex for meat. This is, for Lippert, "the first attempt to establish a true marriage union." The communistic tribe gives way to the matriarchal household, in which "the man appeared only as a guest or even, in view of his services, as a menial member of the household." This is the era of prehistoric "gynecocracy," though Lippert cautions that "we must not allow ourselves to be misled" by this "high-sounding name."[35]

Whatever its flaws, Lippert declares that matriarchal societies provided a very high status for women, comparable to that held by men in patriarchal societies. This was an era of *Frauenherrschaft*, the dominance of women.[36] However, as soon as gynecocracy appears—and Lippert does regard it as an improvement over the more primitive society that came before—it is destined to be destroyed, in true dialectic fashion, by its own contradictions. Under gynecocracy, men are essentially nomads. They are not required on the home front, which is managed by the women of the tribe. They have no grounds for establishing relationships with men or women of other tribes because these people have "alien blood," and, as Lippert says (echoing Bachofen), "strict mother right recognized no bond save that of blood." This set the limits beyond which matriarchal society could not grow. It was left to patriarchy to create an "artificial community of blood." Only in this "artificial community," says Lippert, can large social organizations develop. Lippert discounts the existence of large nations described by classical writers as matriarchal. He says they were "large homogeneous nationalities, each composed of a large number of small organized groups, never . . . unified states of like magnitude."[37]

But it is not the impulse to create large nations that precipitates the transition from mother right to father right. Rather, it is disparities in production between women and men based on the emerging sexed division of labor. In Lippert's account, once man is designated hunter and woman gatherer, a battle of the sexes ensues. The matriarchate survives only as long as women maintain their "control of the food supply" and the "disciplinary weapon" of cutting off food to men. But once men acquire a reliable food supply, they are suddenly put on an equal or superior footing to women.[38] Furthermore, men develop a powerful loyalty to one another as fellow hunters, forming a *Männerbund,* a male society or fraternity. Armed with independent means and their growing identification with one another, men seize the day and establish patriarchal marriage, in which woman "becomes an object of property to the man." The belief that women were alone responsible for procreation eventually swings to the opposite extreme. Men claim to be the sole agent of generation, with women acting as mere incubators for their seed.[39]

Importantly, Lippert did not regard the recognition of paternity as the causal agent in establishing patriarchal social relations (unlike, say, McLennan). The husband first acquires rights of ownership over his children because he owns their mother, and "her children as her fruit are likewise his property." The establishment of women-as-property is due most directly to the domestication of animals, which Lippert views as men's handiwork. Animal husbandry encourages patriarchy for two reasons. First, it opens up the possibility of owning another living being and using it for breeding purposes, a concept that could henceforth be applied to persons. Second—and more importantly in Lippert's theory—it gives men the economic edge that women formerly claimed through their control of agriculture.[40] It is women's taste for meat that eventually despoils them of their social power. In trading sex for meat, women establish "a relation of protection" with men, and, as Lippert says, "a relation of protection . . . tends to become a relation of mastery as soon as the differentiation has become sufficiently great that the protection becomes indispensable."[41]

When patriarchy first stakes its claim, the condition of women is especially grim. Men, says Lippert, were vindictive, and it was through violence that they seized and maintained power over women. Father gods displace mother goddesses as the pantheon is forcibly made to mimic the new social order.[42] Women's earlier status, reliant on "her labor and its value," is replaced by "the charm of her sex," which, for Lippert, is apparently not all that charming. Under patriarchal rule, "she who for untold thousands of years had been the pillar of the history of young mankind now became a weak vessel devoid of a will of her own. . . . She was merely an apparatus, not as yet replaced by another invention, for the propagation of the race, a receptacle for the homunculus." The only lingering survival of the matriarchate is "the high esteem for the woman as mother, which contrasts strongly with the general status of women," and the continued employment of women as religious functionaries (female divinities were still worshipped as a carryover from matriarchal times). "Even after she had been entirely dethroned as stewardess of the domestic *sacra*," Lippert explains, "she was believed to harbor a specifically religious trait in her nature."[43]

As patriarchy develops further, women's lot gradually improves. She "no longer enters [her husband's] house without property like a captured or purchased slave." Instead, she brings a dowry with her, to which is added a bride-price and a "morning gift" from her husband, ensuring her a measure of independence within the marriage. The Roman Empire, according to Lippert, was a great step forward for women. The Romans were learning "how to rule without owning," and they "even dared to introduce this principle into the germ cell of society, the family," by emancipating women from their former status as men's property. Unfortunately, this process was cut short by the fall of the Roman Empire and the invasion of the Germanic peoples. But in nineteenth-century Europe, Lippert predicts, all this will change as women labor alongside men in an industrial environment and form marriages based on mental, emotional, and financial partnership.[44]

Intriguingly, Lippert does not explain the catalyst for the development of more sex egalitarian norms under the Roman Empire. The means of production do not shift dramatically in this era. And up until then, Lippert describes human nature—male and female—as a perpetual seeking of advantage over one another. So it is difficult to understand why, in the absence of coercion or changing material conditions, men would begin to hand over independence and property to women, in whatever small amounts. Nevertheless, Lippert is sanguine about what the future will bring and reconciled to the past abuses of patriarchy. As he argues, property, slavery, and paternal rights were "the only possible starting point for the establishment of larger organizations," which in turn were the only possible context in which "higher civilization" could "blossom forth." Lippert explains, "Many an advance of great moral value has been born of an aberration." The aberration, in this case, was the oppression of women, and the moral value it ushered in was "the requirement of female chastity and marital fidelity," something Lippert deems "a moral attainment of lasting value."[45] The defeat of the matriarchy was also the occasion for ending the practice of blood revenge, another moral advance that Lippert, like Bachofen, celebrates, and one that he feels women could not have managed on their own.[46]

It is when he makes apologies for patriarchy that Lippert hints at an undeveloped theory of sex differences. Without real explanation, or the need to carry any theoretical weight in his argument, Lippert notes in asides that women have a natural knack for religion, that they are detail oriented but cannot see the big picture, and that their intelligence is limited to a specific domain, namely that of the family. Women have a head start in attaining civilization, but in the long run, men, "the bearers of development, progress, wisdom, and spirit," will make up the distance and then some.[47]

Lippert does not gaze back upon the matriarchate nostalgically, as Bachofen (and to a degree, Morgan) did. It was prehistoric, both literally—before the development of written language—and in the sense of coming before what really matters: history. "The historical fact of the matriarchate was easy to overlook," Lippert explains, which is why it was not "discovered" prior to Bachofen. The "history of mankind" begins for Lippert with the "formation of larger organizations, the conflict between them, and its manifold consequences." Thus, he concludes, "it is by no means accidental that the matriarchate falls into the age of prehistory."[48]

SEX, MARRIAGE, AND DARWIN

Lippert's assertion that the earliest human societies were sexually promiscuous did not go unchallenged. Indeed, even before Lippert sketched his synthesis of matriarchal myth, there were those on the continent who disputed or tried to refine the vision of prehistoric sexual relations they had inherited from Bachofen and McLennan. Alexis Giraud-Teulon, hailing from Geneva, was one of the earliest continental entrants into the matriarchal debate with his 1868 article "La Mère chez Certaines Peuples de l'Antiquité." Giraud-Teulon followed Bachofen in interpreting Amazon myth as evidence of ancient female social and political domination. Giraud-Teulon believed that in an era when succession, ownership, and domestic authority inhered in and passed through mothers, men had to have been relegated to subordinate roles.[49] By 1874, in *Histoire du Mariage sous Toutes ses Formes*, Giraud-Teulon moved more into the orbit of the British anthropologists, discussing McLennan's categories of polyandry, exogamy, and female infanticide at length. In its narrative structure, *Histoire du Mariage sous Toutes ses Formes* reads much like Morgan's *Ancient Society* (though it came before), beginning with Hawaiian kinship systems and moving through supposedly later forms of "uterine clans" that represented a gradual restriction of women's sexual activity to a narrower set of potential partners.

Though Giraud-Teulon more or less towed the party line, he was clearly uncomfortable with the promiscuity that other anthropologists assigned to primitive times. He disapproved of women's sexual license in matriarchal societies and marveled that ancient men were willing to tolerate it. He finally put the phenomenon down to the strictures of necessity. Sounding a good bit like Hobbes in his image of prehistoric life, Giraud-Teulon reasoned that men could not afford to antagonize one another in humankind's original condition. They feared the dangers of living outside the tribe and so were forced to endure women's penchant for multiple sexual partners.[50]

Further doubts about a period of primitive promiscuity were raised when continental anthropologists began to pay more serious attention to Darwinian ideas about evolution. One of the first to struggle with this conundrum was M. Kulischer, who, like Giraud-Teulon, was interested in finding a workaround for primitive promiscuity, a way out of Bachofen's hetaeric swamp. In an article published in 1876 titled "Die Geschlechtliche Zuchtwahl bei den Menschen in der Urzeit" (Sexual Selection by Humans in Primitive Times), Kulischer sought to reconcile the views of Lubbock, McLennan, Morgan, and Bachofen with those of Darwin. Darwin never bought into the nearly universal British anthropological opinion that the earliest humans were practitioners of "group marriage" or "communal marriage," in which all the male members of the tribe indiscriminately had sexual relations with all the female members of the tribe. Of course, having spent a lot of time and effort documenting sexual selection among lower animals, Darwin would have had no reason to imagine early human societies in which sexual selection took no part.

Following Darwin, Kulischer asserted that mating was never completely indiscriminate, even during the age of "communal marriage" proposed by Lubbock and friends. Some sexual choice was involved, even if liaisons were short-lived and easily dissolved. Kulischer describes customs from various groups in the Americas of courting dances or games in which men attempt to attract the attention of women, and women—as in other mammalian species—select their sexual partners. He regards male sexual selection, in which men choose and women submit, to belong to a later period of human social development characterized by marriage by capture. For Kulischer, the origin of this reversal of roles is easy to trace. In early times, mating occurred only at specific times of the year, at springtime and harvest. This predictable periodicity allowed for large gatherings in which couples could meet and pair up. But then the sex drive—and here, it would seem, Kulischer is talking specifically about men—"broadened," expanding to fill the entire year. Throughout the year, then, men pursued and acquired women in whatever way they could, including by capture from foreign tribes. This, said Kulischer, initiated the practice of individual marriage. Apparently, once a man captured a woman, he hung on to her, and the free and easy seasonal mating market became a thing of the past. This shift from communal to individual marriage was, in Kulischer's estimation, the beginning of women's oppression.

Though not as given to providing detailed ethnographic examples, Karl Kautsky, writing in 1882, made essentially the same claim as Kulischer, that "group marriage," at least in the form proposed by the British anthropologists, never existed—and could not have—given the prevalence of sexual selection and sexual jealousy documented by Darwin.[51] Kautsky was followed in 1888 by Friedrich von Hellwald, an Austrian historian and the author of *Die Menschliche Familie nach Ihrer Entstehung und Natürlich Entwickelung* (The Human Family in Its Origin and Natural Development). Hellwald's lengthy tome synthesized much of what had come before, both in England and on the continent. Like Kautsky, and in deference to Darwin, Hellwald began his study of marriage and the family with the animal kingdom. He was enthusiastic about the peculiar forms of sex and marriage "discovered" by the British anthropologists and delighted in including all of them in his book: endogamy, exogamy, polyandry, levirate marriage, marriage by capture, marriage by purchase, polygyny, and so on.

Hellwald was particularly concerned to elucidate the phenomenon of *Weibergemeinschaft,* the "sharing of women": something his friend and contemporary Oscar Peschel called simply "the ugly thought."[52] Hellwald tried to carve out a middle ground between Kautsky (who he acknowledged had "abolished the idea" of *Weibergemeinschaft*) and Lubbock, McLennan, Morgan, and Bachofen, who had all stipulated "boundless commingling" for the earliest prehistoric times. Certainly, Hellwald argued, there was never a time of total sexual free-for-all, but Kautsky and Darwin, he said, went a bit too far in imagining that the earliest humans were capable of anything remotely resembling love, friendship, or marriage between women and men.[53] Instead, Hellwald proposed, these remote ancestors lived without benefit of marriage in "sex collectives," keeping their sexual relationships within the group. The only thing that redeemed these sex collectives in Hellwald's eyes was motherhood, and as for Bachofen, it was the mother/child connection—along with a growing aversion to incest—that made it possible for higher social systems to evolve. Hellwald called this stage matriarchal and repeatedly stressed the equality of women and men within the sex collective, save for men's superior physical strength. Men, according to Hellwald, took very little interest in the family during this matriarchal stage, and it was only in the home that women held real authority. Still, women enjoyed the freedoms this system offered them, and they practiced polyandry, not rarely, as Lubbock claimed, but frequently.[54]

Unlike the British anthropologists, and more in keeping with the norms of German ethnology, Hellwald did not regard matriarchy as a necessary stage. Some peoples, he suggested, might have skipped it altogether, moving straight to a patriarchal social system. Some may have practiced marriage by capture or purchase; others not. "Does it not sound more probable," Hellwald asks, "that each people's evolution was different . . . and that some developed certain aspects of cultural life earlier than others?"[55]

True marriage—marriage deserving of the name—did not arise until sexual unions became property relations. Perhaps not incidentally, true marriage did not work to women's benefit, as women were purchased as brides and thereafter treated as property, with which men could do as they pleased. Hellwald felt this situation was ameliorated somewhat with the arrival of Christianity, which saved wives from being their husbands' servants or slaves, but nevertheless left them "completely subject to his will." In discussing the future of marriage at the end of his treatise, Hellwald expresses sympathy for the women's movement, which he regards as an ethical reaction to a former moral humiliation. But he offers no particular form of marriage as superior (as to be desired in the future), nor does he suggest that marriage is destined to evolve in one direction or another.[56]

One of the last German writers of the century to address matriarchal themes, Josef Kohler, offered a ringing restatement of the primacy of promiscuity, completely discarding Darwinian arguments in favor of sexual selection. For Kohler, the salient feature of mother right—apart from its connection to totemic clans— was "free sexual traffic" and the practice of "unrestricted sexual relations before marriage."[57] Kohler was professor of law at the University of Berlin from 1888 to 1919. Prior to his academic appointment, Kohler had studied at Heidelberg and Freiburg and served as a judge in Mannheim.[58] Kohler was a prolific writer, publishing 104 books in his lifetime. Kohler's primary interest was comparative jurisprudence and ethnology, but he also wrote on religion, history, art, and literature; he translated Petrarch, Lao-tzu, and Shakespeare; and he published two novellas and twenty-five songs. In 1897, Kohler turned to matriarchal myth and authored *Zur Urgeschichte der Ehe* (On the Prehistory of Marriage). By this time, Kohler was writing against a turning tide in England. Serious critiques of the theory of prehistoric matriarchy had been raised, and Morgan's evolutionary scheme was in imminent danger of being pitched into the graveyard of discarded anthropological theories. Kohler conceived of his book "as a direct defense of Lewis Henry Morgan" and as an attack against writers such as Westermarck, Durkheim, and Darwin, who had taken exception to the matriarchal claims of the evolutionary anthropologists.[59]

Kohler was, like Morgan, an ardent evolutionist, but in a more Bachofenian vein. That is, he set aside Morgan's materialist bent and instead spoke as Bachofen had done of "spirit" being forged out of "universal substance."[60] Also like Bachofen,

FIGURE 22. Josef Kohler (1849–1919), German jurist and amateur ethnologist

he imagined evolution occurring dialectically, with much see-sawing along the way: "Even if progress appears certain," he wrote, "yet the way is altogether uncertain."[61] Kohler's attitude toward the evidence of ethnography was more cautious than that of the British anthropologists, more in keeping with the tone Bastian set for German ethnology. Peoples who "have not made . . . [much] progress in material and intellectual culture," Kohler cautioned, nevertheless "have long stages of development behind them" and cannot be interpreted simply as living fossils of contemporary European civilizations.[62]

Kohler arrived at his theory of prehistoric mother right via totemism, which he assumed was an ancient and universal institution. Given that a child could have only one totem, Kohler reasoned, it would be impossible to regard him or her as being equally descended from both parents. Since one parent must be chosen, it was—naturally, Kohler asserted—the mother who first assumed this honor: "The mother gave birth to the child and, as is common in tribes, did so away from the house, sundered it from herself, nursed it for years, and then for more years let it play around her while the husband was up to all sorts of tom-foolery. That the relation to her is regarded as decisive is so natural that the contrary must seem highly remarkable to anyone who has ever taken the trouble to imagine what savage life is like."[63] Kohler notes that Australian and American aborigines exhibit both mother right and father right, but he nevertheless claims an original, universal practice of mother right. Assuming that peoples on each continent dispersed from a single source, he is sure that before their dispersal, these peoples practiced matriliny.[64]

PROPERTY AND LAW, WOMEN AND MEN

Law was an interest German ethnologists shared with their British counterparts, and like them, many came from a background of comparative jurisprudence. Questions about property also rose in prominence among German ethnologists, even more so than they did in the work of the British anthropologists. Engels accused the British anthropologists of burying Morgan's work because of its note of materialism, its belief that changes in kinship and technology were linked.[65] Engels undoubtedly overstated this—for example, the British anthropologists were keen on patrilineal inheritance as the trigger for the transition out of the matriarchal stage. But Engels was onto something: most British matriarchalists saw no need to directly link questions of production and property to those of sex and marriage. This was less the case in Germany, where the intellectual environment was alive with the questions socialists posed and the manner in which they framed them. As we have seen, Hellwald set the institutions of marriage and property in lockstep; Lippert also linked shifts in the relation of women and men to changes in technology. The coincidence of notions of property with changes in kinship systems remained a focus of interest on the continent and surfaced in the works of Lothar Dargun and Albert Hermann Post.

Lothar Dargun was a professor of German law at the University of Krakow who had a special interest in property and warfare as they were affected by changes in kinship systems. In contrast to the speculations of other scholars of jurisprudence, Dargun believed that property ownership among the *Naturvölker* was individual before it became communal.[66] This was the opposite of the sequence later proposed by Engels in the *Origin*. Not a socialist himself, Dargun was eager both to begin and end his sequence with individual rather than communal property.

Dargun viewed the equation of matrilineal kinship with women's power and status as utterly false, and the cause of much confusion around the topic of prehistoric matriarchy. Critics who denied the existence of matriarchy because they were aware of ethnographic examples of male domination in the "lowest stages of social development" were missing the point. Kinship and power were two separate and independently variable elements of social life in Dargun's estimation. Matrilineal societies could and did settle social power on men, even in the scenario most often proposed for prehistory, that of indiscriminate sexual relations leading to kinship through mothers alone. For even when individual fatherhood could not be determined, men could still marshal their physical strength to dominate over women. According to Dargun, matriliny sometimes eventuated in women's rule, but more often it did not.[67]

Dargun's earliest work on matriarchal myth, "Zum Problem des Ursprungs der Ehe" (On the Problem of the Origin of Marriage), published in 1879, showed the clear imprint of McLennan. Although Dargun was prepared to quibble with McLennan over the existence of polyandry (many nineteenth-century men thought it improbable that multiple men would ever agree to share a single wife), he was absolutely entranced by the idea of marriage by capture, which he saw as an important instance of property law.[68] (It was from Dargun that Hellwald initially borrowed this idea.) Indeed Dargun's first major book on the topic of matriarchal origins—*Mutterrecht und Raubehe* (Mother Right and Marriage by Capture), published in 1883—focused specifically on this practice.

Albert Hermann Post, another theorist who came to matriarchal myth from a legal background, was born into a well-established family in Bremen in 1839. After studying law at Heidelberg and Göttingen, Post returned to Bremen to serve as a judge.[69] In 1875, Post made his entrée into matriarchal mythmaking with the publication of his book *Die Geschlechtsgenossenschaft der Urzeit und die Entstehung der Ehe* (The Clan of Primitive Times and the Origin of Marriage). In it Post reviewed topics covered by McLennan and Lubbock, including polyandry, endogamy, and the like. Following this early and rather cursory work, Post turned to a different project: investigating indigenous African peoples whose cultures were increasingly coming to the attention of Germany in the mid-1880s as it began to acquire colonies on that continent. Post's *Afrikanische Jurisprudenz* (African Jurisprudence) was published in 1887. It was not until 1889 that Post again directly addressed the topic of prehistoric matriarchy, in his *Studien zur Entwicklungsgeschichte des Familienrechts* (Studies in the Evolution of Family Law). This systematic work divided human history into three main stages, of which the first was the age of matrilineal clans. Post was eager to explain the legal significance of this, namely that the only relationships that counted legally under such a kinship system were blood relations. A family, a clan, could not include people unrelated by blood—it could not, for example, include a husband and wife. Even after marriage, both partners would remain in the clan into which they were born, and the children would belong to the clan of their mother. Post's second stage—that of patrilineal clans—was the mirror image of the first, with children belonging to the clan of their father. Between them Post places an intermediate stage during which matrilineal and patrilineal laws struggled for ascendancy. Nowhere does Post indicate a marked moral preference for either matrilineal or patrilineal clans. In fact, at the outset he leaves open the possibility that patrilineal clans preceded matrilineal ones. Though he believed that the matrilineal system would eventually be proven to be the most primitive family organization and argued that the available evidence supported this sequence, he allowed that there was insufficient data to resolve the question with certainty, a diffidence that would have been unthinkable to most British anthropologists.[70]

Like Bachofen, Post made much of the presumed practice of blood revenge within societies organized according to mother right. Quite unlike Bachofen, though—and unlike Lippert as well—Post did not imagine that father right brought an end to this practice. Bachofen associated the law of blood and blood revenge solely with mother right, imagining father right to be characterized by a more rational, more spiritual, and less material form of kinship. Since Post saw father right as a simple inversion of mother right, he did not imagine anything like "progress" occurring in the transition from matriliny to patriliny.[71] Both systems left people trapped in a world dominated by blood relationship.[72] Recall that for Bachofen, the Roman practice of testamentary adoption, which removes the "natural-sexual basis" of fatherhood, making it "an especially intellectual act," is the hallmark of patriarchy.[73] Post took an entirely different tack. He claimed that artificial forms of kinship are characteristic of societies that are *more* rather than less obsessed with blood relationship. As Post argues, quite sensibly, only where blood kinship is of central importance does it become necessary to make legal arrangements that mimic it. Under later, state-based systems, Post says, artificial forms of kinship are less common because social connections can be made without any pretense of kinship.[74]

It is in his last stage—that of *Elternrecht,* or "parent right"—that true progress occurs in Post's scheme. *Elternrecht* is a bilateral kinship system, characteristic of the *Kulturvölker,* in which children are considered to be related to both parents.[75] Sitting at the pinnacle of his evolutionary sequence, *Elternrecht* is a superior form of kinship whose superiority inheres in, among other things, the improvement in the status of women that occurs in the transition from father right to *Elternrecht*. The position of the wife "changes from an object of property to his [the husband's] equal."[76] Still, like Bachofen, Post deems women's status to have been highest under matrilineal conditions, a stage that he does not hope to see revived.

Post continued his research in law and anthropology into the 1890s. Through his association with the Internationale Vereinigung für Vergleichende Rechtswissenschaft und Volkswirtschaftslehre (International Union for Comparative Law and Political Economy), Post drafted a questionnaire that was sent to European

colonial officials and missionaries in Africa.[77] In it can be found numerous questions that illustrate Post's acceptance of, or at least interest in, key aspects of
McLennan's scheme. "Are there traces," Post asks, "of the custom by which the wife
is abducted, e.g. sham fights at weddings?" "What rules apply in polyandry for the
intercourse of the husbands with the wife? Are the husbands of a wife brothers?"[78]

In the end, Post's story of matriarchal origins is fairly conventional in its por-
trayal of a matriarchal society (in which women's status is comparatively good),
followed by a patriarchal society (in which women's status is comparatively bad),
followed finally by "modern" forms of the family in which women's lot is improving. But everywhere in Post one senses the Germanic flavor of his approach. Yes,
there is an evolutionary sequence from mother right to father right and beyond
that to bilateral kinship *(Elternrecht),* but Post frequently disrupts this sequence.
He gives multiple examples of groups that do not make the transition smoothly
or who skip father right altogether, moving directly from mother right to bilateral kinship. When Post describes various matrilineal societies, about the only
thing they have in common is their matrilineal kinship system; the same is true
for patrilineal societies, which differ widely on all other measures. Diversity—
never schematized into a clear evolutionary sequence—abounds in Post's work,
unlike that of his peers on the other side of the English channel.

MOTHER RIGHT AND THE ETERNAL FEMININE

The notions of gender that lay under later matriarchal myth on the continent did
not vary much from Bachofen's. This was true from the beginning. Bachofen's
earliest respondents, Alexis Giraud-Teulon and Élisée Reclus, both before and
after their encounters with the theories of British anthropologists, continued
Bachofen's love affair with "the mother," even as they undercut his belief in prehistoric female rule. Giraud-Teulon initially agreed with Bachofen's assertions of
women's supremacy in ancient times, and, like Bachofen, he regarded the assertion of paternity as "an indication of moral progress." The man who "first consents
to be recognized as the father" was, for Giraud-Teulon, "a man of genius and
heart, one of the great benefactors of humanity." Later Giraud-Teulon concluded
that prehistoric matriarchy was "not a social organization where women rule
exclusively," but "only a primitive form of the family with the woman at the center." Still, he spoke loftily of the "tender mother and chaste wife" of his own day,
and any greatness he saw in prehistoric times was laid at the foot of mothers.[79]

Élisée Reclus was a French utopian anarchist and "an admirer and correspon-
dent of Bachofen." He was also in regular contact with British anthropological
thought via his teaching of summer seminars in Edinburgh.[80] In "Female Kinship and Maternal Filiation," published in 1877, Reclus discusses the relative

merits of Bachofen's and McLennan's works on prehistoric matriarchy. Although he showers praise on Bachofen (calling his work "delicate and sagacious"), he criticizes him for drawing "from his unexpected formula the most extreme consequences." In particular, says Reclus, Bachofen jumped "from maternal affiliation, a positive fact," to "antique gynocracies,—a doubtful enough affair." In contrast, Reclus describes McLennan as adhering closely "to logic and good sense," presenting his conclusions "in clear and precise language" and offering an argument that "was both sober and vigorous." Reclus suggests that McLennan constructed "a rather narrow foundation" in his theories of female infanticide and marriage by capture for "the large superstructure" of prehistoric matriarchy, but he clearly regarded McLennan as the author of the more serious inquiry into prehistory.[81]

Still, Reclus waxes positively Bachofenian as he describes the role that motherhood plays in the evolution of the human race. "It is the sentiment of maternity which raised mankind from the mire of universal promiscuity," Reclus writes, "and through her will be shaped its final expression." It is "the maternal instinct" that "is the most intelligent and far-sighted of impulses. . . . before this instinct stirred within us, we were among the lowest in the brute creation, more cruel than the tiger, more treacherous than the serpent, more gluttonous than the crocodile. From a mother, smiling on her infant, came the first ray of light which illuminated the human countenance." Reclus describes the shift to patriarchy as no more than a swing of the pendulum: "Because the father had not been made of enough consequence [under mother right], the mother was now to be made next to nothing." But Reclus, like many of the British anthropologists, looked forward to a time in the near future when "slighted motherhood will resume its rights."[82]

This elevation of motherhood—with its vision that allowed little else for women—can perhaps be seen most clearly in the work of Ferdinand Tönnies, one of the best-known German sociologists of the late nineteenth century. Even those unfamiliar with his name are likely to know of his two-part typology of human society: *Gemeinschaft,* the "natural" community of the family and small community life, and *Gesellschaft,* the large, abstract, and impersonal social structure of late industrial society. Tönnies used these concepts to describe how humanity evolved, what was wrong with the present condition, and how it might be changed in the future. His debts to earlier thinkers are several, and intriguing.

Tönnies was a prodigy. Born in 1855 in the far north of Germany, he completed a doctorate at Tübingen at the age of twenty-two. He was keenly interested in the philosophy of Thomas Hobbes, and while in England studying Hobbes's work, he became acquainted with the work of the Scottish philosophers Adam Ferguson and John Millar, both of whom had written comprehensive histories of human evolution that paid special attention to gender relations.[83] Tönnies was shortly moved to write something of his own on the topic, and in 1887 he released

FIGURE 23. Ferdinand Tönnies (1855–1936), German sociologist
and originator of the *Gemeinschaft/Gesellschaft* distinction

Gemeinschaft und Gesellschaft. The book was widely read and quickly became
a classic. Though Tönnies wrote many other works in his lifetime, nothing exceeded the popularity of his earliest effort, which went through eight separate
editions, the final one being released shortly before his death in 1936.[84]

When it came to matriarchal myth, Tönnies had a very light touch indeed. In
the preface to *Gemeinschaft und Gesellschaft,* he expresses his gratitude for the
work of Sir Henry Maine, but adds this disclaimer: "My only regret, in reading
his illuminating comments, is that he unjustly opposes the extraordinary insights offered on the prehistory of the family, community life, and all such institutions by authors from Bachofen's *Matriarchy* through to Morgan's *Ancient Society* and beyond."[85] This would seem to mark Tönnies as a true believer, but there
is actually very little in *Gemeinschaft und Gesellschaft* that describes a universal

human evolution from mother right to father right. Tönnies talks of matrilineal and patrilineal societies, but his time line is fuzzy. He rarely cites ethnographic examples and seems disinterested in the evolutionary scheme, which is only implicit in his work. *Gemeinschaft* and *Gesellschaft,* though associated with feminine and masculine, respectively, function more as ideal types in Tönnies's work than as stages in an upwardly marching (or even downward falling) history of humanity. But what *Gemeinschaft und Gesellschaft* lacks in explicit treatment of matriarchal myth is made up with Tönnies's constant reiterations of notions of sex difference and how they translate into social structures, a set of beliefs shared by proponents of matriarchal myth.

Tönnies begins his description of *Gemeinschaft*—"a complete unity of human wills" that results from "descent and kinship"—with three exemplary relationships: mother and child; husband and wife; and brothers and sisters of a common mother.[86] It is the father who is not included in this *Gemeinschaft,* for a father's love is "mental" rather than physical in character. Father love might resemble the love between siblings except for the fact that the father is older than his children. Because of this, in Tönnies's words, "fatherhood is the clearest foundation for the concept of *authority* within the community."[87] Quickly bypassing matriarchy with a comment that patriliny is not the original pattern of inheritance (since it was preceded by matriliny), Tönnies moves on to "the universal pattern for civilization," that of "paternal authority" and "masculine domination."[88]

Tönnies at first identifies the source of male domination in superior physical strength: men simply bully their way to the top of the social hierarchy by offering to beat up any competition. Men enjoy "the sense of superiority and power to command" that such strength affords them. Within their family relationships men feel "an instinctive, spontaneous *tenderness* toward the weak, a desire to help and protect," which, Tönnies admits, "is bound up with pride of possession and the enjoyment of his own power." Tönnies does not take the common step of imagining that those on the bottom of the social hierarchy like it there, that it accords with their inmost nature to accept subordination. Instead, he says, "those who are being led and *protected,* who *have to* obey, will have a feeling of inferiority and will experience this as something disagreeable, as a form of pressure or compulsion, however much it may be glossed over by habit, gratitude or love."[89]

Nonetheless, things are as they should be, and women, though dissatisfied with their lot, must resign themselves to it, for there is no arguing with nature. "It is a stale cliché," Tönnies remarks, "but all the more important because it is dredged up out of general experience, that women are mostly led by their feelings, while men follow their reason. . . . They alone have the capacity for calculation, cool (abstract) thought, deliberation, strategic thinking and *logic*. As a rule, women are not much good at these things." Women are also "sedentary and awkward" where men are "swifter and more agile."[90] But, Tönnies is quick to add, women have their own sort of strength: in men the muscular system is predominant, but in women the nervous system prevails, and this gives women the edge in creativity.

What this means to Tönnies is that "the finest part, the inner core of *genius,* is usually an inheritance from the mother." However, the person who inherits it is her son—not her daughter. "The person of genius," says Tönnies, "retains a nature that is feminine in many respects." The man who fully integrates femininity into his basic male nature is "the model of the perfect human being." Nowhere does Tönnies suggest that the complementary figure, the masculine woman, is a "person of genius."[91] Instead Tönnies insists that women are at their best when they are at their most feminine: "Staying at home is as natural for women as traveling is unbecoming. . . . All woman's activity involves turning creative energy inwards rather than outwards." *Gesellschaft*—the late nineteenth-century European world, as Tönnies saw it—which invites women into the public workforce, wreaks havoc on women's nature, making women "think in a thoroughly calculating manner." Women become "enlightened, cold-hearted, self-conscious," and, says Tönnies, "nothing is more alien and terrible to her basic nature which, despite all the process of continually acquired modifications, is *inborn.*" For Tönnies, woman belongs in the world of *Gemeinschaft,* in which people are organically bound to one another. She can never participate in the world of *Gesellschaft,* in which people enter into relationships freely and on an individual basis, without destroying her femininity.[92]

Most of this could have been—though it probably wasn't—lifted from the pages of Bachofen. We know that Tönnies read Bachofen, but he read a great many other authors more diligently and with greater interest.[93] It is more probable that Tönnies was simply articulating what were by then very common assumptions about male and female nature. Particularly reminiscent of Bachofen, though, is Tönnies's pervasive mood of nostalgia toward the world of *Gemeinschaft.* Something of infinite value inheres in women within their "natural" sphere of motherhood and the home. Yes, it is limiting; no, society cannot advance beyond a certain (restrictive) point without men using their natural strengths of rationality, intellect, and disinterestedness to create state-level societies. Still, it is sad that "the artificial and mechanical world of *Gesellschaft*" should so completely triumph over the loving and compassionate world of *Gemeinschaft.*[94] Bachofen moodily clings to the glories of the matriarchal era and bemoans the barren and unfeeling present, but never does anything more than to heave a heartfelt sigh of resignation over what has been lost, because it *had* to be lost. Tönnies is less ready to give up on his tender mother world, his *Gemeinschaft.* He looks forward to a time when some of the values of *Gemeinschaft* can be incorporated back into civil society, at least at some level, and when "people of genius" (read: feminine men) can bring their creativity and artistry to bear on the public world.[95] As for women, it would seem that in Tönnies's view, their only task is to keep the hearth warm.

THE ARYAN MOTHER

The Romantic continental infatuation with the mother took a particularly ethnocentric turn in the work of Michael Zmigrodski, a Polish librarian and amateur archaeologist. He drew extensively on Bachofen and to a lesser degree on Lippert, but he added his own views—racist and anti-Semitic ones—to the mix. Zmigrodski would remain nothing more than a curiosity but for the fact that racist, fascist, and anti-Semitic renditions of matriarchal myth continued to be developed in central Europe up to and even through World War II, and that he was not the only matriarchal theorist to concern himself with the matriarchal origins of the Aryan peoples. There is no evidence that Zmigrodski directly influenced the fascist matriarchalists of the early twentieth century. He was little noticed in his own time and disappeared thereafter. But Zmigrodski was the first scholar to locate the unique genius of the Aryan people in its purportedly matriarchal origins.

Zmigrodski's *Die Mutter bei den Völkern des Arischen Stammes: Eine Anthropologisch Historische Skizze als Beitrag zur Lösung der Frauenfrage* (The Mother of the People of the Aryan Tribes: An Anthropological Historical Sketch to Help Resolve the Woman Question) was published in Munich in 1886. Claiming that Europe's Aryan population left its "original Asian dwelling" owing to a social dispute, Zmigrodski concludes that the Aryan society in Asia must have been very advanced indeed, since such a social dispute could only happen within a state, and state-level societies are "usually accompanied by an advanced system of . . . philosophy, religion, and cult."[96] Stating that he intends to examine German and Slavic folk traditions, Zmigrodski turns to marriage—the most important aspect of the Aryan value system, he claims—and from there to the mother, "the fairest part" of the marriage relationship. This is the beginning of a rhapsody to Aryan mother love—both the mother's love of her children and her culture's love for her—that goes on for the full length of the book. "A woman's joy and sorrow, her own history and that of all humanity is the outcome of her becoming a mother" *(Daraus, dass ein Weib zur Mutter wird, entsteht ihr Freud' und Leid, ihre ganze Geschichte, und die Geschichte der Menschheit)*; Zmigrodski repeats this sentence frequently throughout his book. So lofty is the moral status of pregnancy and childbirth that Zmigrodski identifies them as God's chosen instruments in his war with Satan.[97]

Zmigrodski accepts the Bachofenian account of the earliest human societies. Women "were nothing but targets for male lust" in the hetaeric swamp, a nightmare of unregulated sexuality. The fateful step forward for the human race was taken by mothers who objected to child sacrifice. "This," says Zmigrodski, "was the hour of the redemption of humanity. Then the mother became the conscience of humankind."[98] Admirably, she took advantage of her time spent at home—while the men were out hunting—to learn how to domesticate animals, plant fruit trees, and preserve food for the winter. The men couldn't compete with all this industrious innovation, and the "mother era" began.[99]

Zmigrodski cautions his readers not to romanticize the mother era, since men still engaged in warfare (women could not restrain them from that), but he clearly romanticizes it himself, following Bachofen's example. The fact that the mother era had to end is sad, but Zmigrodski reminds his readers that "everything has to consist of three phases: becoming, existence, and decay." In the realm of cultural history, this translated to "fight for power, exercise of power, and abuse of power"; by this natural order of things, the women of the mother era began to behave badly. "Educated in the women's school, the man grew to his full moral maturity, and being aware of his power, started to refuse to obey her orders." In a later era, according to Zmigrodski, women graciously stepped down in the face of male authority, but when men first rebelled, women did not give up so easily. Irritated by men's behavior, they resorted to cruelty and murder. Men, having no other choice—and to their credit, in Zmigrodski's estimation—revolted against this state of affairs and led humanity farther along the path to civilization and state-level societies. Mothers had proven incapable of doing this, as they were too tightly focused on their own homes and children and could not step back to appreciate larger social issues. Women's social power diminished further in the face of state warfare. Fighting, says Zmigrodski, increased men's knowledge and intelligence, while women, kept at home and hearth, experienced a progressive decline in intelligence. "The woman," says Zmigrodski, "was beaten—in every sense."[100]

In making his case that the Aryan peoples were originally matriarchal, Zmigrodski relies on linguistic evidence. Examining the etymology of the Sanskrit terms for "father" and "mother," Zmigrodski concludes that the mother was recognized as the commander and organizer, while the father was seen as worker and protector.[101] Zmigrodski contrasts this to the Semitic view via a materialist interpretation that soon becomes racist. Zmigrodski explains that the Aryans were an agricultural rather than a nomadic people and that Aryan women never had to "sit on the wagon," as Semitic women did.[102] This, says Zmigrodski, is why Aryan and Semitic cultures evolved in different directions. Both had a "mother era," but they did not pass out of it with equally good humor. Aryan women had Christianity—which Zmigrodski regards as an Aryan religion, in spite of its Semitic origins—to help them with the transition. In the early Christian era, Zmigrodski imagines, women chose to side with either the Gnostics or the early church fathers. Semitic, Oriental women sided with the Gnostics, hoping to revive the principle of the mother goddess and regain their lost power. They were defeated and subsequently demeaned by their association with the Gnostic principle of sensuality. Aryan women sided with the early church fathers, who, according to Zmigrodski, appealed to women's good sense and Christian values. The principle of paternity required the complete subordination of women; Aryan women submitted humbly and set about creating the Christian family, thereby providing "the ground for further cultural development." They guarded their modesty and as a result they "glowed" with righteousness—unlike the immodest women of the East.[103] It is in this organic Aryan Christian vision of motherhood that Zmigrodski places his hope for the future. Hope he must, since he takes a rather dim view of the present: men have abandoned themselves to their lusts, he laments; they have dishonored Aryan motherhood and driven Aryan women to lesbianism.[104]

Zmigrodski's later work provides an interesting counterpoint to his 1886 treatise on Aryan motherhood and matriarchy. In 1889 Zmigrodski arranged a display at the Palais des Artes Libéraux during the Paris Exposition consisting of over three hundred drawings of swastikas, or objects Zmigrodski deemed "to have a swastikal origin." Zmigrodski became interested in the symbol of the swastika when Heinrich Schliemann unearthed a great many objects decorated with swastikas from Hissarlik, an archaeological site in Turkey (which Schliemann believed to be the ruins of ancient Troy). Zmigrodski's enthusiasm knew no bounds. The swastika was, in his estimation, a single votive image that captured the essence of the Aryan race and religion. It was a "fly trapped in amber" proving that "in a very ancient epoch, our Indo-European ancestors professed social and religious ideas more noble and elevated than those of other races."[105]

From Schliemann's atlas of the finds at Hissarlik, Zmigrodski claimed to discern "six hundred objects adorned with a swastika." Of these, however, only sixty-five were "of pure form." The others were crosses associated with points or nail holes or had the wrong number of branches. Indeed, there were more objects with three branches than with the four that Zmigrodski deemed to be an unvarying feature of the "pure form."[106] This did not trouble Zmigrodski. As he explains, "I propose that all the figures [of the swastika] are religious symbols and not ornaments, because they are too negligently drawn . . . proving that it was so familiar to everyone that even the most cursory execution was sufficient to effect a recognition." "It is always so with symbols," Zmigrodski asserts.[107] Zmigrodski dated the swastika to the matriarchal epoch of Aryan history.[108] (Indeed, the cover of his earlier *Die Mutter bei den Völkern des Arischen Stammes* was adorned with a swastika.)

Though singular in the enthusiasm with which he promoted the Aryan mother of matriarchal times, Zmigrodski was not entirely alone in his interest in claiming matriarchy for the Aryans and the Aryans for matriarchy. Lothar Dargun diligently sought out survivals of the practice of marriage by capture among the early Germanic tribes.[109] Like Zmigrodski, Dargun believed that linguistic reconstructions of the proto-Indo-European language provided solid evidence that the Aryan peoples were originally matriarchal.[110] Dargun continued to articulate this conviction in his magnum opus, *Mutterrecht und Vaterrecht,* published in 1892.[111] Echoing Dargun, Hellwald declared that the "entire Germanic family system" was based on mother right. Among the Germanic tribes, "traces and remnants of prehistoric matriarchy can be found everywhere," he asserted.[112] The groundwork for a fascistic adaptation of matriarchal myth was laid, though apart from Zmigrodski, this was not intentional.

LATE ENTRANTS TO THE MATRIARCHAL DEBATE

Matriarchal myth on the continent persisted into the early twentieth century even as a sea change occurred within the discipline. Bastian's dominance over German ethnology collapsed shortly before his death in 1905. A new generation of scholars, led by Friedrich Ratzel, rejected Bastian's idea of the fundamental unity of humanity and instead envisioned world history as the diffusion of novel cultural ideas from a small number of centers of creativity.[113] According to historian Andre Gingrich, Ratzel's key concept was *Ideenarmut*—the "mental poverty" or "limited inventiveness" of the human race. This was in pointed contrast to Bastian's *Elementargedanken,* which viewed human creativity as spontaneously springing up everywhere in potentially equal measure.[114] As Ratzel's new school of diffusionism developed in Germany, it turned thoroughly and unapologetically racist, laying the foundation for racial theories that Hitler and his supporters would utilize during the Nazi era.[115] The diffusionist school also took the step Bastian and most of his peers had refused to take: regarding the *Naturvölker* as truly primitive, belonging to an earlier phase of human development.[116] The term *Ethnologie* was gradually set aside in favor of *Völkerkunde,* which had the advantage of being "a uniquely German word" that "was tied to no traditional theoretical stance."[117]

Still, some of Bastian's acceptance of cultural difference and reluctance to impose too heavy a schematic template on human society lived on, for example in Heinrich Zimmer's 1898 essay, "Matriarchy among the Picts." Zimmer found abundant survivals of matriarchy among the pre-Celtic (pre-Aryan) inhabitants of the British Isles. Notably, and unlike Dargun and Hellwald, Zimmer did not find any such matriarchal survivals among the Aryans themselves. He argued, atypically, that it might make more sense to regard matriarchy not as a stage along an evolutionary time line, everywhere superseded by patriarchy, but rather as an alternative and equally stable social form.[118]

More characteristic of matriarchal myth as it would be articulated in the early twentieth century was the work of Heinrich Schurtz, author of *Urgeschichte der Kultur* (The Prehistory of Culture), published in 1900, and *Altersklassen und Männerbünde* (Age Classes and Male Associations), published in 1902. Especially in the latter work, Schurtz showed a great deal more interest in the camaraderie of male-only groups than he did in any prehistoric matriarchy. It was the *Männerbünde* (association of men) that Schurtz believed to be the true evolutionary force behind human history. His work lent itself easily to growing fascist and *völkisch* strains in German society.[119] Schurtz still supported the idea of an earlier, universal matriarchal era, but he did not, like Tönnies, suffer any torments over its passing. The year 1903 brought two more accounts of matriarchal myth, both more conventional than Schurtz's: *Vorgeschichte des Rechts* (The Prehistory of Law), by Paul Wilutzky, and *Mutterrecht: Frauenfrage und Weltanschauung* (Mother Right: The Woman Question and Worldview), by Max Thal. Both works relied explicitly on the work of Bachofen and McLennan. And while both offered evolutionary time lines moving from mother right through to father right, they were generally less doctrinaire than their British counterparts.

These works represented the final echoes of matriarchal myth's initial incursions into German ethnology. Thereafter, they were little heard from again. Notions of prehistoric goddess worship and Amazonian women came to life again on the continent in the first decades of the twentieth century, and vibrantly so. But when they did, they mostly shed their former academic trappings and were embraced as an inspirational vision of what Aryan society once was and could be again. Even later, in the 1980s, when some German feminists began to embrace the myth of matriarchal prehistory, they chose not to revive the work of their fellow countrymen, people like Lippert and Kohler. Instead, they relied on Bachofen and the British evolutionary anthropologists, as well as the psychoanalytic readings of matriarchal myth that emerged in the work of Freud and Jung in the twentieth century. Insofar as late nineteenth-century continental anthropologists lent support to rising fascist and communist ideologies, it could be said that they had a modest influence, even if it was not the one they intended. But as scholars of human prehistory, they were cast aside with finality and without regret as *Ethnologie* gave way to *Völkerkunde,* evolution to diffusion.

7

Struggling to Stay Alive

Anthropology and Matriarchal Myth

Many learned men are too much disposed to seek for the explanation of a given custom in conditions of former times which have now perhaps disappeared. It is certain that customs persist by the force of habit, even when the conditions which first gave birth to them have long ceased to exist; yet it is scarcely necessary to remark that this appeal to early times can only be effective when it has been shown to be impossible to discover the cause of such customs in the conditions under which they still continue. If this main principle is not accepted, we shall be led astray by every idle delusion.

—C. N. STARCKE

Among all the iterations of matriarchal myth that were narrated in the late nineteenth century, it is the myth's heyday in Great Britain among the evolutionary anthropologists that most demands explanation. Bachofen, who brought together so many sources in such a unique—not to say quirky—way had an enormous but delayed impact. His influence on the late nineteenth-century conversation was attenuated; though given a nodding regard by many, he was read and appreciated seriously by very few. This was to change quite dramatically in the twentieth century as he became the mascot for Munich's bohemian subculture and the unsung—and uncited—impetus behind much of the work of Carl Jung and his many followers. But at the turn of the century, Bachofen's work lay fallow. The feminist flirtation with matriarchal myth begun in the 1890s remained low key even after it picked up pace somewhat in the first two decades of the twentieth century in the United States. Matriarchal myth among socialists and communists bifurcated after the work of Bebel: moderate socialists lost interest, while more hard-line twentieth-century communists in the Soviet Union and later in China set down Engels's work as unquestioned (and unquestionable) dogma while in actuality doing little or nothing to further develop the narrative or its implications. And as we have seen, anthropologists on the continent held their matriarchal myth more lightly and gave it up more gently than their colleagues across the English Channel.

What remains a great mystery is this: why did British anthropologists—and an educated British public—fall in love with the idea of prehistoric matriarchies in the mid-1860s only to spurn it almost completely by 1900? On a smaller scale, with less drama, the same thing happened among socialists in a similar time frame, and this too begs for explanation. The relevant questions then are first, how was the grasp of matriarchal myth undone at the turn of the century, and second, why did it take hold in the first place? These are the challenges for this and the following chapter. The myth of matriarchal prehistory did not disappear from the repertoire of the anthropological discipline overnight. It lingered on, enjoying local revivals throughout the twentieth century. But in the 1890s, critics of the matriarchal theory began to get the attention formerly denied them, and with a one-two punch of ethnographic evidence and methodological revision, the myth of matriarchal prehistory was down for the count. Comprehensive defenses of matriarchal myth were offered in 1917 by E. Sidney Hartland and in 1927 by Robert Briffault, but they played to a tiny, resistant audience—unlike the myth's earlier proponents, whose matriarchal perorations were answered with a roar of applause.[1]

It was customary at the time to claim that matriarchal myth was discarded because it was proven wrong, specifically by ethnographic evidence that complicated the clean evolutionary picture painted by early anthropologists. Certainly as more ethnographic fieldwork was done and previous ethnographies were scrutinized more carefully, a body of disconfirming data was compiled that could no longer be explained away as local aberrations having no bearing on the larger evolutionary schema. Ethnographic evidence, however, was as nothing compared to methodological revision when it came to sealing the fate of matriarchal theory within cultural anthropology. The tremendous shift in British anthropology from grand evolutionary theories to cultural relativism and localism left no place for matriarchal myth. Where previously the field had sought to construct a chronology that would simultaneously account for variation between "primitive" peoples and trace the ancestry of "civilized" Europe, it now came to see its task as recording cultural data and describing cultural variety. A new generation of anthropologists rebelled against the old with a determined iconoclasm, stubbornly refusing any suggestion that marriage was ever communal or women ever dominant. The old theories came to be seen, as Robert Lowie put it, as "the shopworn anthropological doctrines of half a century ago," which were now, quite appropriately, "gracing the refuse heaps of anthropological science."[2] The prime locus of anthropological thought shifted away from Britain and toward the United States, with anthropologist Franz Boas of Columbia University leading the charge against cultural evolutionism as the defining framework of anthropological inquiry (no doubt inspired in part by the priorities of his German forerunner, Adolf Bastian).

Matriarchal myth never recovered the high intellectual status it held in the late 1800s within the discipline of cultural anthropology or among the educated public. All twentieth-century matriarchalists have labored under the shadow of the fact that it was cultural anthropologists, the earliest proponents of matriarchal myth, who felt driven not just to abandon the theory, but to passionately disavow its accuracy and hold it up as an example of how anthropologists could be led astray by their enthusiasm to uncover nonexistent evolutionary themes. As cultural anthropologists loosened their grasp on matriarchal theories, though, academics in allied fields—classics, archaeology, and the history of religions—picked it up. Without cultural anthropologists anchoring the debate and claiming it as their private preserve, other academics felt freer to step in and adapt matriarchal myth for their own intellectual and ideological purposes. Rather than ending, the debate about matriarchal prehistory merely shifted across the disciplines.

THE SOCIALIST DEFECTION FROM
MATRIARCHAL MYTH

One might imagine that communists and feminists, with their outsized political commitments, would have continued to support matriarchal myth regardless of where the winds took the discipline of cultural anthropology. Some did, especially in Russia and China. But in Europe, most did not. When matriarchal thought lost its hold in cultural anthropology, it ceased to be given much attention in socialist and other activist circles.

Interestingly, it was feminist socialists who most quickly laid aside matriarchal myth as a rhetorical device to inspire socialist political action. In 1887, Marx's daughter Eleanor Marx-Aveling (and her partner, Edward) took on the task of writing about "the woman question" in *Thoughts on Women and Society*. Marx-Aveling opens her essay by stating that she does "not propose dealing" with the historic portion of Bebel's book, though it is "deeply interesting." She quickly refers readers to Engels's *Origin* as offering a more accurate and scholarly treatment of prehistory. The history thus dispensed with, she moves on to a consideration of the present state of women in capitalist Europe, beginning forcefully: "Society is morally bankrupt, and in nothing does this gruesome moral bankruptcy come out with a more hideous distinctness than in the relation between men and women."[3]

Marx-Aveling spent much of her time in *Thoughts on Women and Society* discussing issues of sexuality, no doubt in part because they played a significant role in her own life. Marx-Aveling had a long engagement to a man she never

FIGURE 24. Eleanor
Marx-Aveling (1855–98),
socialist and feminist
activist, daughter of Karl
Marx

married owing to her father's opposition to the match. Later she became involved with Edward Aveling, her sometime coauthor. Though Edward was already married, she lived openly with him in a common law union for many
years, during which time he was routinely unfaithful to her. The circumstances
of her life being what they were, we can surmise that Marx-Aveling had to
choose between vilifying Edward and vilifying the sexual standards of her day,
against which his behavior was so galling. She chose the latter, speaking sharply
against the sexual double standard in Victorian culture and against sexual re-
pression in the family.[4] However, she did not take the step of comparing an un-
satisfactory Victorian sexual ethic with a prehistoric alternative, as had Bebel (if
only implicitly). Marx-Aveling looked solely to the future for surcease, which she,
like her father, expected would arrive with a law-like certainty, replacing the oppression of women with true equality between the sexes. Though declining to be
specific on the nature of the socialist world to come (regarding future forms of

marriage, Marx-Aveling reassures her readers that "we may be sure that the best form will be chosen, and that by wisdoms riper and richer than ours"), she is certain that "woman will be independent: her education and all other opportunities as those of man."[5]

Marx-Aveling is especially firm on one point: that it is exceedingly misguided to analyze women's position in society or work toward its improvement without first understanding how it is imbricated in economic realities. Marx-Aveling describes all feminist political efforts outside the socialist movement as "palliative, not remedial." "Those who attack the present treatment of women without seeking for the cause of this in the economics of our latter-day society," argues Marx-Aveling, "are like doctors who treat a local affection [sic] without inquiring into the general bodily health." She, like Bebel, views gender and the means of production as phenomena that develop historically rather than being given in nature: "There is no more a 'natural calling' of woman than there is a 'natural' law of capitalistic production, or a 'natural' limit to the amount of the labourer's product that goes to him for means of subsistence." However, Marx-Aveling is convinced that the one—gender—is subsidiary to the other. As she explains: "The position of women rests, as everything in our complex modern society rests, on an economic basis."[6]

Bebel was not as clear on this point. At times, he seemed to privilege gender as the more basic phenomenon, as when he wrote: "Working-class women have more in common with bourgeois women or aristocratic women than do working-class men with men of other social classes."[7] This state of affairs may have been created by economic variables, but for Bebel it appears that gender is at least as relevant as class—maybe more so—in diagnosing social injustice. As Bebel summed up: "Independently of the question whether a woman is oppressed as a proletarian, in this world of private property she is viewed almost exclusively in terms of her gender. . . . A woman suffers as a social being because of her gender, and it is difficult to decide in which of these roles she suffers the most."[8]

Bebel's critics—both his peers and later communist historians—were quick to note this "flaw" in his thinking. Bebel lay accused of that great Marxist crime, reformism: that is, entertaining the idea that one can work within capitalist society to undermine it or that one can work with nonsocialists (such as feminists) to achieve shared goals.[9] This criticism of Bebel's work, more than any other, led to his gradual displacement among late nineteenth-century socialist feminists. One individual in particular was responsible for this: Clara Zetkin. Zetkin was a colleague of Bebel's in the Social Democratic Party in Germany and became known internationally not only as a communist but as an authority on women's rights. It was she who inaugurated March 8 as International Women's Day. Zetkin, like Bebel, was elected to the German Reichstag, and she began her career as an orator by giving speeches about Bebel's *Woman and Socialism*.[10] To many, she was

FIGURE 25. Clara Zetkin
(1857–1933), German
socialist and feminist
activist

Bebel's protégé. But Zetkin and Bebel were not of one mind on issues of gender.
Where Bebel stated quite clearly that women's oppression is ancient, dating to
some of the earliest forms of economic development, Zetkin tended to romanticize women's lot as positive in all economic stages save the capitalist one.[11] Where
Bebel came to promote a straightforward equality between women and men,
Zetkin resurrected an ideal of domesticity that she believed would rightly characterize any coming socialist society. As she said in the 1890s, "It must certainly
not be the task of socialist propaganda for women to alienate the proletarian
woman from her duties as mother and wife. On the contrary, she must be encouraged to carry out these tasks better than ever in the interests of the liberation of the proletariat."[12] Setting aside the issue of domesticity, this statement
captures Zetkin's attitude toward gender very neatly. Whatever women do, their
first obligation is to support a communist revolution. They can do so secure in
the belief that this revolution will bring an end to their oppression as women, but

they must never get these steps out of sequence and seek women's rights first. Bebel writes, by contrast, that *"there can be no liberation of mankind without social independence and equality of the sexes."*[13]

Undoubtedly socialist women were under pressure to prove that their primary loyalty was to the socialist cause. In conversations that took place in the 1920s, Vladimir Lenin instructs Zetkin very precisely on this point: "The thesis must clearly point out that real freedom for women is possible only through Communism. The inseparable connection between the social and human position of the woman, and private property in the means of production, must be strongly brought out. That will draw a clear and ineradicable line of distinction between our policy and feminism."[14] Lenin explicitly chides Zetkin for allowing the themes of matriarchal myth to infect women's socialist gatherings: "I ask you: Is now the time to amuse proletarian women with discussions on how one loves and is loved, how one marries and is married? . . . Now all the thoughts of women comrades, of the women of the working people, must be directed towards the proletarian revolution. It creates the basis for a real renovation in marriage and sexual relations. At the moment other problems are more urgent than the marriage forms of Maoris or incest in olden times."[15] Zetkin accepted Lenin's distinction between feminism and socialism even before Lenin himself made it, regarding the first as bourgeois and the second as revolutionary. In a letter to Engels written in 1895, Zetkin comments, "Despite my great respect for him [Bebel] . . . I cannot shake the impression that with him a little of the author of *Woman,* of the defender of the oppressed female sex, has gotten the best of the marxist."[16]

Ironically, then, matriarchal myth lost its grasp on socialist feminists very early on, which probably contributed to its eclipse in later socialist politics in which "the woman question" increasingly had nothing to do with prehistoric matriarchies or even primitive communist sex-egalitarian paradises. Socialist feminists, once in receipt of matriarchal myth courtesy of Engels and Bebel, could make little use of it without endangering their revolutionary credentials. And so it passed to other women—in socialist terms, bourgeois women—to make pragmatic use of matriarchal myth for the feminist cause. It was they who, in small measure, helped keep matriarchal myth alive through the early decades of the twentieth century.

THE MARGINALIZATION OF MATRIARCHAL MYTH IN ANTHROPOLOGY

Opposition to matriarchal myth within the discipline of anthropology in Great Britain began early—even as it was gaining widespread acceptance, in fact—and gradually crested in the 1920s, by which time it was difficult for cultural anthropologists to champion matriarchal myth without inciting the scorn of their colleagues. In the 1860s and 1870s, criticism of matriarchal myth was mainly internal, the product of in-fighting among those who accepted the myth's basic premises. For example, Lubbock took exception to McLennan's theory of polyandry; McLennan ridiculed Morgan's arguments about paternity in the maternal gens. But once matriarchal myth attained the status of *the* reigning description of prehistoric social life, external criticism surfaced as well. Skeptical voices were raised. They were at first ignored, but in a matter of a few decades, it was they who drowned out the plaintive voices of has-been and would-be matriarchalists. The whole face of anthropology was changing by the close of the nineteenth century, particularly in Britain, where matriarchal myth had been promoted most forcefully. Instead of pronouncing British colonial policy through the voice of high British science, anthropology began to see itself as charged with the preservation of the "noble savages" that formed their primary subject matter.[17] Certainly there was an element of romanticism here, but also a profound rejection of the social Darwinism of thinkers from Herbert Spencer forward.

Sir Henry Sumner Maine was the first to announce his opposition to the matriarchal theory. At face value, this is not surprising, since Maine had made a case for ancient patriarchy just a few years before the matriarchal explosion. But actually, Maine's *Ancient Law* did not necessarily contradict the matriarchal myth of his peers. Maine began in ancient Rome and India and moved to the present; he did not account for what came before (probably because when he first wrote, he did not imagine that there *was* very much that came before).[18] So even in the terms of Maine's own theory, it was entirely possible that "what came before," once the antiquity of the human race was recognized, was matriarchy, and that Maine had merely written the later chapters of the matriarchal drama.[19] Maine himself acknowledged this possibility, at times refraining from taking any firm stand for or against prehistoric matriarchy, and merely defending his own work: "It was not part of my object to determine the absolute origin of human society. I have written very few pages which have any bearing on the subject, and I must confess a certain distaste for inquiries which, when I have attempted to push them too far, have always landed me in mudbanks and fog. The undertaking I have followed . . . has been to trace the real, as opposed to the imaginary, or the arbitrarily assumed, history of the institutions of civilised men."[20]

Here Maine's acknowledgment of the possibility of prehistoric matriarchy is grudging, but elsewhere his disagreement with Morgan and McLennan is explicit.[21] By and large, Maine's critique sticks to the obvious: "The greatest races of mankind, when they first appear to us, show themselves at or near a stage of development in which relationship or kinship is reckoned exclusively through males. They are in this stage; or they are tending to reach it; or they are retreating from it." Groups that practice matriliny are "rare or remote," says Maine, and could as easily result from the degradation of prior patrilineal custom as from entrapment in a putative early evolutionary stage of mother right. Maine appealed later, as he had in *Ancient Law,* to the worship of ancient ancestors, who seemed always to be male.[22]

Maine also goes to the foundation of the matriarchal thesis, expressing serious doubts about the efficacy of the comparative method. First, he questions its evolutionary premise, writing that "so far as I am aware, there is nothing in the recorded history of society to justify the belief that, during that vast chapter of its growth which is wholly unwritten, the same transformations of social constitution succeeded one another everywhere, uniformly if not simultaneously." Second, he wonders how accurate ethnographic reports are or can be, especially on the topic of sexuality: "There is no subject on which it is harder to obtain trustworthy information than the relations of the sexes in communities very unlike that to which the inquirer belongs. The statements made to him are apt to be affected by two very powerful feelings—the sense of shame and the sense of the ludicrous—and he himself nearly always sees the facts stated in the wrong perspective." In support of this claim, Maine notes that the English of his own day misunderstood the character of sexual relations among the French, who were not only their contemporaries, but who lived just a quick hop across the English channel.[23]

Maine offered a direct attack against that which offended him most: the idea of a primordial promiscuous horde. (As we have already seen, this notion titillated and horrified late Victorians, probably in equal measure. Some, out of disgust with the very idea, rejected the matriarchal thesis in its entirety, while others—for example, most first-wave feminists—simply "corrected" this mistake in their adaptations of matriarchal myth.) Maine found it particularly difficult to believe that there were human groups that did not recognize paternity. In a statement widely quoted by his peers, Maine remarked that paternity is a "matter of inference," as opposed to maternity, which is a "matter of observation," a maxim that accorded well with the presuppositions of matriarchal theory. But he also noted that "as soon as intelligent curiosity was directed to the question, it seems to have exaggerated the share of paternity in parentage." He was dismissive of matriarchalist theories on paternity, saying that "Morgan seems almost to suppose that it was introduced by popular vote."[24]

This is where Maine's critique really hits its stride: when he appeals—as most critics after him were to do—to Darwin's descriptions of sexual selection. Ironically, the self-same theory that put the meat on the bones of first-wave feminists' matriarchal myth provided the evidence Maine needed to reject it. This is because Maine looked at the same picture of sexual selection from a different angle. He didn't imagine things from woman's perspective, choosing from among her suitors he who would best advance the human race. He instead looked to the feelings of the triumphant and rejected suitors. He noted that Darwin observed sexual jealousy among all animals on the human branch of the evolutionary tree and concluded that it would be surprising indeed if human beings "in savage conditions" would have broken away from this long-standing tradition of sexual jealousy, only to embrace it again with the rise of patriarchy.[25]

C. Stanisland Wake, writing in 1889, expanded on this Darwinian line of questioning. Wake was less hostile than Maine to the matriarchal theory, probably because he had no prior work to defend. His *Development of Marriage and Kinship* raked over all the familiar territory—wife capture, couvade, polyandry, promiscuity, and so on—concluding that "kinship through females" might be more archaic than "kinship through males." Though this conclusion might seem to place Wake in the matriarchalist camp, it is, in Wake's construction, a very thin conclusion indeed, for he carefully disposes of all the arguments that make mother right a necessary evolutionary stage. Like Maine, Wake projected his particular ire onto the thesis of primitive promiscuity. Wake asserts that paternity "is fully recognised by all races, however uncultured."[26] But what is especially telling for Wake is what he has learned from Darwin: that "promiscuous intercourse in a state of nature is extremely improbable" and is "certainly not taking place among the quadrumana." If promiscuity "is wanting among the lower animals," Wake reasons, "much less can it be asserted of primitive man, who is supposed to inherit and improve on their experiences."[27]

Darwin himself eventually spoke out about the probability of primitive promiscuity and therefore, indirectly, about the matriarchal theory. Darwin was by this time enormously influential. As one scholar commented in 1863, "Darwin is conquering everywhere and rushing in like a flood."[28] Though he was called the "father of evolution," Darwin was not an evolutionist after the manner of the British anthropologists. His brand of evolution was not directed toward social progress, at least not necessarily so. Unlike some of his predecessors (especially Lamarck), who believed that nature created variation when it was needed, Darwin took the position that there was already variation in nature, and how it evolved was due to how well specific variations could survive and reproduce. Darwin's position was therefore marked by considerably more accident and happenstance than the evolutionary theories of the social anthropologists.[29] As a man of his times, however, Darwin speculated along with everyone else about the sexual customs of early humans, and the conclusions he reached with the publication of *The Descent of Man* in 1871 were these: "Judging from the social habits of man as he now exists, and from most savages being polygamists, the most probable view is that primeval man aboriginally lived in small communities, each with as many wives as he could support and maintain, whom he would have jealously guarded against all other men. Or he may have lived with several wives by himself, like the gorilla."[30] Developing this theme, Darwin proceeded to take direct aim at McLennan's matriarchal theories:

> Turning to primeval times, when men had only doubtfully attained the rank of manhood, they would probably have lived . . . either as polygamists or temporarily as monogamists. Their intercourse, judging from analogy, would not then have been promiscuous. . . . They would have been governed more by their instinct, and even less by their reason, than are savages at the present day. They would not at that period have partially lost one of the strongest of all instincts common to all the lower animals, namely, the love of their young offspring; and consequently they would not have practised infanticide. There would have been no artificial scarcity of women and polyandry would not have been followed; there would have been no early betrothals; women would not have been valued as mere slaves; both sexes, if the females as well as the males were permitted to exert any choice, would have chosen their partners, not for mental charms, or property, or social position, but almost solely from external appearance. All the adults would have married or paired, and all the offspring, as far as that was possible, would have been reared.[31]

Clearly Darwin had no intention of offering safe quarter to matriarchal myth, regarding it as a competing rather than complementary account of human evolution.

The first scholar to devote himself to the systematic dismantling of the matriarchal theory was C. N. Starcke. In *The Primitive Family in Its Origins and Development,* published in 1889, Starcke continued Darwin's theme that an age of mother right was a dubious proposition, since such an "unlikely inversion" cannot be supposed to have occurred "at the moment of transition from ape to man."[32] Starcke questioned the basic presuppositions of evolutionary anthropology, casting doubt on an investigator's ability to distinguish "survivals" from customs having a current practical value.[33] But unlike Maine and other, more cautious, critics of matriarchal myth, Starcke was willing to go out on a limb and declare that the primitive family was "ruled by the father in virtue of his physical superiority," by "a strong man, or one who is pre-eminent in other ways, [who] commands respect, and is obeyed by his associates, whether of the family or of the tribe."[34] Though women did not hold a high place in this scheme, they did occupy, according to Starcke, a seemly place, virtually identical with that required of middle- and upper-class women in Victorian England. As he explains, "While the husband's mental capacity exceeded that of his wife, in consequence of his strenuous conflict for subsistence, yet this conflict seemed of less importance to the children in comparison with the woman's quiet influence at home. The female mind gained in this respect what it lost in the sphere of common life, and the slighter exertions demanded by the latter made it possible for the woman to foster the tender germs of childish understanding with constant watchfulness, deep intelligence, and refined feeling."[35]

FIGURE 26. Edward
Westermarck (1862–1939),
Finnish anthropologist
and critic of the
matriarchal theory

What Starcke began, Edward Westermarck finished. More than any other single work, Westermarck's *History of Human Marriage* drew public opinion away
from the matriarchal thesis in England and America, and eventually had an impact on the continent as well.[36] First published in 1891, Westermarck's magnum
opus was reworked and refined over the next three decades in continually en-
larged editions, methodically crushing every argument raised in support of
primitive promiscuity and mother right.[37] Ironically, Westermarck claims that
his decision to write his treatise on marriage "did not spring from a desire for
opposition." "On the contrary," Westermarck asserts, "I commenced my work as
a faithful adherent of the theory of primitive promiscuity and tried to discover
fresh evidence for it in customs which I thought might be interpreted as survivals from a time when individual marriage did not exist." He had a change of
heart, however. Westermarck does not attribute this to the discovery of evidence

against the matriarchal theory, but to questions of methodology: "I perceived that marriage must primarily be studied in its connection with biological conditions, and that the tendency to interpret all sorts of customs as social survivals, without a careful examination into their existing environment, is apt to lead to the most arbitrary conclusions."[38]

Westermarck did not cling to Darwin, his obvious ally; instead, he made generous use of ethnographic arguments and indeed claimed himself to be a practitioner of the comparative method, seeking to explain why "similar customs, beliefs, legends, or arts, are found among different peoples."[39] His argument against primitive promiscuity—which formed the bulk of his work—is summarized by anthropological historian George Murdock as consisting of three interrelated arguments: the "zoological argument," which sees monogamous sexual relationships among "the lower animals"; the "physiological argument," which claims that promiscuous sexual intercourse impairs fertility; and the "psychological argument," which holds that sexual jealousy is "an innate human characteristic."[40] Westermarck admitted the existence of matriliny, but noted that it did not imply the social, political, or even familial dominance of women.[41] Westermarck described "primeval" marriage as "the habit for a man and a woman (or several women) to live together, to have sexual relations with one another, and to rear their offspring in common, the man being the protector and supporter of his family and the woman being his helpmate and the nurse of their children." This was a habit, Westermarck said, "sanctioned by custom, and afterwards by law, and ... thus transformed into a social institution": the institution of patriarchal marriage.[42]

Even before Westermarck, there were chinks in the matriarchal armor among continental anthropologists. The German ethnologist Franz Bernhöft, initially very taken by Morgan's evolutionism, came to have doubts about the priority of mother right as early as 1882 through his study of Indo-European kinship terms, the bulk of which indicated paternal rather than maternal family ties (the opposite conclusion of that reached by his colleague Lothar Dargun).[43] In France, Émile Durkheim objected to the comparative method as "assembling facts from all sources pertaining to the social milieux of the most diversified civilizations ... putting all these disparate data in the same category," and then "implying that all so-called savage or primitive peoples constituted one and the same social type." He also took exception to "the hypothesis of a collective marriage" in which "a confused and enormous group of men [marry] an equally indeterminate group of women."[44]

Back in Britain, where it all started, E. B. Tylor, who had done so much to make matriarchal myth respectable, began to doubt its veracity. Tylor began his 1896 article, "The Matriarchal Family System," by recalling the "shock" that attended the publication of McLennan's *Primitive Marriage,* which "upset the received patriarchal views" and led to the adoption of "primaeval" promiscuity "almost as a fact established by anthropology." But he then noted that "since then . . . a reaction has set in before which the theory is likely to be transformed, or to pass away altogether."[45] Apparently accepting Darwinian-styled criticisms of matriarchal theory, Tylor remarked that "mutual recognition and kindness between the male and female parents of their offspring appear too far down in the animal world for rudimentary ideas of paternity to be accounted a human discovery." Where Tylor previously saw mother right, he now saw patriarchy, patriarchy, and more patriarchy: "However the human race may be classified in stages of culture, whether from the lower to the higher Stone age, and thence on to the Bronze and Iron ages, or from savage life supported by wild fruit or game to agricultural and pastoral prosperity, or from the condition of the roaming family to that of the settled nation, the paternal system is to be found in strong if not exclusive prevalence."[46]

However, even in this late article, Tylor remained fascinated with "maternal" family life, seeing it as a puzzle of large enough dimensions to demand a proper anthropological solution. The "maternal family," said Tylor (though now deemed to be present in only a few tribes, "perhaps not exceeding twenty peoples"), could nevertheless "be found in all the great regions of the barbaric world." Tylor waffled on the issue of the evolutionary precedence of "maternal" cultures. Having first suggested that "the paternal system" seemed dominant in even the earliest human cultures, he nevertheless noted that there had been found "twice or thrice as many imperfect [family] systems, which appear from their fragments of maternal rules to belong to the period of transition into the new paternal stage," implying that matriarchy came first. In a particularly unsatisfying argument, Tylor attributes maternal kinship to exogamy, itself the product of an attempt to curb intertribal conflict. Under conditions of exogamy, maternal kinship is "practically dictated by self-interest," since "there is no loss to the wife's family, who retain her and her children, gaining at the same time help and defence from the husband." Tylor never explains why this solution is preferable to the paternal one, which has the advantage of not giving up its sons to be husbands in another tribe and at the same time gaining wives who can reproduce for them.[47]

FIELDWORK AS THE NEW ANTHROPOLOGICAL IMPERATIVE

Such ambivalence was satisfying to no one and was soon swallowed up in the general move within anthropology toward fieldwork and a theory of cultural specificity. In the same year that Tylor's "Matriarchal Family System" was published, Franz Boas's article, "The Limitations of the Comparative Method of Anthropology," came out. Criticizing the comparative method and the doctrine

FIGURE 27. Franz Boas (1858–1942), German American anthropologist whose work undermined the foundations of the
matriarchal theory

of "survivals," Boas began a wholesale revolution in anthropological method that
effectively pulled the rug out from under the feet of matriarchal myth.

Franz Boas, a German anthropologist who did his fieldwork among the
Kwakiutl of northwestern Canada and who eventually immigrated to the United
States, was initially a dutiful, if less than enthusiastic, follower of the matriarchal
thesis. Early on, he wrote of the Kwakiutl that their marriage ceremonies "seem
to show that originally matriarchate prevailed also among them." He reversed
his thinking in 1895, however, arguing that the Kwakiutl were actually in the process of moving from patriliny to matriliny.[48] From here, Boas began to articulate
a far more sweeping critique of evolutionary anthropology. Complaining that
evolutionists start with the assumption "that the same ethnological phenomena

are always due to the same cause," Boas described the faulty logic of the matriarchal myth as follows: "We find many types of structure of family. It can be proved that paternal families have often developed from maternal ones. Therefore, it is said, all paternal families have developed from maternal ones." Seeing this reasoning behind any evolutionary claim, Boas concluded that "the comparative method . . . has been remarkably barren of definite results, and I believe it will not become fruitful until we renounce the vain endeavor to construct a uniform systematic history of the evolution of culture."[49]

In place of the comparative method, Boas recommended "the much ridiculed historical method" of studying culture, which he described as an "inductive process by which the actual relations of definite phenomena may be derived"—very much the same process advocated by Bastian.[50] Boas cautioned against the mistake made by earlier cultural diffusionists such as Lafitau, that of considering "slight similarities of culture" to be "proofs of relationships." ("The assumption of lost connecting links must be applied most sparingly," said Boas.)[51] Boas made careful room for cross-cultural comparative work as long as it was not prematurely jammed into an evolutionary scheme. But the practical effect of the revolution he introduced was to send anthropologists out into the field to collect data without much attention to systematizing or interpreting it. This was partially motivated by the fact that many non-industrial cultures were rapidly dying out under the impact of Western imperialism and influence and could only be observed for posterity's sake if it were done quickly. But the vogue for fieldwork at the beginning of the twentieth century was also part of a new disciplinary desire to revel in ethnographic details, in all the "quixotic, irrational, and inscrutable ingredients in human life."[52]

Boas, himself trained as a scientist (he had studied physics in Germany before turning to ethnology), was loath to see in human culture any simple, law-like working out of biological destiny. When Boas was studying the Kwakiutl and rethinking his earlier position on matriarchy and evolutionism, he was also reading Kant. In Kant's philosophy, cognition organizes experience and thus logically precedes it. Boas, in a move that is to this day deeply felt in cultural anthropology, placed culture in the position Kant gave to cognition: it is above experience, organizes experience, and creates reality as understood by members of a particular culture. Put simply, Boas argued that nature could only be experienced through culture, effectively putting culture in the front seat and biology in the back. Theories of culture that emphasized predictable chains of evolution in groups widely separated by history and geography could find no place within the Boasian approach. Much less was there any room for a firm separation between "them" and "us," the "primitive" and the "civilized."[53] Even if no other forces had been at work, this alone would have been sufficient to crush the grand ambitions of matriarchal myth. The similar approach of Adolf Bastian had done much to short-circuit any real success the matriarchal theory might have had in continental anthropology.

Boas's revolution was especially successful in the United States, which came into its own, anthropologically speaking. The emphasis on fieldwork accorded well with American tendencies toward empiricism and particularism and took advantage of the proximity of indigenous Americans. Historian of anthropology George Stocking describes the anthropology of this era as "a kind of immigrant science, culturally marginal to its own society as well as to the groups that were the subject of ethnographic fieldwork."[54] As a German Jew, economically and socially privileged but the object of anti-Semitism, Boas was well positioned to deploy a culturally marginal identity in the service of a more relativistic anthropology.[55] In making the United States—a largely immigrant nation—his intellectual base, Boas further emphasized the unique perspective provided by the observer who is never really at home—not when he is "at home," and certainly not in the field.[56]

THE IMPACT OF NEW ETHNOGRAPHY ON
MATRIARCHAL MYTH

Historicist, functionalist anthropology was by definition hostile to universalizing, evolutionary schemes, and thus to the myth of matriarchal prehistory as McLennan and Morgan had characterized it. But in addition, the findings that early twentieth-century anthropologists brought back from the field did not support mother right. Simply put, no matriarchies were found; no group marriage was found; no promiscuous hordes were found; and where matriliny was discovered, its characteristics rarely fit the profile that evolutionary anthropology had laid out for it. For example, some peoples claimed that children were "derived from the father alone," but nevertheless practiced matrilineal descent; others, practicing patriliny, customarily traced inheritance through maternal uncles. Matriliny, where practiced, did not seem to improve women's status; and everywhere, so it seemed, anthropologists found marriage, usually in forms that were not in the least exotic. As Robert Lowie put it, "Marriage between single pairs is not absent but common among the simplest tribes and no ground whatsoever exists for assuming a condition of ancient promiscuity. Indeed, on the lowest cultural plane we frequently encounter matrimonial relations that would be rated exemplary by a mid-Victorian moralist."[57]

Even more troublesome for the evolutionary scheme of matriarchal myth was the unexpected finding that many matrilineal societies were at "higher levels of cultural complexity" than patrilineal ones, and the complementary finding that father right could be found "among a number of backward tribes." The whole chronological sequence of matriarchal myth was thrown off.[58] In theory, the critics of evolutionary anthropology held that all grand schemes were suspect. But in a stunning—and illuminating—exception, American anthropologists temporarily adopted the view that there *was* an evolutionary sequence in kinship systems, and that it ran from patrilineal to matrilineal, with matrilineal societies occupying a higher plane than patrilineal ones.[59] Apparently, critiquing evolutionism competed with nose-thumbing as the primary motivation of the iconoclastic, fieldwork-championing anthropologists at the turn of the century.

For all the pressures combining to defeat matriarchal myth within the discipline of anthropology, there were some who chose to actively defend the matriarchal thesis up to and even after the Second World War. However, across the board, the trend within cultural anthropology was to backpedal, to equivocate, and to hedge matriarchal proclamations with careful disclaimers. Aside from Robert Briffault and Mathilde and Mathias Vaerting, who approached their matriarchal task with revolutionary zeal, anthropologists found ways to say less and to say it less passionately.

8

Matriarchal Myth in the Late Nineteenth Century

Why Then? Why Not Before?

Nothing, perhaps, gives a more instructive insight into the true condition of savages than their ideas on the subject of relationship and marriage; nor can the great advantages of civilisation be more conclusively proved than by the improvement which it has already effected in the relation between the two sexes.

—JOHN LUBBOCK

PRECONDITIONS FOR THE DEVELOPMENT OF MATRIARCHAL MYTH

It is a matter of historical record that in the early 1900s, matriarchal myth lost most of the ground it had gained among anthropologists in the late nineteenth century; but what is perhaps more curious is why it ever attained such currency in the first place. As we have seen, this was no marginal or passing fad, but a theory that sprang up in several places virtually at once (with Bachofen in Switzerland, McLennan in Britain, and Morgan in the United States) and that received an enthusiastic reception not only in the anthropological circles it called home, but also across the humanistic and social scientific disciplines, some of which carried it forward into the twentieth century. The matriarchal thesis even caught on outside the academy, mainly via Engels, Bebel, and first-wave feminists such as Elizabeth Cady Stanton, who took it into the heart of nineteenth- and twentieth-century political movements. What confluence of factors in the late nineteenth century suddenly gave matriarchal myth such widespread appeal? It is not as though the idea of matriarchy had never crossed human minds before. As we have seen, from antiquity on, Amazon legends were a popular form of literature and even of imaginative ethnography. But up until the late nineteenth century this interest in powerful women and gender reversals faced two insurmountable constraints.

First, until Lyell's acceptance of the doctrine of human antiquity in 1859, the six-thousand-year biblical timescale for "Man" was the reigning theory. A few individual thinkers, such as Voltaire in the eighteenth century, had questioned the biblical timescale aggressively, but no academic discipline had risked its reputation by denying it wholesale. Prudence dictated acceptance of the dual scriptural claim that human history went back six thousand years and that it was a history of male domination. If women ruled, then, they could only do so in some place outside the West, where they existed as perversions (or degenerations) of the cultural order set in place by no less a personage than God himself. And if there were places where women ruled, they had not been found. Prior to the flowering of the matriarchal thesis, there had of course been reports of Amazons and matriarchies, but none were corroborated.

Both of these constraints were lifted in the late nineteenth century: prehistory expanded to such a degree that virtually anything could have happened before written records, and ethnographies of different people and their strange customs proliferated, opening up the possibility that men were not everywhere or at all times dominant. Of these two, the discovery of human antiquity was undoubtedly the more important. The idea of prehistory barely existed in Europe prior to 1859. With the Bible taken as a historical text, some information about human history was provided from creation through to civilization. And extensive records began with classical antiquity, which meant that of six thousand years of human history, nearly half were relatively well known even apart from biblical narratives. After the discovery of human antiquity, in contrast, prehistory mushroomed by several orders of magnitude. Suddenly there were hundreds of thousands, even millions of years of human life about which we were ignorant. As archaeologists like to point out, if the history of humanity were a book 400 pages long, beginning with "the first time a human ancestor stood upright on the African savanna," the only part of the book we could read—that is, the only part of human history covered by written texts—would be the last half of the last page. This leaves more than 99 percent of human existence in the vast realm of prehistory, home of bones, tools, and only very late in the game, artwork and habitations.[1] For late nineteenth-century thinkers, this was an enormous blank canvas positively begging to be blocked out and painted. The story of human life on earth, formerly given only to sequels, was abruptly subject to a prequel of truly astonishing length.

The effect this had on matriarchal myth was profound. Scattered, fanciful legends of Amazons and barbarians with strange customs suddenly had room to move, and they did so with enthusiasm and abandon. It may seem problematic at first that the initial salvo in the matriarchal revolution came from Bachofen, who seems to have been operating on a biblical timescale—or at least not on the greatly expanded timescale resulting from the discovery of human antiquity. But this does not ultimately discount the importance of human antiquity in explaining the matriarchal explosion of the late nineteenth century. There is no way to test this hypothesis, of course, but it is worth asking whether or not Bachofen would have received the attention he did if his work had not coincided with the dramatic expansion of human prehistory. In fact, Bachofen's work did *not* receive much attention at the time he published it; he was quickly superseded by McLennan, who was outspoken about the impact that the discovery of human antiquity had on his considerations of the evolution of marriage. Until Bachofen was adopted in the early twentieth century as the patriarch of a group of Munich intellectuals (the *Kosmische Runde*) who resurrected his love affair with the Great Mother, his fame only piggy-backed on that of the British social anthropologists.[2] Like Fourier before him, who had given a mere two centuries to the "Edenic" stage, Bachofen's Demetrian matriarchy, bracketed on the one side by hetaerism and on the other by the triumph of Dionysus and then Apollo, lasted at best one or two thousand years, compared to the ages of male dominance, dated quite dependably to at least two and a half thousand years.[3] The myth of matriarchal prehistory is just not very compelling, as stories go, if the matriarchal era is brief and transitory. With dates like these, matriarchy becomes a mere curiosity rather than a critical benchmark in the evolution of the human race. Quite simply, then, the myth of matriarchal prehistory could not have the power it achieved in the late nineteenth century until there was sufficient prehistoric time available for it to rival the age of the patriarchy, and this did not occur until 1859.

The other enabling condition of late nineteenth-century matriarchal theory was the increased availability of ethnographic reports about "savage" tribal peoples. The myth of matriarchal prehistory flourished during a particular window of opportunity in which there was enough ethnographic information available to anthropologists, but not too much.[4] Too much ethnographic data, as history would later prove, could be devastating for the matriarchal thesis. Putative matriarchies could be discredited, and such "matriarchy" as there was could (and did) fail to occur at the expected level of social evolution. But insufficient ethnographic information—the condition that obtained before the nineteenth century—was also limiting for the matriarchal thesis, since in the absence of a broad base of such data, Europeans could safely imagine that other cultures were more or less the same. As more ethnographies became available, it was clear that cultural variation was not superficial, but quite deep.

Of course, how deeply cultural variation lies is almost wholly a matter of interpretation. British anthropologists, for a variety of reasons, *wanted* cultural variation to be deep, and this is just what they found. Furthermore, they wanted to see "oddities" of sexual behavior and gender roles, and they found these also. British anthropologists could have filled up prehistoric time with nongendered themes, or they could have found other aspects of ethnographic data more enlivening than their pet concerns of sex and marriage—but they didn't. It is their overpowering hunger to investigate sex and gender roles that demands explanation, for it is this interest that lent itself most compellingly to the theory of matriarchal prehistory.

THE PATRIARCHAL FAMILY IN TROUBLE

The most obvious source of anthropological interest in sex and gender is probably also the most significant: that the patriarchal family—long a central institution in British society—was coming under increasing challenge, even as patriarchal custom was being further entrenched into civil law. The seeds of the dislocation of the patriarchal family were sown in the seventeenth century, when British philosophers first developed theories of social contract. Social contract theory inadvertently undermined the patriarchal family as it sought to undermine the divine right of kings. Royalty had long been defended as a macro version of the patriarchal family, in which one male manages the lives and work of his wife, children, other relatives, servants, and employees.[5] The early social contract philosophers—primarily Hobbes and Locke—did not try to argue that the analogy between the patriarchal family and monarchical government was a false one; they generally followed out their own logic, and decried inequality within the household as well as the nation. Individuals, free by nature, necessarily had to "*agree* to be ruled by another." Social contract theory was thus profoundly disruptive of existing defenses of relationships of dominance and subordination.[6] If such relationships were to continue—for example, between husbands and wives—then new defenses for them would have to be found.[7]

One way around this conundrum, favored by later political liberals, was to deny the analogy between political rule and household rule, naming the family home as a "separate sphere," a "refuge from the tensions and turmoil of the larger society," "a sacred place, a vestal temple." If women did not have the same political rights as men, they did not need them, for within the domestic sphere, "women could finally be placed on the pedestal on which they belonged." The "two spheres" ideal was interpreted by its partisans as being very congenial to women's interests. Women were able to avoid or at least minimize physical labor and assaults upon themselves stemming from male lust, and they continued to be cared for in old age.[8] But it also reinforced an ever greater sense of difference between the sexes. As Elizabeth Fox-Genovese asserts, "The Victorians would produce the apotheosis of the female as so unequal as to be naturally of another human order."[9]

The "two spheres" model was lent great credence by an expanding ideology of sex difference, begun a century before the Victorian anthropologists set to work. Sex difference had not been a key factor in the thinking of the early contract theorists. They did not doubt that women, like men, were fully human, nor did they place women below men on an evolutionary tree.[10] But later thinkers did not share their view. By the late eighteenth century, medical commentators began to insist that "women were distinct from men by virtue of their total anatomy and physiology," with their reproductive organs forming "the foundation of incommensurable difference."[11] Where before women had been seen as either fundamentally the same as men or as an (inferior) variation on a male model, it became customary to view the sexes as radically different from each other.[12] And where male supremacy had formerly been a basic matter of superior physical and political power, it increasingly came to be theorized as a psychological and biological reality that was conveniently "beyond the realm of contestation" and thus also beyond efforts at political change.[13]

Theories that located sex difference at a deep biological level had high currency in the late nineteenth century. The most popular of these theories was articulated in a book titled *The Evolution of Sex,* written by Scottish biologist Patrick Geddes and his student, J. Arthur Thomson. Drawing heavily on Spencer's work, Geddes and Thomson argued that sex difference lived within each cell of a man or woman in the form of differing types of metabolism: male cells were "katabolic" ("active, energetic, eager, passionate, variable") while female cells were "anabolic" ("passive, conservative, sluggish and stable"). Women's energy—what there was of it—had to be conserved for the rigors of reproduction, and this prevented them from engaging in social and political activity. Women "were patient because of their passivity and the need to store energy" and "were superior to men in constancy of affection and sympathetic imagination." But male metabolism predisposed men to "greater power of maximum effort, of scientific insight or cerebral experiment with impressions."[14] This was a strong argument for the status quo and its authors knew that. As Geddes remarked, "What was decided among the prehistoric *Protozoa* cannot be annulled by Act of Parliament."[15]

From a somewhat different vantage point, Darwin wrote sex difference into biological evolution via the mechanisms of natural and sexual selection. Arguing that early hunting communities would naturally select for courage and intelligence in men, Darwin posited something he called "the equal transmission of characters": qualities selected for in one sex will be passed, in somewhat inferior form, to the other sex as well, which is why women could retain some slight intelligence of their own.[16] As Darwin wrote: "It is indeed fortunate that the law of equal transmission of characters to both sexes prevails with mammals. Other-

wise it is probable that man would have become as superior in mental endowment to woman as the peacock is in ornamental plumage to the peahen."[17]
The Victorian era thus produced a curious coincidence of interests in what
we might now call "nature" and "nurture" when it came to sex and gender. Both
nature and nurture received fresh injections of practical insight from the corpus
of evolutionary thought. On the one hand, human nature as a biologically determined quantity became newly compelling with Darwin's argument that humans
were evolutionarily related to primates and indeed to all animals. Victorian
thinkers were presented with the possibility that "if mating followed certain exigencies within the animal kingdom, perhaps mankind's complex laws were
simply a human variation of this."[18] On the other hand, it was clear that human
mating patterns and gender roles were not identical to those of any other species
of animal, nor were they everywhere the same.[19] This variation demanded explanation in sociocultural terms. And it was here that matriarchal myth stepped in
to straddle these two discourses, producing a narrative that could promote itself
as a grand unified theory of sex and its evolutionary development.[20]

But if political exigencies created by liberal contract theory had set in motion
a reconceptualization of sex and gender, what provided the motive force for Victorian anthropological obsessions with these same topics was "a fierce and violent debate . . . over the nature of sexual relations, the question of power between
the sexes and the role of the family in relation to other social institutions."[21]
Many women raised the banner of liberal political doctrine in pursuit of their
own emancipation, as well they should have, for women were not faring well in
the Victorian era. Women's lot was actually becoming worse rather than better
as customary political disabilities were being written into law in the first half of
the nineteenth century and as middle-class women progressively lost economic
prerogatives when commerce moved from domestic to dedicated business premises. Marriage involved the near-complete erasure of the female partner: as the
husband and wife were deemed to be "one body" before God, they were "one
person" in the eyes of the law. Someone had to represent that "one person," and it
was the husband. Married women could not sue or be sued on their own account,
sign contracts not also signed by their husbands, or write their own wills. Any
property a woman owned prior to marriage was legally administered by her husband, and any property she acquired after marriage was automatically his. Provi-
sions for "the restitution of conjugal rights" allowed a husband to legally demand
his wife's return to his home in the event that she sought escape. Divorce was
virtually impossible to obtain. Apart from ecclesiastical annulment, the only
option available was a private Act of Parliament, an expensive procedure that
occurred at a rate of roughly one per year since 1697. This situation changed
dramatically with the Matrimonial Causes Act of 1857, but women were still permitted divorce only in cases of adultery, and then only if it were "aggravated by

some further abuse" such as sodomy, rape, or incest. A wife who left her husband without procuring a divorce was "guilty of desertion," and all her property and her rights in her children automatically went to him. The other option—choosing not to marry—was not a real one for most middle- and working-class women, who could not successfully support themselves outside marriage. Women were very much present in the workforce (by the early twentieth century, women constituted one third of the total working population in England), but were rendered invisible by their relegation to the lowest-paying, lowest-status jobs.[22]

Victorian feminists responded to this situation by agitating for change, at first focusing on education and employment, and later directly confronting marriage law and demanding the vote. These efforts were met with predictable distress on the part of the ruling class of men. There was some openness to effecting legal change for women's benefit (in part because some of these changes also benefited men), but there was also fear that things might go too far. Critics claimed that the changes Victorian feminists advocated "would be instrumental in undermining marriage, the family, and the structure of society."[23] This time of agitation about "the woman question" was—not coincidentally, I think—the exact time when the theory of matriarchal prehistory began to be offered up as fact among British anthropologists.[24]

The Victorian era, often remembered as a time of social order and stolidity, was in reality a time of great cultural and political upheaval. Repressive sexual mores hid a world of sexual curiosity and dissent; restrictive gender roles, especially for the middle class, cloaked an enormous debate about women's rights and women's nature; the apparently stable political environment in Britain covered over a recent past of internal political unrest and contested colonialism.[25] Like the 1950s in the United States, the late nineteenth century in Britain appeared to be, and in one sense actually was, an unusually stable time, but it was a forced stability produced by the memory of recent disruption and the fear of future chaos.[26]

It was this environment that was most responsible for producing the myth of matriarchal prehistory and spinning out its attendant theories of sex and gender . . . and often, race, religion, and government as well. The myth of matriarchal prehistory fed both of the (contradictory) social needs of late nineteenth-century Britain: the need to proclaim the essential rightness—in this case, the evolutionary fitness—of Victorian moral and political values; and the need to unsettle these same values, to lift off the lid and examine the simmering stew of cultural alternatives. Users of the myth typically favored one or the other of these elements of the myth, but what is perhaps most intriguing is that frequently both the conservative and the radical implications were intermingled for each of the myth's proponents. What the consumer of the myth of matriarchal prehistory received was neither an uncritical celebration of patriarchy and empire nor a call for its downfall, but rather a spectrum of confused opinion that oscillated between the two.

In spite of much slander heaped upon them in succeeding years, the Victorian anthropologists were not uniformly "in the rearguard on issues relating to gender and marriage." Most of them were politically liberal and regarded themselves as progressives; they felt that conservative arguments against women's emancipation and in favor of the patriarchal family were "reactionary and crude."[27] Some were themselves involved in agitating for change in marriage laws and made common cause with feminists. Lewis Henry Morgan, for example, left a bequest to the University of Rochester upon his death specifically "for the furthering of female education."[28]

However, these men were generally uncomfortable with any too hasty or complete dismantling of the patriarchal family. As we have seen, even most communist proponents of matriarchal myth were content to put off dramatic social change in the arena of sex and the family. And whatever quasi-feminist sentiments Bachofen and the evolutionary anthropologists upheld, their deployment of the matriarchal thesis rested on the Victorian status quo of marriage and gender relations. The same was the case on the continent, too, where a more Romantic view of femaleness obtained. Monogamy was the ideal form of marriage, and it was Western civilization alone that had placed women on the pedestal where they belonged.[29] These familiar assertions persisted while they were at the same time placed on a radically new footing. For if women's position was regarded as a given (possibly by divine fiat) prior to the late nineteenth-century explosion of interest in the matriarchal thesis, it was afterward seen as the culmination of a long evolutionary struggle toward higher and better forms of human society. Women's secondary status, their fitness for the private sphere—formerly secured by natural law or divine authority—was now secured by evolution, by the upward march of civilization.[30]

In the late nineteenth century, the matriarchal thesis was intensely ambivalent in relation to the feminist cause. At times, its advocates used matriarchal theory to denaturalize and historicize women's oppression. Women were not always and everywhere subordinate to men; relationships between the sexes changed over time for specific evolutionary reasons, and could change again. But at other times, the take-home message of the matriarchal thesis was that all history, indeed, the entire apparatus of a highly determined evolutionary track, ran inevitably toward a secondary status for women that neither should nor could be changed at the whim of contemporary feminists.

This Victorian male ambivalence toward feminist concerns is well captured in what was probably the single most popular book on matriarchy published in the late nineteenth century: the novel *She,* by H. Rider Haggard. A minor civil servant in South Africa and later a farmer there before his return to England in 1881, Haggard is best remembered for a trio of novels set in Africa, and featuring English explorers, savage Africans, and regal women. The well-known adventure tales *King Solomon's Mines* and its sequel *Allan Quartermain* flanked Haggard's composition of *She,* written in a mere six weeks and first published in 1887.

Haggard was no scholar of prehistory or the social sciences. Indeed, Haggard was not a scholar of anything. Like Dan Brown writing over a century later, Haggard wrote formulaic genre fiction. And if *The Da Vinci Code* is a synecdoche of late twentieth-century matriarchal myth, *She,* in a more one-sided way, can be read as a synecdoche of late Victorian matriarchal myth.

The matriarchy that emerges in the pages of *She* is not the sex-positive Christian paganism that drives Dan Brown's *Da Vinci Code.* In the late nineteenth century, matriarchy was a far more fearful prospect than this. And patriarchy, the easy target of Brown's *Da Vinci Code* (embodied in the Catholic Church) was in Haggard's day a social system that was lauded as the natural endpoint of human evolution. Racist, anti-Semitic, and antifeminist, Haggard's *She* flirts with matriarchy as with danger: it is a novel of "colonialism and male dread," of "nightmares, suppressed desires, and fantasies."[31]

The heroes in Haggard's narrative are all British men. Ludwig Horace Holly, the narrator of the tale, is a Fellow at Cambridge University. He is a self-confessed "misogynist" who raises Leo Vincey, a friend's son, after his friend's untimely death. Holly is an ugly man: "Women hated the sight of me," he noted, and recounted overhearing one woman say to another that he was a "monster" who "had converted her to the monkey theory." Holly's young charge Leo is, in contrast, beautiful. When Leo first comes to Holly as a toddler, "a perfect child," Holly resolves not to hire a nanny for Leo, saying, "I would have no woman to lord it over me about the child, and steal his affections from me." Instead he employs a young man named Job—also described by Haggard as a misogynist—to help care for Leo.[32]

Leo's childhood, adolescence, and university years all pass in four pages. The real action of the novel begins when Holly retrieves the chest that Leo's father, before his death, had instructed Holly to open on Leo's twenty-fifth birthday. The chest contains a letter to Leo and a few mysterious artifacts. Between the letter and some inscriptions on an ancient potsherd, the three men learn that Leo's heritage reaches back to the fourth century B.C.E., to his ancestors Kallikrates and Amenartas, a royal Egyptian couple. According to the narrative inscribed on the potsherd, Kallikrates and Amenartas left Egypt after their marriage and traveled down the eastern coast of Africa, where they eventually met a queen who held the secret of immortality. The queen fell in love with Kallikrates and offered to make him immortal if he would only kill Amenartas. When Kalli-krates refused, the queen murdered him by magical means, and Amenartas, pregnant with their son, fled from the queen's country, eventually arriving in Athens with her child. When death approached for Amenartas, she entreated her son to find the immortal queen and kill her in revenge for having killed his father.[33] This family legacy, according to the materials in the chest, had been handed from father to son for over two millennia, with some, including Leo's father, attempting to make the journey to Africa to investigate its truth.

The quest now falling to Leo, he resolves to travel to Africa, with Holly and Job insisting on accompanying him. Like *The Da Vinci Code*, Haggard's *She* moves quickly from one precarious situation to another, thrilling the reader with numerous brushes with death and danger as the novel's heroes approach ever closer to the mysterious history of a powerful, misunderstood woman. Whereas *The Da Vinci Code* reveals the matricentric truth behind the secrets kept by Christianity, though, *She* reveals the truth behind darkest Africa and its fearful matriarchy.

On their way to find "She," Leo, Holly, and Job encounter a group of African natives, the Amhagger, who happen to be ruled by the immortal white queen that our heroes seek. And though it is the practice of the Amhagger to kill and eat all strangers who stumble into their country, they refrain from killing Leo, Holly, and Job because the queen has instructed them, "If white men come, slay them not. Let them be brought to the house of 'She-who-must-be-obeyed.'"[34] On the arduous journey to the lair of She-who-must-be-obeyed, our heroes become acquainted with the strange customs of the Amhagger. Among the Amhagger, "descent is traced only through the line of the mother," and "they never pay attention to, or even acknowledge, any man as their father, even when their male parentage is perfectly well known." Women choose their mates and keep them only so long as they wish; all the manual labor is performed by men. As an informant explains to Holly, "In this country the women do what they please. We worship them, and give them their way, because without them the world could not go on; they are the source of life." Haggard's vision of a matriarchal society does not stay romantic for long; when the women become "unbearable" (which they do "about every second generation"), the men kill the older generation of women in order to frighten the younger ones and remind them that men "are the strongest."[35]

All this is prologue to the inevitable encounter with "She." As Leo is ill, "She"—whose name, we learn, is Ayesha—meets first with Holly. Holly's Amhagger guide instructs him to enter Ayesha's presence on his hands and knees, but Holly refuses, reasoning, "I was an Englishman, and why, I asked myself, should I creep into the presence of some savage woman as though I were a monkey in fact as well as in name? I would not and could not do it."[36] Holly soon learns that Ayesha has lived for many centuries, waiting for the return of her lover Kallikrates, who she expects to come back from the dead. Holly eventually asks to look upon Ayesha, who has up until now been wrapped in gauzy white cloth. Holly is instantly transported by her beauty, which he describes as "the beauty of celestial beings . . . only this beauty, with all its awful loveliness and purity, was *evil*." In spite of the evil he senses in her, Holly falls "absolutely and hopelessly in love with this white sorceress" (whose whiteness is emphasized ad nauseam through references to her "ivory arms" and "the snowy argent of her breast").[37] Indeed, Ayesha has this effect on every man who sees her, including Leo (who turns out to be Kallikrates reborn). In thrall to Ayesha, Leo instantly forgets about her murder of his ancestor as well as the Amhagger woman with whom he has partnered during his brief time in Africa. "I am a degraded brute," Leo confesses to Holly. "I know that I am in her power for always; if I never saw her again I should never think of anybody else during all my life; I must follow her as a needle follows a magnet; I would not go away now if I could; I could not leave her, my legs would not carry me, but my mind is still clear enough, and in my mind I hate her—at least, I think so."[38] Holly reflects on Leo's choice: "True, in uniting himself to this dread woman," he had placed "his life under the influence of a mysterious creature of evil tendencies . . . but then that would be likely enough to happen to him in any ordinary marriage."[39]

Ronald Hutton describes *She* as "a profoundly hostile portrait of primitive matriarchy,"[40] and indeed no detective work is required to see its deep suspicion of and hatred toward women. *She* is vastly more one-dimensional and harsh in its attitude toward women than the matriarchal myth articulated by the late nineteenth-century anthropologists. Still, Haggard captured much of the fear and ambivalence that notions of matriarchy conjured in the late nineteenth century. Women, like the "savages" of colonial lands, were both wonderful and dangerous, a marker of how far and how fast late Victorian men feared they might fall, of how tenuous their authority felt to them as they sat atop the peak of cultural evolution.

Feminist critics have been wont to say that evolution proved to be every bit as congenial to the oppression of women as had earlier doctrines of the timeless, original subordination of women. And it is true that whatever its liberal leanings, evolutionary anthropology was unequivocally on the side of the status quo. But there was greater ambiguity in the evolutionary model, more room to negotiate.[41] The theory of evolution was historicizing. If women were in a lower social position than men in the present, this was but a chapter of a longer story in which women held a variety of positions vis-à-vis men. Such "facts" could be—and were—deployed in a variety of ways, some serving to enshroud the status quo in a glow of progressive inevitability, others working to decenter traditional sex roles, drawing "savages" and women into the circle of a broader humanity or reversing established hierarchies altogether.

Some commentators have suggested that the matriarchal thesis fell out of favor precisely because of its interpretive ambiguity, its potential to destabilize the settled verities upon which the patriarchal family rested. For example, V. F. Calverton, writing in 1931, suggested that initially the matriarchal thesis served the need of bolstering the status quo: monogamy and capitalism. However, as anthropologists and others came to appreciate that evolution might not stop with Victorian England, but continue on to who knows what else, it became a matter of some urgency to reground monogamous marriage and private property in something more solid than one (potentially passing) evolutionary stage.[42] Similarly, Raoul Makarius associates the passing of anthropology's fascination with matriarchal prehistory not to any "theoretical dissatisfaction with evolutionism," but to "the material support" its opponents received "from the Colonial Office." Makarius argues that functionalism, the anthropological dogma rapidly replacing evolutionism in the early twentieth century, "suited colonial policy perfectly" because it "studied the conditions of social stability, and therefore made for colonial stability," unlike evolutionism, which was prima facie interested in "studying the conditions of social change."[43]

I believe the historical record shows quite conclusively that the doctrine of cultural evolutionism—and the matriarchal thesis, which flourished in its embrace—was in itself neither reactionary nor revolutionary, conservative nor liberal. Nor, significantly, did it sit solidly, squarely, in the middle, advocating baby steps toward sexual equality while keeping a patriarchal core inviolate. For all its apparent self-satisfaction—the ladder of inevitable progress leading upward to civilization and empire—evolutionary anthropology opened a door to a cultural dynamism that could not be neatly contained or confined to one political cause or another. The subsequent history of the matriarchal thesis bear this out. What was in Lubbock's hands (to take one example) a triumphalist narrative of male British hegemony became in the hands of later feminists, socialists, sexual libertarians, and anarchists the definitive proof that things can, should, and will be different in the future from what they now are. Lest this sound as though the matriarchal thesis was an inherently liberatory story inadvertently formed by men who mistakenly thought it was in their self-interest as the heirs of privilege and empire, it is well to remember that matriarchal myth also fell into the hands of fascists, male supremacists, and misogynists championing the evolutionary fitness of male dominance. Up until its adoption by second-wave feminists in the 1970s, matriarchal myth was antifeminist as often as it was pro-woman, continuing its role as a container for male ambivalence about sexed inequality (or perhaps, more simply, as a container for male ambivalence about women).

From its infancy right up to the present day, the matriarchal thesis has served as a grand thought experiment regarding the nature of sex and gender roles. However much its proponents may seek to disguise it as a story of eventualities—whether

feminist or not—the matriarchal thesis, in the basic core of its narrative structure, opens itself out onto a vista of possibilities. Indeed, I would argue, this has
been and continues to be its principal social, intellectual, and political function:
to act as a vehicle with which its proponents can simultaneously proclaim and
interrogate the received "facts" of sex and gender. So long as we remain interested in teasing out the contours of sex and gender, asking what is given and what
culturally constructed, what is timeless and what subject to change, matriarchal
myth will no doubt remain a compelling story to us.

NOTES

1. THE TRAVELS AND TRAVAILS OF MATRIARCHAL MYTH

1. At the beginning of the novel, Langdon has just completed a lecture on "pagan symbolism hidden in the stones of Chartres Cathedral" (Brown, *Da Vinci Code*, 9).

2. Ibid., 36, 120.

3. Ibid., 23, 46.

4. Ibid., 113. Brown claims that the Priory of Sion was a real organization whose members included Isaac Newton, Sandro Botticelli, Victor Hugo, and Leonardo da Vinci. But most of his "information" about the Priory of Sion seems to draw on the thought and writings of a right-wing Frenchman, Pierre Plantard, who believed himself to be the true heir to the Merovingian throne of France. It was Plantard who, probably quite fancifully, populated a supposedly historical Priory of Sion with figures like Newton and da Vinci. For more information on this and other debates about information contained in *The Da Vinci Code*, see Price, *Da Vinci Fraud*.

5. Brown, *Da Vinci Code*, 124. Constantine is also credited, ironically, with rescuing ancient paganism by fusing it with early Christianity: "nothing in Christianity is original," one of the novel's pedagogues asserts (232).

6. Ibid., 124, 125.

7. According to the novel, the scandal of Mary Magdalene's secret history is, in the eyes of the church, that she "had physical proof that the Church's newly proclaimed *deity* had spawned a mortal bloodline" (ibid., 254).

8. Interestingly, the novel never speculates on why Protestants have remained bound to the sexism and goddess-murder instituted by patriarchal Catholicism, or what role Eastern Orthodoxy played in the suppression of goddess religion. The novel shucks off Christianity's Middle Eastern origins and claims the main action for western Europe as

soon as Mary Magdalene presumably departs Jerusalem, shortly after Jesus's crucifixion, and arrives in France to tend to her secret dynastic line of Christ's heirs (ibid., 255).

9. Ibid., 446.

10. Of course, some people hated *The Da Vinci Code* with the same intensity as those who loved it, mostly those who had a stake in Christian orthodoxy.

11. Brown, *Da Vinci Code*, 444.

12. Actually, Dan Brown regards his novel as historical fiction, resting on many facts. He begins his book with a page titled "FACT," claiming that "all descriptions of artwork, architecture, documents, and secret rituals in this novel are accurate" (*Da Vinci Code*, n.p.). These supposed facts have been thoroughly critiqued. See, for example, Price, *Da Vinci Fraud*.

13. A great many feminists have reiterated this story, from Merlin Stone's 1976 study *When God Was a Woman* to the final summation of the work of Marija Gimbutas in her 1997 book *The Living Goddesses*. Perhaps the most popular summation was Riane Eisler's *The Chalice and the Blade*. For more on recent feminist appropriations of matriarchal myth, see Eller, *Living in the Lap of the Goddess*, 150–184; *Myth of Matriarchal Prehistory*, 30–55.

14. Diop, *Cultural Unity of Black Africa*, 23.

15. Mason, *Unnatural Order*, 11.

16. Shannon, *Great to Be a Girl*, 17–18.

17. Gore, *Earth in the Balance*, 260. Gore explicitly leaves "much room for skepticism about our ability to know exactly what this belief system—or collection of related beliefs—taught."

18. Peake, "Season of the Goddess," 31.

19. As Andre Gingrich writes, "Bachofen can still be seen as a founding spirit of the grand evolutionist debates that intrinsically connected the study of humanity's history with that of the development of gender relations" ("The German-Speaking Countries," in Barth et al., eds., *One Discipline, Four Ways*, 79).

20. The myth of matriarchal prehistory never achieved the sort of prominence in fascist circles that it held in communist circles, but a number of German philosophers and public intellectuals with fascist leanings revived Bachofen in the early twentieth century (including Ludwig Klages, Alfred Schuler, Carl Bernoulli, and Alfred Bäumler). This interest persisted into the era of National Socialism, with some thinkers, such as Ernst Bergmann, insisting that the Aryan race was originally matriarchal and that under matriarchal conditions, proper "racial hygiene" was practiced (*Erkenntnisgeist und Muttergeist;* "Deutung des nationalsozialistischen Gedankens," 36).

21. When Dan Brown was sued for copyright infringement, it was by two of the authors of *Holy Blood, Holy Grail* (Michael Baigent and Richard Leigh), whose book Brown did indeed follow very closely. But Brown's broader attention to goddess and matriarchalist themes is far more indebted to feminist matriarchal writings than to the work of Baigent and Leigh.

22. Stocking, *Victorian Anthropology*, 301–2.

23. For an overview, see Segal, *Myth*. In *The Politics of Myth*, Robert Ellwood makes the case that the entire idea of "myth" as a particular sort of story is thoroughly modern

and that the cultures that created the "myths" that scholars reflected upon did not necessarily distinguish these stories from folklore, fairy-tales, or legends (21).

24. Bruce Lincoln describes this as the "pejorative and condescending usage" of the term *myth* (*Discourse and the Construction of Society,* 24), but notes that it goes back to classical times, among later Greeks and Romans, and certainly among early Christians (*Theorizing Myth,* 47). Anthropologist Annette Hamilton describes this usage well: "A myth is usually described as a series of statements which some people might think are true, but which to others, privileged as to wisdom, know to be false" ("Knowledge and Misrecognition: Mythology and Gender in Aboriginal Australia," in Gewertz, ed., *Myths of Matriarchy Reconsidered,* 57).

25. James George Frazer, quoted in Burkert, *Structure and History in Greek Mythology and Ritual,* 143, n. 3.

26. According to Bruce Lincoln, the ancient Sophist philosopher Gorgias asserted just this view: myth is "a narrative that is (1) emotionally moving, (2) deceptive or misleading, but (3) misleading toward a good end" (*Theorizing Myth,* 34).

27. Paden, *Religious Worlds,* 70. Georg Friedrich Creuzer, who influenced Bachofen, offered a similar definition of myth (see Ellenberger, *Discovery of the Unconscious,* 729).

28. Others who have questioned the historical veracity of matriarchal myth include Conkey and Tringham, "Archaeology and the Goddess"; Ehrenberg, *Women in Prehistory;* Fagan, "Sexist View of Prehistory"; Hayden, "Archaeological Evaluation of the Gimbutas Paradigm"; Lefkowitz, "Twilight of the Goddess"; Meskell, "Goddesses, Gimbutas"; Townsend, "The Goddess"; Walters, "Caught in the Web."

29. Lincoln, *Theorizing Myth,* 147. Many scholars take issue with this definition, arguing that calling myth "ideological" is as pejorative as summarily rejecting it as untrue. A number of anthropologists make such arguments in Gewertz, ed., *Myths of Matriarchy Reconsidered* (see especially articles by Young, Weiner, Reay, Hamilton, and Thomas).

30. Burkert, *Structure and History in Greek Mythology and Ritual,* 2–3; Lévi-Strauss, *Structural Anthropology,* 216ff.; *Myth and Meaning,* 41–43.

31. Burkert, *Structure and History in Greek Mythology and Ritual,* 18. Lévi-Strauss regards these "strong contrasts" as an inherent component of myth. As Wendy Doniger explains Lévi-Strauss's view, "All mythology is dialectic in its attempt to make cognitive sense out of the chaotic data provided by nature, and . . . this attempt inevitably traps the human imagination in a web of dualisms" (foreword to Lévi-Strauss, *Myth and Meaning,* viii).

32. Lincoln, *Discourse and the Construction of Society,* 24–25.

33. See Malinowski, *Myth in Primitive Psychology,* 76; Wendy Doniger, foreword to Lévi-Strauss, *Myth and Meaning,* x.

34. Malinowski uses the case of sex inequality to articulate his view of the function of myth: "Nothing is more familiar to the native than the different occupations of the male and female sex; there is nothing to be *explained* about it. But though familiar, such differences are at times irksome, unpleasant, or at least limiting, and there is the need to justify them, to vouch for their antiquity and reality, in short to buttress their validity" (*Myth in Primitive Psychology,* 32–33). In my view, differences in sex roles are more than irksome, and are thus even more in need of explanation.

35. Perhaps to say that sex inequality is inexplicable is an exaggeration, for many things we once believed were inexplicable have been explained, and the dynamics and perpetuation of sex inequality have been extensively analyzed. But having spent many years searching for and digesting various accounts of the "why" of sex inequality, I still find the existing explanations wanting.

36. Bruce Lincoln recognizes this as a fundamental characteristic of myth, that "narrators ... modify details of the stories that pass through them, introducing changes in the classificatory order as they do so, most often in ways that reflect their subject position and advance their interests" (*Theorizing Myth*, 149).

2. AMAZONS EVERYWHERE

Epigraph: Lafitau, *Customs of the American Indians*, 73.

1. Pembroke, "Women in Charge," 1.

2. Kenyatta, *Facing Mount Kenya*, 5–10.

3. For Africa, see Colin M. Turnbull, "Mbuti Womanhood," in Dahlberg, ed., *Woman the Gatherer*. For Australia, see Annette Hamilton, "Knowledge and Misrecognition," in Gewertz, ed., *Myths of Matriarchy Reconsidered*, 59–60. Melanesian examples are given in Juillerat, "Odor of Man"; Terence Hays, "Myths of Matriarchy," in Gewertz, ed., *Myths of Matriarchy Reconsidered*; Tuzin, *Voice of the Tambaran*; Gillison, "Cannibalism among Women"; Meigs, *Food, Sex, and Pollution*; and Panoff, "Patrifiliation." South American examples are given in Reichel-Dolmatoff, *Amazonian Cosmos*; Chapman, *Drama and Power*; and Murphy, "Social Structure and Sex Antagonism."

4. Augustine, *City of God*, 616. In *Women at the Beginning*, Patrick J. Geary notes that a number of legends that circulated in eastern Europe from the sixth to the twelfth centuries C.E. also featured female rulers, ancestresses who eventually had to pass their power on to men so that history proper could begin (26–42).

5. Lefkowitz, *Women in Greek Myth*, 1st ed., 22.

6. Blok, *Early Amazons*, 1–2; Weigle, *Spiders and Spinsters*, 269–71; Pomeroy, *Goddesses, Whores*, 24; Lefkowitz, *Women in Greek Myth*, 1st ed., 23; Lefkowitz, *Women in Greek Myth*, 2nd ed., 3–4.

7. Lefkowitz, *Women in Greek Myth*, 2nd ed., 3.

8. Blok, *Early Amazons*, 1–2, 31.

9. Cantarella, *Pandora's Daughters*, 17; Lefkowitz, *Women in Greek Myth*, 2nd ed., 4–5; Blok, *Early Amazons*, 21–26, 36.

10. Lysias, quoted in Lefkowitz, *Women in Greek Myth*, 1st ed., 23; Samson, "Superwomen," 61; Vidal-Naquet, "Slavery and the Role of Women," 190; Tyrrell, *Amazons*, 40; Pomeroy, "Classical Scholar's Perspective on Matriarchy," 221; Yalom, *History of the Breast*, 23; Blok, *Early Amazons*, ix.

11. Although the name *Amazon* belongs to the ancient Greeks, stories about woman-only or woman-dominant societies are not unique to the West. For example, in the Trobriand Islands in Melanesia (themselves legendary owing to the pioneering work of anthropologist Bronislaw Malinowski), there are stories of "the marvelous land of Kaytalugi" to the north, where a group of "sexually rabid women" live alone with their children,

eventually killing any men who happen upon them through their sexual excesses. This is the fate of their male children, too, who are "sexually done to death" before they can "attain ripeness" (Malinowski, *Father in Primitive Psychology*, 51–52). Michael W. Young gives further examples of such "island of women" mythologies in New Guinea ("The Matriarchal Illusion in Kalauna Mythology," in Gewertz, ed., *Myths of Matriarchy Reconsidered*, 2).

12. On Pizan's treatment of Amazons, see Kleinbaum, "Amazon Legends and Misogynists," 95, 97; Weinbaum, *Islands of Women and Amazons*, 128.

13. Barber, *"Amadis de Gaule" and the German Enlightenment*, 1–2, 12.

14. Weinbaum, *Islands of Women and Amazons*, 128–29.

15. Barber, *"Amadis de Gaule" and the German Enlightenment*, 93–94.

16. Taufer, "The Only Good Amazon," 35, 41, 45–48.

17. Ibid., 42.

18. Ibid., 37–38, 43–44.

19. Ibid., 37; Weinbaum, *Islands of Women and Amazons*, 131. Josine Blok points out that Western colonials were finding Amazons outside the Americas too, in India and Tibet (*Early Amazons*, 63–64).

20. Raleigh, *Discoverie of Guiana*, 282–83. Andrew Hadfield suggests that Raleigh might have included this story of the Amazons "to flatter [Queen] Elizabeth and incite her interest in the area" (*Amazons, Savages, and Machiavels*, 279). Raleigh had displeased the queen and was eager to win back her favor.

21. This was Sir Walter Raleigh's opinion (*Discoverie of Guiana*, 282).

22. Kleinbaum, "Amazon Legends and Misogynists," 94; Weinbaum, *Islands of Women and Amazons*, 131,

23. Taufer, "The Only Good Amazon," 36.

24. Shepherd, *Amazons and Warrior Women*, 5. Spenser might have been inspired to write the *Faerie Queene's* Amazon characters by Sir Walter Raleigh's reports of Amazon societies from his travels to Guiana in 1595 (Woods, "Amazonian Tyranny," 53).

25. Spenser, *Faerie Queene*, V.vii.42.

26. Ibid., V.v.25.

27. Shepherd, *Amazons and Warrior Women*, 133–39. Christine de Pizan's *Book of the City of Ladies* draws on such a catalogue of famous women. A Tuscan writer, Boccaccio, had produced a book titled *De Claris Mulieribus* (Concerning Famous Women) in 1375, one of the earliest in this genre of compendiums of biographies of strong female figures (Rosalind Brown-Grant, introduction to Pizan, *City of Ladies*, xviii).

28. Ellenberger, *Discovery of the Unconscious*, 219.

29. Weinbaum, *Islands of Women and Amazons*, 131.

30. Ter Horst, *Lessing, Goethe, Kleist*, 1, 6.

31. Barber, *"Amadis de Gaule" and the German Enlightenment*, 13.

32. Brown, *Kleist and the Tragic Ideal*, 14.

33. Ibid., 37–38; Ter Horst, *Lessing, Goethe, Kleist*, 128.

34. Kleist, *Penthesilea: A Tragic Drama*, 38.

35. Ibid., 29–30.

36. Ibid., 58.

37. Ibid., 78.

38. Ibid., 91.

39. "She sinks—tearing the armor off his body—/Into his ivory breast she sinks her teeth,/She and her savage dogs in competition,/Oxus and Sphinx [her dogs] chewing into his right breast,/And she into his left" (ibid., 128). The original German is especially evocative: "Sie schlägt, die Rüstung ihm vom Liebe reißend,/Den Zahn schlägt sie in seine weiße Brust,/Sie und die Hunde, die wetteifernden,/Oxus und Sphinx den Zahn in seine rechte,/In seine linke sie" (Kleist, *Penthesilea: Ein Trauerspiel*, 102).

40. Kleist, *Penthesilea: A Tragic Drama*, 144.

41. Lafitau, *Customs of the American Indians*, 69. Although he labels Iroquois society a gynecocracy, Lafitau recognizes that the Iroquois had male leaders. He explains this phenomenon as follows: "The real authority is in the women's hands, but they choose chiefs in their families to represent them and be, as it were, the repositories of this authority with the senate. . . . The women choose their chiefs among their maternal brothers or their own children and it is the latter's brothers or their nephews who succeed them in the mother's household" (70). Another explorer, John Lederer, had earlier noted the phenomenon of matriliny among Native Americans, in this case the Sioux, but he did not speak of rule by women or posit any grand evolutionary or diffusionary schemes for what he apparently regarded as an oddity (Tax, "From Lafitau to Radcliffe-Brown," 445).

42. William N. Fenton and Elizabeth L. Moore, introduction to Lafitau, *Customs of the American Indians*, xxxiii, xlv.

43. Lafitau, *Customs of the American Indians*, 69.

44. Pembroke, "Women in Charge," 3, and "Early Human Family," 277; Borgeaud, "From Lafitau to Bachofen." The more Lafitau examined the classical sources for signs of gynecocracy, the more he found them: in Egypt, where marriage contracts forced men "to swear that they would obey their wives in everything"; in Scythia, Sarmatia, Spain, and Asia Minor generally; and among the Amazons, whom Lafitau speculates gave up being an exclusively female society when the Greeks destroyed their empire, but who continued to hold all the political power in the cultures and nations they established with men (*Customs of the American Indians*, 73, 285).

45. Van Amringe, *Natural History of Man*, 632. Other "races"—such as the Hindoos and Turks—are mentioned, but these four—Shemite, Ishmaelite, Japhethite, and Canaanite—are the principal ones discussed by van Amringe.

46. Ibid., 639, 658, 660–61.

47. Ibid., 595, 597.

48. Ibid., 629–30.

49. Everyone, that is, except mothers and their children. In direct contradiction to the rule of individuality, mothers and children stick together in Hobbes's state of nature, the mother agreeing to let the child live on the condition that the child will not become her enemy in adulthood. This sense that mothers and their children are the first and only social unit among early humans is frequently found in different versions of matriarchal myth.

50. Hobbes, *Leviathan*, 199. See also Gorman, "Theories of Prehistoric Inequality," 46–47; Cantarella, *Pandora's Daughters*, 3; Pateman, *Sexual Contract*, 45. Most early

modern European philosophers did not voice such clear portents of the matriarchal myth to come, but some (like Rousseau and Locke) included lengthy reflections on the status of women in human society, and how it came to be as it was (see Katz, "Ideology," 34–35).

51. Ferguson, *History of Civil Society*, 283.

52. Ibid., 137, 138. See also Fishbane, "Mother-Right, Myth, and Renewal," 515–16; Pembroke, "Early Human Family," 279.

53. Borgeaud, "From Lafitau to Bachofen"; Ferguson, *History of Civil Society*, 139.

54. "It seems unnecessary to observe, that what is here said with regard to marriage, together with many other Remarks which follow concerning the manners of early nations, can only be applied to those who had lost all knowledge of the original institutions, which, as the sacred scriptures inform us, were communicated to mankind by an extraordinary revelation from heaven" (Millar, *Origin of the Distinction of Ranks*, 185).

55. Ibid., 175–76.

56. Ibid., 193, 192, 183, 184.

57. Ibid., 199, 200.

58. Ibid., 201. Anticipating Bachofen, Millar draws the reader's attention to the myth of the naming of Athens, which indicates that "women had . . . a share in public deliberations" in ancient Attica; Millar also mentions Amazons, those of both ancient Greek and medieval European myth, and asserts that "though these accounts are evidently mixed with fable, and appear to contain much exaggeration, we can hardly suppose that they would have been propagated by so many authors, and have created such universal attention, had they been entirely destitute of real foundation" (202).

59. Ibid., 219.

60. Ibid., 222–23.

61. Ibid., 225.

62. Gamble, *Timewalkers*, 20. See Vico, *Selected Writings*, 82–83, 200, for his speculations regarding gender relations in prehistory.

63. Harris, *Rise of Anthropological Theory*, 29. This tripartite typology formed the basis of Lewis Henry Morgan's *Ancient Society* and was generally accepted throughout nineteenth-century evolutionary anthropology. Bachofen's time line, as we shall see, is somewhat different from Montesquieu's.

64. Smith demonstrated almost no interest in gender relations. Early in *An Inquiry into the Nature and Causes of the Wealth of Nations*, in a discussion of the succession of monarchy, Smith quickly disposes of women as contenders to the throne, explaining the rule of primogeniture as follows: "The male sex is universally preferred to the female; and when all other things are equal, the elder everywhere takes place of the younger" (158). Thereafter, Smith has nothing to say about women and proceeds with his discussion of the origin of the division of labor as though women did not exist.

65. Smith, *Lectures on Jurisprudence*, 27. Later anthropologists who discussed matriarchal myth in terms of economic changes often used Smith's typology (hunting and gathering; pastoralism or animal husbandry; agriculture; and capitalism or civilization), usually collapsing animal husbandry and agriculture into "barbarism." Bachofen, in contrast, showed only the most fleeting concern with prehistoric forms of subsistence, attributing large-scale changes in social relations to exclusively social causes.

66. Riasanovsky, *Teaching of Charles Fourier,* 139. Though Fourier preceded Bachofen, there is no evidence that he influenced him. Fourier did, however, have a direct influence on a later champion of matriarchal myth: Friedrich Engels. Pembroke notes that by 1843, Engels was already recommending Fourier to his English readers as "scientific research, cool, unbiassed, systematic thought" ("Early Human Family," 290–91).

67. Riasanovsky, *Teaching of Charles Fourier,* 2, 5–7, 19.

68. Fourier, *Théorie des Quatre Mouvements,* 285.

69. Robertson, *Experience of Women's Pattern and Change,* 292–93.

70. There are some important exceptions, such as Lewis Morgan, who subdivided the familiar savagery, barbarism, and civilization into seven stages, and shaved these even more finely as he analyzed the evolution of kinship terminology *(Ancient Society, Systems of Consanguinity).*

71. Fourier, *Selections,* 50–51; Riasanovsky, *Teaching of Charles Fourier,* 140–41.

72. Fourier, *Selections,* 51–52.

73. Ibid., 78; Fourier, *Théorie des Quatre Mouvements,* 131. In spite of the central role Fourier gave to women's emancipation, he did not advocate feminist change before its duly appointed time, arguing that "each social period should fashion its youth to reverence the dominant absurdities," even if these include "brutalizing" or "stupefying" women (*Selections,* 78).

74. Fourier, *Selections,* 76, 79; Robertson, *Experience of Women's Pattern and Change,* 292–93.

75. Pembroke, "Early Human Family," 288–89; Riasanovsky, *Teaching of Charles Fourier,* 141, 144.

76. *La Politique Universelle* was published again in 1854 under the title *La Liberté dans le Mariage par l'Egalité des Enfants devant la Mère.*

77. De Girardin, *Politique Universelle;* Pembroke, "Early Human Family," 283; Robertson, *Experience of Women's Pattern and Change,* 346. Fathers' contribution to the estate of the mother of their children was voluntary in de Girardin's scheme, so one wonders how effective his proposed solution would have been.

78. Davis, *Goddess Unmasked,* 276–79. Bachofen did not himself favor de Girardin's proposal, which he saw as a step backward rather than forward.

79. Bachofen was also familiar with Lafitau's work through the writings of Johannes Müller, primarily *History of the Primitive Religions of America* (Borgeaud, "From Lafitau to Bachofen").

80. Graf, "Materia come Maestra," 27; Blok, "Quests for a Scientific Mythology," 28.

81. In *Pandora's Daughters,* Eva Cantarella relates the myth of the murder of the Lemnian men as follows: "The Lemnian women once had husbands, but, punished for an offense against Aphrodite with a foul odor (dysosmia), they had been deserted by their men for Thracian slave girls. In revenge, the Lemnian women cut the throats of every man on the island, and from that moment Lemnos was a community of women alone. They were governed by the virgin Hypsipyle, until one day Jason and the *Argo* landed and that was the end of female power. The Argonauts married the Lemnian women (the foul odor disappeared the moment they welcomed the men) and Jason married Hypsipyle" (16–17).

82. Borgeaud, "From Lafitau to Bachofen."

83. Phillipe Borgeaud, "Quelques Théories du Symbole et du Mythe dans l'Allemagne du XIXe Siècle," in Borgeaud et al., *Mythologie du Matriarcat,* 56–57; Williamson, *Longing for Myth in Germany,* 148; Hutton, *Triumph of the Moon,* 35–36. Bachofen and Gerhard had both been students of August Böckh at the University of Berlin. K. O. Müller had anticipated Gerhard's theory of a prehistoric goddess monotheism, though he treated it rather lightly, merely suggesting that the earliest Greek farmers worshipped a single deity, probably Demeter (Feldman and Richardson, eds., *Rise of Modern Mythology,* 417).

84. Phillipe Borgeaud, "Quelques Théories du Symbole et du Mythe dans l'Allemagne du XIXe Siècle," in Borgeaud et al., *Mythologie du Matriarcat,* 59.

85. Josine H. Blok attributes this view to Georg Friedrich Creuzer, who influenced Bachofen (*Early Amazons,* 44).

3. ON THE LAUNCHING PAD

Epigraph: Bachofen, *Myth, Religion, and Mother Right,* 70.

1. Eckstein-Diener, *Mütter und Amazonen,* 28. *Mütter und Amazonen* was originally published in German in 1932 under the pen name "Sir Galahad."

2. Andreas Cesana, quoted in Gossman, "Orpheus Philologus," 11, n. 17.

3. Bachofen, quoted in Gossman, "Basle, Bachofen, and the Critique of Modernity," 162. See also 145, 151, 157.

4. Bachofen had withdrawn from the family business in deference to a younger brother, with the approval of his father, who was himself an amateur scholar (Gossman, "Basle, Bachofen, and the Critique of Modernity," 158).

5. Knight, review of *Das Mutterrecht,* 145.

6. Cesana, *Bachofens Geschichtsdeutung,* 25–26; Gossman, "Basle, Bachofen, and the Critique of Modernity," 158; Borgeaud, "From Lafitau to Bachofen"; Bachofen, *Selbstbiographie,* 14–19.

7. Borgeaud, "From Lafitau to Bachofen"; Gossman, "Basle, Bachofen, and the Critique of Modernity," 163. Gossman suggests that prior to his resignation from the University of Basel, Bachofen was probably politically liberal, in spite of his conservative family and class associations, being still under the influence of his mentors (especially Savigny). Afterward, Gossman says, Bachofen's liberal faith collapsed and he was a political conservative for the remainder of his life (12–14).

8. Bachofen, *Selbstbiographie,* 9.

9. Though he no longer had any official connection with the University of Basel after 1858, it seems that Bachofen was still consulted on university matters (Gossman, "Orpheus Philologus," 13, n. 23).

10. Momigliano, review of "Orpheus Philologus," 329; Borgeaud, "From Lafitau to Bachofen"; Eckstein-Diener, *Mothers and Amazons,* xiii–xiv, n. 2. Bachofen's *Unsterblichkeit der Orphischen Theologie,* for example, was published in 1867 in an edition of fifty copies (Gossman, "Basle, Bachofen, and the Critique of Modernity," 175).

11. Bremmer, "Importance of the Maternal Uncle," 173, n. 3.

12. Bachofen, *Selbstbiographie,* 10, 14.

13. Gossman, "Orpheus Philologus," 46.

14. Bachofen, *Selbstbiographie,* 11, 15.

15. See especially the 5 July 1859 letter from Bachofen to Gerhard, in Bachofen, *Bachofens Gesammelte Werke,* vol. 10, 192–97.

16. Borgeaud, "From Lafitau to Bachofen."

17. Gossman, "Orpheus Philologus," 22, n. 42; Pembroke, "Early Human Family," 282–83; Borgeaud, "From Lafitau to Bachofen."

18. Fishbane, "Mother-Right, Myth, and Renewal," 488.

19. Bachofen, quoted in Fishbane, "Mother-Right, Myth, and Renewal," 489.

20. Georgoudi, "Myth of Matriarchy"; Knight, review of *Das Mutterrecht,* 145; Weigle, *Spiders and Spinsters. Das Mutterrecht* was reprinted in 1897 by Benno Schwabe in Basel, who published Bachofen's collected works between 1943 and 1967. A Bachofen "reader," including an excerpted version of *Das Mutterrecht,* was published in Stuttgart in 1926; this reader was translated and published in English in 1967 and was for decades the only portion of Bachofen's writings that was available in English. Another abridged version of *Das Mutterrecht* has since been edited and translated by David Partenheimer and is available in a five-volume set from Edwin Mellen Press, published from 2003 to 2007.

21. Fromm, "Theory of Mother Right," 93–94; Juillerat, "Odor of Man," 85–86; Stocking, review of *Myth, Religion, and Mother Right,* 1189. Bachofen married Louise Elizabeth Burckhardt, daughter of another illustrious Baselite family and thirty years his junior, in 1865, when she was twenty years old. She gave birth to a son, Wilhelm, a year later (Gossman, "Orpheus Philologus," 16).

22. Gossman, personal communication, 11 December 1996.

23. For opinions on *Mutterrecht*'s confusing structure and prose, see Hays, *From Ape to Angel,* 35; Howard, *History of Matrimonial Institutions,* 39–40; Anonymous, "Bachofen," 52; Knight, review of *Das Mutterrecht,* 145; Dareste, review of *Das Mutterrecht,* 101; Hyman, "Myths and Mothers," 550; Ettlinger, review of *Das Mutterrecht,* 46. As John Ferguson McLennan, a later matriarchalist, complained, "The general exposition [of *Das Mutterrecht*] . . . is of so mystic a nature that it is difficult to obtain from it distinct propositions" ("Bachofen's *Das Mutterrecht,*" 320). Gossman believes the text's opacity is intentional, that Bachofen wanted to speak "to an elect of initiates" ("Orpheus Philologus," 24).

24. Bachofen, *Mutterrecht,* 12, 72. (All translations are by the author.)

25. Ibid., 103.

26. Ibid., 3. Given that Bachofen does not, at least in *Das Mutterrecht,* recognize any living peoples as being fully matriarchal, it would seem that all peoples have evolved not only through, but also out of, this stage.

27. Hyman, "Myths and Mothers," 549. See also Georgoudi, "Myth of Matriarchy," 455–56; Fishbane, "Mother-Right, Myth, and Renewal," 544; Campbell, introduction to Bachofen, *Myth, Religion, and Mother Right,* xlvii; Blok, "Sexual Asymmetry," 29.

28. Blok, "Sexual Asymmetry," 30. Hegel passed away in 1831, before Bachofen went to Berlin to study. Bachofen's mentor, Friedrich Karl von Savigny, had opposed Hegel's appointment at the University of Berlin, so it is doubtful that Bachofen explicitly identified himself with Hegel's work; the signs of Hegel's influence, though, are unmistakable (Ziolkowski, *Clio the Romantic Muse,* 123). Gossman suggests that Bachofen was influenced by

Hegel via August Böckh, with whom he also studied at the University of Berlin ("Orpheus Philologus," 72). At any rate, it would have been impossible for Bachofen *not* to be familiar with Hegelian thought, as it was so much in the air during his formative years.

29. Magli, *Matriarcato e Potere delle Donne*, 28; Borgeaud, personal communication. 20 November 1996; Schiavoni, "Il Logos nel Labirinto," 138; Hyman, "Myths and Mothers," 549.

30. Bachofen appeals to the nature of human reproduction to support this distinction, noting that "just as the carpenter, although an individual, can make many tables, but the wood always provides material for just one table, so too a man can fertilize many women, but the material always has only enough to bear one fruit. The movement of life begins with the influence of the male power on the female material" (quoted in Heine, *Christianity and the Goddesses*, 90).

31. This stage is alternatively called "tellurian" and is characterized by "chthonic materialism."

32. Bachofen, quoted in Georgoudi, "Myth of Matriarchy," 451–53; Remys, *Hermann Hesse's "Das Glasperlenspiel,"* 35.

33. Bachofen, *Mutterrecht*, 90, 93. See also Fishbane, "Mother-Right, Myth, and Renewal," 561; Hartley, *Age of Mother-Power*, 32–33; Warren, "Johann Jacob Bachofen," 53.

34. Lionel Gossman argues convincingly that Bachofen created the stage of hetaerism because he was very attached to the idea of a frightening, lawless, primitive prehistory. If he planned to redeem a portion of prehistory by rewriting it as an orderly, harmonious society ruled by benevolent mothers, the frightening past would have to be pushed farther back, deeper into prehistory ("History as Decipherment," 41–42).

35. Gossman, "Basle, Bachofen, and the Critique of Modernity," 175.

36. Bachofen, *Mutterrecht*, 12.

37. Ibid., 109. Bachofen is quite clear on this point ("government of the state was also entrusted to the women"), but his commentators often muddy the waters. They complain that the term *matriarchy* (in German, *matriarchat*) was never used by Bachofen, and that *mutterrecht* (literally, "mother right" or "mother law") does not connote the public rule of women but rather "maternal dominance" (see, for example, Juillerat, "Odor of Man," 66). Bachofen does not separate the two, however. As Stella Georgoudi notes, "Bachofen used the terms 'maternal law' *[Mutterrecht]* and 'gynecocracy' *[Gynaikokratie]* often side by side, without establishing any firm distinction between them" ("Myth of Matriarchy," 450–51). See also Fluehr-Lobban, "Marxism and the Matriarchate," 7.

38. Bachofen, *Mutterrecht*, 30.

39. "Das Weib wählt sich den Mann, über den sie in der Ehe zu herrschen berufen ist" (ibid., 233).

40. Ibid., 43. The reigning matriarchs did, however, make allowances for prostitution, which Bachofen interprets as "an important step toward a higher morality," since it "transferred the obligation of all womanhood" (to satisfy men's sexual impulses) and allowed women in general to "lead a more dignified life" (32).

41. Remys, summarizing Bachofen, in *Hermann Hesse's "Das Glasperlenspiel,"* 35.

42. Heiler, *Die Frau in den Religionen der Menschheit*, 7–11; Fromm, "Theory of Mother Right," 88. In "From Lafitau to Bachofen," Philippe Borgeaud suggests that Bachofen borrowed

204 NOTES TO PAGES 44-46

this reasoning from Friedrich Gottlieb Welcker. Welcker does focus on "Nature" as the source of the oldest portion of Greek mythology (Müller, *Scientific System of Mythology,* 276).

43. Bachofen, *Mutterrecht,* 76 ("Der Vater ist stets eine juristische Fiktion, die Mutter dagegen ein physische Tatsache").

44. Ibid., 72, 319.

45. Bachofen, quoted in Fishbane, "Mother-Right, Myth, and Renewal," 558.

46. Georgoudi, "Myth of Matriarchy," 451.

47. Bachofen, *Mutterrecht,* 126.

48. Bachofen, *Myth, Religion, and Mother Right,* 144.

49. Bachofen, *Mutterrecht,* 17. Bachofen is clear in saying that the Demetrian matriarchy practiced warfare: "Far from excluding military bravery, gynecocracy is a mighty supporter of it. At all times, a knightly ethos goes hand in hand with the cult of woman. To face the enemy courageously and to serve the woman is ever the common honor of youthful, vital peoples" (104). He later suggests that warfare helped keep the matriarchy alive, since it removed men from their homes, leaving women to "preside over the children and the goods which are most often entrusted to her exclusive care" (105). Bachofen's Demetrian matriarchy is often described by others as a peaceful, harmonious age (see, for example, Bean, "Children of the Goddess," 15; Adler, *Drawing Down the Moon,* 188), but this view of matriarchy is a later development and is not found in Bachofen.

50. Georgoudi, "Myth of Matriarchy," 454.

51. Of course, Freud's Oedipal theory draws on many of the same cultural beliefs held by Bachofen. Bachofen may have even directly influenced Freud.

52. Bachofen, quoted in Janssen-Jurreit, *Sexism,* 53-54.

53. Bachofen, *Mutterrecht,* 315.

54. Ibid., 53.

55. Ibid., 41.

56. Ibid., 43. Indeed, these two stages of Bachofen's chronology, the Dionysian and Amazonian, are more insubstantial than the other three stages (the hetaeric, Demetrian, and finally, Apollonian). They seem more like shifts of power within Demetrian matriarchy than evolutionary stages in their own right. However, the distinction Bachofen draws between the Dionysian and the Apollonian forms of male power is a key aspect of his theory.

57. Bachofen, *Mutterrecht,* 63.

58. Ibid., 315.

59. Bachofen, quoted in Georgoudi, "Myth of Matriarchy," 454; Bachofen, *Mutterrecht,* 73, 258.

60. Bachofen, quoted in Janssen-Jurreit, *Sexism,* 57 (original in Bachofen, *Mutterrecht,* 129).

61. Bachofen, *Mutterrecht,* 53, 318. This does not mean that there cannot *also* be a blood relation, for Bachofen sees a spiritual component even in men's very material contribution to conception. It is not only sperm he donates to the project; it is "fecundating virility," an energy that is "immaterial, noncorporeal . . . the expression of a pure spirituality" (Georgoudi, "Myth of Matriarchy," 450). Still, for Bachofen, there is something su-

perior about paternity that has no tie whatsoever to matter, which is how Bachofen understood the conception of Christ, formed by paternity without maternity, spirit unmixed by the matter of motherhood (Borgeaud, personal communication, 20 November 1996). It is unclear what role Jesus's flesh, gestated in his mother's womb, plays in Bachofen's theology, if any.

62. Bachofen, *Mutterrecht*, 48.

63. Ibid., 318.

64. Ibid., 72.

65. Ibid., 58.

66. Ibid., 163.

67. Ibid., 164.

68. Ibid., 173, 220–21. Bachofen softens this somewhat by giving women credit for engineering the transition from mother right to father right behind the scenes. Though men fought the necessary battles, Bachofen insists that women understood the necessity for the change first, and that "everything is completed in her inside long before it gains external validation" (240). Women welcomed male domination because it allowed them, like Kleist's Penthesilea, to recover their true femininity.

69. Cantarella, "Potere Femminile," 112. See also Magli, *Matriarcato e Potere delle Donne*, 28.

70. Philippe Borgeaud describes the *Oresteia* as "the centerpiece of *Mutterrecht*" ("From Lafitau to Bachofen," 14).

71. The story was also told by additional writers before Aeschylus's time (Hesiod, Stasinus of Cyprus, Agias, Xanthus, and Simonides), but their works have not survived (see Wolfe, "Woman, Tyrant, Mother, Murderess").

72. In the *Odyssey*, Agamemnon was killed not by Clytemnestra, but by her lover Aegisthus. However, even in this version, Clytemnestra ends up with blood on her hands, as she is named as the murderer of Agamemnon's consort, Cassandra, a woman her husband had won in battle at Troy.

73. Sheila Murnaghan, personal communication, 21 January 1997; Alan Sommerstein, introduction to Aeschylus, *Eumenides*, 1; Aeschylus, *Oresteian Trilogy*, 169–70, 172.

74. This raises the possibility that Bachofen, by drawing attention to these myths, did not create a new myth, but simply gave new life to a classical Greek tradition of matriarchal myth. Stella Georgoudi makes this case. Bachofen, she says, recovered "the obsession of the good Greek citizen with all that was thought to be primitive, chaotic, obscure, undisciplined, and dangerous in the 'female element.'" And he did this through classical Greek myths that "placed this fearsome female element at the beginning of time and endowed it with venerable primordial power" ("Myth of Matriarchy," 463; see also Zeitlin, "Dynamics of Misogyny," 161). It seems probable to me that the ancient Greeks and Bachofen shared similar anxieties about women and male power. But given their chronological and geographical separation, I think we have to regard classical Greek and modern European matriarchal myths as substantially different traditions rather than seeing the latter as a revival of the former.

75. Joan Bamberger calls these "mainly poetic and frequently dubious historical sources." The sources thus characterized include Hesiod, Pindar, Ovid, Virgil, Horace,

the *Iliad* and the *Odyssey,* Herodotus, and Strabo ("Myth of Matriarchy," 263–64). See also Pembroke, "Last of the Matriarchs," 217.

76. Butler, *Tyranny of Greece.*

77. Gossman, "Orpheus Philologus," 41; Williamson, *Longing for Myth in Germany,* 8; Noll, *Jung Cult,* 24. George S. Williamson suggests that "the fascination with all things Greek might have remained a passing fad had it not acquired institutional roots in the German educational system." Williamson points especially to Göttingen, where several highly respected figures taught in the classics and where Bachofen studied for a time before his return to Basel (37).

78. See Lowie, *History of Ethnological Theory,* 42; Graf, "Materia come Maestra," 29–30; Coward, *Patriarchal Precedents,* 50. Ethnographic material became crucial to Bachofen's case for prehistoric matriarchy later, but by then Bachofen was imitating rather than initiating trends in matriarchal myth.

79. Bachofen, with his study of classical myth, believed himself capable not only of speculating on prehistory but also providing convincing documentation of his views (Bourgeaud, "Quelques Théories du Symbole et du Mythe dans l'Allemagne du XIXe Siècle," in Borgeaud et al., *Mythologie du Matriarcat,* 45).

80. As Bachofen explains, "The parts of the old system that withstand the spirit of the time the longest are the ones which are inseparably linked to religion. They are protected from demise by the higher sanction attached to everything cultic" (*Mutterrecht,* 46). See also Firth, *Symbols,* 103–4; Graf, "Materia come Maestra," 32.

81. Bachofen, *Mutterrecht,* 9.

82. Bachofen, *Sage von Tanaquil,* vi. See also Graf, "Materia come Maestra," 18–19.

83. Gossman, "Basle, Bachofen, and the Critique of Modernity," 177.

84. As Josine Blok writes of the nineteenth-century philological encounter with classical myths, "Myths seemed to call for decipherment: a liberation from language rather than translation from one language to another" (*Early Amazons,* 18).

85. Bachofen, *Selbstbiographie,* 11–12. Myth was the ideal mode for investigating the ethos of the ancient world, since for Bachofen it worked via symbols, which have the unique ability to pluck "all the strings of the human spirit at once," unlike ordinary speech or writing, which "is compelled to take up a single thought at a time" (Firth, *Symbols,* 105).

86. Borgeaud, "From Lafitau to Bachofen."

87. Lowie, *History of Ethnological Theory,* 41.

88. Firth, *Symbols,* 103–4. See also Croce, "Il Bachofen e la Storiografia Afilologica," 162; Hays, *From Ape to Angel,* 35; Graf, "Materia come Maestra," 32.

89. Phillipe Borgeaud, "Quelques Théories du Symbole et du Mythe dans l'Allemagne du XIXe Siècle," in Borgeaud et al., *Mythologie du Matriarcat,* 64.

90. Momigliano, review of "Orpheus Philologus," 328; Bäumler and Schröter, *Mythos von Orient und Okzident;* Moretti, *Heidelberg Romantica.*

91. Malinowski, *Sex, Culture, and Myth,* 250. The term *euhemerism* derives from a classical Greek novel by Euhemerus suggesting that the gods and goddesses of the Greco-Roman pantheon were divinized versions of previously living men and women (see

Sharpe, *Comparative Religion*, 6). One of the first modern Europeans to argue for reading myth as the "mirror of history" was the Italian Giambattista Vico, writing in the early eighteenth century (see Cantarella, *Pandora's Daughters*, 18).

92. Heyne was instrumental in training the next generation of German philologists. Among Heyne's students were Friedrich and August Schlegel, Georg Friedrich Creuzer, and Wilhelm von Humboldt (Feldman and Richardson, eds., *Rise of Modern Mythology*, 216).

93. Feldman and Richardson, eds., *Rise of Modern Mythology*, 166.

94. Phillipe Borgeaud, "Quelques Théories du Symbole et du Mythe dans l'Allemagne du XIXe Siècle," in Borgeaud et al., *Mythologie du Matriarcat*, 48.

95. Williamson, *Longing for Myth in Germany*, 32. See also Blok, *Early Amazons*, 14.

96. Phillipe Borgeaud, "Quelques Théories du Symbole et du Mythe dans l'Allemagne du XIXe Siècle," in Borgeaud et al., *Mythologie du Matriarcat*, 46.

97. Thornhill, *German Political Philosophy*, 131.

98. Smith, *Politics and the Sciences of Culture in Germany*, 25.

99. Koepping, *Bastian and the Psychic Unity of Mankind*, 80, 86; Feldman and Richardson, eds., *Rise of Modern Mythology*, 226; Penny and Bunzl, eds., *Worldly Provincialism*, 11.

100. Williamson, *Longing for Myth in Germany*, 33. There was a strong Orientalizing thread in Herder's thought. Herder was fascinated with India, its epics, and its language (Olender, *Languages of Paradise*, 3; Halbfass, *India and Europe*, 69).

101. Friedrich W. J. Schelling, quoted in Feldman and Richardson, eds., *Rise of Modern Mythology*, 327.

102. Koepping, *Bastian and the Psychic Unity of Mankind*, 80.

103. Feldman and Richardson, eds., *Rise of Modern Mythology*, 302; Williamson, *Longing for Myth in Germany*, 23.

104. Ellenberger, *Discovery of the Unconscious*, 215; Heinrichs, *Materialen zu Bachofens "Das Mutterrecht,"* n.p. See also Hermand, *"All Power to the Women,"* 652; Stocking, review of *Myth, Religion, and Mother Right*, 1188.

105. Beiser, *Romantic Imperative*, 66.

106. Roger Wines, introduction to Ranke, *Secret of World History*, 8.

107. Cesana, *Bachofens Geschichtsdeutung*, 27–28; Gossman, "Orpheus Philologus," 51, 62–63; Gossman, "History as Decipherment," 44.

108. Böckh, *Encyklopädie und Methodologie der Philologischen Wissenschaften*, 86.

109. "Je weiter sich die Darstellung vom Charakter des Historischen entfernt, in desto höherem Maasse erfordert sie die historische Auslegung" (ibid., 113).

110. Gossman, "Orpheus Philologus," 75.

111. Ibid., 21. Gossman notes that Bachofen centered his rancor on Theodor Mommsen, saying that he "should stick to his inscriptions" and complaining of him to Savigny and to Gerhard, another former student of Böckh's (26).

112. Savigny was born into wealth and into the law: his father was lawyer for several German princes. However, Savigny was orphaned at the age of thirteen, when his parents and twelve of his siblings died (Ziolkowski, *Clio the Romantic Muse*, 109).

113. Ibid., 122.

114. Rahmatian, "Savigny's *Beruf* and *Volksgeistlehre*," 1, 5.

115. Savigny, quoted in Rahmatian, "Savigny's *Beruf* and *Volksgeistlehre*," 5 ("organischer Zussamenhang des rechts mit dem Wesen und Charakter des Volkes"). See also Smith, *Politics and the Sciences of Culture in Germany*, 68–69; Thornhill, *German Political Philosophy*, 135; Koepping, *Bastian and the Psychic Unity of Mankind*, 82; Cesana, *Bachofens Geschichtsdeutung*, 29. Savigny passed these views on to others of his students, also, including Jakob and Wilhelm Grimm (Williamson, *Longing for Myth in Germany*, 81).

116. Gossman, "Orpheus Philologus," 61, 64. In his political leanings, Bachofen was closer to another of his professors at the University of Berlin, Leopold von Ranke (Smith, *Politics and the Sciences of Culture in Germany*, 67).

117. Gossman, "Orpheus Philologus," 73; Feldman and Richardson, eds., *Rise of Modern Mythology*, 387. Gossman suggests that Creuzer was "the philologist with whom he [Bachofen] had perhaps the greatest affinity."

118. Goethe was less kind, describing Creuzer's theory as a "dark-poetic-philosophical-priestly-labyrinth" that led nowhere (Williamson, *Longing for Myth in Germany*, 137).

119. Ibid., 122–23, 126; Blok, "Quests for a Scientific Mythology," 29–30.

120. Bäumler, *Mythische Weltalter*, chapter 4. Creuzer had ties not only with Romanticism and the *Historische Schule*, but also with the *Philosophische Schule*. He engaged Hegel with his ideas about symbols and aesthetics. Critics have long found it difficult to say whether Creuzer should be considered as belonging to the Enlightenment or to Romanticism. For a discussion of this point, see Blok, "Quests for a Scientific Mythology," 28.

121. Feldman and Richardson, eds., *Rise of Modern Mythology*, 387–90; Williamson, *Longing for Myth in Germany*, 128–29, 134; Blok, "Quests for a Scientific Mythology," 30. Leopold von Ranke, the highly esteemed German historian who taught Bachofen at the University of Berlin and who lived long enough to write a universal history well after Bachofen's *Mutterrecht*, rejected Creuzer's thesis of Oriental religious influence, claiming that the Orient influenced ancient Greek science, but not its mythology (*Geschichte des Altertums*, 301–2).

122. Creuzer, *Symbolik und Mythologie*, 556.

123. Williamson, *Longing for Myth in Germany*, 133.

124. Phillipe Borgeaud, "Quelques Théories du Symbole et du Mythe dans l'Allemagne du XIXe Siècle," in Borgeaud et al., *Mythologie du Matriarcat*, 51, 53–54; Gossman, "Basle, Bachofen, and the Critique of Modernity," 158; Momigliano, review of "Orpheus Philologus," 329; Gossman, "History as Decipherment," 46; Blok, *Early Amazons*, 45, 47–48. One commentator, Josine Blok, goes so far as to claim that "only the methods introduced by Creuzer enabled the discovery of the preceding stage of mother-right" ("Sexual Asymmetry," 29).

125. Williamson, *Longing for Myth in Germany*, 145; Feldman and Richardson, eds., *Rise of Modern Mythology*, 416. Müller's three-volume *Geschichten Hellenischer Stämme und Städte*, published between 1820 and 1824, focused on specific Greek tribes and their role in creating ancient Greek myth, as did a later work, *Die Dorier*, on Doric and Amazon tribes (Williamson, *Longing for Myth in Germany*, 145; Blok, "Quests for a Scientific Mythology," 26).

126. Müller, *History of the Literature of Ancient Greece*, 18–19. On the controversy over Creuzer's *Symbolik*, see Williamson, *Longing for Myth in Germany*, 14; Feldman and Richardson, eds., *Rise of Modern Mythology*, 388; Marchand, *Down from Olympus*, 45–48. As Williamson explains, "The Creuzer affair combined issues of sexuality, race, and religion, as the Greek gods were linked to the seemingly grotesque world of Egyptian oriental deities, and liberal Philhellenists battled a philology that was both theologically heterodox and politically conservative" (17). Creuzer's most hostile interlocutor was his colleague Johann Heinrich Voss (121–22), a poet and translator of the *Odyssey* (139), but even K.O. Müller showed signs of a racism that would have predisposed him to disagree with Creuzer. In one work he accused the ancient Greek historian Herodotus of having "an unrestrained admiration for the Orient" (145).

127. Phillipe Borgeaud, "Quelques Théories du Symbole et du Mythe dans l'Allemagne du XIXe Siècle," in Borgeaud et al., *Mythologie du Matriarcat*, 53; Blok, *Early Amazons*, 55; Feldman and Richardson, eds., *Rise of Modern Mythology*, 388; Blok, "Quests for a Scientific Mythology," 42.

128. Some commentators have disagreed with this assessment. Alfred Bäumler and Manfred Schröter, who revived Bachofen in the early twentieth century, dismiss the significance of Creuzer and state categorically that "from Karl Müller, the path leads to Bachofen" (*Mythos von Orient und Okzident*, 151).

129. Müller, quoted in Blok, "Quests for a Scientific Mythology," 38–39.

130. Blok, "Quests for a Scientific Mythology," 51, n. 98.

131. Williamson, *Longing for Myth in Germany*, 212.

132. Bachofen, *Mutterrecht*, 108. Erich Fromm interprets Bachofen's analysis of motherhood as consisting of not only a claim about who women are by nature, but also a claim about how women come to develop certain traits through the *practice* of motherhood: traits that men might also develop if they filled the same social roles (Fromm, "Theory of Mother Right," 91–92). This conceptualization never receives a hearing in Bachofen's thought, because for him biological and social motherhood are inextricably linked.

133. The notion of a "higher rebirth" is not what differentiates these two views. Elsewhere as well, Bachofen alternately speaks in admiring and critical tones of women's mourning of the dead (see Blok, "Sexual Asymmetry," 28–29).

134. Bachofen, quoted in Fishbane, "Mother-Right, Myth, and Renewal," 550–51.

135. Bean, "Children of the Goddess," 11; Bamberger, "Myth of Matriarchy," 265; Merrill, "Theoretical Explanations of the Change from Matriarchy to Patriarchy," 14.

136. Hyman, "Myths and Mothers," 552; Juillerat, "Odor of Man," 85–86.

137. Bachofen, *Mutterrecht*, 19, 22. See also Lowie, *History of Ethnological Theory*, 41.

138. Engels, *Origin*, 77.

139. Bachofen, *Mutterrecht*, 19, 278.

140. Schefold, *Religion des Archäologen J.J. Bachofen*, 5; Fishbane, "Mother-Right, Myth, and Renewal," 27; Lowie, review of *Das Mutterrecht*, 628. Andreas Cesana goes so far as to say that the transition from mother right to father right was just the first of two crucial transitions in Bachofen's world history, the other being the coming to earth of God in human form, as Jesus (*Bachofens Geschichtsdeutung*, 189).

141. Fishbane, "Mother-Right, Myth, and Renewal," 220, 292–93.

142. Gossman, "Basle, Bachofen, and the Critique of Modernity," 165. Bernard Juillerat argues that Bachofen's conservative orientation could not have been tied to the ongoing nineteenth-century "challenge to the urban patrician society to which he belonged," because Bachofen so distanced himself from contemporary politics. Juillerat notes that Bachofen's presence in Italy during Garibaldi's entry into Rome "did not succeed in distracting from his evolutionist and maternal reveries this conservative protected by his milieu and his fortune" ("Odor of Man," 84). But disinterest is hardly the only reason one might insulate him- or herself from contemporary politics. Bachofen appears to have suffered not from disinterest, but from despair. For a contrary opinion, that Bachofen was self-consciously intervening in contemporary politics through his scholarship, see Davies, *Myth, Matriarchy, and Modernity,* n.p.

143. Bachofen, quoted in Fromm, "Theory of Mother Right," 93.

144. Gossman, "Orpheus Philologus," 56.

145. Schefold, *Religion des Archälogen J. J. Bachofen,* 5. See also Cesana, "l'Antico e il Nuova Stato," 88.

146. Bachofen, *Mutterrecht,* 278.

147. Gossman, "Basle, Bachofen, and the Critique of Modernity," 152. Gossman attributes this view in part to Bachofen's roots in Basel: "Because of its peculiar situation, the view of the world from the 'Dreiländerecke' of Basel was different from those which could be enjoyed from the great centres of European power—from Paris, London, Berlin, or Vienna. It was not the dominating view of the hero and conqueror; but the cautious, questioning, mistrustful view of the prosaic anti-hero among giants whose dangerous games threaten his livelihood and his very existence" (136).

148. Gossman, "Orpheus Philologus," 84–85; Borgeaud, personal communication, 20 November 1996.

149. Fishbane, "Mother-Right, Myth, and Renewal," 247; Gossman, "Basle, Bachofen, and the Critique of Modernity," 171.

150. Bachofen, *Mutterrecht,* 18, 97; Gossman, "Orpheus Philologus," 33; Bachofen, quoted in Gossman, "Basle, Bachofen, and the Critique of Modernity," 183; Cesana, *Bachofens Geschichtsdeutung,* 189.

151. Jordanova, *Sexual Visions,* 73–74.

152. Elizabeth Millán-Zaibert, introduction to Frank, *Philosophical Foundations of Early German Romanticism,* 10; Thornhill, *German Political Philosophy,* 130; Koepping, *Bastian and the Psychic Unity of Mankind,* 81.

153. Gossman, "History as Decipherment," 25, 41; Bäumler, *Mythische Weltalter,* 178; Felski, *Gender of Modernity,* 57.

154. Halbfass, *India and Europe,* 88. Halbfass notes that Hegel does not regard the Orient as entirely obsolete; instead it "can function as a corrective and antidote," helping "to supplement and rectify deficiencies and one-sided developments" in Western thought (93–94). Bachofen's position is similar.

155. Bachofen, letter to Meyer-Ochsner, quoted in Gossman, "Basle, Bachofen, and the Critique of Modernity," 166; Bachofen, letter to Hornung, quoted in Fishbane, "Mother-Right, Myth, and Renewal," 779. The letters can also be found in *Bachofens Gesammelte*

Werke, vol. 10, 319–22, 453–55. The chassepot was a military rifle invented around the time of Bachofen's writing.

156. Gossman, "Orpheus Philologus," 63; Jules Michelet, quoted in Gossman, "History as Decipherment," 25.

157. Bachofen, *Mutterrecht,* 18; Bachofen, quoted in Gossman, "Basle, Bachofen, and the Critique of Modernity," 170–71.

158. Attempts to rewrite Bachofen in this manner have been undertaken by Fritz Kramer, who sees Bachofen as having created a space for contemporary feminism by "breaking down the idea of a primary patriarchal society," and by Erich Fromm, who suggests that Bachofen "largely overcame the potential reactionary interpretation of his theory by exploring the principle of the differences between the sexes in a radical way and by discovering earlier social and cultural structures in which women's superiority and authority were evident" (Kramer, "Empathy," 344; Fromm, "Theory of Mother Right," 91).

159. Williamson, *Longing for Myth in Germany,* 2–3.

160. Felski, *Gender of Modernity,* 16.

161. Blok, *Early Amazons,* 12–13.

162. Rosaldo, "Imperialist Nostalgia," 70. Rita Felski differs from Rosaldo in arguing that it is possible for nostalgia "to serve a critical rather than a simply conservative purpose" (*Gender of Modernity,* 59).

163. Rosaldo, "Imperialist Nostalgia," 70.

164. Bachofen, *Myth, Religion, and Mother Right,* 79.

165. Gossman, "Orpheus Philologus," 3.

166. Early reviews were given by Felix Liebrecht in 1862 and Rudolphe Dareste in 1865. Dareste praised Bachofen's erudition, but tossed off the review very quickly, saying that "it is enough to just indicate the thesis: scholars who want to know more should go to the book itself" (review of *Das Mutterrecht,* 101). For more on the reception of Bachofen's work in his own era, see Fishbane, "Mother-Right, Myth, and Renewal," 488, 593, and Kees Bolle, "Great Goddess," in Dexter and Polomé, eds., *Varia on the Indo-European Past,* 89–90.

167. Bernard Juillerat calls Bachofen's work on matriarchy "no more than one of the most unusual pieces of the historical museum of anthropology" ("Odor of Man," 65–66). McLennan himself referred to *Das Mutterrecht* as a "ponderous German quarto" ("Bachofen's *Das Mutterrecht,*" 320, n. 1).

168. "Very many of our scholars are now familiar with the German, and if I had my life to live over, I should not fail to master it to obtain access to German thought and German works, which are now so necessary to us. . . . those who do not read the language are necessarily shut out from the body of your literature. This is a great privation" (letter from Morgan to Bachofen, 27 January 1881, in *Bachofens Gesammelte Werke,* vol. 10, 510–12).

169. Bachofen, *Antiquarische Briefe,* n.p. See also Fishbane, "Mother-Right, Myth, and Renewal," 775, 781–82, 813; Bachofen, quoted in Fluehr-Lobban, "Marxist Reappraisal of the Matriarchate," 354; Borgeaud, "From Lafitau to Bachofen."

170. As George Eliot Howard writes in *A History of Matrimonial Institutions,* "His [Bachofen's] work is fantastic and almost wholly devoid of scientific method. . . . Though

the general results of the investigation are summarized in a short introduction, the argument is so loose, the arrangement so confusing, and the style so obscure that it is with the utmost difficulty the author's meaning can be gathered" (39–40). See also Anonymous, "Johann Jakob Bachofen," in *European Authors*, 52; Knight, review of *Das Mutterrecht*, 145; Hyman, "Myths and Mothers," 550; Ettlinger, review of *Das Mutterrecht*, 46. Sir James Frazer (himself a major player in the history of matriarchal myth) confessed, "To be frank, I have not had the patience to read through his long dissertation" (quoted in Anonymous, "Bachofen," 52).

171. Borgeaud, "From Lafitau to Bachofen."

172. Reclus, "Female Kinship and Maternal Filiation," 219–22.

173. It was through Giraud-Teulon's writings that several influential English scholars, including John Lubbock and John F. McLennan, first became acquainted with Bachofen's work. Giraud-Teulon was also read in the German-speaking world (see, for example, Zmigrodski, *Mutter bei den Völkern des Arischen Stammes*).

174. Bachofen, *Bachofens Gesammelte Werke*, vol. 10, 517–18, 523, 527, 531–33, 539–40; Giraud-Teulon, *Histoire du Mariage*, 12; George Murdock, "Appendix A: Primitive Promiscuity," in Lippert, *Evolution of Culture*, 645; Fishbane, "Mother-Right, Myth, and Renewal," 775, 784–85, 787; Stagl, "Notes on Johann Jakob Bachofen's *Mother Right*," 191. For more information on Reclus and Giraud-Teulon, see Georgoudi, "Myth of Matriarchy," 450; Gossman, "Basle, Bachofen, and the Critique of Modernity," 139, n. 8; 169–70; Ellenberger, *Discovery of the Unconscious*, 221.

175. Durkheim, *Contributions to l'Année Sociologique*, 249.

176. Fishbane, "Mother-Right, Myth, and Renewal," 775.

177. Burckhardt, "Bachofen e Burckhardt," 10–11. Kohler was polite but reserved with Bachofen and did not rely on *Das Mutterrecht* in his own matriarchal theories (see chapter 6).

178. *Basler Nachrichten*, quoted in Gossman, "Basle, Bachofen, and the Critique of Modernity," 164.

179. Wagner, quoted in Fishbane, "Mother-Right, Myth, and Renewal," 764.

180. Vogel, *Apollonisch und Dionysisch*, 98.

181. Gossman, "Orpheus Philologus," 4–5.

182. Starcke, *Primitive Family*, 243. Some reviewers are rather kinder to Bachofen, attributing some of his errors to a lack of resources: "*Mutterrecht* was published before scientific archaeology really existed . . . leaving Bachofen with little more than Homer to inform him about pre-Hellenic Europe" (Davis, "Goddess and the Academy," 58). Jan Herman Ronhaar also lets Bachofen off the hook by saying that his "literature was not good." For this reason Ronhaar refrains from passing "a crushing judgment in very hard words on Bachofen" (*Woman in Primitive Motherright Societies*, 505). But even those sympathetic to Bachofen admit that his work was little known in the decades after his death (see, for example, Casimir von Kelles-Krauz, "Bachofen," in Heinrichs, ed., *Materialen zu Bachofens "Das Mutterrecht,"* 75).

183. Stella Georgoudi refers to a "Bachofenian vulgate," a "simplified, often inaccurate" version of Bachofen's work that has been passed around by matriarchalists for over a hundred years ("Myth of Matriarchy," 455, 459–60).

184. See, for example, Firth, *Symbols,* 106; Lefkowitz, "Twilight of the Goddess," 30. The connections between Bachofen and Jung, and Jung and contemporary spiritual feminists, will be discussed in a later work.

185. Certain of Jung's followers, especially Erich Neumann and Joseph Campbell, have been considerably more interested in both historical trajectories and female archetypes.

186. Bachofen is not popular in contemporary feminist circles, but it is not as though he is never praised or cited anywhere. Karl Schefold's 1987 treatment of Bachofen's work *(Die Religion des Archäologen J. J. Bachofen)* is positively worshipful in its discussion of Bachofen.

4. THE MATRIARCHAL EXPLOSION

Epigraph: McLennan, *Primitive Marriage,* 67.

1. Murdock, "Priority of Mother-Right," in Lippert, *Evolution of Culture,* 656–57. See also Murdock, "Correlations of Matrilineal and Patrilineal Institutions," 445.

2. Histories of anthropology as a discipline, beginning in the 1930s and continuing to the present day, all confirm the central role of the matriarchal debate in the discipline's emerging self-consciousness (see, for example, Lowie, *History of Ethnological Theory;* Penniman, *A Hundred Years of Anthropology;* Hays, *From Ape to Angel;* Harris, *Rise of Anthropological Theory;* Stocking, *Race, Culture, and Evolution;* Tax, "From Lafitau to Radcliffe-Brown," 466).

3. I refer to them as "British anthropologists" for convenience. Sociocultural anthropology's fascination with matriarchal prehistory began in Great Britain, and British anthropologists dominated the discussion, especially in the early years. As anthropological matriarchalists emerged in continental Europe and the United States, they mainly followed Britain's lead (see chapter 6).

4. Stocking, *Victorian Anthropology,* 188. See also Fraser, *Making of "The Golden Bough,"* 73.

5. See, for example, Lubbock, *Origin of Civilisation,* 160; McLennan, "Early History of Man," 528.

6. Fritz Graf explains that for Bachofen ethnographic material "only serves as an amplification of the matter," but does not add anything new to what can be learned from classical antiquity ("Materia come Maestra," 29–30).

7. Mary A. Warren claims that Bachofen "accepted the biblically derived estimate that the Creation occurred about 4000 B.C." ("Johann Jakob Bachofen," 52; see also Knight, "Matriarchate and the Perversion of History," 569). I have not been able to confirm this claim, but suspect that it is true. In her 1976 master's thesis, "Children of the Goddess," Lynne Bean complains of the imprecision of Bachofen's evolutionary stages and attempts—unsuccessfully, by her own reckoning—to link them up with now standard archaeological periodizations such as the Upper Paleolithic, the Mesolithic, and the Neolithic eras (12). These periodizations did not exist when Bachofen wrote *Das Mutterrecht:* C. J. Thomsen and J. J. A. Worsaae spoke of the Stone Age, Bronze Age, and Iron Age, but it was not until 1865 that John Lubbock (one of the British matriarchalists) broke the Stone Age down into Paleolithic, Mesolithic, and Neolithic (see Lowie, *History of Ethnological*

Theory, 70; Ammerman and Cavalli-Sforza, *Neolithic Transition,* 34). *Mutterrecht* gives no sign that Bachofen was either aware of or had accepted the vastly expanded time-depth of human history yielded by new geological evidence. Donald K. Grayson dates widespread acceptance of this evidence and its accompanying timelines for human antiquity to 1859 (*Establishment of Human Antiquity,* 1–2). At this time, Bachofen was hard at work on *Das Mutterrecht,* and given his notorious penchant for scholarly seclusion, it seems likely that he would have missed either the news about human antiquity or its import for his own work. Philippe Borgeaud, who has worked extensively in the Bachofen archives, says he knows of no explicit claim on Bachofen's part that human history was restricted to six thousand years, but also no sign that Bachofen was *not* reasoning on this foreshortened timescale, at least at the time he wrote *Das Mutterrecht* (personal communication, 20 November 1996).

8. This theory—that one's own ancestry can be observed in "primitive" tribes—is as old as Thucydides, who thought less progressive Greek states and the non-Greek world could shed light on the past of Athenians (Pomeroy, "Classical Scholar's Perspective on Matriarchy," 218).

9. This is the model that Lafitau, for example, relied upon.

10. Joseph Campbell attributes this innovation to Bachofen, likening him to Darwin: "Like his contemporary in the biological field [Darwin], he [Bachofen] . . . [argued that] the representatives of the various periods of [cultural] development lay scattered over the earth, having undergone in the various provinces of diffusion local adjustments to environment and independent secondary developments and regressions" (introduction to Bachofen, *Myth, Religion, and Mother-Right,* xxxviii). Campbell is here reading the work of the evolutionary anthropologists backwards into Bachofen, who argued nothing of the kind until after he came under the influence of these same evolutionary anthropologists.

11. Boas, "Limitations of the Comparative Method of Anthropology," 270.

12. This endeavor was not always successful; as Tylor complained in 1889, "there has still to be overcome a certain not unkindly hesitancy on the part of men engaged in the precise operations of mathematics, physics, chemistry, biology, to admit that the problems of anthropology are amenable to scientific treatment" ("Development of Institutions," 1).

13. See Coward, *Patriarchal Precedents,* 53; Fee, "Sexual Politics," 90–91.

14. McLennan, "Bachofen's *Das Mutterrecht,*" 323–24.

15. G. Bertin, quoted in Tylor, "Development of Institutions," 24. Bertin was responding to a paper Tylor presented to the Royal Anthropological Institute (circa 1889). This raises the question of how matriarchal myth can be taken to include both those who envision the rule of women and those who imagine a society in which women are "little better than a slave or beast of burden, condemned to hard labour, bought as a commodity with no redress against her husband's brutality" (Coward, *Patriarchal Precedents,* 108). The simplest answer is that the various matriarchalists believed their work to be mutually supportive. Though they were not making identical assessments of the status of women in "primitive" cultures, they still felt themselves to be talking about roughly the same thing. For example, Tylor lists both Bachofen and McLennan as "the pioneers of the investigation" into "the antiquity of the maternal system" ("Development of Institutions," 11). Edward Westermarck—a contemporary, if not a partisan—claims that McLennan "set forth the

same hypothesis" as Bachofen (*History of Human Marriage*, 275); Lester F. Ward lists Bachofen, McLennan, and Morgan as all having "contributed to our knowledge of the remarkable institution or historic phase called the matriarchate" (*Pure Sociology*, 300). The tradition of regarding Bachofen's and McLennan's theories of matriarchy as two instances of the same thesis began with McLennan, who himself wrote that he had "been anticipated by Herr Bachofen" in the "discovery" of "kinship through females" and "ancient gynaikocracy" ("Bachofen's *Das Mutterrecht*," 319, n. 1; 324–25).

16. When such consensus as there was arrived, it took the form that Tylor gave it in 1896: "The term 'matriarchal' was an improvement on earlier definitions, but takes it too much for granted that the women govern the family. It is true that in these communities women enjoy greater consideration than in barbaric patriarchal life, but the actual power is rather in the hands of their brothers and uncles on the mother's side" ("Matriarchal Family System," 90).

17. M. Kay Martin and Barbara Voorhies comment, "It may well be said that [Victorian evolutionary] anthropology brought discussions of reproductive activities out of the brothel and into the respectability of scientific discourse" (*Female of the Species*, 154). Most of the evolutionary anthropologists included at least one chapter on sex in their treatises, whether they stood for or against the matriarchal thesis (see, for example, Wake, *Development of Marriage and Kinship*).

18. Fraser, "Anthropology as Consolation," 104. Or as Hays says, "It is amusing to note with what horrified but fascinated insistence the Victorian anthropologists contemplated the sexual free-for-all that they attributed to primitive man" (*From Ape to Angel*, 42).

19. Harris, *Rise of Anthropological Theory*, 186–87.

20. Some commentators are more defensive about the bad reputation given to nineteenth-century evolutionary anthropologists. Peter Rivière says that McLennan "started people thinking, and we are still thinking about McLennan's thoughts today" (introduction to McLennan, *Primitive Marriage*, xliv–xlv). R. H. Barnes, speaking more generally, notes: "In a superficial reading of the works of the era, we may be impressed only by a few lurid fallacies and thus carry away the comforting view that it was left to the twentieth century to set scholarship on a right footing. A closer look, however, shows that we are heirs to a rich body of hard analytic criticism in many essential issues, and it is this collective product of the inspired controversies of the nineteenth century which may be taken as the true foundation of modern anthropology" (introduction to Kohler, *Prehistory of Marriage*, 69).

21. As Elizabeth Fee puts it, "They [evolutionary anthropologists] aimed at nothing less than an understanding of the entire history of the human race; and if in the end they succeeded in telling us more about themselves than about human pre-history or the cultures they ostensibly studied, we may still admire their daring, their forthrightness, and their intellectual ambition" ("Sexual Politics," 86).

22. As E. B. Tylor later remarked, Maine laid out "the received patriarchal views . . . with especial force and strictness" ("Matriarchal Family System," 82).

23. Maine was followed in 1864 by Numa Denis Fustel de Coulanges, who made similar arguments regarding the antiquity of patriarchy and its gradual loosening in the face of women's growing emancipation, and who relied on essentially the same sources from

classical antiquity and Vedic law (*Ancient City,* see especially 38-39, 396). His work, however, never attained the currency that Maine's had.

24. Maine, *Ancient Law,* 119.

25. Lawrence Rosen, foreword to Maine, *Ancient Law,* x–xi.

26. As George Stocking comments, Maine's thinking was "defined in a preevolutionary epoch ... [but] it quickly found a place in the post evolutionary milieu" (*Victorian Anthropology,* 117). Maine's place was not a lofty one. His influence never entirely died out, but for many years he functioned as a straw man for thinkers like McLennan, Lubbock, and Morgan to knock down.

27. Stocking, *Victorian Anthropology,* 168; Bamberger, "Myth of Matriarchy," 264; Cavin, *Lesbian Origins,* 28.

28. Fraser, *Making of "The Golden Bough,"* 23.

29. Maine, *Ancient Law,* 3; see also ix.

30. Ibid., 118-19, 121-22, 147; Fraser, *Making of "The Golden Bough,"* 23.

31. Coward, *Patriarchal Precedents,* 26; Maine, *Ancient Law,* 148-50; Stocking, *Victorian Anthropology,* 205-6; Kuklick, *Savage Within,* 113.

32. Maine is surprisingly double-voiced about the value of ethnography. On the one hand, he regards "primitive" peoples as "mere waifs and strays of humanity" and discounts "the slippery testimony concerning savages which is gathered from travelers tales" (Stocking, *Victorian Anthropology,* 125-26; Fee, "Sexual Politics," 88). But on the other hand, Maine complains—in words that foreshadow the anti-evolutionary strain that emerged in anthropology only at the turn of the century—that "the lofty contempt which a civilised people entertains for barbarous neighbours has caused a remarkable negligence in observing them, and this carelessness has been aggravated at times by fear, by religious prejudice, and even by the use of these very terms—civilisation and barbarism—which convey to most persons the impression of a difference not merely in degree but in kind" (*Ancient Law,* 116-17).

33. Stocking, *Victorian Anthropology,* 125-26; Lawrence Rosen, foreword to Maine, *Ancient Law,* xiii; Harris, *Rise of Anthropological Theory,* 143.

34. Fraser, "Anthropology as Consolation," 105.

35. See John Burrow, quoted in Pembroke, "Early Human Family," 275; Peter Rivière, introduction to McLennan, *Primitive Marriage,* x, xxxii–xxxiii; Fraser, *Making of "The Golden Bough,"* 22; Hays, *From Ape to Angel,* 36-37.

36. McLennan did not discover the work of Millar until 1871, six years after the publication of *Primitive Marriage,* and one hundred years after Millar himself wrote *Origin of the Distinction of Ranks* (Pembroke, "Early Human Family," 284; McLennan, "Bachofen's *Das Mutterrecht,*" 325, n. 1; Peter Rivière, introduction to McLennan, *Primitive Marriage,* xxviii–xxix).

37. McLennan first read *Das Mutterrecht* in 1866 (Fraser, "Anthropology as Consolation," 105; Pembroke, "Early Human Family," 284; Peter Rivière, introduction to McLennan, *Primitive Marriage,* xxviii–xxix). McLennan had, however, read and absorbed Lafitau's *Les Moeurs des Sauvages Amériquains* prior to writing *Primitive Marriage* (William N. Fenton and Elizabeth L. Moore, introduction to Lafitau, *Customs of the American Indians,* cvii).

38. Lowie, *History of Ethnological Theory*, 44; Rivière, introduction to McLennan, *Primitive Marriage*, xliv–xlv. Rivière adds that McLennan "became a more aggressive disputant as he grew older so that he ended his life a virtual paranoiac" (xv–xvi). An obituary in *The Scotsman* described McLennan in this way: "On the surface he was occasionally aggressive and denunciatory, and people who did not know him, or were incapable of appreciating him, were apt to think him disagreeable; especially as he had no respect whatever for persons. But in reality these surface asperities arose entirely from simple earnestness and a somewhat dangerous habit of saying precisely what he thought in the strongest language which occurred to him at the time" (xiii).

39. Rivière, introduction to McLennan, *Primitive Marriage*, xix.

40. *The Patriarchal Theory* was completed after McLennan's death by his brother Donald. Interestingly, McLennan's acknowledged zeal for crushing opposing views did not always prevent him from maintaining cordial relationships with those who disagreed with him, the anecdote about Spencer notwithstanding. McLennan met with Lewis Henry Morgan in London in 1871 and introduced him to Maine (see Hays, *From Ape to Angel*, 49). He also attempted to secure introductions to John Lubbock and Herbert Spencer. And, in spite of many years of pointed intellectual conflict, McLennan wrote to Maine in 1881, saying that he was working on a refutation of Maine's work and would like to discuss it with him (Rivière, introduction to McLennan, *Primitive Marriage*, xiv–xv).

41. Lowie, *History of Ethnological Theory*, 50.

42. Rivière, introduction to McLennan, *Primitive Marriage*, x, xiv–xv, xxxv. See also Hays, *From Ape to Angel*, 36–37.

43. Bennett, "Geologists and Folklorists," 26; Stocking, *Victorian Anthropology*, 73–74, 169; McLennan, "Early History of Man," 522.

44. There were rumblings as early as the late eighteenth century that six thousand years was simply insufficient to account for the geological and biological changes that had clearly occurred, and there had long been tension between the biblical account and the chronologies of other ancient peoples, which reached back much farther in time (Grayson, *Establishment of Human Antiquity*, 28). But in general these rumblings were quieted by extending geological time back indefinitely, while still dating the creation of human beings to the biblically appointed time (Stocking, *Victorian Anthropology*, 12).

45. Of the two, human antiquity was more important to the evolutionary anthropologists than Darwinian evolution. One could assent to the first without implying the second (for example, even if humans were deemed to have existed on earth for hundreds of thousands of years, it could still be believed that they were created at that time by God and had existed unchanged since, or that they had evolved through some mechanism other than natural selection). Stocking and Grayson both argue that human antiquity and human evolution were elided by the early 1860s (*Victorian Anthropology*, 147; *Establishment of Human Antiquity*, 210–11), but the British anthropologists had a somewhat complicated relationship to Darwin, especially since by 1871, Darwin was critiquing anthropologists' theories based on his own (see Rivière, introduction to McLennan, *Primitive Marriage*, xxviii–xxix). Stocking describes human antiquity as both a boon and a problem for Darwin: it provided the necessary time for evolution, but it also led humankind "back to the pliocene, or even the miocene" without providing a way out (*Victorian*

Anthropology, 172–73). Sociocultural anthropologists were intent on providing this pathway.

46. Grayson, *Establishment of Human Antiquity,* 1–2, 27, 28; Stocking, *Victorian Anthropology,* 73–74, 147; Mallory, *In Search of the Indo-Europeans,* 9.

47. McLennan, "Early History of Man," 516, 518–19, 521, 522.

48. William N. Fenton and Elizabeth L. Moore, introduction to Lafitau, *Customs of the American Indians,* xlvii. Degenerationism takes nonbiblical forms as well. Indeed, it is the mainspring of any golden age theory (of which the myth of matriarchal prehistory is arguably one, particularly in its feminist manifestations), and it is found in Hesiod and Virgil (see Fraser, *Making of "The Golden Bough,"* 12–13). In the late nineteenth century, some individuals, such as George Campbell, the Duke of Argyll, were willing to accede to an expansion of human antiquity, but not to the doctrine of evolutionism. As Campbell stated, "I know of no one moral or religious truth which depends on a short estimate of man's antiquity." However, the evidence unearthed in support of human antiquity—stone tools—did not support the degenerationist theory (see Grayson, *Establishment of Human Antiquity,* 217–18). At any rate, for McLennan and the other British anthropologists, it was crucial to defeat both the biblical chronology and the doctrine of degenerationism.

49. McLennan speaks of this frequently. See "Early History of Man," 525–32.

50. Harris, *Rise of Anthropological Theory,* 54–55.

51. McLennan, "Early History of Man," 532.

52. Julia Wedgwood, quoted in Grayson, *Establishment of Human Antiquity,* 217.

53. In "The Early History of Man," McLennan compares the evolution of human societies to that of individuals, a move that became increasingly common in later versions of the myth of matriarchal prehistory (especially for Erich Neumann and for contemporary matriarchalists who are more psychologically oriented). This analogy to the individual's growth and development is partially responsible for the gendered nature of matriarchalists' evolutionary stages. As McLennan puts it, "The infant has his mother's arms; the child his father's hearth." However, for McLennan this is a relatively unimportant aspect of matriarchal myth: "The analogies between the evolution of the life of the specimen and the species are suggestive rather than instructive, and need not seriously occupy the student of history" (540–41).

54. McLennan, "Early History of Man," 531. McLennan nevertheless defends "savages," assiduously incorporating these ancestors of his into the human family. As he explains, "In reaching a time indefinitely more remote, we have come on a condition of man indefinitely lower. Yet . . . we find man still distinctively human, a tool-user, an artist, a thinker, an ingenious craftsman" (523).

55. Field research was not common at the time among anthropologists. Bastian traveled a great deal (Kramer, "Empathy," 342), and Morgan and Tylor had some brief exposures to native cultures (Griesman, "Matriarchate as Utopia," 323; Lowie, *History of Ethnological Theory,* 69), but most anthropologists worked from the library.

56. Lowie, *History of Ethnological Theory,* 44; Fraser, *Making of "The Golden Bough,"* 92–93; Reclus, "Female Kinship and Maternal Filiation," 221–22.

57. Rivière, introduction to McLennan, *Primitive Marriage,* xl. Marvin Harris claims that "the evolutionists were perpetrators and victims of massive ethnographic errors

which, far from being canceled out by appeal to a large number of cases, became that much more entrenched by reiteration" (*Rise of Anthropological Theory*, 161).

58. The term *primitive horde*, later to be widely used, was invented by McLennan (Hays, *From Ape to Angel*, 39).

59. McLennan did endeavor to find—or at least imagine—the stipulated promiscuity among the lower classes in London, which he believed could illustrate "the phases through which the more advanced [classes] have passed." He reflects: "In that centre of arts, sciences, industries, and intelligence, are predatory bands, leading the life of the lowest nomads. The night street-prowlers are nearly as low in their habits as the jackals of Calcutta. The city might be made to furnish illustrations of the progress of the family in every phase, from the lowest incestuous combinations of kindred to the highest group based on solemn monogamous marriage. It contains classes that know not marriage, classes approximating to marriage through habits of settled concubinage, and classes for whom promiscuity is an open, unabashed organization" ("Early History of Man," 541–43).

60. McLennan, *Primitive Marriage*, 67.

61. Ibid., 65.

62. McLennan, "Bachofen's *Das Mutterrecht*," 324.

63. McLennan, *Primitive Marriage*, 65, n. 2. McLennan himself did not understand sexual reproduction as we do now. In the same footnote, he writes: "It has been doubted whether the blood-tie through the father is entitled to rank with that through the mother. It may be that the connection between father and child is less intimate than that between mother and child as regards the transmission of characteristics, mental or physical. And the former tie is unquestionably less obvious than the latter." In this era before Mendelian genetics was widely accepted and disseminated in a scholarly context, there was no agreement on who—mother or father—furnished the substance and soul of a child produced through their sexual relations. More common than McLennan's suggestion of maternal dominance was that of paternal dominance, according to which most or all of a child's traits came from its father. Numa Denis Fustel de Coulanges, a contemporary of McLennan's, notes that "the idea that generation was due entirely to males" was prevalent in "primitive ages" recorded in the Vedas and Greek and Roman law (*Ancient City*, 38–39). Certainly the ancient Greek belief that the father planted a *homunculus*—a miniature person—in a woman's womb, which she nourished but did not significantly alter, favors the father's role in procreation at the expense of the mother's.

64. Martin and Voorhies, *Female of the Species*, 151. McLennan agrees with Bachofen that "women, revolting from hetairism, introduced monogamous marriage" ("Bachofen's *Das Mutterrecht*," 323–24).

65. McLennan, *Primitive Marriage*, 69–70; McLennan, "Bachofen's *Das Mutterrecht*," 325, n. 1.

66. McLennan, *Primitive Marriage*, 69.

67. Ibid., 57–58.

68. Ibid., 58–59, 68; Fee, "Sexual Politics," 93. As late as 1863, McLennan had not yet developed these ideas. In an article titled "Hill Tribes of India," he said that female infanticide was based in superstition and "that marriage by capture was practiced only by the

rudest societies, and even among them was the exception rather than the rule" (Rivière, introduction to McLennan, *Primitive Marriage*, xxxi–xxxiii).

69. Coward, *Patriarchal Precedents*, 35–36; Penniman, *A Hundred Years of Anthropology*, 158; McLennan, *Primitive Marriage*, 58–59, 114–15.

70. Fee, "Sexual Politics," 95.

71. McLennan, *Primitive Marriage*, 71, 78; Penniman, *A Hundred Years of Anthropology*, 158–59; Lowie, *History of Ethnological Theory*, 46. Stocking suggests that "the 'grosser copartneries' of Victorian prostitution were an obvious model for primitive polyandrous marriage" (*Victorian Anthropology*, 202).

72. McLennan, *Primitive Marriage*, 97–98. Anne Merrill notes that McLennan was the first to connect changes in kinship systems with property ("Theoretical Explanations of the Change from Matriarchy to Patriarchy," 15). He was certainly not the last.

73. McLennan, *Primitive Marriage*, 91.

74. McLennan, "Early History of Man," 526, 527; McLennan, *Primitive Marriage*, 91.

75. McLennan, "Early History of Man," 527. McLennan was himself politically active in the effort to reform marriage law (Stocking, *Victorian Anthropology*, 164–65, 203; Rivière, introduction to McLennan, *Primitive Marriage*, xxxv; Fraser, *Making of "The Golden Bough,"* 22).

76. McLennan, quoted in Hartland, "Matrilineal Kinship," 4; Bachofen, *Bachofens Gesammelte Werke*, 479–80; Fishbane, *Mother-Right, Myth, and Renewal*, 775.

77. Kuklick, *Savage Within*, 46; Daniel, *Origins and Growth of Archaeology*, 107–11; Kuklick, ed., *New History of Anthropology*, 54.

78. Lubbock, *Origin of Civilisation*, 158–59; Fee, "Sexual Politics," 91. Bachofen apparently reached out to Lubbock in the post-*Mutterrecht* years as he struggled to bring himself up to speed with ethnographic supports for his theory of mother right (Borgeaud, "From Lafitau to Bachofen").

79. Lubbock, *Origin of Civilisation*, 103, 134, 135, 160; Harris, *Rise of Anthropological Theory*, 162.

80. Lubbock, *Origin of Civilisation*, 74, 86, 151, 158–59, 160–61.

81. According to Lubbock, women do not mind being won in contests or sold as property; they "never dream of protesting against this, which, indeed, seems to them perfectly natural" (*Origin of Civilisation*, 102).

82. Ibid., 99.

83. Ibid., 136.

84. Ibid., 105–6.

85. Ibid., 157, 158–59.

86. Lubbock was dubbed "Darwin's Mercury" for his close relationship to and promotion of Darwin's work.

87. Stocking, *Victorian Anthropology*, 237.

88. Most of the evolutionary anthropologists were more ambivalent about "savages," at once noting their vast inferiority to the nineteenth-century British and commenting upon their unique accomplishments.

89. Stocking, *Victorian Anthropology*, 153; John Lubbock, quoted in Lowie, *History of Ethnological Theory*, 70.

90. Lubbock, *Origin of Civilisation,* 9, 20; Lubbock, quoted in Swain, *Interpreting Aboriginal Religion,* 45.

91. Between 1865, when Lubbock's *Prehistoric Times* was published, and 1870, when his *Origin of Civilisation* came out, Lubbock made a distinct shift toward more universalism and evolutionism and less localism and diffusionism. Though Lubbock did not straightforwardly adapt Darwin to the study of human society—none of the evolutionary anthropologists did that—Darwin was an important part of Lubbock's overall mind-set, particularly since Lubbock knew Darwin from the time he was young, as their families were neighbors (Stocking, *Victorian Anthropology,* 150, 156).

92. Lubbock, *Origin of Civilisation,* 486.

93. Ibid., 485.

94. Gordon Marsden, quoted in Young, "Spencer and 'Inevitable' Progress," 149; Stocking, *Victorian Anthropology,* 135, 149. As Marvin Harris notes, "It was Spencer and not Darwin who popularized the term 'evolution'. . . . It was also Spencer and not Darwin who introduced the phrase 'survival of the fittest'" (*Rise of Anthropological Theory,* 128–29). Darwin himself did not interpret evolutionary processes in the way that Spencer did; Darwin "was insistent in his biological writings that evolution had no goal and followed no great design" (Gamble, *Timewalkers,* 29). Spencer, in contrast, was certain that evolution had the great design of producing Victorian England (Duffin, "Prisoners of Progress," 59).

95. Fee, "Sexual Politics," 97; Young, "Spencer and 'Inevitable' Progress," 149–50.

96. Young, "Spencer and 'Inevitable' Progress," 151; Fee, "Sexual Politics," 97.

97. Spencer, quoted in Fee, "Sexual Politics," 98; Spencer, *Principles of Sociology,* 276, 279.

98. Fee, "Sexual Politics," 99. Spencer sees a survival of this stage in Victorian England, where some married men support mistresses or patronize prostitutes.

99. Duffin, "Prisoners of Progress," 59; Robertson, *Experience of Women's Pattern and Change,* 151. Robertson notes that Spencer "described how a man of refined feeling would strive to put his poorer neighbors at their ease, encouraging them to be less submissive and more self-respecting. (Such a man even says 'please' and 'thank you' to domestics!)."

100. Duffin, "Prisoners of Progress," 66–67; Fee, "Sexual Politics," 98. Émile Durkheim articulated the same view in 1893, saying that "the farther we look into the past, the smaller becomes the difference between men and women. The woman of past days was not at all the weak creature she has become with the progress of morality" (quoted in Nelson, *Gender in Archaeology,* 116).

101. Spencer, quoted in Conway, "Stereotypes of Femininity," 141; Spencer, quoted in Duffin, "Prisoners of Progress," 66–67.

102. Spencer, *Principles of Sociology,* 221, 645–46; Conway, "Stereotypes of Femininity," 141; Young, "Spencer and 'Inevitable' Progress," 154.

103. Duffin, "Prisoners of Progress," 60; Stocking, *Victorian Anthropology,* 207; Robertson, *Experience of Women's Pattern and Change,* 151; Janssen-Jurreit, *Sexism,* 62; Hofstadter, *Social Darwinism,* 40–41.

104. Lowie, *History of Ethnological Theory,* 55. Morgan was never affiliated with a university, but he was nevertheless a respected scholar. In 1880 he was elected president of

the American Association for the Advancement of Science (Griesman, "Matriarchate as Utopia," 323).

105. See, for example, Fluehr-Lobban, "Marxism and the Matriarchate," 5; Joseph Campbell, introduction to Eckstein-Diener, *Mothers and Amazons*, viii. Morgan himself thought his fieldwork important to his theories. As he wrote to Bachofen on 4 June 1878, "I have endeavoured to commence with the institution in its archaic form and descend with it to its maturity. My residence in the land of the American aborigines gave this advantage" (Bachofen, *Bachofens Gesammelte Werke*, 481).

106. Regna Darnell, "North American Traditions in Anthropology," in Kuklick, ed., *New History of Anthropology*, 38. Though more extensive, Morgan's research on the Iroquois was not necessarily for this reason more accurate. As Margaret Jolly points out, "Morgan's empirical data on the Iroquois was not subject to . . . critical scrutiny by his contemporaries" ("Matriarchy," 5). Morgan was a great supporter of Indian rights, though he believed that their way of life was evolutionarily destined for oblivion (Coward, *Patriarchal Precedents*, 39-40). In contrast, Morgan was contemptuous of African Americans; he promoted abolitionism "in the hope that unprotected by slavery, the negro race would disappear" (Harris, *Rise of Anthropological Theory*, 139).

107. Morgan, quoted in Lowie, *History of Ethnological Theory*, 60-61.

108. Penniman, *A Hundred Years of Anthropology*, 163-64; Kriukov, "Types of Kinship Systems," 111-12.

109. See, for example, Kriukov, "Types of Kinship Systems," 111.

110. Morgan, *Ancient Society*, v-vii.

111. Vogel, *Marxism and the Oppression of Women*, 75; Morgan, *Ancient Society*, 12; Gough, "An Anthropologist Looks at Engels," 108.

112. Morgan, *Ancient Society*, 6; Merrill, "Theoretical Explanations of the Change from Matriarchy to Patriarchy," 15.

113. Morgan, *Ancient Society*, 393-94; Gough, "An Anthropologist Looks at Engels," 108; Tiffany, "Power of Matriarchal Ideas," 140; Cavin, *Lesbian Origins*, 26; Grossman, "Morgan and Bachofen," 986; Krader, *Ethnological Notebooks*, 31; Starcke, *Primitive Family*, 179.

114. Fedigan, "Changing Role of Women," 30-31; Tiffany, "Power of Matriarchal Ideas," 140; Morgan, *Ancient Society*, 516; letter from Morgan to Bachofen, 21 June 1880, in *Bachofens Gesammelte Werke*, vol. 10, 501.

115. Morgan, *Ancient Society*, 390, 474; Vogel, *Marxism and the Oppression of Women*, 78-79; Ellis, *Women and Marriage*, 16; Starcke, *Primitive Family*, 179.

116. Morgan, *Ancient Society*, 390; Krader, *Ethnological Notebooks*, 14; Morgan, quoted in Fromm, "Theory of Mother Right," 97.

117. Fee, "Sexual Politics," 96-97. Further information on the relationship between Bachofen and Morgan can be found in Lanza, "Matriarcato, Mito, Mito del Matriarcato," and Fluehr-Lobban, "Marxist Reappraisal of the Matriarchate," 354.

118. Rivière, introduction to McLennan, *Primitive Marriage*, xiv-xv; Hays, *From Ape to Angel*, 49; William N. Fenton and Elizabeth L. Moore, introduction to Lafitau, *Customs of the American Indians*, cvii; Harris, *Rise of Anthropological Theory*, 195; Lowie, *Primitive Society*, 58-59.

119. Howitt and Fison, "Mother-Right to Father-Right," 32, 33, 38; Hays, *From Ape to Angel*, 86; Kuklick, "British Tradition," in Kuklick, ed., *New History of Anthropology*, 57.

120. Morton Smith, "William Robertson Smith," in Calder, ed., *Cambridge Ritualists Reconsidered*, 251–52, 260; Robert Ackerman, "Anthropology and the Classics," in Kuklick, ed., *New History of Anthropology*, 146; Sharpe, *Comparative Religion*, 79; Ivan Strenski, "The Spiritual Dimension," in Kuklick, ed., *New History of Anthropology*, 120.

121. Fraser, "Anthropology as Consolation," 97, 106; Rivière, introduction to McLennan, *Primitive Marriage*, xlii; Smith, *Kinship and Marriage in Early Arabia*, 178.

122. Smith's work on matriarchy among the Arabs was preceded by the Dutch ethnologist G. A. Wilken in his *Das Matriarchat: Bei den Alten Arabern*, published in 1884.

123. Smith, *Kinship and Marriage in Early Arabia*, 37, 99, 139–40, 147.

124. Ibid., 142, 177.

125. Ibid., 86–87, 97, 120, 129, 205.

126. Ivan Strenski, "The Spiritual Dimension," in Kuklick, ed., *New History of Anthropology*, 116; Robert Ackerman, "Anthropology and the Classics," in Kuklick, ed., *New History of Anthropology*, 143.

127. Robert Fraser, introduction to Frazer, *Golden Bough*, xiii; Malinowski, *Scientific Theory of Culture*, 179.

128. Robert Fraser, introduction to Frazer, *Golden Bough*, xiv–xv. Even before this, however, Frazer was familiar with the debate between Henry Sumner Maine and John Ferguson McLennan, if only in passing, via his study of Greco-Roman law (Fraser, "Anthropology as Consolation," 105). Frazer's initial interest in the work of Maine and McLennan, according to Fraser, stemmed from his Scottish background. Scottish law was more similar to ancient Roman law than to its modern British counterpart (*Making of "The Golden Bough,"* 22).

129. Fraser, "Anthropology as Consolation," 106; Sharpe, *Comparative Religion*, 81.

130. Frazer, *Golden Bough*, 3.

131. Robert Fraser, introduction to Frazer, *Golden Bough*, xl–xli.

132. Robert Ackerman, "The Cambridge Group," in Calder, *Cambridge Ritualists*, 8.

133. Vickery, *Literary Impact of "The Golden Bough,"* 84.

134. Fraser, "Anthropology as Consolation," 106.

135. Divale, *Matrilocal Residence in Pre-Literate Society*, 3.

136. In 1896, with "The Matriarchal Family System," Tylor is already equivocal about the matriarchal thesis.

137. Ivan Strenski, "The Spiritual Dimension," in Kuklick, ed., *New History of Anthropology*, 116; Penniman, *A Hundred Years of Anthropology*, 179; Lowie, *History of Ethnological Theory*, 69; Tylor, "Development of Institutions," 11.

138. Tylor, *Primitive Culture*, 16, 17. Ronald Hutton sees Tylor's dissenting religious roots in the Society of Friends as an important source for his doctrine of survivals. A "puritan preacher, reclad as a Victorian liberal humanist," Tylor delighted in pointing up the primitivism and paganism living on in Christianity as survivals of earlier times (*Triumph of the Moon*, 114). See also Kuklick, *Savage Within*, 79.

139. Fraser, *Making of "The Golden Bough,"* 24.

140. In 1889, when asked by American scholar Edward D. Cope what work he should consult to learn about matriarchal prehistory, Tylor recommended McLennan's *Primitive Marriage* (Cope, "What Was Matriarchy?" 1519).

141. In his discussion of couvade, Tylor was drawing on Bachofen ("Development of Institutions," 10; see also Pembroke, "Early Human Family," 277–78; Coward, *Patriarchal Precedents*, 33).

142. Tylor, "Development of Institutions," 5, 7.The term often applied to maternal kinship by the evolutionary anthropologists was *motherkin*, a term also used as "a Victorian endearment for the *mater familias*" (Fraser, personal communication, 24 March 1996).

143. Tylor, "Matriarchal Family System," 90, 93–94.

144. Tylor, *Primitive Culture*, 21, 27–29, 58; Tylor, quoted in Penniman, *A Hundred Years of Anthropology*, 183–84; Fraser, *Making of "The Golden Bough,"* 14; Tylor, quoted in Harris, *Rise of Anthropological Theory*, 149.

5. MAKING MATRIARCHAL MYTH WORK

Epigraph: Engels, *Origin*, 83.

1. Joachim Müller and Edith Schotte, "Epilogue," in Marx-Aveling and Aveling, *Thoughts on Women and Society*, 32. This debate surfaced in socialist circles as early as the Third Congress of the Workingmen's Clubs in Stuttgart in 1865, in which a resolution on women's suffrage and emancipation sparked the longest debate of the congress. The resolution was passed (Bebel, *My Life*, 69).

2. Bachofen allowed for regress within the confines of his theory: for example, the Amazonian rebellion and Dionysian matriarchy were regressions from Demetrian matriarchy. But from these moments of regression, progress was always destined to break forth. Regressions in Bachofen's schema—and in those of many continental anthropologists— were ebbs and flows, Hegelian theses and antitheses whose conflicts could only yield to progress in the long run.

3. Steenson, *Kautsky*, 14–16, 41; Geary, *Kautsky*, 4–5.

4. As Kautsky biographer Dick Geary points out, "Only two Marxist works circulated widely in Imperial Germany: Bebel's *Die Frau und der Socialismus* (Woman and Socialism) and Kautsky's *Die Ökonomischen Lehren von Karl Marx* (Marx's Economic Doctrines)" (*Kautsky*, 10). Maurice Bloch regards Kautsky as "the foremost Marxist theoretician and heir to Engels" in the period from 1890 to 1905, while Gary P. Steenson notes that Kautsky's work "was probably the first full-length marxian work translated into Chinese" (Bloch, *Marxism and Anthropology*, 100–101; Steenson, *Kautsky*, 3).

5. It was Höchberg who introduced Kautsky to the work of Herbert Spencer, arguing that although Engels was of a different opinion on the matter, Spencer was a "fine and wise psychological observer" and a "brilliant philosopher" (Kautsky, *Erinnerungen und Erörterungen*, 493).

6. Bloch, *Marxism and Anthropology*, 100–101; Steenson, *Kautsky*, 5, 7, 31.

7. Geary, *Kautsky*, 4–5; Steenson, *Kautsky*, 4.

8. Friedrich Engels and Karl Marx, quoted in Steenson, *Kautsky*, 47–48.

9. Kautsky, *Erinnerungen und Erörterungen*, 492–93; Steenson, *Kautsky*, 45.

10. Steenson, *Kautsky*, 27. Marx had earlier received a doctoral degree via correspondence from the University of Jena, which is most likely what inspired Kautsky to make the attempt.

11. Steenson believes that Haeckel might have arranged for the publication of Kautsky's article since he was closely associated with *Kosmos* (*Kautsky*, 27).

12. Kautsky, "Entstehung der Ehe," 257.

13. Ibid., 205.

14. Ibid., 338, 347. The connection Kautsky drew between various forms of marriage and the development of private property is perhaps the only socialist element in his article (see Coward, *Patriarchal Precedents*, 134). However, Kautsky did not see private property as linked directly to patriarchy, as later socialists would.

15. Engels and Kautsky, *Frühzeit des Marxismus*, 78. This letter from Engels to Kautsky was written on 10 February 1883.

16. Ibid., 81–83. This letter from Engels to Kautsky was written on 2 March 1883.

17. Ibid., 85.

18. Kautsky, *Engels*, 25.

19. Harris, *Rise of Anthropological Theory*, 246; Vogel, *Marxism and the Oppression of Women*, 81.

20. It is profoundly ironic that Bachofen in particular could become the hero (though sometimes unsung) of a whole host of left-wing radicals. As Philippe Borgeaud remarks, "How could a theory so revolutionary, capable of interesting an Engels, have been born in a mind so conservative, not to say reactionary?" ("From Lafitau to Bachofen"). See also Hyman, "Myths and Mothers," 533; Hays, *From Ape to Angel*, 36.

21. Fluehr-Lobban, "Marxism and the Matriarchate," 5.

22. Coward, *Patriarchal Precedents*, 130–31.

23. Indeed, Marx wrote very little on anything after he suffered a nervous collapse in 1873 (Eugene Kamenka, introduction to Marx, *Portable Karl Marx*, xxii).

24. These notes are compiled in Krader, *Ethnological Notebooks*. See also Fromm, "Theory of Mother Right," 96; Harris, *Rise of Anthropological Theory*, 229; Julia Petrova-Averkieva, quoted in Gellner, "Soviet and the Savage," 610.

25. Engels praises Morgan's *Ancient Society* in a February 1884 letter to Kautsky, crediting Marx with having discovered the book and saying that it "destroyed all the lies made by Tylor and Lubbock." He even suggested that Tylor and Lubbock were suppressing the publication of Morgan's work in England (Engels and Kautsky, *Frühzeit des Marxismus*, 99).

26. Nikolai Ssorin-Chaikov, "Political Fieldwork, Ethnographic Exile, and State Theory," in Kuklick, ed., *New History of Anthropology*, 194; Bloch, *Marxism and Anthropology*, 45; Joachim Müller and Edith Schotte, "Epilogue," in Marx-Aveling and Aveling, *Thoughts on Women and Society*, 37; Vogel, *Marxism and the Oppression of Women*, 74.

27. On Kautsky and *Die Neue Zeit*, see Geary, *Kautsky*, 4–5; Steenson, *Kautsky*, 50–52. Kautsky remained as editor of and contributor to *Die Neue Zeit* until 1917, when he broke ranks with the socialist party in Germany by opposing the war.

28. Engels and Kautsky, *Frühzeit des Marxismus*, 103–9.

29. Engels, "Preface to the First Edition," *Origin*, 71.

30. Marx's continuing thoughts on this historical sequence were recorded in *The Communist Manifesto* (1848), written with Engels, and in the unpublished *Grundrisse*, written by Marx in 1858 (portions of the latter have since been published in English translation as *Pre-Capitalist Economic Formations*, with an introduction by E. Hobsbawm [Bloch, *Marxism and Anthropology*, 33]). When Engels wrote *The Origin* he was self-consciously updating the never published "German Ideology," which he had recently come across in Marx's papers (Vogel, *Marxism and the Oppression of Women*, 90–91).

31. Engels and Marx, "The German Ideology," in Marx, *Portable Karl Marx*, 172.

32. Krader, *Ethnological Notebooks*, 31, 43–44; Bloch, *Marxism and Anthropology*, 46; Fluehr-Lobban, "Marxist Reappraisal of the Matriarchate," 344.

33. Friedrich Engels, quoted in Marx, *Portable Karl Marx*, 69; Engels, *Origin*, 96. See also Harris, *Rise of Evolutionary Theory*, 228; Semenov, "Doctrine of Morgan," 3. Marx himself consistently thought of his work as "scientific" (see Eugene Kamenka, introduction to Marx, *Portable Karl Marx*, xxxix–xl).

34. Krader, *Ethnological Notebooks*, 11; Fluehr-Lobban, "Marxist Reappraisal of the Matriarchate," 343.

35. Krader, *Ethnological Notebooks*, 11. Engels's debt to Morgan's *Ancient Society* is transparent and unapologetic throughout *The Origin*. Indeed, Engels's original intention in writing *The Origin* seems to have been to summarize Morgan's lengthy *Ancient Society* for socialist readers. It was only later that he decided to treat "the matter critically instead with the socialist perspective" (Fluehr-Lobban, "Marxist Reappraisal of the Matriarchate," 343).

36. Bloch, *Marxism and Anthropology*, 8.

37. This is Krader's opinion (*Ethnological Notebooks*, 84) as well as my own.

38. Engels, *Origin*, 74.

39. Engels read Bachofen, but didn't find it pleasant, remarking that it was "a tough and by no means grateful task to plow through Bachofen's solid tome" (*Origin*, 77).

40. Bachofen's entire historical trajectory pointed toward diminishing human dependence on the material, which he regarded as vastly inferior to the spiritual. In his earlier years, Marx also relished this sense of human control over human destiny. Even as a mature thinker, Marx marveled at the technological accomplishments of capitalism while looking forward to capitalism's demise (Eugene Kamenka, introduction to Marx, *Portable Karl Marx*, xxiii, xxxv).

41. Engels, *Origin*, 77.

42. Ibid., 77–78. Engels was certainly more tolerant of Bachofen than of McLennan, for example, whom he dismissed, somewhat contradictorily, as both dull and overly fanciful (79–80, 84; Fluehr-Lobban, "Marxism and the Matriarchate," 8). Since many of McLennan's ideas about primitive promiscuity were the same as Bachofen's, one has to assume that Engels was reacting to something other than McLennan's actual theories. Most probably, Engels saw McLennan as a real political threat—belonging to the British liberal elite—in contrast to Bachofen, who was ensconced in Switzerland, barely read, and generally dismissed (*Origin*, 84).

43. Engels, *Origin*, 79–80.

44. Ibid., 113. See also Fraser, "Anthropology as Consolation," 114; Hermand, "All Power to the Women," 653–54.

45. Karl Marx and Friedrich Engels, "The German Ideology," in Marx, *Portable Karl Marx*, 175.

46. Engels, *Origin*, 218.

47. Both Marx and Engels are said to have admired Darwin and felt that his concern with the bare material facts of species survival complemented their own materialist approach. Indeed, Marx considered dedicating his monumental *Capital* to Darwin (Harris, *Rise of Anthropological Theory*, 222–23; Reed, *Problems of Women's Liberation*, 15).

48. Bloch, *Marxism and Anthropology*, 115.

49. Ibid., 78–79.

50. Karl Marx and Friedrich Engels, "The German Ideology," in Marx, *Portable Karl Marx*, 173.

51. This division of reproduction and production onto two related but separate tracks of social evolution is evident in Engels's remark in *The Origin* that "the reports of travelers and missionaries, I may add, to the effect that women among savages and barbarians are overburdened with work in no way contradict what has been said. The division of labor between the two sexes is determined by quite other causes than by the position of woman in society" (113).

52. Ibid., 71–72.

53. See Cavin, *Lesbian Origins*, 26.

54. See, for example, Engels, *Origin*, 112.

55. For a critique of Engels on this point, see Silverblatt, "Women in States," 430–31.

56. Engels, *Origin*, 137.

57. Ibid., 120–21, 137.

58. Bloch, *Marxism and Anthropology*, 54, 98, 115.

59. Engels, *Origin*, 118–19, 220–21. Both Marx and Engels believed that pastoralism preceded agriculture rather than the opposite, a view they derived from biblical sources and from an influential 1840 volume by W. Cooke Taylor (*The Natural History of Society in the Barbarous and Civilized State*) that Marx read in 1851 (Bloch, *Marxism and Anthropology*, 33, 65–66). This was not the prevailing view among the Victorian anthropologists, who believed the domestication of plants preceded that of animals.

60. Engels, *Origin*, 117; Bloch, *Marxism and Anthropology*, 55.

61. Ibid. As Engels points out, "It has never occurred to them [men], even to this day, to renounce the pleasures of actual group marriage."

62. Ibid., 120–21.

63. Ibid., 129. For a further exposition of this point, see Coward, *Patriarchal Precedents*, 158.

64. Engels, *Origin*, 222–25.

65. Ibid., 220. This connection between sex oppression and war (in Engels, it was rather indirect) forged a new link in the chain of matriarchal myth that increased in importance throughout the twentieth century to eventually become a received opinion about the development of warfare in the transition from matriarchy to patriarchy.

66. Karl Marx, quoted in Krader, *Ethnological Notebooks*, 14.

67. Engels, *Origin*, 145.

68. Ibid., 139.

69. Ibid., 145.

70. Karl Marx to Friedrich Engels, quoted in Janssen-Jurreit, *Sexism*, 108.

71. Karl Marx, quoted in Joachim Müller and Edith Schotte, "Epilogue," in Marx-Aveling and Aveling, *Thoughts on Women and Society*, 34.

72. Marx, *Portable Karl Marx*, 53.

73. Quoted in Coward, *Patriarchal Precedents*, 174.

74. Janssen-Jurreit, *Sexism*, 103.

75. Karl Marx and Friedrich Engels, *Manifesto of the Communist Party*, in Marx, *Portable Karl Marx*, 239. In their first collaborative work, *The Holy Family* (written in 1845), Marx and Engels accepted Fourier's thesis that the status of women was the leading indicator of social progress, paraphrasing him as follows: "The change in a historical epoch can always be determined by women's progress toward freedom, because here, in the relation of woman to man, of the weak to the strong, the victory of human nature over brutality is most evident. The degree of emancipation of women is the natural measure of general emancipation" (Marx and Engels, quoted in Vogel, *Marxism and the Oppression of Women*, 42; Engels echoed this sentiment in 1878 [ibid., 73–74]). This appears to be a feminist sentiment, but is not. It relies on the prior belief that men are strong and women weak—and this in an apparently immutable way, since the treatment of women (weak) by men (strong) can be used transhistorically as a measure of society's advance. Engels did acknowledge Fourier in a footnote in *The Origin*, explaining that he "originally intended to place the brilliant criticism of civilization which is found scattered through the work of Charles Fourier beside that of Morgan and my own," but he lacked the time to do so. For more on Marx and Engels's reception of Fourier, see Riasanovsky, *Teaching of Charles Fourier*, 139; Pembroke, "Early Human Family," 290–91.

76. Lopes and Roth, *Men's Feminism*, 29.

77. Bebel, *Woman in the Past, Present and Future*, 6; Lopes and Roth, *Men's Feminism*, 73.

78. Bebel, *My Life*, 15ff.; Maehl, *Bebel*, 9–15; Stalin, "Bebel," 112.

79. Maehl, *Bebel*, 2, 16; Lopes and Roth, *Men's Feminism*, 35 (pp. 13–17 offer an excellent chronology of Bebel's life).

80. Bebel, *My Life*, 66–67.

81. For details on Müller and his feminist activities, see Lopes and Roth, *Men's Feminism*, 93–100.

82. August Bebel, quoted in Lopes and Roth, *Men's Feminism*, 122; Bebel, *My Life*, 167–69.

83. Lopes and Roth, *Men's Feminism*, 19, 217.

84. Maehl, *Bebel*, 126. Lopes and Roth note that the bourgeois feminist movement was more inclined to build its politics around the "specialness" of women and the virtues thought to be implicitly feminine (*Men's Feminism*, 96).

85. Bebel, *My Life*, 302.

86. Bebel's classic went by many titles both in German and in translation. In the text I refer to it as *Woman and Socialism*, though it is cited under other titles, including *Women in the Past, Present and Future*, and *Woman under Socialism*.

87. Bebel, *My Life*, 79. This is Bebel's account of what he read in prison in the early 1870s: "I studied history and political economy principally. I read Marx's 'Capital' for the second time; only the first volume was then published; Engels' 'Condition of the Working Classes in England'; Lassalle's 'System of Acquired Rights'; Mill's 'Political Economy'; the works of Dühring and Carey; Lavelaye's 'Primitive Property'; Stein's 'History of Socialism and Communism in France'; Plato's 'Republic'; Aristotle's 'Politics'; Machiavelli's 'Prince'; Sir Thomas More's 'Utopia'; von Thünen's 'The Isolated State'; and others. Of the historical works which I then read I was most captivated by Buckle's 'History of Civilisation' and Wilhelm Zi[m]mermann's 'History of the German Peasants' War.' The last book inspired me to write a popular essay with the title 'The German Peasants' War,' with special regard to the chief social movements of the Middle Ages. It was published in book form, but confiscated later on under the anti-Socialist laws. I did not neglect natural science. I read Darwin's 'Origin of Species'; Haeckel's 'Story of Creation'; Büchner's 'Force and Matter' and 'Man's Position in Nature'; Liebig's 'Letters on Chemistry'; and part of my time I devoted to reading the classics. I was seized by a veritable passion for reading and learning" (258–59). Henry Ellenberger (*Discovery of the Unconscious*, 292) reports that Bebel also read Bachofen, but this seems not to have happened until after Engels wrote *The Origin*.

88. Lopes and Roth, *Men's Feminism*, 33, 128.

89. Bebel, *My Life*, 259–60. See also Maehl, *Bebel*, 124.

90. Lopes and Roth, *Men's Feminism*, 33; Bebel, *My Life*, 318–19; Maehl, *Bebel*, 123–24.

91. Sombart, "Max Weber and Otto Gross," 140; Bebel, *My Life*, 259–60; Lopes and Roth, *Men's Feminism*, 33.

92. Vogel, *Marxism and the Oppression of Women*, 96–97; Maehl, *Bebel*, 124.

93. Coward, *Patriarchal Precedents*, 171; Vogel, *Marxism and the Oppression of Women*, 96–97.

94. Vogel, *Marxism and the Oppression of Women*, 96–97.

95. Marx-Aveling and Aveling, *Thoughts on Women and Society*, 10–11.

96. Lopes and Roth, *Men's Feminism*, 33, 35, 37; Maehl, *Bebel*, 124.

97. Lopes and Roth report that *Woman and Socialism* was translated into Danish, English, and Swedish during the 1880s; Bulgarian, Czech, Dutch, French, Greek, Hungarian, Italian, Polish, Rumanian, and Russian during the 1890s; and Armenian, Finnish, Georgian, Lettish, Norwegian, Serbo-Croatian, and Spanish in the 1900s (*Men's Feminism*, 38).

98. Vogel, *Marxism and the Oppression of Women*, 75; Lopes and Roth, *Men's Feminism*, 22, 33.

99. Bebel, *Woman in the Past, Present and Future*, 1. In the first and second editions of his classic, Bebel mentioned cases of women's equality or dominance in his first chapter, but tossed these off briefly as anomalies in the face of near total male dominance throughout history (and before it).

100. Bebel, *Woman under Socialism*, 9.

101. Ibid., 3, 10.

102. Ibid., 9–46. Bebel does add one curious "fact" to both pre- and post-*Origin* editions of *Woman and Socialism*: that "savage" and "barbarian" women and men were more similar in brain size and weight than the women and men of "civilized" societies (*Woman*

in the Past, Present and Future, 2–3; *Woman under Socialism*, 26–27). This was a claim made by Darwin and popularized by Herbert Spencer (Duffin, "Prisoners of Progress," 66–67; Fee, "Sexual Politics," 98).

103. See, for example, Vogel, *Marxism and the Oppression of Women*, 75.

104. Lopes and Roth, *Men's Feminism*, 74–76. See Vogel, *Marxism and the Oppression of Women* (98) for a conflicting account of the relationship between Bebel and Engels.

105. Maehl estimates that two fifths of *Woman and Socialism* is "an exegesis on the class state and society in the aristocratic-bourgeois era," which only comes around to the issue of gender again in the end, long enough to say that a socialist revolution will bring equality for women (*Bebel*, 127–28).

106. Lopes and Roth note that the first edition of Engels's *Origin* contained fewer than five pages scattered throughout the work on women's condition in capitalist society. By the time of the second edition (1891), this had increased to about eight pages (*Men's Feminism*, 82, n. 5).

107. This is not to say that Bebel always accepted Engels's authority on all matters. The relationship between them as fellow activists was sometimes strained, as Engels accused the German Social Democratic Party of becoming reformist rather than revolutionary, while Bebel defended its actions as *realpolitik*. In his autobiography, *My Life*, Bebel remarks of Marx and Engels, "It will be seen that it was not an easy matter to satisfy the two old gentlemen in London. What was really a clever tactical move on our part and the result of prudent calculation they regarded as mere weakness" (286–87). Later, Bebel states that "Marx and Engels . . . were too far away to hold a correct view of persons and things" (309).

108. Bebel, *Woman under Socialism*, 58. This tendency to make early Christianity (or, just as often, Jesus) an exception, feminist before its time, is quite widespread in later versions of matriarchal myth. Nobody in Western Christian societies—least of all August Bebel—seems to have the stomach to blame Jesus and his followers for much of anything.

109. Ibid., 17, 20. In *Men's Feminism*, Lopes and Roth credit Bebel with being a forerunner to a generation of European sexologists, including Richard Krafft-Ebing, Magnus Hirschfeld, and Havelock Ellis.

110. Bebel, *Woman under Socialism*, 97.

111. Lopes and Roth, *Men's Feminism*, 81, n. 47.

112. The royalties from *Woman and Socialism* supported Bebel and his family throughout his later years (Maehl, *Bebel*, 124, 361).

113. It is interesting to note that there were eleven people in attendance at Karl Marx's funeral, while at August Bebel's funeral, there were five hundred wreath-bearers and the funeral procession took more than an hour to pass any one point (Eugene Kamenka, introduction to Marx, *Portable Karl Marx*, xxii; Maehl, *Bebel*, 5). Janssen-Jurreit argues that it was Bebel who first put the myth of matriarchal prehistory before a popular audience, Bachofen's and Morgan's work being relatively unknown (*Sexism*, 111). She almost certainly overstates this. Morgan was not the only anthropologist disseminating matriarchal myth, and many of the Victorian anthropologists were widely read in England and

the United States. In Germany, however, where anthropologists were less likely to adopt matriarchal myth, Bebel probably did introduce more readers to matriarchal myth than did Morgan, Bachofen, or any of the British or German anthropologists.

114. Bloch, *Marxism and Anthropology*, 100; Coward, *Patriarchal Precedents*, 164. Bloch suggests that Lafargue followed Engels rather slavishly in his *La Propriété, Origines et Evolution*, with the exception of some "totally fallacious evidence" about sexual dimorphism in the brain size of "primitives." Most likely, Lafargue took this material from Bebel.

115. Fromm, "Theory of Mother Right," 96.

116. Coward, *Patriarchal Precedents*, 298, n. 10. Cunow was a friendly critic; he was one of the few later matriarchalists who actually praised Bachofen (Andre Gingrich, "The German-Speaking Countries," in Barth et al., eds., *One Discipline, Four Ways*, 79).

117. Matilda Joslyn Gage, who stands out as one of the most ardent first-wave feminist narrators of matriarchal myth, was appropriated in the 1970s and 1980s, but she was mainly revived by Christian feminists, who were less interested in Gage's matriarchal views than in her critique of Christianity.

118. For example, a French feminist group (Groupe Français d' Études Féministes) published a translation of Bachofen's *Mutterrecht* in 1903 and disseminated it as a feminist text (Georgoudi, "Myth of Matriarchy," 450; Borgeaud, "From Lafitau to Bachofen").

119. The most important feminist critic of matriarchal myth was Marianne Weber (spouse of sociologist Max Weber), who in 1907 published *Ehefrau und Mutter in der Rechtsentwicklung* (Wives and Mothers in the Development of Law).

120. Eliza Burt Gamble (*Evolution of Woman*) includes a chapter on Bachofen, though she seems to be relying on secondary sources. Scholars sometimes mention Bachofen in connection with Elizabeth Cady Stanton (see, for example, Love and Shanklin, "Answer Is Matriarchy," 183, n. 1), but I have not been able to find any evidence that Stanton was familiar with Bachofen's work.

121. See, for example, Gamble, *Evolution of Woman*, 129. Matilda Joslyn Gage also seems to have been aware of Morgan's work (*Woman, Church and State*, 19).

122. Eliza Burt Gamble, Anna Garlin Spencer, Catherine Gasquoine Hartley, and Charlotte Perkins Gilman all made reference to McLennan, Lubbock, and/or Tylor in their writings on matriarchy.

123. Stanton, "Matriarchate," 4.

124. Ibid.

125. Gage, *Woman, Church and State*, 39; Bennett, *Religious Cults*, 73–76; Swiney, *Awakening of Woman*, 81, 110.

126. This is borne out particularly clearly in the theories that Marx and Engels developed regarding the "Asiatic" mode of production. When Marx and Engels noticed that traditional Chinese economics did not fit neatly into the schematic stages they had created for Western society, they simply added on an additional, different mode of production which they termed "Asiatic" (Bloch, *Marxism and Anthropology*, 37). One suspects that as long as they kept encountering new forms of economic structure, Marx and Engels would have continued to make additions to their schema.

127. For a review of the impact of Darwin on late nineteenth-century feminist theorists, see Bland, *Banishing the Beast,* 85; Deutscher, "Descent of Man and Evolution of Woman."

128. For example: "The chief distinction in the intellectual powers of the two sexes is shewn by man's attaining to a higher eminence, in whatever he takes up, than can woman—whether requiring deep thought, reason, or imagination, or merely the use of the senses and hands" (Darwin, *Descent of Man,* 726).

129. Gamble, *Evolution of Woman,* v–vi.

130. Darwin, *Origin of Species,* 218.

131. Gamble, *Evolution of Woman,* 29.

132. Swiney, *Awakening of Woman,* 121. This was a consistent theme in Swiney's work, which came to include a series of writings on "racial problems" and "racial poisons."

133. Gamble, *Evolution of Woman,* 78–79.

134. Stanton, "Matriarchate," 3.

135. Ibid.

136. But a glimpse of things to come can be seen in Elizabeth Blackwell's assertion that it is not actual motherhood, but the mere possession of a womb that creates maternal instinct, and with it, female superiority (Bland, *Banishing the Beast,* 69). Blackwell herself did not promote matriarchal myth, but shared some of its assumptions regarding femaleness (see her book, *The Sexes throughout Nature,* published in 1875).

137. See, for example, Stanton, "Matriarchate," 5; Gamble, *Evolution of Woman,* 58–59. The relationship between goddess and god was frequently imagined as one of mother and son, probably owing to the rising influence of Sir James Frazer's *The Golden Bough.* During the first wave of feminism, actual worship of goddesses or the Goddess was virtually unheard of; interest in goddesses was historical. Feminists looked to the past not for a religion to replicate in the future, but simply for the evidence that everything male—including God—was once female. Some few feminists arriving on the scene after the turn of the twentieth century (for example, Frances Swiney) came to advocate goddess worship, but as they did so they tended to move out of the social orbit of feminism and into that of theosophy.

138. Stanton, "Matriarchate," 8; Gage, *Woman, Church and State,* 42.

139. Gage, *Woman, Church and State,* 22, 32; Gage, "Matriarchate," 1481. Gage rarely acknowledged other theorists when describing the "matriarchate." An exception can be found in a printed exchange between Matilda Joslyn Gage and Edward Cope published in *The Open Court,* in which Gage cites W. Robertson Smith as supporting the notion that ancient religions put their gods in the role of sons ("Matriarchate," 1481).

140. See, for example, Gage, "Matriarchate," 1481.

141. Gamble, *Evolution of Woman,* 91, 210.

142. Ibid., 208–209.

143. Gage, *Woman, Church and State,* 43–44.

144. Stanton, "Matriarchate," 6.

145. Gamble, *Evolution of Woman,* 29, 139, 169.

146. Stanton, "Matriarchate," 1. Stanton actually claimed that the patriarchal victory over matriarchal culture was only truly completed with the Protestant Reformation in the sixteenth century (6–7).

147. Gage, *Woman, Church and State*, 12–13.

148. Stanton, *Woman's Bible*, 25.

6. MOTHER RIGHT ON THE CONTINENT

Epigraph: Dargun, *Mutterrecht und Raubehe*, 77.

1. Fredrik Barth calls their discussions "remarkably acrimonious" ("Britain and the Commonwealth," in Barth et al., eds., *One Discipline, Four Ways*, 9). Some historians have regarded Tylor as a bridge between British and continental anthropology, mainly because he made occasional reference to the work of Bastian and Theodor Waitz, but others claim that Tylor's linguistic abilities were limited and that he did not really read or understand German anthropology at any significant level (see Koepping, *Bastian and the Psychic Unity of Mankind*, 3–4; 126–27).

2. Smith, *Sciences of Culture in Germany*, 60; H. Glenn Penny, "Bastian's Museum," in Penny and Bunzl, eds., *Worldly Provincialism*, 101.

3. Smith, *Sciences of Culture in Germany*, 116–17; Koepping, *Bastian and the Psychic Unity of Mankind*, 7–11.

4. The Museum für Völkerkunde opened in Berlin in 1886, but was in the planning stages well before then (H. Glenn Penny, "Bastian's Museum," in Penny and Bunzl, eds., *Worldly Provincialism*, 87).

5. H. Glenn Penny, "Traditions in the German Language," in Kuklick, ed., *New History of Anthropology*, 84–85; Koepping, *Bastian and the Psychic Unity of Mankind*, 26–27.

6. Koepping, *Bastian and the Psychic Unity of Mankind*, 11, 13, 26, 117.

7. Smith, *Sciences of Culture in Germany*, 59; Koepping, *Bastian and the Psychic Unity of Mankind*, 3.

8. Zimmerman, "German Anthropology and the 'Natural Peoples,'" 96; Smith, *Sciences of Culture in Germany*, 100–103.

9. Andre Gingrich, "The German-Speaking Countries," in Barth et al., eds., *One Discipline, Four Ways*, 86; Koepping, *Bastian and the Psychic Unity of Mankind*, 69; Zimmerman, "German Anthropology and the 'Natural Peoples,'" 99. On the parallel situation in England, see Kuklick, *Savage Within*, 5.

10. James Whitman, "From Philology to Anthropology," in Stocking, ed., *Functionalism Historicized*, 224; Andrew Zimmerman, "Adventures in the Skin Trade," in Penny and Bunzl, eds., *Worldly Provincialism*, 159; H. Glenn Penny, "Traditions in the German Language," in Kuklick, ed., *New History of Anthropology*, 83. The discipline of philology still retained a higher status than that accorded to ethnology, partly because, as Robert Ackerman explains, "a classical education acted as an explicit class marker, serving to differentiate those who shared a privileged social background regardless of their actual knowledge of the classical world from those who did not" ("Anthropology and the Classics," in Kuklick, ed., *New History of Anthropology*, 143). And although German ethnology was read and appreciated outside its native context, German philology had a greater impact abroad (Smith, *Sciences of Culture in Germany*, 61).

11. Penny and Bunzl, eds., *Worldly Provincialism*, 14.

12. This terminology originated with Herder (see chapter 3).

13. Andrew Zimmerman, "Adventures in the Skin Trade," in Penny and Bunzl, eds., *Worldly Provincialism*, 161.

14. Koepping, *Bastian and the Psychic Unity of Mankind*, 19.

15. See H. Glenn Penny, "Bastian's Museum," in Penny and Bunzl, eds., *Worldly Provincialism*, 96.

16. Bastian promoted ethnological fieldwork not just for himself, but for his students. As H. Glenn Penny explains, Bastian was convinced "that the creation of universal theories about human history were secondary to the accumulation of knowledge about its particulars" ("Bastian's Museum," in Penny and Bunzl, eds., *Worldly Provincialism*, 94; see also H. Glenn Penny, "Traditions in the German Language," in Kuklick, ed., *New History of Anthropology*, 87).

17. Adolf Bastian, quoted in H. Glenn Penny, "Bastian's Museum," in Penny and Bunzl, eds., *Worldly Provincialism*, 97.

18. Koepping, *Bastian and the Psychic Unity of Mankind*, 47; Zimmerman, "German Anthropology and the 'Natural Peoples,' " 102; James Whitman, "From Philology to Anthropology," in Stocking, ed., *Functionalism Historicized*, 221.

19. Adolf Bastian, quoted in H. Glenn Penny, "Bastian's Museum," in Penny and Bunzl, eds., *Worldly Provincialism*, 95. See also Zimmerman, "German Anthropology and the 'Natural Peoples,' " 100.

20. Smith, *Sciences of Culture in Germany*, 118.

21. Koepping, *Bastian and the Psychic Unity of Mankind*, 47, 98.

22. Penny and Bunzl, eds., *Worldly Provincialism*, 2.

23. Andrew D. Evans, "Anthropology at War," in Penny and Bunzl, eds., *Worldly Provincialism*, 203; Smith, *Sciences of Culture in Germany*, 50; Koepping, *Bastian and the Psychic Unity of Mankind*, 126–27.

24. Adolf Bastian, quoted in H. Glenn Penny, "Bastian's Museum," in Penny and Bunzl, eds., *Worldly Provincialism*, 93–94.

25. Zimmerman, "German Anthropology and the 'Natural Peoples,' " 102.

26. Andre Gingrich, "The German-Speaking Countries," in Barth et al., eds., *One Discipline, Four Ways*, 87.

27. Koepping, *Bastian and the Psychic Unity of Mankind*, 54; Penny and Bunzl, eds., *Worldly Provincialism*, 11–12; H. Glenn Penny, "Traditions in the German Language," in Kuklick, ed., *New History of Anthropology*, 81; Smith, *Sciences of Culture in Germany*, 4, 25–26.

28. See Koepping, *Bastian and the Psychic Unity of Mankind*, 209–10.

29. Ibid., 17, 53–54, 96, 98, 137–39. Bastian's analysis of the evolution of human religious thought was highly influential for Frazer's work, culminating in *The Golden Bough* and giving German ethnology a direct impact in England.

30. Indeed, in 1872, Bastian and Bachofen exchanged cordial greetings praising one another's work. Bastian provided Bachofen with information about the cultural history of matrilineal societies and polyandry in Burma for Bachofen to use in his continuing investigations into the principle of mother right (letter from Adolf Bastian to Johann Jakob Bachofen, 10 May 1872, in *Bachofens Gesammelte Werke*, 10:462–65; Koepping, *Bastian and the Psychic Unity of Mankind*, 233, n. 1).

31. Both before and after his works on matriarchal prehistory, Lippert published works on religion. In the early twentieth century he wrote a significant work on the Muslim philosopher Ibn Sina and a biography of Mohammed. Of course the British anthropologists were interested in religion, too. Lubbock devoted two thirds of *The Origin of Civilisation* to the topic, and McLennan and Robertson Smith wrote at length about totemism. But the British anthropologists did little to tie together the story they developed about religion and the one they told about changing patterns of marriage (Harris, *Rise of Anthropological Theory*, 200–201), as Bachofen and then Lippert did.

32. Lippert, *Geschichte der Familie*, 71.

33. Ibid., 4–5, 19, 50. Lippert was explicit about his debt to Bachofen, saying in the preface to *Geschichte der Familie* that he is mainly repeating Bachofen, though adding some material of which Bachofen was unaware when he wrote *Das Mutterrecht*.

34. Lippert, *Evolution of Culture*, 201, 203–4, 207, 212, 227, 290–91.

35. Ibid., 209, 225, 227–29. The "sex for meat" exchange became a very popular explanation of the sexed division of labor in the "man the hunter" version of evolutionary anthropology developed during the 1960s. It is still popular today.

36. Lippert, *Geschichte der Familie*, 30–31, 38.

37. Lippert, *Evolution of Culture*, 223–24, 240–41. Lippert takes the approach of Bachofen, that mother right is characterized by blood relationship and father right by adoptive kinship.

38. Lippert, *Geschichte der Familie*, 40.

39. Lippert, *Evolution of Culture*, 285, 290–91.

40. Lippert, *Geschichte der Familie*, 36.

41. Lippert, *Evolution of Culture*, 230, 237–38, 277–78, 285, 323, 356, 357.

42. Lippert, *Geschichte der Familie*, 73–94.

43. Ibid., 43, 48; Lippert, *Evolution of Culture*, 247, 248, 331, 358, 360. This notion that goddess worship outlasted the matriarchy and gave evidence of its prior existence becomes key in later versions of the myth of matriarchal prehistory.

44. Lippert, *Evolution of Culture*, 274–75, 319, 320–21, 346–47, 351.

45. Ibid., 323.

46. Lippert, *Geschichte der Familie*, 78–79, 86, 93–94, 181.

47. Ibid., 37, 57.

48. Lippert, *Evolution of Culture*, 246; *Geschichte der Familie*, 259–60.

49. Giraud-Teulon, *Histoire du Mariage*, 12. Giraud-Teulon was never entirely consistent on this point.

50. Ibid., 21–22.

51. Kautsky, "Entstehung der Ehe," 205.

52. Hellwald, *Menschliche Familie*, 124.

53. Ibid., 126–29.

54. Ibid., 175, 196, 209, 227. Hellwald distinguished matriarchy, which he believed was a key stage in human social development, from gynecocracy, to which he gave no place in his schema.

55. Ibid., 225–26, 240.

56. Ibid., 568, 575, 578, 580–81.

57. Kohler, *Prehistory of Marriage*, 209; Howard, *History of Matrimonial Institutions*, 44–45.

58. Lyall, "Early German Legal Anthropology," 115, n. 2.

59. R. H. Barnes, introduction to Kohler, *Prehistory of Marriage*, 3–5, 19, 23, 29, 45–46; Kohler, *Prehistory of Marriage*, 75, 79.

60. Kohler, quoted in R. H. Barnes, introduction to Kohler, *Prehistory of Marriage*, 13.

61. Penniman, *A Hundred Years of Anthropology*, 171; Kohler, quoted in R. H. Barnes, introduction to Kohler, *Prehistory of Marriage*, 15. Barnes reports that Kohler had personal contact with Bachofen (20); undoubtedly Kohler read and absorbed *Das Mutterrecht* before embarking on his own treatise on the topic.

62. Kohler, *Prehistory of Marriage*, 76–77.

63. Ibid., 115, 129.

64. Ibid., 137–38.

65. Engels, *Origin*, 71.

66. Young, *Malinowski*, 33.

67. Smith, review of *Studien zum Ältesten Familienrecht*, 572–73; Howard, *History of Matrimonial Institutions*, 44–45.

68. This overlapped with Dargun's other main interest, war, because he believed, along with McLennan, that marriage by capture developed when women were taken captive in warfare ("Ursprungs der Ehe," 129).

69. Lyall, "Early German Legal Anthropology," 116.

70. Post, *Entwicklungsgeschichte des Familienrechts*, 7, 42, 45.

71. Ibid., 19.

72. Ibid., 105–14, 129, 134. Post does draw one important distinction between *Mutterrecht* and *Vaterrecht:* he imagines that sexual promiscuity or lack of regulated marriage would always imply mother right, since only the mother of an individual child could be known with certainty. Father right, by comparison, is more "artificial." In this, Post sounds more like Bachofen (ibid., 54–55).

73. Bachofen, *Mutterrecht*, 327.

74. Post, *Entwicklungsgeschichte des Familienrechts*, 25–29.

75. Ibid., 20, 44. Here Post follows Morgan. Overall, Morgan, rather than Bachofen, seems to have had the stronger influence on Post's work (Penniman, *A Hundred Years of Anthropology*, 170, 171; R. H. Barnes, introduction to Kohler, *Prehistory of Marriage*, 19).

76. Post, *Entwicklungsgeschichte des Familienrechts*, 326.

77. Lyall, "Early German Legal Anthropology," 116, 119.

78. Post's questionnaire is reproduced as an appendix in Lyall's "Early German Legal Anthropology."

79. Alexis Giraud-Teulon, quoted in Fishbane, "Mother-Right, Myth, and Renewal," 787. See also Howard, *History of Matrimonial Institutions*, 44–45; Murdock, "Appendix A," in Lippert, *Evolution of Culture*, 645.

80. Gossman, "Basle, Bachofen. and the Critique of Modernity," 139, n. 8, 169–70. Fritz Kramer describes Reclus as a "Belgian anarchist" ("Empathy," 344).

81. Reclus, "Female Kinship and Maternal Filiation," 211, 219–22.

82. Ibid., 213–14, 218.

83. See chapter 2.

84. Cahnman, ed., *Tönnies*, 51–52; Jose Harris, introduction to Tönnies, *Community and Civil Society*, xii, xv.

85. Tönnies, *Community and Civil Society*, 12. Tönnies also notes the influence of Karl Marx, whom he describes as "the most outstanding and profound social philosopher," thereby winning himself an undeserved reputation as a Marxist (Jose Harris, introduction to Tönnies, *Community and Civil Society*, xxiv).

86. The first and even the third are consistent with the assumptions of matriarchal myth, but the second is unusual. Tönnies, *Community and Civil Society*, 22.

87. Ibid., 24–25.

88. Ibid., 25.

89. Ibid., 26–27.

90. Ibid., 152–54. Tönnies credits men's hunting activities with sharpening men's intellect. Believing in the inheritance of acquired characteristics, he asserts that increased intelligence is passed to subsequent generations, including women, which somewhat undercuts his own argument about sex differences (153; see n. 2, translators' note).

91. Ibid., 155–56.

92. Ibid., 166, 170, 187.

93. As we have seen, Bachofen was mentioned by Tönnies in the introduction to his *Gemeinschaft und Gesellschaft*, but as Werner J. Cahnman points out, he never cites Bachofen in his text (*Tönnies*, 42).

94. The quoted phrase is Rita Felski's (*Gender of Modernity*, 55).

95. Tönnies, *Community and Civil Society*, 260.

96. Zmigrodski, *Mutter bei den Völkern des Arischen Stammes*, 95ff.

97. Ibid., 151–56.

98. Ibid., 194–97.

99. Ibid., 201.

100. Ibid., 209–15.

101. Ibid., 177.

102. Ibid., 180. Zmigrodski's view contradicts most theories about the proto-Indo-Europeans, who are generally imagined as a nomadic people.

103. Ibid., 297, 312.

104. Ibid., 333–45.

105. Quinn, *Swastika*, 22–24. Zmigrodski's drawings were later deposited in the St. Germain Museum of Prehistory.

106. Zmigrodski, *Zur Geschichte der Swastika*, quoted in Quinn, *Swastika*, 25.

107. Ibid., 49.

108. Quinn, *Swastika*, 52.

109. Wagner-Hasel, ed., *Matriarchatstheorien der Altertumswissenschaft*, 353, n. 79.

110. See, for example, Dargun, *Mutterrecht und Raubehe*, 72, 77.

111. The question of the original kinship system of the Aryan peoples was not limited to those who favored the matriarchal thesis. The renowned linguist Otto Schrader and German anthropologist Franz Bernhöft both claimed that all Indo-European languages reveal a patriarchal family system and that it is thus probable that the speakers

of proto-Indo-European were patriarchal in social organization. Some partisans of matriarchal myth responded by placing matriarchy further back in prehistory or in a geographically separate place from the Indo-European homeland; as we have seen here, Dargun and Zmigrodski responded by detecting the priority of mother right in Indo-European linguistics. See Szemerényi, "Kinship Terminology of the Indo-European Languages," 195; Renfrew, *Archaeology and Language*, 15.

112. Hellwald, *Menschliche Familie*, 235.

113. H. Glenn Penny, "Bastian's Museum," in Penny and Bunzl, eds., *Worldly Provincialism*, 109–14.

114. Andre Gingrich, "The German-Speaking Countries," in Barth et al., *One Discipline, Four Ways*, 90.

115. Penny and Bunzl, eds., *Worldly Provincialism*, 10, 17–18; H. Glenn Penny, "Traditions in the German Language," in Kuklick, ed., *New History of Anthropology*, 91.

116. H. Glenn Penny, "Bastian's Museum," in Penny and Bunzl, eds., *Worldly Provincialism*, 113–14. Penny attributes this view especially to Willy Foy.

117. Smith, *Sciences of Culture in Germany*, 101; H. Glenn Penny, "Traditions in the German Language," in Kuklick, ed., *New History of Anthropology*, 91. Penny also draws attention to the role played by the rediscovery of Gregor Mendel's theories of biological inheritance, which were easily pressed into service for racist purposes.

118. Zimmer, "Matriarchy among the Picts," 36–41.

119. Davies, "Männerbund and Mutterrecht," 102.

7. STRUGGLING TO STAY ALIVE

Epigraph: Starcke, *Primitive Family*, 18–19.

1. Stocking dates the demise of matriarchal myth to the 1920s, when "the priority of matrilineal kinship was no longer taken for granted in mainstream anthropology, and the problem of primitive promiscuity had been replaced by the universality of the incest taboo" (*Victorian Anthropology*, 204–5). Divale claims that the Hartland-Kroeber debate—an exchange of articles and letters published in *American Anthropologist* in 1918—marked the end of the theory of matriarchy in anthropology (*Matrilocal Residence in Pre-Literate Society*, 2–3). Malinowski names Robert Briffault's *The Mothers*, published in 1927, "the swan-song of mother-right hypotheses" (quoted in Coward, *Patriarchal Precedents*, 47–48). Others writing in the 1910s, 1920s, and 1930s—including Westermarck, Lowie, Hartley, Murdock, and Calverton—reported that "the former belief in mother-power has been transformed, and now seems likely to disappear altogether" (Hartley, *Age of Mother-Power*, 111; see also Murdock, "Correlations of Matrilineal and Patrilineal Institutions," 446; Calverton, "Modern Anthropology," 20; Westermarck, *History of Human Marriage*, 279; Lowie, *Primitive Society*, 171, 186). I date the end of the matriarchal thesis in anthropology to the turn of the century because this is when it ceased to be regarded as dogma, becoming just one theory among others—and a theory whose doom was pretty well sealed.

2. Lowie, *Primitive Society*, 171, 186.

3. Marx-Aveling and Aveling, *Thoughts on Women and Society*, 11–12.

4. Ibid., 19–22. Eleanor Marx-Aveling did not extend her critique beyond the sexual double standard and the separation of the sexes in society, accepting, for example, the heterosexism of her time. "The effeminate man and masculine woman," she declared, are produced by a society that separates the genders, and they "are two types from which even the average person recoils with a perfectly natural horror of the unnatural" (23).

5. Ibid., 25–28.

6. Ibid., 12–15.

7. August Bebel, quoted in Lopes and Roth, *Men's Feminism*, 199.

8. Ibid., 39.

9. As Lise Vogel, a twentieth-century Marxist scholar, complains: "Bebel often pictures the solution to the so-called woman question in terms of achieving equal rights to participate in society without distinction of sex. This approach fails to differentiate socialist aims from the liberal feminist goal of sex equality in capitalist society. . . . He conceptualized the so-called woman question as an issue pertaining to woman's situation as an individual, on the one hand, and to social conditions in general, on the other, but he was unable to construct a reliable bridge between the two levels of analysis (*Marxism and the Oppression of Women*, 103). Orthodox Marxist commentators tend to blame the influence of Charles Fourier on Bebel as the source of this "weakness" in his work (Vogel, *Marxism and the Oppression of Women*, 101; Moira Donald, quoted in Lopes and Roth, *Men's Feminism*, 40).

10. N. Krupskaya, introduction to Lenin, *Women and Society*, 8; Lopes and Roth, *Men's Feminism*, 70, 201–2.

11. Vogel, *Marxism and the Oppression of Women*, 107–11.

12. Lopes and Roth, *Men's Feminism*, 200.

13. August Bebel, quoted in Lopes and Roth, *Men's Feminism*, 7.

14. Vladimir Lenin, quoted in Zetkin, *Lenin on the Woman Question*, 14–15.

15. Ibid., 8–9.

16. Clara Zetkin to Friedrich Engels, quoted in Lopes and Roth, *Men's Feminism*, 219.

17. Stocking, *Victorian Anthropology*, 289.

18. Maine was operating on the biblical time line (Stocking, *Victorian Anthropology*, 125–26).

19. Indeed, some matriarchalists used Maine in just this way, as the author of the last segment of the matriarchal narrative (see Fee, "Sexual Politics," 94). Starcke (see below) makes this apology for Maine, but George Elliott Howard notes—accurately, I think—that "obviously his [Maine's] language will not bear that construction" (*History of Matrimonial Institutions*, 14).

20. Maine, *Dissertations on Early Law and Government*, 192–93, 195. See also Hartland, "Matrilineal Kinship," 5; Coward, *Patriarchal Precedents*, 43; Starcke, *Primitive Family*, 95.

21. Maine first took note of the matriarchal theory in *Village Communities*, published in 1871, but did not offer any critique. As Penniman notes, in *Lectures on the Early History of Institutions*, published in 1875, Maine "prefers to leave unsettled the question of kinship in the more primitive races, still maintaining that his own plan of development is unshaken, applying as it does to the evolution of the higher races with which history is

properly concerned." It was later, in *Dissertations on Early Law and Custom* (1883), that Maine first offered a clear argument against McLennan and Morgan (Penniman, *A Hundred Years of Anthropology*, 157).

22. Maine, *Dissertations on Early Law and Government*, 72–75, 149–50; Maine, quoted in Coward, *Patriarchal Precedents*, 43. See also Lawrence Rosen, foreword to Maine, *Ancient Law*, xvi. Maine cites Fustel de Coulanges in support of his theories about male ancestor worship (*Dissertations on Early Law and Government*, 75–76).

23. Maine, *Dissertations on Early Law and Government*, 218–19; Maine, quoted in Lowie, *History of Ethnological Theory*, 53.

24. Maine, *Dissertations on Early Law and Government*, 199–200, 202–3, 217. Maine's comment on maternity and paternity is quoted by, for example, Westermarck (*History of Human Marriage*, 285–86) and Montagu (*Coming into Being*, 10).

25. Maine, *Dissertations on Early Law and Government*, 205. See also Stocking, *Victorian Anthropology*, 176–77; Coward, *Patriarchal Precedents*, 43.

26. Wake, *Development of Marriage and Kinship*, vi, 15, 17, 20, 52, 260.

27. Ibid., 52.

28. Charles Kingsley, quoted in Stocking, *Victorian Anthropology*, 147.

29. Gamble, *Timewalkers*, 29. (See also Feder and Park, *Human Antiquity*.)

30. Darwin, *Descent of Man*, 760. In his earlier *On the Origin of Species*, Darwin refrained from discussing human evolution at any length, "fearful that godless nature and a simian ancestry would be too much reality for most Victorians to stomach all at once." Darwin left it to Thomas Huxley—known as "Darwin's bulldog"—to articulate the implications of his theory for human evolution (see Shreeve, *Neandertal Enigma*, 32). By the time of *The Descent of Man*, Darwin had been influenced in his turn by the writings of McLennan and his ilk. Though he clearly disagreed with them, it is likely that his earliest thoughts on human social evolution were inspired by the British matriarchalists (see Fedigan, "Changing Role of Women," 29).

31. Charles Darwin, quoted in Wake, *Development of Marriage and Kinship*, 6. See also Krader, *Ethnological Notebooks*, 63; Fedigan, "Changing Role of Women," 29.

32. Coward, *Patriarchal Precedents*, 57–58; Starcke, *Primitive Family*, 255.

33. Starcke, *Primitive Family*, 18–19.

34. Ibid., 53. It was only here that Starcke saw some possibility of mother right, as patriarchal family groups are formed into clans who may practice matrilineal descent.

35. Ibid., 270–71.

36. George Peter Murdock, writing in 1931, describes Westermarck as "the unquestioned leader" of "the critics of original mother-right" ("Priority of Mother-Right," in Lippert, *Evolution of Culture*, 657). See also Calverton, "Modern Anthropology," 8–9.

37. In the preface to the fifth edition of *The History of Human Marriage*, Westermarck writes: "The book has been rewritten throughout to such an extent that very few sentences of the earlier editions have remained unchanged. . . . the customs which have been represented as survivals of such a [promiscuous] state in the past have been more fully discussed. Thus the subjects of the *jus primae noctis*, religious prostitution, and the lending or exchange of wives now occupy sixty-nine pages instead of nine. . . . Polyandry, which was dealt with on a few pages, now forms the subject-matter of two whole chapters; and

the question of group-marriage, which of late has much occupied the minds of sociologists, has been discussed in a chapter by itself" (v–vii).

38. Ibid., vii–viii. This was a refrain that Westermarck sang routinely: where evolutionary anthropologists perceived "survivals," Westermarck saw "more or less arbitrary inferences" and insisted that "the burden of proof lies on him who asserts the former existence of something which does not exist at present, and not on him who professes ignorance as regards the past" (279–80).

39. Ibid., 1–2.

40. Murdock, "Primitive Promiscuity," in Lippert, *Evolution of Culture,* 647–48. A fourth argument, which Murdock terms "ethnological" but which he does not find in Westermarck, "maintains that most savage peoples are actually monogamous or else tend in that direction." Penniman claims, incorrectly, that this is Westermarck's principal argument against primitive promiscuity, "that no tribes of men in a normal state live thus, and that the customs and relationship terms which have been taken as proof of such promiscuity do not, in fact, prove it" (*A Hundred Years of Anthropology,* 167).

41. Westermarck, *History of Human Marriage,* 276; Bamberger, "Myth of Matriarchy," 264.

42. Westermarck, *History of Human Marriage,* 27–28; Murdock, "Priority of Mother-Right," in Lippert, *Evolution of Culture,* 657; Cavin, *Lesbian Origins,* 28. Engels complains that Westermarck "applies the term 'marriage' to every relationship in which the two sexes remain mated until the birth of the offspring," even though "this kind of marriage can very well occur under the conditions of promiscuous intercourse without contradicting the principle of promiscuity" (*Origin,* 101).

43. Szemerényi, *Kinship Terminology of the Indo-European Languages,* 195; Penniman, *A Hundred Years of Anthropology,* 170.

44. Durkheim, *Contributions to l'Année Sociologique,* 184; Durkheim, quoted in R. H. Barnes, introduction to Kohler, *Prehistory of Marriage,* 45–46.

45. Tylor, "Matriarchal Family System," 82. Tylor consistently used passive constructions such as these when discussing the matriarchal debate, either not seeing himself as a principal player in that debate or wishing to downplay his role in the eyes of others. See also Stocking, *Victorian Anthropology,* 204–5; Coward, *Patriarchal Precedents,* 57–58.

46. Tylor, "Matriarchal Family System," 83, 84–85.

47. Ibid., 90, 93–94.

48. Harris, *Rise of Anthropological Theory,* 304–5; Stocking, *Victorian Anthropology,* 287.

49. Boas, "Limitations of the Comparative Method," 273, 275, 280. As Simon Pembroke comments of evolutionary anthropology, "Inference in these theories, provided not only mortar, but bricks" ("Women in Charge," 1).

50. Boas had worked as an assistant at Berlin's Museum für Völkerkunde when Bastian was its director (H. Glenn Penny, "Bastian's Museum," in Penny and Bunzl, eds., *Worldly Provincialism,* 91).

51. Boas, "Limitations of the Comparative Method," 276, 277. See also Bell, *Reconstructing Prehistory,* 143. Interestingly, among those Boas cites as practitioners of this

historical method is E. B. Tylor (278). In fact, Tylor only shed his evolutionism under the pressure of arguments against it.

52. Bell, *Reconstructing Prehistory*, 143; Fedigan, "Changing Role of Women," 32–33; Harris, *Rise of Anthropological Theory*, 2. Harris points out that Boasian fieldwork anthropology, "while ostensibly operating within a restricted theoretical frame," actually permitted the formulation of "conclusions of the widest possible significance bearing on the nature of history and culture," since Boasian anthropologists spurned materialist explanations of culture and "stressed the inner, subjective meaning of experience to the exclusion of objective effects and relations."

53. Baker, *From Savage to Negro*, 5, 100, 148.

54. Stocking, *Victorian Anthropology*, 289.

55. di Leonardo, *Exotics at Home*, 161; Baker, *From Savage to Negro*, 101.

56. A parallel movement took place in Britain under the name of "functionalism," with Malinowski and Radcliffe-Brown—very different from each other—uniting to lead the charge against "conjectural history": a.k.a., evolutionary anthropology. Kay and Voorhies, *Female of the Species*, 155; Schneider, preface to Schneider and Gough, eds., *Matrilineal Kinship*, xi; Fluehr-Lobban, "Marxism and the Matriarchate," 8–9; Leacock, introduction to Engels, *Origin*, 16; Moore, *Feminism and Anthropology*, 12–13.

57. Westermarck, *History of Human Marriage*, 294–95; Lowie, "Matrilineal Complex," 30, 32–33, 45; Coward, *Patriarchal Precedents*, 62; Wake, *Development of Marriage and Kinship*, 297; Schneider, preface to Schneider and Gough, eds., *Matrilineal Kinship*, viii; Lowie, *Primitive Society*, 167–68, 170, 184.

58. Divale, *Matrilocal Residence in Pre-Literate Society*, 2; Murdock, "Priority of Mother-Right," in Lippert, *Evolution of Culture*, 662. See also Starcke, *Primitive Family*, 28; Lowie, *Primitive Society*, 167–68.

59. Harris, *Rise of Anthropological Theory*, 305; Lowie, *History of Ethnological Theory*, 82; Murdock, "Correlations of Matrilineal and Patrilineal Institutions," 448–49. This view was not universally accepted. W. J. McGee argued in 1896 in his article "The Beginning of Marriage" for a generalized matriliny-to-patriliny scheme for the Native American tribes. The key articles advancing the theory of a patriliny-to-matriliny trajectory were by Jon Swanton and were published in 1905.

8. MATRIARCHAL MYTH IN THE LATE NINETEENTH CENTURY

Epigraph: Lubbock, *Origin of Civilisation*, 69.

1. Feder and Park, *Human Antiquity*.

2. This group of poets and philosophers, initially centered around Stefan George, became fascinated with Bachofen, less for his matriarchal views than for his Romantic cosmology.

3. Bachofen never specifies dates for the stages he describes, but given his apparent dependence on the biblical timescale—and more importantly, the timescale his contemporaries would have attributed to him—these are the dates that make sense.

4. British colonial expansion between 1760 and 1860 involved systematic recording of data from a great number of cultures (Coward, *Patriarchal Precedents,* 26).

5. Fox-Genovese, "Property and Patriarchy," 36–39, 55.

6. Pateman, *Sexual Contract,* 39–40.

7. Hobbes was the only contract philosopher to regard women and men as "naturally free and equal." Other contract theorists continued to find some natural basis for male dominance. Locke came close to asserting sexual equality, claiming that husbands and wives should theoretically have equal rights. He wormed his way out of the implications of this by arguing that when husbands and wives disagree, since there are only two of them, majority rule cannot bring any resolution. Someone's will must triumph, and Locke says that it should be the husband's, since rule "naturally falls to the Man's share, as the abler and stronger" (Pateman, *Sexual Contract,* 41; Shanley, *Feminism, Marriage, and the Law,* 11; Fox-Genovese, "Property and Patriarchy," 50).

8. Fox-Genovese, "Property and Patriarchy," 55; Shanley, *Feminism, Marriage, and the Law,* 4, 8; Fee, "Sexual Politics," 100; Tiffany and Adams, *Wild Woman,* 8.

9. Fox-Genovese, "Property and Patriarchy," 40.

10. Pateman, *Sexual Contract,* 226.

11. Jordanova, *Sexual Visions,* 27; Laqueur, *Making Sex,* 149. Thomas Laqueur ties this revolution specifically to the political needs of the era, arguing that when "a preexisting transcendental order or time-immemorial custom became a less and less plausible justification for social relations, the battleground of gender roles shifted to nature, to biological sex" (152).

12. Fromm, "Theory of Mother Right," 90; Gossman, personal communication, 11 December 1996. Laqueur describes the old view (which reigned for two millennia) as one in which the sexes were "a matter of degree, gradations of one basic male type . . . [with] men and women . . . arrayed according to their degree of metaphysical perfection, their vital heat" (*Making Sex,* 4–6).

13. Coward, *Patriarchal Precedents,* 56, 79, 81.

14. Conway, "Stereotypes of Femininity," 142–43, 147; Duffin, "Prisoners of Progress," 63; Tiffany and Adams, *Wild Woman,* 13–14.

15. Patrick Geddes, quoted in Conway, "Stereotypes of Femininity," 146.

16. Late nineteenth-century thinkers, including Darwin and Spencer (see Fedigan, "Changing Role of Women," 29; Conway, "Stereotypes of Femininity," 141), did not understand human reproduction the way we do today. It was not until the mid-nineteenth century, with the discovery of the ovum, that it was "proven" that women and men both contributed something to the fetus. That these contributions were equal was not established until the early twentieth century, when experiments on fruit flies isolated chromosomes. Prior to this, Mendel posited equal parental contributions on the basis of his genetic experiments, but his theories were essentially mathematical rather than biological and did not attain general acceptance in scientific circles In the meantime, individuals like McLennan were free to speculate that mothers contributed more to their children than did fathers (*Primitive Marriage,* 65, n. 2).

17. Charles Darwin, quoted in Fedigan, "Changing Role of Women," 29; Arwill-Nordbladh, *Montelius and the Liberation of Women,* 133; Taylor, *Prehistory of Sex,* 26.

These same theories were used in a racist as well as a misogynist way. "Natural selection" was a convenient way to disarm imperialist policies of any morally objectionable overtones; it was, as George Stocking characterized it, "a grimly optimistic, but morally ambiguous doctrine, which could be used to justify the worst excesses of expropriation and colonial rule" (*Victorian Anthropology*, 237; see also Harris, *Rise of Anthropological Theory*, 128–29; Appiah, "Race," 276, 282).

18. Coward, *Patriarchal Precedents*, 97–98.

19. Duffin, "Prisoners of Progress," 74; Fee, "Sexual Politics," 87, 89.

20. A discussion of the overlap between biological and social explanations in matriarchal myth can be found in Coward, *Patriarchal Precedents*, 79–81.

21. Ibid., 9–10.

22. Stocking, *Victorian Anthropology*, 197–98, 201; Shanley, *Feminism, Marriage, and the Law*, 3, 8–10; Tiffany and Adams, *Wild Woman*, 13; Fedigan, "Changing Role of Women," 60–61. Attitudes and laws were not substantially different in continental Europe. See Allen, *Feminism and Motherhood in Germany, 1800–1914* and Allen, *Feminism and Motherhood in Western Europe, 1890–1970*.

23. Shanley, *Feminism, Marriage, and the Law*, 15–17; Duffin, "Prisoners of Progress," 58–60, 83; Stocking, *Victorian Anthropology*, 201.

24. Coward, *Patriarchal Precedents*, 52; Lefkowitz, *Women in Greek Myth*, 15; Merrill, "Theoretical Explanations of the Change from Matriarchy to Patriarchy," 13; Blok, "Sexual Asymmetry," 22.

25. Remarks on the relationship between colonialism and evolutionary anthropology can be found in Stocking, *Victorian Anthropology*, 237, 240–41, 273.

26. For a description of this unease in Victorian Britain, see Young, "Spencer and 'Inevitable' Progress," 149–50, 156–57. For a perspective on the 1950s in the United States, see Breines, *Young, White, and Miserable*, 1–24. Another factor contributing to the unease in Victorian Britain was the renewed challenge to Christian doctrine. After some hard questioning in the late eighteenth century, Christianity had reasserted itself with new force through the early and mid-nineteenth century. But in the late nineteenth century, it was once again under siege (see Harris, *Rise of Anthropological Theory*, 54–55, 210; Fraser, *Making of "The Golden Bough,"* 15, 44; Stocking, *Victorian Anthropology*, 76–77, 196, 207; Calverton, "Modern Anthropology," 3; Swain, *Interpreting Aboriginal Religion*, 42; McLennan, "Early History of Man," 516).

27. Stocking, *Victorian Anthropology*, 207; Fee, "Sexual Politics," 88.

28. Fee, "Sexual Politics," 96–97.

29. As Robert Lowie says, "For the mid-Victorian thinker it was a foregone conclusion requiring only statement not proof that monogamy is the highest form of marriage in the best of conceivable universes" (*Primitive Society*, 56). See also Coward, *Patriarchal Precedents*, 108.

30. Calverton, "Modern Anthropology," 3–5, 13; Duffin, "Prisoners of Progress," 57, 74; Fee, "Sexual Politics," 89; Magli, *Matriarcato e Potere delle Donne*, 28.

31. Daniel Karlin, introduction to Haggard, *She*, xiv–xv.

32. Haggard, *She*, 8, 19, 21.

33. Ibid., 23–45.

34. Ibid., 74.
35. Ibid., 81, 89, 114.
36. Ibid., 140.
37. Ibid., 155, 159.
38. Ibid., 230, 241.
39. Ibid., 242–43.
40. Hutton, *Triumph of the Moon*, 151.
41. Fee, "Sexual Politics," 89; Duffin, "Prisoners of Progress," 74.
42. Calverton, "Modern Anthropology," 7–9, 13.
43. Raoul Makarius, quoted in Gellner, "Soviet and the Savage," 606–7.

Adler, Margot. *Drawing Down the Moon: Witches, Druids, Goddess-Worshippers, and Other Pagans in America Today.* Boston: Beacon Press, 1979.

Aeschylus. *Eumenides.* Translated and edited by Alan H. Sommerstein. Cambridge: Cambridge University Press, 1989.

———. *The Oresteian Trilogy.* Translated by Philip Vellacott. Hammandsworth, UK: Penguin, 1956.

Allen, Ann Taylor. *Feminism and Motherhood in Germany, 1800–1914.* New Brunswick, NJ: Rutgers University Press, 1991.

———. *Feminism and Motherhood in Western Europe, 1890–1970.* New York: Palgrave Macmillan, 2005.

Amadiume, Ifi. *Afrikan Matriarchal Foundations: The Igbo Case.* London: Karnak House, 1987.

———. *Male Daughters, Female Husbands: Gender and Sex in an African Society.* London: Zed Books, 1987.

———. *Reinventing Africa: Matriarchy, Religion, and Culture.* London: Zed Books, 1997.

Ammerman, Albert J., and L. L. Cavalli-Sforza. *The Neolithic Transition and the Genetics of Populations in Europe.* Princeton, NJ: Princeton University Press, 1984.

Anonymous. "Johann Jakob Bachofen." In *European Authors 1000–1900,* edited by Stanley J. Kunitz and Vineta Colby, 52–53. New York: Wilson, 1967.

Appiah, Kwame Anthony. "Race." In *Critical Terms for Literary Study,* edited by Frank Lentricchia and Thomas McLaughlin, 274–87. Chicago: University of Chicago Press, 1995.

Arwill-Nordbladh, Elisabeth. *Oscar Montelius and the Liberation of Women: An Example of Archaeology, Ideology, and the Early Swedish Women's Movement.* London: British Archaeological Reports, 1989.

Augustine. *The City of God*. Translated by Marcus Dods. New York: Random House, 1950.

Bachofen, Johann Jakob. *Antiquarische Briefe, Vornemlich zur Kenntniss der Ältesten Verwandtschaftsbegriffe*. Strasburg: K. J. Trübner, 1880.

———. *An English Translation of Bachofen's "Mutterrecht" (Mother Right): A Study of the Religious and Juridical Aspects of Gynecocracy in the Ancient World*. Ed. and trans. by David Partenheimer. 5 vols. Lewiston, NY: Edwin Mellen Press, 2003–7 [1861].

———. *Johann Jakob Bachofens Gesammelte Werke: Mit Benützung des Nachlasses unter Mitwirkung von Max Burckhardt, Matthais Gelzer, Olof Gigon Herausgegeben von Karl Meuli*. 10 vols. Basel: Schwabe & Co., 1943–67.

———. *Das Mutterrecht: Eine Untersuchung über die Gynaikokratie der Alten Welt nach Ihrer Religiosen und Rechtlichen Natur*. Edited by Hans-Jürgen Heinrichs. Frankfurt: Suhrkamp, 1975 [1861].

———. *Myth, Religion, and Mother Right: Selected Writings of J. J. Bachofen*. Translated by Ralph Manheim. Princeton, NJ: Princeton University Press, 1967.

———. *Die Sage von Tanaquil. Eine Untersuchung über den Orientalismus in Rom und Italien*. Heidelberg: J. C. B. Mohr, 1870.

———. *Selbstbiographie und Antrittsrede über das Naturrecht*. Halle, Germany: Max Niemeyer Verlag, 1927 [1854].

Baigent, Michael, Richard Leigh, and Henry Lincoln. *Holy Blood, Holy Grail*. New York: Delacorte Press, 1982.

Baker, Lee D. *From Savage to Negro: Anthropology and the Construction of Race, 1896–1954*. Berkeley: University of California Press, 1998.

Bamberger, Joan. "The Myth of Matriarchy: Why Men Rule in Primitive Society." In *Woman, Culture, and Society*, edited by Michelle Zimbalist Rosaldo and Louise Lamphere, 263–80. Stanford: Stanford University Press, 1974.

Barber, Sigmund J. *"Amadis de Gaule" and the German Enlightenment*. Berne: Peter Lang, 1984.

Barth, Fredrik, Andre Gingrich, Robert Parkin, and Sydel Silverman, eds. *One Discipline, Four Ways: British, German, French, and American Anthropology*. Chicago: University of Chicago Press, 2005.

Bäumler, Alfred. *Das Mythische Weltalter: Bachofens Romantische Deutung des Altertums, 1926*. Munich: Verlag C. H. Beck, 1965 [1926].

Bäumler, Alfred, and M. Schröter. *Der Mythus von Orient und Occident: Eine Metaphysik der Alten Welt aus den Werken von J. J. Bachofen*. Munich: Verlag C. H. Beck, 1956 [1926].

Bean, Lynne. "Children of the Goddess: A Critical Examination of Feminist Writings on the Matriarchy." Master's thesis. University of California, Northridge, 1976.

Bebel, August. *My Life*. New York: Howard Fertig, 1973 [1912].

———. *Woman in the Past, Present and Future*. Edited by Subrata Mukherjee and Sushila Ramaswamy. New Delhi: Deep and Deep Publications, 1996 [1883].

———. *Woman under Socialism*. Translated by Meta L. Stern. New York: Socialist Literature Co., 1910.

Beiser, Frederick C. *The Romantic Imperative: The Concept of Early German Romanticism*. Cambridge, MA: Harvard University Press, 2003.

Bell, James A. *Reconstructing Prehistory: Scientific Method in Archaeology*. Philadelphia: Temple University Press, 1994.

Bennett, Florence Mary. *Religious Cults Associated with the Amazons*. New York: Columbia University Press, 1967.

Bennett, Gillian. "Geologists and Folklorists: Cultural Evolution and 'the Science of Folklore.'" *Folklore* 105 (1994): 25–37.

Bergmann, Ernst. "Die Deutung des nationalsozialistischen Gedankens aus dem Geiste des Mutterrechts." *Deutsches Arzteblatt* 64 (1934): 35–37.

———. *Erkenntnisgeist und Muttergeist*. Breslau: Ferdinand Hirt, 1932.

Blackwell, Antoinette Brown. *The Sexes throughout Nature*. New York: G.P. Putnam's Sons, 1875.

Bland, Lucy. *Banishing the Beast: English Feminism and Sexual Morality, 1885–1914*. London: Penguin, 1995.

Bloch, Maurice. *Marxism and Anthropology: The History of a Relationship*. New York: Oxford University Press, 1983.

Blok, Josine H. *The Early Amazons: Modern and Ancient Perspectives on a Persistent Myth*. Leiden: E.J. Brill, 1995.

———. "Quests for a Scientific Mythology: F. Creuzer and K.O. Müller on History and Myth." *History and Theory* 33, no. 4 (2001): 26–52.

———. "Sexual Asymmetry: A Historiographical Essay." In *Sexual Asymmetry: Studies in Ancient Society*, edited by Peter Mason, 1–57. Amsterdam: J.C. Gieben, 1987.

Boas, Franz. "The Limitations of the Comparative Method of Anthropology." In *Race, Language, and Culture*, 270–80. New York: Macmillan, 1940.

Boccaccio, Giovanni. *De Claris Mulieribus*. Tübingen: Litterarischer Verein, 1895 [1362].

Böckh, August. *Encyklopädie und Methodologie der Philologischen Wissenschaften*. Leipzig: B.G. Teubner, 1877.

Borgeaud, Phillipe. "From Lafitau to Bachofen: Primitive Matriarchy." Lecture given at Columbia University, 6 December 1996.

Borgeaud, Phillipe, Nicole Durisch, Antje Kolde, and Grégoire Sommer. *La Mythologie du Matriarcat: L'atelier de Johann Jakob Bachofen*. Geneva: Librairie Droz, 1999.

Bramley, William. *The Gods of Eden: A New Look at Human History*. San Jose, CA: Dahlin Family Press, 1989.

Breines, Wini. *Young, White, and Miserable: Growing up Female in the Fifties*. Boston: Beacon Press, 1992.

Bremmer, Jan. "The Importance of the Maternal Uncle and Grandfather in Archaic and Classical Greece and Early Byzantium." *Zeitschrift für Papyrologie und Epigraphik* 50 (1983): 173–86.

Briffault, Robert. *The Mothers: A Study of the Origins of Sentiments and Institutions*. New York: Macmillan, 1927.

Brown, Dan. *The Da Vinci Code*. New York: Doubleday, 2003.

Brown, H.M. *Kleist and the Tragic Ideal: A Study of "Penthesilea" and Its Relationship to Kleist's Personal and Literary Development 1806–1808*. Berne: Peter Lang, 1977.

Burckhardt, Max. "Johann Jakob Bachofen e Jacob Burckhardt." *Quaderni di Storia* 14, no. 28 (1988): 7–16.

Burkert, Walter. *Structure and History in Greek Mythology and Ritual*. Berkeley: University of California Press, 1979.

Butler, E. M. *The Tyranny of Greece over Germany: A Study of the Influence Exercised by Greek Art and Poetry over the Great German Writers of the Eighteenth, Nineteenth, and Twentieth Centuries*. New York: Macmillan, 1935.

Cahnman, Werner J., ed. *Ferdinand Tönnies: A New Evaluation*. Leiden: E.J. Brill, 1973.

Calder, William M., III., ed. *The Cambridge Ritualists Reconsidered: Proceedings of the First Oldfather Conference*. Atlanta: Scholars Press, 1989.

Calverton, V. F. "Modern Anthropology and the Theory of Cultural Compulsives." In *The Making of Man*, 1–40. Westport, CT: Greenwood, 1931.

Cantarella, Eva. *Pandora's Daughters: The Role and Status of Women in Greek and Roman Antiquity*. Baltimore: Johns Hopkins University Press, 1987.

———. "Potere Femminile, Diritto e Stato tra Mito e Antropologia." *Quaderni di Storia* 14, no. 28 (1988): 107–20.

Cavin, Susan. *Lesbian Origins*. San Francisco: Ism Press, 1985.

Cesana, Andreas. "L'Antico e il Nuova Stato: La Critica del Moderno e la sua Motivazione Storico-Universale in Johann Jakob Bachofen." *Quaderni di Storia* 28 (1988): 87–105.

———. *Johann Jakob Bachofens Geschichtsdeutung: Eine Untersuchung Ihrer Geschichtsphilosophischen Voraussetzungen*. Basel: Birkhäuser, 1983.

Chapman, Anne MacKaye. *Drama and Power in a Hunting Society: The Selk'nam of Tierra del Fuego*. Cambridge: Cambridge University Press, 1982.

Conkey, Margaret W., and Ruth E. Tringham. "Archaeology and the Goddess: Exploring the Contours of Feminist Archaeology." In *Feminisms in the Academy: Rethinking the Disciplines,* edited by A. Stewart and D. Stanton, 199–247. Ann Arbor: University of Michigan Press, 1995.

Conway, Jill. "Stereotypes of Femininity in a Theory of Sexual Evolution." In *Suffer and Be Still: Women in the Victorian Age,* edited by Martha Vicinus, 140–54. Bloomington: Indiana University Press, 1972.

Cope, Edward D. "What Was Matriarchy?" *The Open Court* 3 (1889): 1518–19.

Coward, Rosalind. *Patriarchal Precedents*. Boston: Routledge and Kegan Paul, 1983.

Creuzer, Georg Friedrich. *Symbolik und Mythologie der Alten Völker, Besonders der Griechen*. Vol. 4. Leipzig and Darmstadt: Heyer and Leske, 1836–1842 [1819–23].

Croce, Benedetto. "Il Bachofen e la Storiografia Afilologica." *Atti della Reale Accademia di Scienze Morali e Politiche* 51 (1928): 158–76.

Dahlberg, Frances, ed. *Woman the Gatherer*. New Haven, CT: Yale University Press, 1981.

Daniel, Glyn. *The Origins and Growth of Archaeology*. New York: Galahad Books, 1967.

Dareste, Rudolphe. "Review of *Das Mutterrecht* by Johann Jakob Bachofen." *Revue Historique de Droit Français et Étranger* 11 (1865): 100–101.

Dargun, Lothar. *Mutterrecht und Raubehe und ihre Reste im Germanischen Recht und Leben*. Breslau: W. Koebner, 1883.

———. *Mutterrecht und Vaterrecht*. Leipzig: von Duncker and Humblot, 1892.

———. "Zum Problem des Ursprungs der Ehe." *Archiv für Anthropologie* 11, no. 1 (1879): 125–31.

Darwin, Charles. *The Descent of Man, and Selection in Relation to Sex*. Vol. 2. New York: American Home Library Co., 1902 [1871].

———. *On the Origin of Species by Means of Natural Selection, or, the Preservation of Favoured Races in the Struggle for Life*. New York: D. Appleton, 1861 [1859].

Davies, Peter. "Männerbund and Mutterrecht: Herman Wirth, Sophie Rogge-Börner and the *Ura-Linda-Chronik*." *German Life and Letters* 60, no. 1 (2007): 98–115.

———. *Myth, Matriarchy, and Modernity: The Work of Johann Jakob Bachofen in German Culture, 1860–1945*. Berlin: de Gruyter, 2009.

Davis, Philip G. "The Goddess and the Academy." *Academic Questions (Canada)* 6, no. 4 (1993): 49–66.

———. *Goddess Unmasked: The Rise of Neopagan Feminist Spirituality*. Dallas: Spence Publishing Co., 1998.

de Girardin, Émile. *La Politique Universelle: Décrets de l'Avenir*. 3rd ed. Paris: Librairie Nouvelle, 1855 [1852].

Deutscher, Penelope. "The Descent of Man and the Evolution of Woman." *Hypatia* 19, no. 2 (2004): 35–55.

Dexter, Miriam Robbins, and Edgar C. Polomé, eds. *Varia on the Indo-European Past: Papers in Memory of Marija Gimbutas*. Washington, DC: The Institute for the Study of Man (Journal of Indo-European Studies monograph no. 19), 1997.

di Leonardo, Micaela. *Exotics at Home: Anthropologies, Others, American Modernity*. Chicago: University of Chicago Press, 1998.

Diop, Cheikh Anta. *The Cultural Unity of Black Africa: The Domains of Patriarchy and of Matriarchy in Classical Antiquity*. London: Karnak House, 1989.

Divale, William. *Matrilocal Residence in Pre-Literate Society*. Ann Arbor, MI: UMI Research Press, 1984.

Duffin, Lorna. "Prisoners of Progress: Women and Evolution." In *The Nineteenth-Century Woman: Her Cultural and Physical World*, edited by Sara Delamont and Lorna Duffin, 57–91. London: Croom Helm, 1978.

Durkheim, Émile. *Contributions to l'Année Sociologique*. Edited by Yash Nandan. New York: Free Press, 1980.

Eckstein-Diener, Berta [Helen Diner]. *Mothers and Amazons: The First Feminine History of Culture*. Translated by John Philip Lundin. New York: Julian Press, 1965.

Eckstein-Diener, Berta [Sir Galahad]. *Mütter und Amazonen: Ein Umriß Weiblicher Reiche*. Munich: Non-Stop Verlag, 1975.

Ehrenberg, Margaret. *Women in Prehistory*. Norman: University of Oklahoma Press, 1989.

Eisler, Riane. *The Chalice and the Blade: Our History, Our Future*. San Francisco: Harper and Row, 1987.

Ellenberger, Henry F. *The Discovery of the Unconscious: The History and Evolution of Dynamic Psychiatry* New York: Basic Books, 1970.

Eller, Cynthia. *Living in the Lap of the Goddess: The Feminist Spirituality Movement in America*. Boston: Beacon Press, 1995.

———. *The Myth of Matriarchal Prehistory: Why an Invented Past Won't Give Women a Future*. Boston: Beacon Press, 2000.

Ellis, Havelock. *Women and Marriage*. London: W. Reeves & Co., 1888.

Ellwood, Robert S. *The Politics of Myth: A Study of C. G. Jung, Mircea Eliade, and Joseph Campbell*. Albany: State University of New York Press, 1999.

Engels, Friedrich. *The Origin of the Family, Private Property, and the State*. New York: International Publishers, 1972 [1884].

Engels, Friedrich, and Karl Kautsky. *Aus der Frühzeit des Marxismus: Engels Briefwechsel mit Kautsky*. Prague: Orbis-Verlag, 1935.

Ettlinger, Ellen. "Review of *Das Mutterrecht* by Johann Jakob Bachofen." *Folklore* 61 (1950): 46–47.

Fagan, Brian. "A Sexist View of Prehistory." *Archaeology* 45, no. 2 (1992): 14–15, 18, 66.

Feder, Kenneth L., and Michael Alan Park. *Human Antiquity: An Introduction to Physical Anthropology and Archaeology*. 5th ed. New York: McGraw-Hill, 2006.

Fedigan, Linda Marie. "The Changing Role of Women in Models of Human Evolution." *Annual Review of Archaeology* 15 (1986): 25–66.

Fee, Elizabeth. "The Sexual Politics of Victorian Social Anthropology." In *Clio's Consciousness Raised: New Perspectives on the History of Women*, edited by Mary S. Hartman and Lois W. Banner, 86–102. New York: Harper and Row Colophon, 1974.

Feldman, Burton, and Robert D. Richardson, eds. *The Rise of Modern Mythology, 1680–1860*. Bloomington: Indiana University Press, 1972.

Felski, Rita. *The Gender of Modernity*. Cambridge, MA: Harvard University Press, 1995.

Ferguson, Adam. *Essays on the History of Civil Society*. Edinburgh: University of Edinburgh Press, 1966 [1767].

Firth, Raymond. *Symbols: Public and Private*. London: Allen and Unwin, 1973.

Fishbane, Jonathan D. "Mother-Right, Myth, and Renewal: The Thought of Johann Jakob Bachofen and Its Relationship to the Perception of Cultural Decadence in the Nineteenth Century." PhD diss., University of Michigan, 1981.

Fluehr-Lobban, Carolyn. "Marxism and the Matriarchate: 100 Years after *The Origin of the Family, Private Property, and the State*." *Critique of Anthropology* 7, no. 1 (1987): 5–14.

———. "A Marxist Reappraisal of the Matriarchate." *Current Anthropology* 20 (1979): 341–59.

Fourier, François Marie Charles. *Selections from the Works of Fourier*. Translated by Julia Franklin. London: Swan Sonnenschein & Co., 1901.

———. *Théorie des Quatre Mouvements*. Paris: Librairie sociétaire, 1841 [1808].

Fox-Genovese, Elizabeth. "Property and Patriarchy in Classical Bourgeois Political Theory." *Radical History Review* 4 (1977): 36–59.

Frank, Manfred. *The Philosophical Foundations of Early German Romanticism*. Translated by Elizabeth Millán-Zaibert. Albany: State University of New York Press, 2004.

Fraser, Robert. "Anthropology as Consolation: The Strange Case of Motherkin." In *Sir James Frazer and the Literary Imagination*, edited by Robert Fraser, 101–20. New York: St. Martin's Press, 1991.

———. *The Making of "The Golden Bough": The Origins and Growth of an Argument*. London: Macmillan, 1990.

Frazer, James George. *The Golden Bough*. Edited by Robert Fraser. Oxford: Oxford University Press, 1994.

Fromm, Erich. "The Theory of Mother Right and Its Relevance for Social Psychology." In *The Crisis of Psychoanalysis*, chapter 7. New York: Holt, Rinehart and Winston, 1970.

Fustel de Coulanges, Numa Denis. *The Ancient City: A Study on the Religion, Laws, and Institutions of Greece and Rome*. Garden City, NY: Doubleday, 1956 [1864].

Gage, Matilda Joslyn. "The Matriarchate." *The Open Court* 2 (1888): 1480–81.

———. *Woman, Church, and State: A Historical Account of the Status of Woman through the Christian Ages: With Reminiscences of the Matriarchate*. New York: Arno Press, 1972 [1893].

Gamble, Clive. *Timewalkers: Prehistory of Global Colonization*. Stroud, UK: Alan Sutton, 1993.

Gamble, Eliza Burt. *The Evolution of Woman: An Inquiry into the Dogma of Her Inferiority to Man*. New York: G.P. Putnam's, 1894.

Geary, Dick. *Karl Kautsky*. Manchester, UK: Manchester University Press, 1987.

Geary, Patrick J. *Women at the Beginning: Origin Myths from the Amazons to the Virgin Mary*. Princeton, NJ: Princeton University Press, 2006.

Geddes, Patrick, and J. Arthur Thomson. *The Evolution of Sex*. London: W. Scott, 1889.

Gellner, Ernest. "The Soviet and the Savage." *Current Anthropology* 16 (1973): 595–617.

Georgoudi, Stella. "Creating a Myth of Matriarchy." In *A History of Women in the West. Vol. 1: From Ancient Goddesses to Christian Saints*, edited by Pauline Schmitt Pantel, 449–63. Cambridge, MA: Belknap Press of Harvard University Press, 1992.

Gerhard, Eduard. *Griechische Mythologie*. Berlin: G. Reimer, 1855.

Gewertz, Deborah, ed. *Myths of Matriarchy Reconsidered*. Sydney: University of Sydney Press, 1988.

Gillison, Gillian. "Cannibalism among Women in the Eastern Highlands of Papua New Guinea." In *The Ethnography of Cannibalism*, edited by Paula Brown and Donald Tuzin, 33–50. Washington, DC: Society for Psychological Anthropology, 1983.

Gimbutas, Marija. *The Living Goddesses*, edited by Miriam Robbins Dexter. Berkeley: University of California Press, 1997.

Giraud-Teulon, Alexis. *Histoire du Mariage sous Toutes ses Formes*. Paris: Raymond Castells Éditions, 1998 [1874].

———. *La Mère chez Certaines Peuples de l'Antiquité* (Paris: Ernest Thorin, 1867).

Gore, Al. *Earth in the Balance: Ecology and the Human Spirit*. Boston: Houghton Mifflin, 1992.

Gorman, Alice C. "Theories of Prehistoric Inequality: Hobbes, Freud, and Engels." In *Women and Archaeology: A Feminist Critique*, edited by Hilary du Cros and Laurajean Smith, 46–50. Canberra: Australian National University, 1993.

Gossman, Lionel. "Basle, Bachofen, and the Critique of Modernity in the Second Half of the Nineteenth Century." *Journal of the Warburg and Courtauld Institutes* 47 (1984): 136–85.

———. "History as Decipherment: Romantic Historiography and the Discovery of the Other." *New Literary History* 18, no. 1 (1986).

———. "Macht der Kultur gegen Kultur der Macht." In *Johann Jakob Bachofen (1815–1887)*, 41–57. Basel: Historischen Museum, 1987.

———. "Orpheus Philologus: Bachofen versus Mommsen on the Study of Antiquity." *Transactions of the American Philosophical Society* 73, no. 5 (1983): 1–89.

Gough, Kathleen. "An Anthropologist Looks at Engels." In *Woman in a Man-Made World: A Socioeconomic Handbook*, edited by Nona Glazer and Helen Youngelson Waehrer. Chicago: Rand McNally, 1977.

Graf, Fritz. "La Materia come Maestra: La Teoria del Simbolo e Dei Miti di Johann Jakob Bachofen e i suoi Presupposti Storico-Scientifici." *Quaderni di Storia* 14, no. 28 (1988): 17–39.

Grayson, Donald. *The Establishment of Human Antiquity*. New York: Academic Press, 1983.

Griesman, Harvey. "Matriarchate as Utopia, Myth, and Social Theory." *Sociology* 15, no. 3 (1981): 321–36.

Grossman, Julian A. "Morgan and Bachofen." *American Anthropologist* 73 (1971): 986.

Hadfield, Andrew, ed. *Amazons, Savages, and Machiavels: Travel and Colonial Writing in English, 1550–1630: An Anthology*. Oxford: Oxford University Press, 2001.

Haggard, H. Rider. *Allan Quartermain*. New York: McKinlay, Stone and Mackenzie, 1887.

———. *King Solomon's Mines*. London: Cassell and Co., 1907 [1885].

———. *She*. New York: Oxford University Press, 1991 [1887].

Halbfass, Wilhelm. *India and Europe: An Essay in Understanding*. Albany: State University of New York Press, 1988.

Harris, Marvin. *The Rise of Anthropological Theory*. New York: Thomas Crowell, 1968.

Hartland, E. S. "Matrilineal Kinship and the Question of Its Priority." *Memoirs of the American Anthropological Association* 4 (1917): 1–87.

———. *Primitive Paternity*. London: Folk-Lore Society, 1909.

Hartley, Catherine Gasquoine. *The Age of Mother-Power: The Position of Woman in Primitive Society*. New York: Dodd Mead, 1914.

Hayden, Brian. "An Archaeological Evaluation of the Gimbutas Paradigm." *Pomegranate*, no. 6 (1998): 35–46.

Hays, Hoffman. *From Ape to Angel: An Informal History of Social Anthropology*. New York: Knopf, 1958.

Heiler, Friedrich. *Die Frau in den Religionen der Menschheit*. Berlin: Walter de Gruyter, 1977.

Heine, Susanne. *Christianity and the Goddesses: Systematic Criticism of a Feminist Theology*. Translated by John Bowden. London: SCM Press, 1988.

Heinrichs, Hans-Jürgen. *Materialen zu Bachofens "Das Mutterrecht."* Frankfurt: Suhrkamp, 1975.

Hellwald, Friedrich von. *Die Menschliche Familie nach Ihrer Entstehung und Natürlich Entwickelung*. Leipzig: Ernst Günthers Verlag, 1888.

Hermand, Jost. "All Power to the Women: Nazi Concepts of Matriarchy." *Journal of Contemporary History* 19, no. 4 (1984): 649–67.

Hobbes, Thomas. *Leviathan: Or the Matter, Forme, and Power of a Common-Wealth Ecclesiastical and Civill*. Radford, VA: Wilder Publications, 2007 [1651].

Hofstadter, Richard. *Social Darwinism in American Thought*. Boston: Beacon Press, 1955.

Hays, Hoffman, R. *From Ape to Angel: An Informal History of Social Anthropology.* New York: Knopf, 1958.

Howard, George E. *A History of Matrimonial Institutions.* Vol. 1. Chicago: University of Chicago Press, 1904.

Howitt, Alfred W., and Lorimer Fison. "From Mother-Right to Father-Right." *Journal of the (Royal) Anthropological Institute* 12 (1883): 30–46.

Hutton, Ronald. *The Triumph of the Moon: A History of Modern Pagan Witchcraft.* Oxford: Oxford University Press, 1999.

Hyman, Stanley E. "Myths and Mothers." *Kenyon Review* 30 (1968): 547–53.

Janssen-Jurreit, Marielouise. *Sexism: The Male Monopoly on History and Thought.* New York: Farrar Straus Giroux, 1982.

Jolly, Margaret. "Matriarchy: Myth and History." *Refractory Girl* 11 (1976): 3–8.

Jordanova, Ludmilla. *Sexual Visions: Images of Gender in Science and Medicine between the Eighteenth and Twentieth Centuries.* Madison: University of Wisconsin Press, 1989.

Juillerat, Bernard. "An Odor of Man: Melanesian Evolutionism, Anthropological Mythology, and Matriarchy." *Diogenes,* no. 144 (1988): 65–91.

Katz, Marilyn A. "Ideology and 'the Status of Women' in Ancient Greece." In *Women and Antiquity: New Assessments,* edited by Richard Hawley and Barbara Levick, 21–43. New York: Routledge, 1995.

Kautsky, Karl. "Die Entstehung der Ehe und Familie." *Kosmos* 2 (1882): 190–207, 256–72, 329–48.

———. *Erinnerungen und Erörterungen.* The Hague: Mouton, 1960.

———. *Friedrich Engels: His Life, His Work and His Writings.* Chicago: Charles H. Kerr & Co., 1899.

Kazantzakis, Nikos. *The Last Temptation of Christ.* Oxford: Bruno Cassirer, 1961 [1951].

Kenyatta, Jomo. *Facing Mount Kenya: The Tribal Life of the Gikuyu.* New York: Random House, 1965.

Kleinbaum, Abby Wettan. "Amazon Legends and Misogynists: The Women and Civilization Question." In *Views of Women's Lives in Western Tradition: Frontiers of the Past and the Future,* edited by Frances Richardson Keller, 83–109. New York: Edwin Mellen, 1990.

Kleist, Heinrich von. *Penthesilea: A Tragic Drama.* Translated by Joel Agee. New York: HarperCollins, 1998 [1808].

Kleist, Heinrich von. *Penthesilea: Ein Traverspiel.* Stuttgart: J. Hoffman, 1923 [1808].

Knight, Melvin M. "The Matriarchate and the Perversion of History." *Social Forces* 2 (1923): 569–74.

Knight, William F. J. "Review of *Das Mutterrecht* by Johann Jakob Bachofen." *Journal of Hellenic Studies* 72 (1952): 145–46.

Koepping, Klaus-Peter. *Adolf Bastian and the Psychic Unity of Mankind: The Foundations of Anthropology in Nineteenth Century Germany.* Hong Kong: University of Queensland Press, 1983.

Kohler, Josef. *On the Prehistory of Marriage: Totemism, Group Marriage, Mother Right.* Edited by R. H. Barnes. Chicago: University of Chicago Press, 1975 [1897].

Krader, Lawrence. *The Ethnological Notebooks: Studies of Morgan, Phear, Maine, Lubbock, by Karl Marx*. Assen, The Netherlands: Van Gorcum, 1974.

Kramer, Fritz. "Empathy—Reflections on the History of Ethnology in Prefascist Germany: Herder, Creuzer, Bastian, Bachofen, and Frobenius." *Dialectical Anthropology* 9 (1985): 337–47.

Kriukov, M. V. "Types of Kinship Systems and Their Historical Interrelationship." *Soviet Anthropology and Archaeology* 11 (1972): 107–50.

Kuklick, Henrika, ed. *A New History of Anthropology*. Oxford: Blackwell, 2008.

———. *The Savage Within: The Social History of British Anthropology, 1885–1945*. Cambridge: Cambridge University Press, 1991.

Kulischer, M. "Die Geschlechtliche Zuchtwahl bei den Menschen in der Urzeit." *Zeitschrift für Ethnologie* 8 (1876): 140–57.

Lafargue, Paul. *La Propriété, Origines et Evolution, Thèse Communiste*. Paris: Bibliothèque Rouge, 1895.

Lafitau, Joseph François. *Customs of the American Indians Compared with the Customs of Primitive Times*. Vol. 1. Translated and edited by William N. Fenton and Elizabeth L. Moore. Toronto: Champlain Society, 1974 [1724].

Lanza, Diego. "Matriarcato, Mito, Mito del Matriarcato: Annotazioni Marginali." *Quaderni di Storia* 28 (1988): 121–35.

Laqueur, Thomas. *Making Sex: Body and Gender from the Greeks to Freud*. Cambridge, MA: Harvard University Press, 1990.

Lefkowitz, Mary. "The Twilight of the Goddess." *The New Republic* (1992): 29–33.

———. *Women in Greek Myth*. 1st ed. Baltimore: Johns Hopkins University Press, 1986.

———. *Women in Greek Myth*. 2nd ed. Baltimore: Johns Hopkins University Press, 2007.

Lenin, V. I. *Women and Society*. New York: International Publishers, 1938.

Lévi-Strauss, Claude. *Myth and Meaning: Cracking the Code of Culture*. New York: Schocken, 1979.

———. *Structural Anthropology*. New York: Basic Books, 1963 [1958].

Liebrecht, Felix. "Review of *Das Mutterrecht* by Johann Jakob Bachofen." *Göttingische Gelehrte Anzeigen* (1862): 383–99.

Lincoln, Bruce. *Discourse and the Construction of Society: Comparative Studies of Myth, Ritual, and Classification*. New York: Oxford University Press, 1989.

———. *Theorizing Myth: Narrative, Ideology, and Scholarship*. Chicago: University of Chicago Press, 2000.

Lippert, Julius. *Die Geschichte der Familie*. Stuttgart: F. Enke, 1884.

———. *The Evolution of Culture*. New York: Macmillan, 1931 [1886–87].

Lopes, Anne, and Gary Roth. *Men's Feminism: August Bebel and the German Socialist Movement*. Amherst, NY: Humanity Books, 2000.

Love, Barbara, and Elizabeth Shanklin. "The Answer Is Matriarchy." In *Our Right to Love: A Lesbian Resource Book Produced in Cooperation with Women of the National Gay Task Force*, edited by Ginny Vida, 183–86. Englewood Cliffs, NJ: Prentice-Hall, 1978.

Lowie, Robert H. *The History of Ethnological Theory*. New York: Farrar and Rinehart, 1937.

———. *The Matrilineal Complex.* Berkeley: University of California Press, 1919.

———. *Primitive Society.* New York: Boni and Liveright, 1920.

———. "Review of *Das Mutterrecht,* 3d ed., by Johann Jakob Bachofen." *American Anthropologist* 51, no. 4 (1949): 628–29.

Lubbock, John. *The Origin of Civilisation.* London: Longmans Green & Co., 1870.

Lyall, Andrew. "Early German Legal Anthropology: Albert Hermann Post and His Questionnaire." *Journal of African Law* 52, no. 1 (2008): 114–38.

Lyell, Charles. *The Geological Evidences of the Antiquity of Man.* Philadelphia: George W. Childs, 1863.

Maehl, William Harvey. *August Bebel: Shadow Emperor of the German Workers.* Philadelphia: American Philosophical Society, 1980.

Magli, Ida. *Matriarcato e Potere delle Donne.* Milan: Feltrinelli, 1978.

Maine, Henry Sumner. *Ancient Law: Its Connection with the Early History of Society, and Its Relation to Modern Ideas.* Tucson: University of Arizona Press, 1986 [1861].

———. *Dissertations on Early Law and Government.* New York: Arno Press, 1975 [1883].

———. *Lectures on the Early History of Institutions.* London: John Murray, 1875.

———. *Village Communities in the East and West: Six Lectures Delivered at Oxford.* London: John Murray, 1871.

Malinowski, Bronislaw. *The Father in Primitive Psychology.* New York: W.W. Norton, 1927.

———. *Myth in Primitive Psychology.* Westport, CT: Negro Universities Press, 1971.

———. *A Scientific Theory of Culture and Other Essays.* Chapel Hill: University of North Carolina Press, 1944.

———. *Sex, Culture, and Myth.* New York: Harcourt Brace and World, 1962.

Mallory, J. P. *In Search of the Indo-Europeans.* London: Thames and Hudson, 1989.

Marchand, Suzanne L. *Down from Olympus: Archaeology and Philhellenism in Germany, 1750–1970.* Princeton, NJ: Princeton University Press, 1996.

Martin, M. Kay, and Barbara Voorhies. *Female of the Species.* New York: Columbia University Press, 1975.

Marx, Karl. *The Portable Karl Marx.* Edited by Eugene Kamenka. New York: Penguin Books, 1983.

———. *Pre-Capitalist Economic Formations.* New York: International Publishers 1965 [1859].

Marx, Karl, and Friedrich Engels. *The Communist Manifesto.* New York: Penguin Books, 1967 [1848].

Marx, Karl, [Friedrich] Engels, V. I. Lenin, and Joseph Stalin. *The Woman Question.* New York: International Publishers, 1951.

Marx-Aveling, Eleanor, and Edward Aveling. *Thoughts on Women and Society.* Edited by Joachim Müller and Edith Schotte. New York: International Publishers, 1987 [1887].

Mason, Jim. *An Unnatural Order: Uncovering the Roots of Our Domination of Nature and Each Other.* New York: Simon and Schuster, 1993.

McGee, W. J. "The Beginning of Marriage." *American Anthropologist* 9 (1896): 371–83.

McKenna, Terence. *Food of the Gods: The Search for the Original Tree of Knowledge: A Radical History of Plants, Drugs, and Human Evolution.* New York: Bantam Books, 1992.

McLennan, John Ferguson. "Bachofen's *Das Mutterrecht*," in *Studies in Ancient History*. London: Macmillan, 1886.

―――. "The Early History of Man." *North British Review* 50 (1869): 516–49.

―――. *Primitive Marriage*. Edited by Peter Rivière. Chicago: University of Chicago Press, 1970 [1865].

McLennan, John Ferguson, and Donald McLennan. *The Patriarchal Theory*. London: Macmillan, 1885.

McVickar, Harry Whitney. *The Evolution of Woman*. New York: Harper and Brothers, 1896.

Meigs, Anna S. *Food, Sex, and Pollution: A New Guinea Religion*. New Brunswick, NJ: Rutgers University Press, 1984.

Merrill, Anne W. "Theoretical Explanations of the Change from Matriarchy to Patriarchy." *Kroeber Anthropological Society Papers* 59/60 (1979): 13–18.

Meskell, Lynn. "Goddesses, Gimbutas, and 'New Age' Archaeology." *Antiquity* 69 (1995): 74–86.

Millar, John. *Origin of the Distinction of Ranks*. Edited by William C. Lehmann. Cambridge: Cambridge University Press, 1960 [1771].

Momigliano, Arnaldo D. "Review of 'Orpheus Philologus: Bachofen versus Mommsen on the Study of Antiquity' by Lionel Gossman." *Journal of Modern History* 57 (1985): 328–30.

Montagu, M. F. Ashley. *Coming into Being among the Australian Aborigines*. London: Routledge, 1974.

Montesquieu, Charles de Secondat. *The Spirit of the Laws*. New York: Free Press, 1970 [1748].

Moore, Henrietta L. *Feminism and Anthropology*. Minneapolis: University of Minnesota Press, 1988.

Moretti, Giampiero. *Heidelberg Romantica: Josef Görres, Friedrich Creuzer, Jacob E. Wilhelm Grimm, Johann J. Bachofen*. Rome, 1984.

Morgan, Lewis Henry. *Ancient Society or Researches in the Lines of Human Progress from Savagery through Barbarism to Civilization*. New York: Henry Holt & Co., 1878.

―――. *Systems of Consanguinity and Affinity of the Human Family*. Washington, DC: Smithsonian Museum, 1871.

Müller, Karl Otfried. *Die Dorier*. Zurich: Georg Olms Verlag AG, 1989 [1824].

―――. *Geschichten Hellenischer Stämme und Städte*. Breslau: J. Max, 1844 [1820].

―――. *History of the Literature of Ancient Greece*. London: R. Baldwin, 1846 [1841].

―――. *Introduction to a Scientific System of Mythology*. Translated by John Leitch. London: Longman, Brown, Green, and Longmans, 1844 [1825].

Murdock, George P. "Correlations of Matrilineal and Patrilineal Institutions." In *Studies in the Science of Society*, edited by George P. Murdock, 445–70. New Haven, CT: Yale University Press, 1937.

Murphy, Robert F. "Social Structure and Sex Antagonism." *Southwestern Journal of Anthropology* 15, no. 1 (1959): 89–98.

Nelson, Sarah Milledge. *Gender in Archaeology: Analyzing Power and Prestige*. Walnut Creek, CA: Sage Publications, 1997.

Noll, Richard. *The Jung Cult: Origins of a Charismatic Movement.* Princeton, NJ: Princeton University Press, 1994.

Olender, Maurice. *The Languages of Paradise: Race, Religion, and Philology in the Nineteenth Century.* Translated by Arthur Goldhammer. Cambridge, MA: Harvard University Press, 1992.

Paden, William E. *Religious Worlds: The Comparative Study of Religion.* Boston: Beacon Press, 1988.

Panoff, Michel. "Patrifiliation as Ideology and Practice in a Matrilineal Society." *Ethnology* 15 (1976): 175–88.

Pateman, Carole. *The Sexual Contract.* Stanford: Stanford University Press, 1988.

Peake, Rhea. "Season of the Goddess: Rediscovering the Divine Feminine." *Healing Retreats and Spas Magazine* (2000).

Pembroke, Simon. "The Early Human Family: Some Views, 1770–1870." In *Classical Influences on Western Thought 1650–1870,* edited by R. R. Bolgar, 275–91. Cambridge: Cambridge University Press, 1979.

———. "Last of the Matriarchs: A Study in the Inscriptions of Lycia." *Journal of the Economic and Social History of the Orient* 8 (1965): 217–47.

———. "Women in Charge: The Function of Alternatives in Early Greek Tradition and the Ancient Idea of Matriarchy." *Journal of the Warburg and Courtald Institutes* 30 (1967): 1–35.

Penniman, T. K. *A Hundred Years of Anthropology.* London: Duckworth, 1952.

Penny, H. Glenn, and Matti Bunzl, eds. *Worldly Provincialism: German Anthropology in the Age of Empire.* Ann Arbor: University of Michigan Press, 2003.

Pizan, Christine de. *The Book of the City of Ladies.* Translated by Rosalind Brown-Grant. London: Penguin Books, 1999 [1405].

Pomeroy, Sarah B. "A Classical Scholar's Perspective on Matriarchy." In *Liberating Women's History,* edited by Berenice A. Carroll, 217–23. Urbana: University of Illinois Press, 1976.

———. *Goddesses, Whores, Wives, and Slaves: Women in Classical Antiquity.* New York: Schocken, 1994.

Post, Albert Hermann. *Afrikanische Jurisprudenzs: Ethnologisch-juristische Beiträge zur Kenntniss der Einheimischen Rechte Afrikas.* Leipzig: Schulze, 1887.

———. *Die Geschlechtsgenossenschaft der Urzeit und die Entstehung der Ehe: Ein Beitrag zu Einer Allgemeinen Vergleichenden Staats- und Rechtswissenschaft.* Leipzig: Schulz, 1875.

———. *Studien zur Entwicklungsgeschichte des Familienrechts. Ein Beitrag zu Einer Allgemeinen Vergleichenden Rechtswissenschaft auf Ethnologischer Basis.* Leipzig: A. Schwartz, 1889.

Price, Robert M. *The Da Vinci Fraud: Why the Truth Is Stranger than Fiction.* Amherst, NY: Prometheus Books, 2005.

Quinn, Malcolm. *The Swastika: Constructing the Symbol.* London and New York: Routledge, 1994.

Rahmatian, Andreas. "Friedrich Carl von Savigny's *Beruf* and *Volksgeistlehre*." *The Journal of Legal History* 28, no. 1 (2007): 1–29.

Raleigh, Sir Walter. *Discoverie of Guiana*. Edited by Joyce Lorimer. Surrey, UK: Hakluyt Society, 2006 [1595].

Ranke, Leopold von. *Geschichte des Altertums*. Essen, Germany: Phaidon-Akademische, 1990 [1886].

———. *The Secret of World History: Selected Writings on the Art and Science of History*. Translated by Roger Wines. New York: Fordham University Press, 1981.

Reclus, Élisée. "Female Kinship and Maternal Filiation." *The Radical Review* 1, no. 11 (1877): 205–23.

Reed, Evelyn. *Problems of Women's Liberation: A Marxist Approach*. New York: Pathfinder Press, 1970.

Reichel-Dolmatoff, Gerardo. *Amazonian Cosmos: The Sexual and Religious Symbolism of the Tukano Indians*. Chicago: University of Chicago Press, 1971.

Remys, Edmund. *Hermann Hesse's "Das Glasperlenspiel": A Concealed Defense of the Mother World*. Berne: Peter Lang, 1983.

Renfrew, Colin. *Archaeology and Language: The Puzzle of Indo-European Origins*. New York: Cambridge University Press, 1987.

Riasanovsky, Nicholas V. *The Teaching of Charles Fourier*. Berkeley: University of California Press, 1969.

Rich, Adrienne. *Of Woman Born: Motherhood as Experience and Institution*. New York: Norton, 1986.

Robertson, Priscilla. *An Experience of Women's Pattern and Change in Nineteenth-Century Europe*. Philadelphia: Temple University Press, 1982.

Ronhaar, Jan Herman. *Woman in Primitive Motherright Societies*. The Hague: J.B. Wolters, 1931.

Rosaldo, Renato. "Imperialist Nostalgia." In *Culture and Truth: The Remaking of Social Analysis*, chapter 3. Boston: Beacon Press, 1989.

Samson, Ross. "Superwomen, Wonderwomen, Great Women, and Real Women." *Archaeological Review from Cambridge* 7, no. 1 (1988): 60–66.

Schefold, Karl. *Die Religion des Archäologen J.J. Bachofen*. Munich: Verlag der Bayerischen Akademie der Wissenschaften, 1987.

Schiavoni, Giulio. "Il Logos nel Labirinto." *Quaderni di Storia* 14, no. 28 (1988): 137–39.

Schneider, David M., and Kathleen Gough, eds. *Matrilineal Kinship*. Berkeley: University of California Press, 1961.

Schurtz, Heinrich. *Altersklassen und Männerbünde: Eine Darstellung der Grundformen der Gesellschaft*. Berlin: G. Reimer, 1902.

———. *Urgeschichte der Kultur*. Leipzig and Vienna: Bibliographisches Institut, 1900.

Segal, Robert A. *Myth: A Very Short Introduction*. Oxford: Oxford University Press, 2004.

Semenov, Iu I. "The Doctrine of Morgan, Marxism, and Contemporary Ethnography." *Soviet Anthropology and Archaeology* 4, no. 2 (1965): 3–15.

Shanley, Mary Lyndon. *Feminism, Marriage, and the Law in Victorian England*. Princeton, NJ: Princeton University Press, 1989.

Shannon, Jacqueline. *Why It's Great to Be a Girl: Fifty Eye-Opening Things You Can Tell Your Daughter to Increase Her Pride in Being Female*. New York: Warner Books, 1994.

Sharpe, Eric J. *Comparative Religion: A History*. 2nd ed. London: Duckworth, 1986.

Shepherd, Simon. *Amazons and Warrior Women: Varieties of Feminism in Seventeenth-Century Drama*. Sussex, UK: Harvester Press, 1981.

Shreeve, James. *The Neandertal Enigma: Solving the Mystery of Modern Human Origins*. New York: Morrow, 1995.

Silverblatt, Irene. "Women in States." *Annual Review of Anthropology* 17 (1988): 427–60.

Smith, Adam. *An Inquiry into the Nature and Causes of the Wealth of Nations*. Edinburgh: Thomas Nelson, 1843 [1776].

———. *Lectures on Jurisprudence*. Edited by Ronald L. Meek, David Daiches Raphael, and Peter Stein. Oxford: Oxford University Press, 1978 [1762–66].

Smith, Munroe. "Review of *Studien zum Ältesten Familienrecht. Erster Teil: Mutterrecht und Vaterrecht*, by Lothar von Dargun." *Political Science Quarterly* 8 (1893): 572–75.

Smith, William Robertson. *Kinship and Marriage in Early Arabia*. London: Darf Publishers, 1990 [1885].

Smith, Woodruff D. *Politics and the Sciences of Culture in Germany 1840–1920*. New York: Oxford University Press, 1991.

Sombart, Nicolaus. "Max Weber and Otto Gross: On the Relationship between Science, Politics and Eros in Wilhelmine Germany." *History of Political Thought* 8, no. 1 (1987): 131–52.

Spencer, Herbert. *Principles of Sociology*. Edited by Stanislav Andreski. London: Macmillan, 1969 [1874–96].

———. *Social Statics*. New York: D. Appleton, 1865 [1851].

Spenser, Edmund. *The Faerie Queene*. New York: Penguin, 1979 [1590–1609].

Stagl, Justin. "Notes on Johann Jakob Bachofen's Mother Right and Its Consequences." *Philosophy of Social Sciences* 19 (1989): 183–200.

Stalin, J. V. "August Bebel." *Labour Monthly* 32, no. 3 (1950): 111–16.

Stanton, Elizabeth Cady. "The Matriarchate or Mother-Age." Address of Mrs. Stanton before the National Council of Women. February 1891.

———. *The Woman's Bible*. New York: European Publishing Co., 1895–98.

Starcke, C. N. *The Primitive Family in Its Origins and Development*. New York: D. Appleton, 1901 [1889].

Steenson, Gary P. *Karl Kautsky, 1854–1938: Marxism in the Classical Years*. Pittsburgh: University of Pittsburgh Press, 1978.

Stocking, George W., Jr. *Race, Culture, and Evolution: Essays in the History of Anthropology*. Chicago: University of Chicago Press, 1968.

———. "Review of *Myth, Religion, and Mother Right* by Johann Jakob Bachofen." *American Anthropologist* 70 (1968): 1188–90.

———. *Victorian Anthropology*. New York: Free Press, 1987.

———, ed. *Functionalism Historicized: Essays on British Social Anthropology*. Madison: University of Wisconsin Press, 1984.

Stone, Merlin. *When God Was a Woman*. New York: Harcourt, Brace, Jovanovich, 1976.

Swain, Tony. *Interpreting Aboriginal Religion: An Historical Account*. South Australia: Australian Association for the Study of Religions, 1985.

Swiney, Frances. *The Awakening of Woman or Women's Part in Evolution*. London: William Reeves, 1908.

Szemerényi, Oswald. "Studies in the Kinship Terminology of the Indo-European Languages with Special References to Indian, Iranian, Greek, and Latin." *Acta Iranica* 16 (1977): 1–240.

Taufer, Alison. "The Only Good Amazon Is a Converted Amazon: The Woman Warrior and Christianity in the *Amadís Cycle*." In *Playing with Gender: A Renaissance Pursuit,* edited by Jean R. Brink, Maryanne C. Horowitz, and Allison P. Coudert, 35–51. Urbana: University of Illinois Press, 1991.

Tax, Sol. "From Lafitau to Radcliffe-Brown: A Short History of the Study of Social Organization." In *Social Anthropology of North American Tribes,* edited by Fred Eggan, 445–81. Chicago: University of Chicago Press, 1937.

Taylor, Timothy. *The Prehistory of Sex: Four Million Years of Human Sexual Culture.* New York: Bantam, 1996.

Ter Horst, Eleanor E. *Lessing, Goethe, Kleist, and the Transformation of Gender.* New York: Peter Lang, 2003.

Thal, Max. *Mutterrecht: Frauenfrage und Weltanschauung.* Breslau: Schleische Verlags, 1903.

Thornhill, Chris. *German Political Philosophy: The Metaphysics of Law.* New York: Routledge, 2007.

Tiffany, Sharon W. "The Power of Matriarchal Ideas." *International Journal of Women's Studies* 5, no. 2 (1982): 138–47.

Tiffany, Sharon W., and Kathleen J. Adams. *The Wild Woman: An Inquiry into the Anthropology of an Idea.* Cambridge, MA: Schenkman Publishing Co., 1985.

Tönnies, Ferdinand. *Community and Civil Society.* Translated by Jose Harris and Margaret Hollis. Cambridge: Cambridge University Press, 2001 [1887].

Townsend, Joan B. "The Goddess: Fact, Fallacy, and Revitalization Movement." In *Goddesses in Religions and Modern Debate,* edited by Larry W. Hurtado, 179–203. Atlanta: Scholars Press, 1990.

Tuzin, Donald F. *The Voice of the Tambaran: Truth and Illusion in Ilahita Arapesh Religion.* Berkeley: University of California Press, 1980.

Tylor, Edward Burnett. "The Matriarchal Family System." *Nineteenth Century* 40 (1896): 81–96.

———. "On a Method of Investigating the Development of Institutions: Applied to Laws of Marriage and Descent." In *Readings in Cross-Cultural Methodology,* edited by Frank W. Moore, 221–45. New Haven, CT: HRAF Press, 1961 [1889].

———. *Primitive Culture: Researches into the Development of Mythology, Philosophy, Religion, Language, Art, and Custom.* New York: Holt, 1889 [1871].

Tyrrell, William Blake. *Amazons, a Study in Athenian Mythmaking.* Baltimore: Johns Hopkins University Press, 1989.

Vaerting, Mathilde and Mathias. *The Dominant Sex.* Westport, CT: Hyperion Press, 1981 [1921].

Van Amringe, William Frederick. *An Investigation of the Theories of the Natural History of Man.* New York: Baker and Scribner, 1848.

Vickery, John B. *The Literary Impact of "The Golden Bough."* Princeton, NJ: Princeton University Press, 1973.

Vico, Giambattista. *Vico: Selected Writings*. Translated and edited by Leon Pompa. Cambridge: Cambridge University Press, 1982.

Vidal-Naquet, Pierre. "Slavery and the Role of Women in Tradition, Myth, and Utopia." In *Myth, Religion, and Society*, edited by R. L. Gordon, 187–200. Cambridge: Cambridge University Press, 1981.

Vogel, Lise. *Marxism and the Oppression of Women*. New Brunswick, NJ: Rutgers University Press, 1987.

Vogel, Martin. *Apollonisch und Dionysisch: Geschichte eines Genialen Irrtums*. Regensburg, Germany: Gustav Bosse Verlag, 1966.

Voltaire. *Candide*. New York: Penguin, 1950 [1759].

Wagner-Hasel, Beate, ed. *Matriarchatstheorien der Altertumswissenschaft*. Darmstadt: Wissenschaftliche Buchgesellschaft, 1992.

Wake, C. Stanisland. *The Development of Marriage and Kinship*. London: George Redway, 1889.

Walters, Suzanne Danuta. "Caught in the Web: A Critique of Spiritual Feminism." *Berkeley Journal of Sociology* 30 (1985): 15–40.

Ward, Lester. *Pure Sociology: A Treatise on the Origin and Spontaneous Development of Society*. New York: Macmillan, 1903.

Warren, Mary Ann. "Johann Jakob Bachofen." In *The Nature of Woman: An Encyclopedia and Guide to the Literature*, 51–54. Pt. Reyes, CA: Edgepress, 1980.

Weber, Marianne. *Ehefrau und Mutter in der Rechtsentwicklung*. Tübingen: J. C. B. Mohr, 1907.

Weigle, Marta. *Spiders and Spinsters: Women and Mythology*. Albuquerque: University of New Mexico Press, 1982.

Weinbaum, Batya. *Islands of Women and Amazons: Representations and Realities*. Austin: University of Texas Press, 1999.

Welcker, Friedrich Gottlieb. *Die Aeschylische Trilogie: Prometheus und die Kabirenweihe zu Lemnos, nebst Winken über die Triologie des Aeschylus Überhaupt*. Darmstadt: Drud und Verlag von C. B. Leste, 1824.

Westermarck, Edward. *The History of Human Marriage*. 5th ed. Vol. 1. New York: Johnson Reprint Corp., 1971 [1921; 1st ed., 1891].

Wilken, G. A. *Das Matriarchat: Bei den Alten Arabern*. Leipzig: Schulze, 1884.

Williamson, George S. *The Longing for Myth in Germany: Religion and Aesthetic Culture from Romanticism to Nietzsche*. Chicago: University of Chicago Press, 2004.

Wilutzky, Paul. *Vorgeschichte des Rechts: Prähistorisches Recht*. Breslau: Eduard Trewendt, 1903.

Wolfe, Rachel. "Woman, Tyrant, Mother, Murderess: An Exploration of the Mythic Character of Clytemnestra in All Her Forms." *Women's Studies* 38, no. 6 (2009): 692–719.

Woods, Susanne. "Amazonian Tyranny: Spenser's Radigund and Diachronic Mimesis." In *Playing with Gender: A Renaissance Pursuit*, edited by Jean R. Brink, Maryanne C. Horowitz, and Allison P. Coudert, 52–61. Urbana: University of Illinois Press, 1991.

Yalom, Marilyn. *A History of the Breast*. New York: Knopf, 1997.

Young, Michael W. *Malinowski: Odyssey of an Anthropologist, 1884–1920*. New Haven, CT: Yale University Press, 2004.

Young, Robert M. "Herbert Spencer and 'Inevitable' Progress." In *Victorian Values*, edited by Gordon Marsden, 147–57. London: Longman, 1990.

Zeitlin, Froma I. "The Dynamics of Misogyny: Myth and Mythmaking in the Oresteia." In *Women in the Ancient World: The Arethusa Papers*, edited by John Peradotto and J. P. Sullivan, 149–84. Albany: State University of New York Press, 1984.

Zetkin, Clara. *Lenin on the Woman Question*. New York: International Publishers, 1934.

Zimmer, Heinrich. "Matriarchy among the Picts." In *Leabhar Nan Gleann: The Book of the Glens*, edited by George Henderson, 1–42. Edinburgh: Norman MacLeod, 1898.

Zimmerman, Andrew. "German Anthropology and the 'Natural Peoples': The Global Context of Colonial Discourse." *European Studies Journal* 16, no. 2 (1999): 95–112.

Ziolkowski, Theodore. *Clio the Romantic Muse: Historicizing the Faculties in Germany*. Ithaca, NY: Cornell University Press, 2004.

Zmigrodski, Michael. *Die Mutter bei den Völkern des Arischen Stammes: Eine Anthropologisch Historische Skizze als Beitrag zur Lösung der Frauenfrage*. Munich: T. Ackermann, 1886.

INDEX

Malthus, Thomas, 103
Männerbund, 142, 161
marriage, 31, 65, 68, 70, 72, 77–81, 84, 90, 100,
102–5, 111, 116, 134, 143, 145–47, 149, 157,
165–66, 173–74, 178, 182–83, 199n54, 25n31;
absence of, 42, 90, 146–47, 219n59, 225n14,
235n31, 236n72, 241n42; as arranged by
women, 25; by capture, 68, 72, 77–78, 80, 91,
95, 98–99, 104, 123, 130, 145–47, 150, 152–53,
160, 171, 219n68, 236n68; future of, 79, 91,
166, 168, 187; group (or communal), 66,
68–69, 81, 92, 104–5, 111, 113, 121, 145–46, 163,
174, 178, 227n61, 240n37; levirate, 146;
monogamous, 33, 43, 45, 65, 67, 70, 77, 79,
80–82, 86, 90–92, 95, 104, 113, 121, 125,
129–30, 144, 146, 172, 174, 178, 187, 191,
219n59, 219n64, 241n40, 244n29; origin of,
31, 33, 43–44, 67, 74, 81, 94, 102–103, 105, 107,
116, 139, 141, 150, 225n14; patriarchal, 33, 90,
95, 142, 146, 174–75, 185–86; "primitive," 29,
68, 92, 95, 180, 198n44; by purchase, 146–47;
"visit," 68, 150. *See also* endogamy;
exogamy; polyandry; promiscuity
Martin, M. Kay, 215n17
Marx, Karl, 7, 9, 100, 103, 107–16, 108f15, 118,
120, 122, 164, 224n4, 225n10, 225n23, 225n25,
226n30, 226n33, 226n40, 227n47, 227n59,
228n75, 229n87, 230n107, 230n113, 231n126,
237n85; as non-feminist, 114–15, 228n75
Marx, Laura, 122
Marx-Aveling, Eleanor, 107, 119, 164–66, 165f24,
239n4
marxism, 8, 102–103, 106–107, 111–13, 120,
166–68
Marxism and Anthropology, 112
Mary Magdalene, 1–4, 193n7, 193n8
masculinity and femininity, 42, 45, 46, 55,
58–60, 141, 144, 155–56, 172, 184, 205n68,
228n75, 228n84, 239n4
Mason, Jim, 5
materialism, 42, 44, 62, 90, 105, 106, 109, 111,
120, 123, 140, 147, 149, 158, 166, 203n31,
226n40, 227n47, 242n52
maternal uncle. *See* avunculate
matriarchy, 4, 8, 10, 13, 34–35, 39, 41, 43–48,
56–57, 59–60, 62, 65–66, 68–69, 80, 86–87,
104, 107, 110, 112, 119, 122, 124–26, 129, 131–32,
140, 144, 146–47, 149–50, 152–55, 158, 160–61,
169, 175, 177, 180, 182, 187–90, 198n44,
203n37, 204n49, 205n68, 235n43, 235n54; as
communal, 84, 110–11, 141; German/Aryan,

133, 157–61, 194n20, 237n102, 237n111,
237n111; status of women in, 43, 67–68, 77,
85, 90–91, 95, 99, 104, 110, 122, 134, 141, 146,
149, 151–53, 174, 214n15, 215n16
matriliny, 25, 34, 42–43, 61–62, 67–69, 76, 81,
84–85, 91–94, 96, 99, 104, 109, 144, 148–52,
153, 155, 170–71, 174–76, 178–79, 198n41,
214n15, 224n142, 234n30, 236n72, 238n1,
240n34, 242n59
matrilocality, 69, 98–99
McGee, W. J., 242n59
McKenna, Terence, 5
McLennan, John Ferguson, 7, 60–61, 65, 67,
72–82, 73f7, 84, 86–87, 90–92, 94–95, 98, 103,
109, 123, 130, 132, 134, 137, 142, 144–46, 150,
152–53, 161, 169, 172, 174, 178, 180, 182,
202n23, 211n167, 212n173, 214n15, 215n20,
216n26, 216n36, 216n37, 217n38, 217n40,
218n48, 218n53, 218n54, 219n58, 219n59,
219n63, 219n64, 219n68, 220n72, 220n75,
223n128, 224n140, 226n42, 231n122, 235n31,
236n68, 240n30, 243n16
Mead, Margaret, 87
Mendel, Gregor, 219n63, 238n117, 243n16
*Menschliche Familie nach Ihrer Entstehung und
Natürlich Entwickelung, Die,* 146
Merian, Valeria, 40
Merrill, Anne, 220n72
Meyer-Ochsner, Heinrich, 59
Michelet, Jules, 59
Mill, John Stuart, 70
Millar, John, 27–30, 153, 199n58, 216n36
misogyny. *See* antifeminism
Moeurs des Sauvages Amériquains, Les, 25
Mohawks, 25
Mommsen, Theodor, 207n111
monogamy, 33, 43, 45, 65, 67, 70, 77, 79, 80–82,
86, 90–92, 95, 104, 113, 121, 125, 129–30, 144,
146, 172, 174, 178, 187, 191, 219n59, 219n64,
241n40, 244n29
monotheism, 4, 53, 65, 201n83
Montalvo, Garcia Rodríguez de, 19, 21
Montesquieu, baron of (Charles de Secondat),
30, 90, 199n63
Morgan, Lewis Henry, 61, 74, 79, 87–92, 88f10,
105, 107, 109–11, 119, 123–24, 132, 134, 140,
144–47, 149–50, 154, 169–70, 174, 178, 180,
187, 199n63, 200n70, 211n168, 214n15,
216n26, 217n40, 218n55, 221n104, 222n105,
222n106, 222n117, 221n117, 225n25, 226n35,
228n75, 230n113, 231n121, 236n75, 239n21

Secondat, Charles de (Baron of Montesquieu), 30, 90, 199n63

sedentism, 78, 175

separate spheres, 59, 87, 111, 113, 115, 156, 172, 183–84, 187

sex differences, 84, 86, 111, 124, 140, 155–56, 172, 184, 221n100, 243n7, 243n12

sex equality, 17, 27–28, 32–33, 71–72, 104, 115, 124, 131, 143, 151, 180, 230n104, 239n9, 243n7; in the future, 34, 79, 87, 91, 114, 118, 122, 165, 167–68, 191, 230n105; in the past, 46, 67, 104, 146, 229n99

sex inequality, 9–10, 14, 86, 183, 191, 195n34, 196n35

sexual freedom, 25, 31, 33, 68, 79, 104, 114, 120–21, 130, 165–66, 191, 230n109, 239n4

sexual jealousy, 104–5, 146, 171, 174

sexual reproduction, 68, 111–13, 122, 140, 145–46, 184, 215n17, 219n63, 227n51, 243n16; metaphors for, 42, 43, 46, 203n30

sexual selection, 126–27, 129, 145–47, 170, 172, 184

Sexual Visions, 58

Shakespeare, William, 147

Shannon, Jacqueline, 6

She, 188–90

Shekhinah, 4

Silva, Feliciano de, 19

slavery, 17, 25, 33, 70, 113, 130, 143, 172, 222n106. *See also* women: as slaves

Smith, Adam, 30–31, 199n64

Smith, William Robertson, 92–96, 93f11, 223n122, 232n139, 235n31

social contract theory, 183

social Darwinism, 83, 85, 103–4, 169

Social Democratic Party, 116–17, 166, 230n107

socialism, 57, 101–22, 123, 133–34, 149, 162–64, 191, 224n1, 225n14, 226n35, 230n105; feminist, 164–68, 239n9

Social Statics, 87

sociobiology, 125

Socrates, 11

Soviet Union, 8, 10, 134, 162, 164

Sozialdemokrat, Der, 103

Spencer, Anna Garlin, 231n122

Spencer, Herbert, 73, 83–87, 85f9, 93, 103, 140, 169, 184, 217n40, 221n94, 221n98, 221n99, 224n5, 229n102, 243n16

Spenser, Edmund, 21, 197n24

Spirit of the Laws, 30

Stanton, Elizabeth Cady, 123, 124f17, 127–28, 130–32, 180, 231n120, 232n146

Starcke, C. N., 162, 172–73, 239n19, 240n34

status of women: in "matriarchal" cultures, 43, 67–68, 77, 85, 90–91, 95, 99, 104, 110, 122, 134, 141, 146, 149, 151–53, 174; as measure of social progress, 32, 39, 91, 180, 228n75; in Victorian England, 185–86

Steenson, Gary P., 224n4, 225n11

Stocking, George, 9, 65, 74, 178, 216n26, 217n45, 220n71, 238n1, 243n17, 243n25

Stone, Merlin, 194n13

Strabo, 25

structuralism, 13

Studien zur Entwicklungsgeschichte des Familienrechts, 150

survivals, 88, 93, 97, 99, 109, 129, 143, 160, 162, 172, 174, 176, 214n8, 223n138, 235n43, 240n37, 241n38

Swanton, Jon, 242n59

swastika, 159

Swiney, Frances, 127, 232n132, 232n137

Symbolik und Mythologie der Alten Völker, 52–53, 209n126

Systems of Consanguinity and Affinity of the Human Family, 89

Tahiti, 33–34, 76

Taylor, W. Cooke, 227n59

Thal, Max, 161

theosophy, 122, 232n137

Thomson, J. Arthur, 184

Thoughts on Women and Society, 164–66

Thucydides, 214n8

Tönnies, Ferdinand, 153–57, 154f23, 161, 237n85, 237n90, 237n93

totemism, 66, 92, 96, 100, 147–48

"two spheres" model. *See* separate spheres

Tylor, E. B., 96–99, 98f12, 174–75, 214n12, 214n15, 215n16, 215n22, 215n23, 218n55, 223n138, 224n140, 224n141, 225n25, 231n122, 233n1, 241n45, 241n51

Tyranny of Greece over Germany, 48

universalism, 50, 58, 74–75, 97

University of Basel, 37–38, 201n7, 201n9

University of Berlin, 51, 53, 58, 147, 201n83, 202n28, 208n116, 208n121

University of Bonn, 34

University of Calcutta, 70

University of Geneva, 61

University of Göttingen, 34, 50, 53

University of Heidelberg, 52

TEXT

10/12.5 Minion Pro

DISPLAY

Minion Pro

COMPOSITOR

Westchester Book Group

PRINTER AND BINDER

IBT Global